T0240049

# 3-D Computer Vision

Yu-Jin Zhang

# 3-D Computer Vision

## Principles, Algorithms and Applications

 Springer

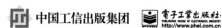 中国工信出版集团

Yu-Jin Zhang
Department of Electronic Engineering
Tsinghua University
Beijing, China

ISBN 978-981-19-7582-0        ISBN 978-981-19-7580-6   (eBook)
https://doi.org/10.1007/978-981-19-7580-6

Jointly published with Publishing House of Electronics Industry
The print edition is not for sale in China (Mainland). Customers from China (Mainland) please order the
print book from: Publishing House of Electronics Industry.

This Springer imprint is published by the registered company Springer Nature Singapore Pte Ltd.
The registered company address is: 152 Beach Road, #21-01/04 Gateway East, Singapore 189721,
Singapore

# Preface

This book is a specialized textbook that introduces the basic principles, typical methods, and practical techniques of 3-D computer vision. It can provide an advanced/second course service of computer vision for graduate students of related majors in higher engineering colleges and universities, after studying *2D Computer Vision: Principles, Algorithms and Applications*.

This book mainly covers the higher level of computer vision from the selection of materials. This book is self-contained, mainly for information majors, but also takes into account learners of different professional backgrounds, and also considers the needs of self-study readers. After learning the fundamental content of computer vision in this book, readers can carry out scientific research and solve more and even difficult specific problems in practical applications.

This book pays more attention to practicality in writing. Considering that computer vision technology has been involved in many professional fields in recent years, but many working people are not specialized in computer vision technology, this book does not emphasize the theoretical system too much, minimizes the formula derivation, and focuses on commonly used techniques. This book has many sample questions and uses intuitive explanation to help readers understand abstract concepts. A subject index list is given at the end of the book, and those corresponding terms are marked in bold in the text.

This book provides a large number of self-test questions (including hints and answers). In terms of purpose: on the one hand, it is convenient for self-study to judge whether they have mastered the key content; on the other hand, it is also convenient for teachers to carry out online teaching and strengthen teacher-student interaction during lectures. The types of questions are multiple-choice questions, which can be easily judged by a computer. In terms of content, many questions express the basic concepts in a different way, supplementing the text, so that learners can deepen their understanding. Some questions list descriptions that are similar but not the same, or even have opposite meanings. Through dialectical thinking of pros and cons, learners can also deeply understand the essence. The hints have been provided for all self-test questions, allowing readers to obtain more information to further identify the meaning of the questions. At the same time, each question can be said to be divided into two levels in this way. Readers can complete the self-test after reading the hints to show that they basically understand it, and to complete the self-test without looking at the hints indicates that they have an even better grasp.

From the structure of this book, there are 12 chapters in total, plus one appendix, answers to self-test questions, and subject index. Under these 15 first-level headings, there are a total of 103 second-level headings (sections), and there are 141 third-level headings (subsections) underneath. The book has a total of about 500,000 words (including pictures, drawings, tables, formulas, etc.) and a total of (numbered) 228 figures, 22 tables, and 566 formulas. In order to facilitate teaching and learning, this book provides a total of 68 examples of various types and 157 self-test questions (all with hints and answers). In addition, there are a list of more than 100 directly related references and a list of more than 500 subject terms for indexing, at the end of the book.

This book can consider three aspects from the knowledge requirements of the prerequisite courses: (1) Mathematics: including linear algebra and matrix theory, as well as basic knowledge about statistics, probability theory, and random modeling; (2) Computer science: including the mastery of computer software technology, the understanding of computer structure system, and the application of computer programming methods; (3) Electronics: On the one hand, the characteristics and principles of electronic equipment; on the other hand, circuit design and other content. In addition, the book *2D Computer Vision: Principles, Algorithms and Applications* can be counted as the discipline prerequisite of this book.

Thanks to the editors of the publisher for carefully composing the manuscript, seriously reviewing, and attentively modifying.

Finally, the author thanks his wife Yun HE and daughter Heming ZHANG for their understanding and support in all aspects.

Beijing, China                                                        Yu-Jin Zhang

# Contents

# Chapter 1
# Computer Vision Overview

Computer vision is an information subject/discipline that uses computers to realize the functions of human vision system (HVS). This book mainly introduces the high-level content of computer vision, which can be used as a textbook for in-depth study of computer vision. Readers can read this book after studying *2D Computer Vision: Principles, Algorithms and Applications*.

The process of human vision (in brief, **vision**) can be regarded as a complex process from sensation (obtaining the image by the 2-D projection of the 3-D world) to perception (gaining the content and meaning of the 3-D world from the 2-D image) process. The ultimate goal of vision in a narrow sense is to make a meaningful explanation and description of the scene for the observer, and in a broad sense, it is also to make a behavior plan based on these explanations and descriptions, as well as the surrounding environment and the wishes of the observer. **Computer vision** is artificial vision or human-made vision. It is to use computers to realize human visual functions, hoping to make meaningful judgments about actual targets and scenes based on the perceived images.

The sections of this chapter are arranged as follows:

Section 1.1 introduces the characteristics of human vision, the brightness properties of vision, the spatial properties of vision, and the temporal properties of vision, as well as makes some discussions on visual perception.

Section 1.2 discusses the research purpose, research tasks, and research methods of computer vision. It also introduces the visual computational theory proposed by Marr in more detail. Moreover, a combined presentation for some improvement ideas is provided.

Section 1.3 gives a general introduction to the 3-D vision system that obtains 3-D spatial information and realizes the understanding of the scene. It compares and discusses the layers of computer vision and image technology, leading to the main content of this book.

Section 1.4 presents the structure of the book and gives the brief summaries of each chapter.

## 1.1   Human Vision and Characteristics

Computer vision (also called artificial vision or human-made vision) is developed on the basis of human vision. There are two meanings here. One is that computer vision needs to realize the functions of human vision, so it could imitate the system structure and functional modules of human vision; the other is that computer vision needs to extend the functions of human vision, so it could use the features of human vision to improve the efficiency and effectiveness of these functions.

   The following first gives an overview of the functional characteristics of human vision and then discusses some important visual brightness, spatial, and temporal properties.

### 1.1.1   Visual Characteristics

First compare **vision** with some related concepts.

#### 1.1.1.1   Vision and Other Sensations

It is generally believed that humans have five senses of vision, hearing, smell, taste, and touch and the corresponding sensory organs, for obtaining information from the objective world. Among them, vision provides humans with most of the data they receive; in other words, humans often rely more on vision than other senses when they acquaint the world. For example, the input information obtained by humans from eye observation often reaches several million bits, and the data rate during continuous viewing can exceed tens of million bits per second. The human brain has more than $10^{10}$ cells/neurons, some of which have more than 10,000 connections (or synapses) with other neurons. It is estimated that the amount of visual information the brain receives from the eyes is at least two orders of magnitude larger than all the information obtained from other sense organs.

#### 1.1.1.2   Vision and Computer Vision

Although computer vision needs to realize the functions of human vision, there are still differences between human vision and computer vision. Human vision first receives light stimulation in a certain wavelength range from the external environment through the sensory organs (eyes) of the visual system to the retina and then encodes and processes the perceptive organs (brain or cerebral visual cortex) of the visual system to obtain subjective feelings. Therefore, vision involves not only physics and chemistry but also psychophysiology. Computer vision mainly relies on photoelectric conversion for image acquisition, then uses processing and analysis functions to obtain objective data, and makes stricter reasoning and judgments based on these results.

### 1.1.1.3 Vision and Machine Vision

In the early days, computer vision put more emphasis on the research of vision science and design system software, while **machine vision** not only considered design system and software but also considered hardware environment and image acquisition technology as well as the integration of vision systems. Therefore, from the perspective of vision system integration, machine vision systems are more comparable to human vision systems (human visual systems). However, with the development of electronic technology and computer technology, true and real-time applications can be realized to a considerable extent on a stand-alone PC. Due to the increase in knowledge in related fields, the difference between machine vision and computer vision has been significantly reduced, and they are more interchangeably used nowadays.

### 1.1.1.4 Vision and Image Generation

Vision can be regarded as a process of obtaining description and explanation of the scene from the image of the scene with the help of the knowledge of the law of image formation. The image generation in graphics can be seen as the process of generating images from the abstract description of the scene with the help of the knowledge of the law of image formation. Although they have some parallels/similarities, certain people regard them as inverse processes, but their complexity is quite different. The image generation process is completely deterministic and predictable, and the visual process involves not only providing a list of all possible explanations but also providing the most likely interpretation. This search process is one to many and may be accompanied by combinatorial explosion. Therefore, vision is inherently more complex than image generation in graphics.

## *1.1.2 Brightness Properties of Vision*

The brightness of vision corresponds to the light intensity that the human eye feels from the scene. A psychological term closely related to brightness is **subjective brightness** or **subjective luminance** The subjective brightness refers to the brightness of the observed object, which is judged by the human eyes according to the intensity of the light stimulation of the retina. Examples of three typical brightness properties in which the perception of brightness is related to multiple factors are as follows.

### 1.1.2.1  Simultaneous Contrast

The subjective brightness felt from the surface of an object is not only related to the brightness of the surface itself but also to the relative relationship (ratio) between the brightness of the surface and the surrounding environment (background). If two objects with different brightness have a similar relative relationship with their respective backgrounds, they can appear to have the same brightness. At this time, the subjective brightness perceived by people has nothing to do with the absolute value of the object brightness. Conversely, the surface of the same object will appear brighter if it is placed on a darker background and will appear darker if it is placed on a brighter background. This phenomenon is called **simultaneous contrast**, also called **conditional contrast**.

**Example 1.1 Simultaneous Contrast Example**
All the small squares in the center of big squares (background) in Fig. 1.1 have exactly the same brightness. However, it looks brighter when it is on a dark background and looks darker when it is on a bright background. So, it feels like when these four pictures are viewed from left to right, the small square in the center gradually darkens. This is just the result of simultaneous contrast.

### 1.1.2.2  Mach Band Effect

At the boundary of the touch regions with different brightness in the object, human vision may estimate the brightness value too high or too low. In other words, the subjective brightness felt from the surface of an object is not a simple proportional function of the illuminance the object receives. This phenomenon was discovered by Mach, so it is called the **Mach band effect**.

**Example 1.2 Example of Mach Band Effect**
Figure 1.2a is a Mach band pattern, which includes three parts: the left side is a uniform low-brightness area, the right side is a uniform high-brightness area, and the middle is a gradual transition from low brightness to high brightness. Fig. 1.2b shows the actual brightness distribution (three straight lines) from left to right. If one looks at Fig. 1.2a with the eyes, one will find that there is a darker band at the junction of the left and middle bands than the left band and a darker band at the junction of the middle and right bands than the right band. The subjective brightness

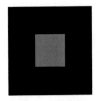 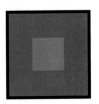  

**Fig. 1.1**  Example of simultaneous contrast

**Fig. 1.2**  Schematic
diagram of Mach band effect

(a)

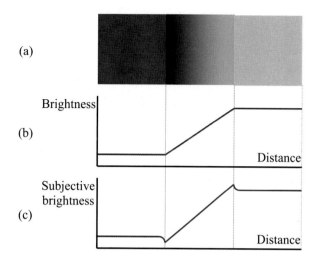

(b)

Brightness

Distance

(c)

Subjective
brightness

Distance

obtained should be as shown in Fig. 1.2c. In fact, the darker band and the brighter
band do not exist objectively; it is the result of subjective brightness perception.

### 1.1.2.3  Contrast Sensitivity

**Contrast sensitivity** (also called **contrast susceptibility**) reflects the ability of the
human eye to distinguish differences in brightness. It is affected by the observation
time and the size of the observed object. If a grid composed of lines of different
thickness and contrast is used for testing, the closer the contrast between the bright
and dark lines of the grid perceived by the eyes is to the contrast between the bright
and dark lines of the original test grid, the greater the contrast sensitivity. Under ideal
conditions, people with good eyesight can distinguish a brightness contrast of 0.01,
which means that the contrast sensitivity can reach up to 100.

If the abscissa represents the thickness of the bright and dark lines of the test grid
and the ordinate represents the contrast sensitivity, then the measured result will give
the modulation transfer function of the visual system, that is, the ability that human
visual system accurately converts the test grid into an optical image. Here the grid
thickness can be expressed by **spatial frequency**, and its unit is the number of circles
(number of lines) contained in each degree of viewing angle, that is, circle/degree
(CPD).

The contrast sensitivity can be regulated by the light modulation factor $M$. If $L_{max}$,
$L_{min}$, and $L_{av}$ are, respectively, the maximum, minimum, and average brightness
values, then

$$M = \frac{L_{max} - L_{min}}{L_{av}} \tag{1.1}$$

### 1.1.3  Spatial Properties of Vision

Vision is first and foremost a spatial experience, so the spatial properties of vision have a great influence on visual effects.

#### 1.1.3.1  Spatial Cumulative Effect

Vision has a cumulative effect in space. The range of light stimulus intensity experienced by the human eye can reach about 13 orders of magnitude. If described by light illuminance, the lowest absolute stimulus threshold is $10^{-6}$ lx (lux), and the highest absolute stimulus threshold exceeds $10^7$lx. Under the best conditions, every light quantum in the peripheral region of the retina will be absorbed by a rod cell, and a visual response can be caused by only a few light quanta. This is considered to have taken place in a complete spatial accumulation, and it can be described by the law of the inverse ratio of light intensity and area. This law can be written as

$$E_c = kAL \tag{1.2}$$

where $E_c$ is the absolute threshold of vision, which is the critical light energy required for 50% detection probability (i.e., the light energy when the light stimulation is observed once in every two tests in multiple experiments); $A$ is the cumulative area; $L$ is the brightness; and $k$ is a constant, which is related to the units used by $E_c$, $A$, and $L$. Note that the area that can satisfy the above law has a critical value $A_c$ (corresponding to a round **solid angle** with a diameter of about 0.3 rad). When $A < A_c$, the above law holds; otherwise the above law does not hold.

It can be seen that the **spatial cumulative effect** can be understood as follows: when a small and weak light spot is presented alone, it may be invisible (cannot cause a visual response), but when multiple such light spots are connected together as a large spot at the same time, one can see it. Its functional significance lies in: large objects may be seen in a dark environment even if the outline is blurred.

#### 1.1.3.2  Spatial Frequency

The **spatial frequency** corresponds to the changing speed of the visual image in space. This can be tested with stripes whose brightness sinusoidally changes in space. The brightness function $Y(x, y) = B(1 + m\cos2\pi fx)$. Among them, $B$ is the basic brightness, $m$ is the amplitude (corresponding to black and white contrast), and

$f$ is the fringe frequency (corresponding to the fringe width). The spatial resolution capability can be tested by changing $m$ when $f$ is given as a fixed value. Obviously, the larger $m$, the stronger the spatial resolution ability. In practice, to test the minimum $m$ value that can distinguish bright and dark stripes at different angles and frequencies, one can define $1/m$ minute (1′) as the contrast sensitivity. Usually the human eye, in terms of spatial frequency felling, is equivalent to a band-pass filter (more sensitive to the intermediate thickness of the stripes), the most sensitive is 2 ~ 5 CPD, and the spatial cut-off frequency is 30 CPD.

When a person observes a still image, the eyeball is not still in one place, usually after staying in one place for a few hundred milliseconds to complete the image acquisition, the eyeball will move to another place to take another image, and so on. This kind of movement is called **saccadic eye movement**. Studies have shown that jumping movement can increase contrast sensitivity, but the peak sensitivity will decrease.

### 1.1.3.3   Visual Acuity

**Visual acuity** is usually defined as the reciprocal of the viewing angle value corresponding to the smallest detail that can be distinguished under certain conditions. The smaller the viewing angle, the greater the visual acuity. If $V$ is used for visual acuity, then $V = 1/$(viewing angle). It represents the ability of the human eye to correctly distinguish the details and contours of objects. A visual acuity of 1 indicates the resolution capability at a standard distance when the corresponding viewing angle is 1°. The actual viewing angle of the human eye is 30″ ~ 60″ (this is basically consistent with the cone cell diameter of about 0.004 mm), that is, the best visual acuity can reach 2.0.

Visual acuity is affected by many factors, including the following:

1. Distance: When the distance of the object from the observer increases, the visual acuity of the human eye decreases. This phenomenon is most obvious at about 10 m, and beyond a certain distance limit, the details of the object can no longer be recognized.
2. Brightness: Increasing the brightness of the object (or enlarging the pupil) will increase the visual acuity. The relationship between visual acuity and brightness $I$ is

$$V = a \log I + b \tag{1.3}$$

where $a$ and $b$ are constants. Visual acuity increases with increasing brightness, and the relationship between the two is logarithmic. If the brightness continues to increase to a certain level, the visual acuity will be close to saturation and will not increase.

3. The contrast between the object and the background: Increasing the contrast will increase the visual acuity; decreasing the contrast will decrease the visual acuity.
4. Retina: Different parts of the retina have different visual acuity. The sensory cell density near the **fovea** is the highest, and the visual acuity is also the highest; the farther away from the fovea, the lower the visual acuity.

When a person observes an object, the best visual acuity is obtained when the object is located 0.25 m in front of the eye, and the illumination is 500 lx (equivalent to placing a 60 W incandescent lamp at 0.4 m away). At this time, the distance between the two points that can be distinguished by the human eye is about 0.00016 m.

### 1.1.4   Temporal Properties of Vision

The time factor is also very important in visual perception. This can be explained in three ways:

1. Most visual stimuli change over time or are generated sequentially.
2. The eyes are generally in constant motion, which makes the information acquired by the brain constantly changing.
3. Perception itself is not an instantaneous process, because information processing always takes time.

In addition, the rapid arrival of light stimuli in visual perception may affect each other. For example, the latter light stimulus may reduce the sensitivity to the previous light stimulus. This phenomenon is often referred to as **visual masking**, which reduces the perceived contrast, thereby reducing the perceived visual acuity.

#### 1.1.4.1   Visual Phenomena That Change Over Time

There are some visual phenomena that change over time. Here are two more obvious examples.

Brightness Adaptation

The human eye is sensitive to the external brightness in a wide range, from the dark vision threshold to the dazzling limit which is about $10^{-6} \sim 10^7$ cd/m$^2$. However, the human eye cannot work in such a large range at the same time. It relies on changing its specific sensitivity range to achieve **brightness adaptation**. See Fig. 1.3. Under certain conditions, the current sensitivity of the human eye is called the brightness adaptation level. The brightness range (subjective brightness range, two specific

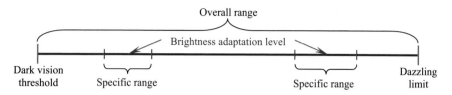

**Fig. 1.3**   The sensitive brightness range of human eye

ranges are given in the figure) that the human eye can feel at a certain moment is a small segment centered on this adaptation level.

At any moment in reality, the ratio of the maximum brightness to the minimum brightness perceived by the human eye rarely exceeds 100. The minimum brightness and maximum brightness are 1–100 cd/m$^2$ in a bright room, 10–1000 cd/m$^2$ outdoors, and 0.01–1 cd/m$^2$ at night (without lighting). Note that as the eye traverses the image, the change in the average background will cause different incremental changes at each adaptation level. As a result, the eye has the ability to distinguish a much larger total brightness level.

When the eye encounters a sudden change in brightness, the eye will temporarily lose sight to adapt to the new brightness as quickly as possible. The adaptation to bright light is faster than the adaptation to dark light. For example, when you leave the movie theater and enter a place under the sun, your normal vision can be restored quickly, but entering the movie theater from the outside under the sun may take a rather long time to see everything clearly. Quantitatively speaking, it only takes a few seconds to adapt to bright light, while it takes 35 to 45 min to fully adapt to dark light (about 10 min for cone cells to reach maximum sensitivity, plus another 30 min for rod cells to reach maximum sensitivity).

## Time Resolution of the Eyes

Many experiments have shown that the eyes can perceive two kinds of asynchronous brightness phenomena, as long as they can be separated in time. Among them, it normally takes at least 60–80 μs (microsecond) to distinguish them with confidence and about 20–40 μs to determine which brightness phenomenon appears first. In terms of absolute time, this interval does not seem to be long, but it is quite long if compared with other perception processes. For example, the time resolution of the auditory system is only a few microseconds.

In addition, when the frequency of the intensity of the incident light changes not too fast, the visual system can perceive the change in the intensity of the incident light, and its effect is like letting people see intermittent "flicker." When the frequency of light increases and exceeds a critical frequency (its value depends on the intensity of the light), this effect disappears, and people seem to observe continuous and steady light. For medium-intensity light, the above critical frequency is about 10 Hz, but for strong light, this frequency can reach 1000 Hz.

### 1.1.4.2   Time Cumulative Effect

Vision also has a **cumulative effect of time**. When observing an object with general brightness (light stimulation is not too large), the total energy $E$ of the received light is directly proportional to the visible area $A$, surface brightness $L$, and time interval (length of observation time) $T$ of the object, such as let $E_c$ be 50% probability of perceiving the required critical light energy; then there is

$$E_c = ALT \qquad\qquad (1.4)$$

Equation (1.4) is established under the condition that $T < T_c$, and $T_c$ is the critical time interval. Equations (1.1)–(1.4) shows that the degree of stimulating eye in the time less than $T_c$ is directly proportional to the stimulating time. When the time interval exceeds $T_c$, there is no longer a time cumulative effect.

### 1.1.4.3   Time Frequency

**Time frequency** corresponds to the speed of visual image changes over time. This can be tested with stripes whose brightness changes sinusoidally with time. The brightness function $Y(t) = B(1 + m\cos 2\pi ft)$. Among them, $B$ is the basic brightness, $m$ is the amplitude (corresponding to black and white contrast), and $f$ is the fringe frequency (corresponding to the fringe width). The time resolution can be tested by changing $m$ when $f$ is a fixed value to determine the **contrast sensitivity**.

Experiments show that the time frequency response is also related to the average brightness. Under normal indoor light intensity, the human eye's response to time and frequency is similar to a band-pass filter. It is most sensitive to 15–20 Hz signal and has a strong sense of flicker. When it is greater than 75 Hz, the response is 0 and the flicker disappears. The frequency at which the flicker disappears is called the **critical flicker frequency/critical fusion frequency** (CFF). In a darker environment, the response has more low-pass characteristics, and CFF is reduced. At this time, the 5 Hz signal is most sensitive, and the flicker above 25 Hz basically disappears. For example, if the movie theater environment is very dark, the projector's refresh rate is 24 Hz, and there will be no flicker, which can reduce the amount of film and the speed of the machine. The brightness of the computer monitor is larger, and then the refresh rate of 75 Hz is needed to make flicker disappear. After the flicker disappears, the brightness perception is equal to the time average of brightness. This low-pass characteristic can also be parsed as a persistent visual characteristic, that is, when the image disappears/changes, the brain image does not disappear immediately but remains for a short period of time. Motion blur and afterimages often felt in life are also related to this property.

## *1.1.5   Visual Perception*

Vision is an important function for humans to comprehend the world. Vision includes "sensation" and "perception," so it can be further divided into visual sensation and visual perception. In many cases, visual sensation is often referred to as vision, but in fact, visual perception is more important and more complicated.

### 1.1.5.1   Visual Sensation and Visual Perception

People not only need to obtain information from the outside world but also need to process the information to make judgments and decisions. Therefore, the human vision, hearing, smell, taste, touch and other functions can be divided into two levels of sensation and perception. Sensation is at lower level; it mainly receives external stimuli. Perception is at a higher level; it converts external stimuli into meaningful content. In general, the sensation is to completely receive the external stimulus basically without distinction, while the perception is to determine which parts of the external stimulus should be combined into the "target" of concern or to analyze and judge the nature of the source of the external stimulus.

Human **visual sensation** is mainly to understand the basic properties (such as brightness, color) of people's response to light (visible radiation) from a molecular perspective, which mainly involves physics, chemistry, etc. The main research contents in visual sensation are as follows:

1. The physical properties of light, such as light quantum, light wave, spectrum, etc.
2. The degree of light stimulation on visual receptors, such as photometry, eye structure, visual adaptation, visual intensity and sensitivity, the temporal and spatial properties, etc.
3. The sensations produced by the visual system after light acts on the retina, such as brightness, color tone, etc.

**Visual perception** mainly discusses how people react after receiving visual stimuli from the objective world, as well as the methods and results obtained in response. It studies how to form people's appearance of the external world space through vision, so it has also psychological factors. Visual perception is a group of activities carried out in the nerve center. It organizes some scattered stimuli in the field of vision to form a whole with a certain shape and structure and to cognize the world accordingly. As early as 2000 years ago, Aristotle defined the task of visual perception as determining "What is where." In recent years, both its connotation and extension have been expanded.

The objective things that people use vision to perceive have many characteristics. To the light stimulation, the human visual system will produce different forms of response, so visual perception can be divided into brightness perception, color perception, shape perception, space perception, motion perception, etc. It should be noted that some of the various perceptions change in accordance with the changes in the physical quantity of the stimulus. For example, the brightness depends on the intensity of the light, and the color depends on the wavelength of the light. However, for some perceptions, such as the perception of space, time, and motion, there is no exact correspondence between them and the physical quantity of the stimulation. Perceptions with correspondences are easier to analyze, while perceptions without exact correspondences must be considered comprehensively in conjunction with other knowledge.

### 1.1.5.2  The Complexity of Visual Perception

The visual process includes three sub-processes, namely, optical process, chemical process, and neural processing process (see *2D Computer Vision: Principles, Algorithms and Applications*). In the optical process, the radiation energy received by the human eye will pass through the refractive system (including the lens, pupil, cornea, aqueous humor, vitreous, etc.) in the human eye and finally be imaged on the retina according to geometric rules. The visual pattern formed on the retina can be called a retinal image, which is an optical projection received through a system composed of the lens and pupil in the eye. This purely optical image is then transformed into a completely different form/type by the chemical system on the retina. Note that the retinal image is only an intermediate result of the visual system's processing of light. It can be regarded as the boundary between visual sensation and visual perception. Unlike the "images" used in other occasions, people cannot see their own retinal images. Only ophthalmologists who use special devices can see this "image." One of the most obvious differences between the retinal optical image and the artificial image is that the retinal image is only focused in the center while the artificial image (used to represent a moving eye's field of view) is evenly focused.

Visual perception is a complicated process. In many cases, it is difficult to fully explain all (perception) processes only by relying on the retinal image formed by the light projected on the retina and the known mechanisms of the eye or nervous system. Here are two examples of perception to help illustrate this problem.

Perception of the Visual Edge

The **visual edge** refers to the boundary between two surfaces with different brightness observed from a point of view. There can be many reasons for the difference in brightness, such as different illumination and different reflection properties. When the visual edge is observed from a viewpoint, the visual edge may change its position by changing the point of view and then observing again. In this way, the cognition of the observed object may vary depending on the observation position. In the perception of the visual edge, there are both objective factors and subjective factors.

Perception of Brightness Contrast

The visual system feels mainly the change of brightness rather than the brightness itself. The psychological brightness of an object's surface is basically determined by its relationship with the brightness of the surrounding environment (especially the background). If two objects have similar brightness ratios to their respective backgrounds, then they appear to have similar brightness, which has nothing to do with their own absolute brightness. Conversely, if the same object is placed on a darker background, it will appear brighter than on a brighter background (such as simultaneous contrast phenomenon).

The visual system can also link the perception of brightness with the perception of visual edges. The brightness of two visual surfaces can be compared using perception only when they are considered to be on the same visual plane. If they are considered to be at different distances from the eyes, it is difficult to compare their relative brightness. Similarly, when a visual edge is considered to be caused by illumination on the same surface (the two sides of the edge are illuminated and shadowed respectively), then the brightness difference on both sides of the edge will automatically appear stronger.

## 1.2   Computer Vision Theory and Framework

**Computer vision** refers to the realization of human visual functions with computers, that is, the perception, recognition, and understanding of 3-D scenes in the objective world.

### 1.2.1   Reaserch Goals, Tasks, and Methods of Computer Vision

The original purpose of computer vision research is to grasp the images of the scene; identify and locate/extract the objects in it; and determine their structure, spatial arrangement and distribution, and the relationship between the objects. The goal of computer vision research is to make meaningful judgments about actual objects and scenes based on perceived images.

The main research tasks of computer vision can be summarized into two, which are related to each other and complement each other. The first research task is to build a computer vision system to complete various vision tasks. In other words, it is necessary to enable the computer to obtain images of the scene with the help of various visual sensors (such as CCD, CMOS camera devices, etc.); to perceive and restore the geometric properties, posture structure, movement, and mutual position of objects in the 3-D environment; identify, describe, and explain the objective scene; and then make the required judgments and decisions. The main research here is the technical mechanism. The current work in this domain is focused on building various special systems to complete the special vision tasks proposed in various practical situations, and in the long run, it is necessary to build more general systems. The second research task is to use this research as a means to explore the working mechanism of human brain vision and to further deepen the grasp and understanding of human brain vision (such as computational neuroscience). The main research here is the biological mechanism. For a long time, a large number of researches have been conducted on the human brain visual system from the aspects of physiology, psychology, nerves, cognition, etc., but all the mysteries of the visual process have not been revealed. It can be said that the research and understanding of the visual mechanism are still far behind for the research and mastery of visual information processing. It needs to be pointed out that a full understanding of human brain vision will also promote the in-depth study of computer vision. This book mainly considers the first research task.

It can be seen from the above discussions that computer vision needs to use computers to realize human vision functions, and its research has also gained a lot of inspiration from human vision. Many important researches in computer vision are realized by understanding the human visual system. Typical examples are the use of pyramids as an effective data structure, the use of local orientation concepts to analyze the shape of objects, and filtering techniques to detect motion. In addition, with the help of research on the huge understanding of the human visual system, it can help people to develop new image understanding and computer vision algorithms.

There are two main research methods of computer vision: one is the bionics method, which refers to the structural principles of the human visual system and establishes corresponding processing modules to complete similar functions and tasks, and the other is the engineering method, which starts by analyzing the functions of human vision process; it does not deliberately simulate the internal structure of the human visual system but only considers the input and output of the system and uses any existing feasible means to achieve system functions. This book mainly discusses the second method.

## 1.2.2  Visual Computational Theory

Research on computer vision did not have a comprehensive theoretical framework in the early days. The research on object recognition and scene understanding in the 1970s basically detected linear edges as the primitives of the scene and then combined them to form more complex scene structure. However, in practice, comprehensive primitive detection is difficult and unstable, so the visual system can only input simple lines and corners to form the so-called building block world.

The book *Vision* published by Marr in 1982 summarized a series of results based on the research of human vision by him and his colleagues and proposed the **visual**

**computational theory/computational vision theory**, which outlined a framework for understanding visual information. This framework is both comprehensive and refined and is the key to make the research of visual information understanding more rigorous and improve the visual research from the level of description to the level of mathematical science. Marr's theory states that one must first understand the purpose of vision and then understand the details inside. This is suitable for various information processing tasks. The main points of this theory are as follows.

### 1.2.2.1 Vision Is a Complex Information Processing Process

Marr believes that vision is a far more complicated information processing task and process than human imagination, and its difficulty is often not considered squarely. One of the main reasons here is that although it is difficult to understand images with computers, it is often easy for humans.

In order to understand the complex process of vision, two problems must be solved first. One is the representation of visual information; the other is the processing of visual information. The representation here refers to a formal system (such as the Arabic number system, binary number system) that can clearly represent certain entities or types of information and several rules that explain how the system works. Some information in the representation can be prominent and clear, while other information may be hidden and vague. Representation has a great influence on the difficulty of subsequent information processing. As for visual information processing, it must achieve its goal by continuously processing, analyzing, and understanding information, transforming different forms of representation, and gradually abstracting it.

Solving the problem of visual information representation and processing of visual information is actually to solve the problem of computability. If a task needs to be completed by a computer, then it should be computable. This is the problem of computability. Generally speaking, if there is a program and the program can give output in a finite step for a given input of a particular problem, the problem is computable.

### 1.2.2.2 Three Essential Factors of Visual Information Processing

To fully understand and interpret visual information, three essential factors need to be grasped at the same time, namely, computational theory, algorithm implementation, and hardware implementation.

The highest level of visual information understanding is abstract computational theory. The question of whether vision can be computed by modern computers needs to be answered by computational theory, but there is no clear answer yet. Vision is a process of sensation plus perception. People have very little grasp of the mechanism of human visual function in terms of micro-anatomical knowledge and objective visual psychological knowledge. Therefore, the discussion on visual computability

**Table 1.1** The meaning of the three essential factors of visual information processing

| Essential factor | Name | Meaning and problems to be solved |
|---|---|---|
| 1 | Computational theory | What is the computation goal? Why is it computed like this? |
| 2 | Representation and algorithm | How to realize computational theory? What is input and output representation? What algorithm is used to realize the conversion between representations? |
| 3 | Hardware implementation | How to physically implement representations and algorithms? What are the specific details of computing structures? |

is still relatively limited, mainly focusing on completing certain specific visual tasks with the digital and symbol processing capabilities of existing computers nowadays.

Secondly, the objects operated by computers today are discrete digits or symbols, and the storage capacity of computers is also limited. Therefore, with the computational theory, the realization of the algorithm must be considered. For this reason, it is necessary to choose a suitable type of representation for the entity operated by the processing. Here, on the one hand, the input and output representation of processing must be selected; on the other hand, the algorithm for completing the representation conversion must be determined. Representation and algorithm are mutually restrictive. Three points need to be paid attention to:

1. There can be many alternative representations in general.
2. The determination of the algorithm often depends on the selected representation.
3. Given a representation, there can be multiple algorithms to complete the task.

From this point of view, the selected representations and the processing methods are closely related. In general, the instructions and rules used for processing are called algorithms.

Finally, with the representation and algorithm, how to implement the algorithm physically must also be considered. Especially with the continuous improvement of real-time requirements, the problem of special hardware implementation is often raised. It should be noted that the determination of an algorithm often depends on the hardware characteristics of physically implementing the algorithm, and the same algorithm can also be implemented by different technical approaches.

After summarizing the above discussion, Table 1.1 can be obtained.

There is a certain logical causal connection between the above three essential factors, but there is no absolute dependence. In fact, there are many different options for each essential factor. In many cases, the problems involved in explaining each essential factor are basically irrelevant to the other two essential factors (each essential factor is relatively independent), or one or two essential factors can be used to explain certain visual phenomena. The above three essential factors are also called by many people the three levels of visual information processing, and they point out that different problems need to be explained at different levels. The relationship among the three essential factors is often shown in Fig. 1.4 (in fact, it is more appropriate to regard it as two levels), in which the positive arrow indicates

**Fig. 1.4** The relationship of the three essential factors of visual information processing

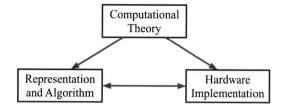

that it has a guiding meaning, and the reverse arrow has a meaning of as basic. Note that once there is a theory of computation, representations and algorithms as well as hardware implementations influence each other.

### 1.2.2.3    Three-Level Internal Expression of Visual Information

According to the definition of visual computability, the visual information processing process can be broken down into multiple conversion steps from one representation to another. Representation is the key to visual information processing. A basic theoretical framework for research of visual information understanding with computer is mainly composed of the three-level representation structure of the visible world established, maintained, and interpreted by visual processing. For most philosophers, what is the essence of visual representation, how they relate to perception, and how they support action can all have different interpretations. However, they all agree that the answers to these questions are related to the concept of **representation**.

1. Primal Sketch

The **primal sketch** denotes a 2-D representation, which is a collection of image features and describes the contour part where the properties of the object surface change. The primal sketch representation provides the information of the contour of each object in the image and is a form of sketch representation of the 3-D object. This way of representation can be proven from the human visual process. When people observe a scene, they always notice the drastic changes in it. Therefore, primal sketch should be a stage of the human visual process.

2. 2.5-D Sketch

The **2.5-D sketch** is completely proposed to adapt to the computing functions of the computer. It decomposes the object according to the principle of **orthogonal projection** according to a certain sampling density, so that the visible surface of the object is decomposed into many facets (face element) of a certain size and geometric shape; each facet has its own orientation. Using a normal vector to represent the orientation of the facet in which it is located and composing a set of needles (the vector is shown with an arrow/needle) constitutes a 2.5-D sketch map (also called a needle diagram). In this type of diagram, the normal of each

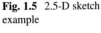

**Fig. 1.5**  2.5-D sketch example

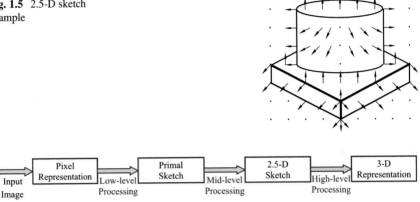

**Fig. 1.6**  The three-level representation decomposition of the Marr's framework

orientation takes the observer as the center. The specific steps to obtain the 2.5-D sketch map (Fig. 1.5 shows an example) are as follows:

1. Decompose the orthogonal projection of the visible surface of the object into a collection of facets.
2. Use the normal lines to represent the orientation of the facet.
3. Draw each normal line, and superimpose all normal lines on the visible surface within the outline of the object.

The 2.5-D sketch map is actually an intrinsic image (see Sect. 3.2), because it shows the orientation of the surface element of the object, thus giving the information of the surface shape. Surface orientation is an intrinsic characteristic, and depth is also an intrinsic characteristic. The 2.5-D sketch map can be converted into a (relative) depth map.

## 3. 3-D Representation

**3-D representation** is a representation form centered on the object (i.e., it also includes the invisible part of the object). It describes the shape and spatial organization of 3-D objects in the object-centered coordinate system. Some basic 3-D entity representations can be found in Chap. 9.

Now come back to the problem of visual computability. From the perspective of computer or information processing, the problem of visual computability can be divided into several steps. Between the steps is a certain form of representation, and each step consists of a calculation/processing method that connects the two forms of representation (see Fig. 1.6).

**Table 1.2** Representation framework of visual computability problem

| Representation | Goal | Primitive |
|---|---|---|
| Image | Represent the brightness of the scene or the illuminance of the object | Pixel (values) |
| Primal sketch | Represent the location of brightness changes in the image, the geometric distribution of the object outline, and the organizational structure | Zero crossing point, end point, corner point, inflection point, edge segment, boundary, etc. |
| 2.5-D sketch | Represent the orientation, depth, contour, and other properties of the visible surface of the object in the observer-centered coordinate system | Local surface orientation ("needle" primitives), surface orientation discontinuities, depth, discontinuous point in depth, etc. |
| 3-D representation | Represent the object shapes and their spatial organization, by using voxels or surface elements, in a coordinate system centered on an object | 3-D model, with the axis as the skeleton, attach the volume element or face element to the axis |

According to the above-mentioned three-level representation viewpoint, the problem to be solved by visual computability is how to start from the pixel representation of the original image, through the primal sketch representation and 2.5-D sketch representation, and finally obtain the 3-D representation. They can be summarized in Table 1.2.

### 1.2.2.4 Visual Information Understanding Is Organized in the Form of Functional Modules

The idea of viewing the visual information system as a set of relatively independent functional modules is not only supported by the evolutionary and epistemological arguments in computing, but also some functional modules can be separated by experimental methods.

In addition, psychological research also shows that people obtain various intrinsic visual information by using a variety of clues or a combination of them. This suggests that the visual information system should include many modules. Each module obtains a specific visual cues and performs certain processing, so that different weight coefficients can be combined with different modules to complete the visual information understanding task according to the environment. According to this point of view, complex processing can be completed with some simple independent functional modules, which can simplify research methods and reduce the difficulty of specific implementation. This is also very important from an engineering perspective.

### 1.2.2.5    The Formal Representation of Computational Theory Must Consider Constraints

During the image acquisition process, the information in the original scene will undergo various changes, including the following:

1. When a 3-D scene is projected as a 2-D image, the depth of the object and the invisible part of the information are lost.
2. Images are always obtained from a specific viewing directions. Different perspective images of the same scene will be different. In addition, information will be lost due to mutual occlusion of objects or mutual occlusion of various parts.
3. Imaging projection makes the illumination, object geometry, and surface reflection characteristics, camera characteristics, and the spatial relationship between the light source, the object, and the camera all integrated into a single image gray value, which are difficult to be distinguished.
4. Noise and distortion will inevitably be introduced in the imaging process.

For a problem, if its solution is existing; unique; continuously dependent on the initial data, then it is well-posed. If one or more of the above is not satisfied, it is ill-posed (under-determined). Due to the information changes in the various original scenes mentioned above, the method of solving the vision problem as the inverse problem of the optical imaging process becomes an ill-posed problem (becoming an ill-conditioned problem), so it is very difficult to solve. In order to solve this problem, it is necessary to find out the constraints of the relevant problems according to the general characteristics of the external objective world and turn them into precise assumptions, so as to draw conclusive and testable conclusions. Constraints are generally obtained with the aid of prior knowledge. The use of constraints can change ill-conditioned problems. This is because by adding constraints to the computation problem, whose meaning could become clear and suitable solution could be found.

### 1.2.3    Framework Problems and Improvements

Marr's visual computational theory is the first theory that has a greater impact on visual research. This theory has actively promoted research in this field and has played an important role in the research and development of image understanding and computer vision.

Marr's theory also has its shortcomings, including four problems about the overall framework (see Fig. 1.6):

1. The input in the framework is passive, what image is input, the system will process what image.
2. The processing goal in the framework remains unchanged, and the position and shape of the objects in the scene are always restored.

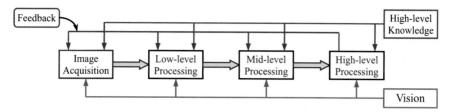

**Fig. 1.7**  Improved visual computational framework

3. The framework lacks or does not pay enough attention to the guiding role of high-level knowledge.
4. The information processing process in the entire framework is basically bottom-up, one-way flow, and no feedback.

In response to the above problems, people have proposed a series of improvement ideas in recent years. Corresponding to the framework of Fig. 1.6, these improvements can be incorporated into new modules to obtain the framework of Fig. 1.7.

The following is a detailed discussion of the improvements in the four aspects of the framework of Fig. 1.6 in conjunction with Fig. 1.7.

1. Human vision has initiative.
      People will change the line of sight or perspective as needed to help observation and cognition. **Active vision** means that the vision system can determine the movement of the camera according to the existing analysis results and the current requirements of the vision task to obtain the corresponding image from the appropriate position and perspective. Human vision is also selective, one can stare (observing the region of interest at a higher resolution), or one can turn a blind eye to certain parts of the scene. **Selective vision** means that the vision system can determine the focus of the camera to obtain the corresponding image based on the existing analysis results and the current requirements of the vision task. Taking these factors into account, an image acquisition module is added to the improved framework, which is also considered together with other modules in the framework. This module should choose the image acquisition modes according to the visual purpose.
      The aforementioned active vision and selective vision can also be regarded as two forms of active vision: one is to move the camera to focus on a specific object of interest in the current environment; the other is to focus on a specific region in the image and dynamically interact with it to get an interpretation. Although the two forms of active vision look very similar, in the first form, the initiative is mainly reflected in the observation of the camera, while in the second form, the initiative is mainly reflected in the processing level and strategy. Although there is interaction in both forms, that is, vision has initiative, mobile cameras need to record and store all the complete scenes, which is a very expensive process. In addition, the overall interpretations obtained in this way are not necessarily used. Collecting only the most useful part of the scene, narrowing its scope, and

enhancing its quality to obtain useful interpretations mimics the process of human interpretation of the scene.

2. Human vision can be adjusted for different purposes.

   **Purposive vision** means that the vision system makes decisions based on the purpose of vision, such as whether to fully recover information like the position and shape of objects in the scene or just detect whether there is an object in the scene. It may give a simpler solution to vision problems. The key issue here is to determine the purpose of the task. Therefore, a visual purpose box (vision goal) is added to the improvement framework. Qualitative analysis or quantitative analysis can be determined according to different purposes of understanding (in practice, there are quite a lot of occasions where only qualitative results are sufficient; no complex quantitative result is needed). However, the current qualitative analysis still lacks complete mathematical tools. The motivation of purposive vision is to clarify only part of the information that is needed. For example, the collision avoidance of autonomous vehicles does not require precise shape descriptions, and some qualitative results are sufficient. This kind of thinking does not have a solid theoretical basis, but the study of biological vision systems provides many examples.

   **Qualitative vision**, which is closely related to purposive vision, seeks a qualitative description of an object or scene. Its motivation is not to express geometric information that is not needed for qualitative (non-geometric) tasks or decisions. The advantage of qualitative information is that it is less sensitive to various unwanted transformations (such as slightly changing perspectives) or noise than quantitative information. Qualitative or invariant can allow easy interpretation of observed events at different levels of complexity.

3. Humans have the ability to completely solve visual problems with only partial information obtained from images.

   Humans have this ability due to the implicit use of various knowledge. For example, after obtaining object shape information with the aid of CAD design data (using object model library), it can help solve the difficulty of restoring the object shape from a single image. The use of high-level (domain) knowledge can solve the problem of insufficient low-level information, so a high-level knowledge frame (module) is added to the improved framework.

4. There is an interaction between the sequential processing processes in human vision.

   The human visual process has a certain sequence in time and different levels in meaning, and there is a certain interaction between the various steps. Although the mechanism of this interaction is not yet fully understood, the important role of high-level knowledge and feedback from the later results to low-level processing has been widely recognized. From this perspective, the feedback control flow is added to the improvement framework, and the existing results and high-level knowledge are used to improve visual efficiency.

# 1.3   Three-Dimensional Vision System and Image Technology

In practical applications, in order to complete the vision task, a corresponding vision system needs to be constructed, in which various image technologies are used.

## 1.3.1   Three-Dimensional Vision System Process

Although in many cases, people can only directly acquire images produced by 2-D projection of the 3-D world, the objective world itself is in the 3-D space. To accurately understand the objective world, it is necessary to grasp the 3-D spatial information of the scene. Therefore, a 3-D vision system needs to be studied and used.

In order to obtain 3-D spatial information, on the one hand, one can directly acquire it; on the other hand, one can also use 2-D images to understand the content and meaning of the 3-D world. Considering these two aspects separately, there are two types of schemes for obtaining 3-D spatial information. One type is to build special equipment to directly collect 3-D images, which will be discussed in Chap. 3; the other type is to collect one or a series of 2-D images first and then try to obtain 3-D spatial information from these images (i.e., to reconstruct and restore the objective scene). There are two technical routes in this latter method. One is to collect multiple related 2-D images and obtain the 3-D spatial information in these images according to their correlation. Some typical methods in this technical route will be introduced in Chaps. 6 and 7. The other is to collect only a single 2-D image, but use some relevant prior knowledge to obtain hidden 3-D spatial information. Some typical methods in this technical route will be introduced in Chap. 8.

Obtaining 3-D spatial information lays the foundation for the realization of visual tasks. On this (perceptual) basis, computer vision also needs to make meaningful interpretations and judgments of actual goals and scenes based on the perceived images to help to make decisions and take actions. This is a high-level work that requires learning, reasoning, and matching with models to explain the content, characteristics, changes, and trends of the scene.

**Scene interpretation** is a very complicated process, and the difficulties mainly come from two aspects: one is that there is a large amount of multi-sided data to be processed, and the other is the lack of the basic tools for operations from known low-level pixel matrix to the required high-level results (to grasp the details of image content for the information reflecting the scene). Since there is no universal tool for understanding unstructured images, it is necessary to compromise between the two, that is, on the one hand, the generality of the problem needs to be restricted and, on the other hand, human knowledge needs to be introduced into the understanding process. It is relatively straightforward to limit the generality of the problem. People can limit the unknown conditions in the problem or limit the scope or precision of the

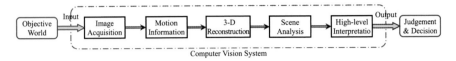

**Fig. 1.8** 3-D vision system flow chart

expected result, but the introduction of knowledge is more difficult and worthy of serious study.

Combining the above discussion, a 3-D vision system flowchart as shown in Fig. 1.8 can be given. Here, the image acquisition should consider 3-D images or 2-D images containing 3-D information. Obtaining motion information is also to obtain more comprehensive information about the objective world. 3-D reconstruction is to restore the original appearance of the objective world and then through objective analysis of the scene, to realize the interpretation and understanding of the scene, and to help to make decisions and to take actions to deal with the environment and transform the world.

### 1.3.2   Computer Vision and Image Technology Levels

In order to complete the functions of the vision system, a series of technologies are required. After years of development, computer vision technology has made great progress, and there are many types. There are some classification methods for these technologies, but it seems that they are not stable and consistent. For example, different researchers divide computer vision technology into three levels, but the three levels are not uniform. For example, someone divides computer vision into low-level vision, middle-level vision, and 3-D vision. Some other people divide computer vision into early vision (which is divided into two parts: only one image; multiple images), middle vision, and high-level vision (geometric methods). Even the same researcher is not consistent at different times. For example, someone once divided the computer vision into early vision (which is divided into two parts: only one image; multiple images), middle vision, and high-level vision (which is divided into two parts, geometric methods; probability and inference methods).

Relatively speaking, in **image engineering** (a new cross-discipline that systematically studies various image theories, technologies, and applications), a classification method for image technology has been relatively consistent for the past 27 years. This method divides various image technologies into three levels: image processing, image analysis, and image understanding. As shown in Fig. 1.9, each level has its own characteristics in terms of operation objects, data volume, semantic level, and abstraction.

**Image processing** (IP) is at the low level, basically focusing on the conversion between images, with the intent to improve the visual effects of images and lay the foundation for subsequent tasks.

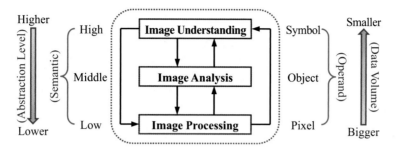

**Fig. 1.9**  Schematic diagram of three levels of image engineering

**Image analysis** (IA) is at the middle level, mainly considering the detection and measurement of objects of interest in the image to obtain their objective information to establish a description of the image.

**Image understanding** (IU) is at a high level and emphasizes the grasping the meaning of the image content and the interpretation of the original objective scene, which has many similarities with human thinking and reasoning.

As mentioned above, image processing, image analysis, and image understanding have their own characteristics in terms of abstraction degree and data volume, and their operation objects and semantic levels are different. For their interrelationships, see Fig. 1.9. Image processing is a relatively low-level operation, which is mainly worked at the pixel level of the image, and the amount of processed data is very large. Image analysis enters the middle level. Segmentation and feature extraction transform the original image described by pixels into a more concise description of the object. Image understanding is mainly a high-level operation. The operation object is basically a symbol abstracted from the description. Its processing process and method have many similarities with human thinking and reasoning. In addition, it can be seen from Fig. 1.9 that the amount of data gradually decreases as the degree of abstraction increases. Specifically, the original image data is gradually transformed into a more organized and more abstract representation through a series of processing procedures. In this process, semantics are continuously introduced/upgraded, operation objects are changed, and the amount of data is compressed. On the other hand, higher-level operations have a guiding role for low-level operations and can improve the efficiency of lower-level operations.

## *1.3.3   Image Technology Category*

According to the latest overview of statistical study of image engineering literature, the classification of image technology in the three levels of image processing, image analysis, and image understanding can be seen in Table 1.3. In addition to the 16 subcategories in these three levels, image engineering also includes various technical applications subcategories, so there are 23 subcategories in total.

**Table 1.3** Current image technology categories studied in the three levels of image processing, image analysis, and image understanding

| Three layers | Image technology categories and names |
|---|---|
| Image processing | **Image acquisition** (including various imaging methods, image capturing, representation and storage, camera calibration, etc.) |
| | Image reconstruction (including image reconstruction from projection, indirect imaging, etc.) |
| | Image enhancement/image restoration (including transformation, filtering, restoration, repair, replacement, correction, visual quality evaluation, etc.) |
| | Image/video coding and compression (including algorithm research, implementation and improvement of related international standards, etc.) |
| | Image information security (including digital watermarking, information hiding, image authentication and forensics, etc.) |
| | Image multi-resolution processing (including super-resolution reconstruction, image decomposition and interpolation, resolution conversion, etc.) |
| Image analysis | Image segmentation and primitive detection (including edges, corners, control points, points of interest, etc.) |
| | **Object representation, object description, feature measurement** (including binary image morphology analysis, etc.) |
| | **Object feature extraction and analysis** (including color, texture, shape, space, structure, motion, saliency, attributes, etc.) |
| | **Object detection** and **object recognition** (including object 2-!D positioning, tracking, extraction, identification and classification, etc.) |
| | Human body biological feature extraction and verification (including detection, positioning and recognition of human body, face and organs, etc.) |
| Image understanding | **Image matching and fusion** (including registration of sequence and stereo image, mosaic, etc.) |
| | **Scene recovering** (including 3-D scene representation, modeling, reconstruction, etc.) |
| | **Image perception and interpretation** (including semantic description, scene model, machine learning, cognitive reasoning, etc.) |
| | Content-based image/video retrieval (including corresponding labeling, classification, etc.) |
| | **Spatial-temporal techniques** (including high-dimensional motion analysis, object 3-D posture detection, spatial-temporal tracking, behavior judgment and behavior understanding, etc.) |

This book involves some contents of three levels. In image processing technology, it mostly discusses camera calibration and 3-D image acquisition. In image analysis technology, it mainly discusses the promotion of some 2-D analysis technologies to 3-D space. This book focuses on some technologies in image understanding. It generally involves image matching and image fusion, scene restoration, image perception and image interpretation, and spatial-temporal technology. These categories are shown in bold letters in Table 1.3.

Among the three levels of image engineering, the level of image understanding has the closest relationship with current computer vision technology. This book will mainly introduce the content of this level. This also has many historical origins. In establishing an image/visual information system and using computers to assist humans in completing various visual tasks, image understanding and computer vision require the use of projective geometry, probability theory and random processes, artificial intelligence, and other theories. For example, they all rely on two types of intelligent activities: perception, such as perceiving the distance, orientation, shape, movement speed, and mutual relationship of the visible part of the scene; thinking, such as analyzing the behavior of subjects and objects based on the structure of the scene; inferring the development and changes of the scene; and determining and planning the subject actions.

Computer vision began to be studied as an artificial intelligence problem, so it is often called image understanding. In fact, the terms image understanding and computer vision are often mixed. In essence, they are connected to each other. In many cases, they have overlapped coverages and contents, and they have not absolute boundary in concept or practicality. In many occasions and situations, although they have their own emphasis, they often complement each other. Therefore, it is more appropriate to regard them as different terms used by people with different professions and backgrounds. They are not deliberately distinguished in this book.

## 1.4 Overview of the Structure and Content of This Book

This book mainly introduces the three-dimensional part of computer vision and also corresponds to the basic concepts, basic theories, and practical techniques of high-level image engineering. Through the comprehensive use of these theories and technologies, various computer vision systems can be constructed to explore and solve practical application problems. In addition, through the introduction of the high-level content of image engineering, it can also help readers to obtain more information based on the results obtained from the low-level and middle-level technologies of image engineering, as well as combine and integrate the technologies at all levels.

### 1.4.1 Structural Framework and Content of This Book

According to the 3-D vision system flow chart in Fig. 1.8, this book selects some related technologies for introduction. The structural framework and main contents of this book are shown in Fig. 1.10.

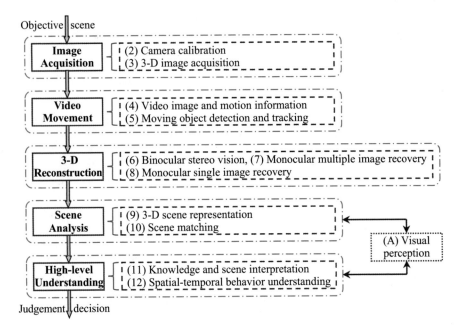

**Fig. 1.10** The structure and main contents of this book (the number in parentheses corresponds to the specific chapter number)

## 1.4.2  Chapter Overview

This book has 12 chapters and 1 appendix.

Chapter 1 introduces some elementary concepts and knowledge of human vision. It first discusses some important features and characteristics of vision and then introduces visual perception combined with visual sensation. On this basis, an overview discussion of computer vision and the main content of this book are provided.

Chapter 2 discusses the camera calibration scheme, followed by the reviewing of the basic linear camera model and the typical non-linear camera model, respectively. It also introduces a traditional camera calibration method and a simple active vision-based calibration method.

Chapter 3 introduces 3-D image acquisition, especially depth image acquisition. Among them, it includes not only the method of directly collecting depth images but also the two-camera stereo imaging method with reference to human vision.

Chapter 4 introduces the video image that is another form of 3-D (2-D space and 1-D time) image that contains motion information. This chapter analyzes the characteristics of video and discusses the principles and methods of motion information classification, detection, and filtering.

Chapter 5 discusses the detection and tracking technology for moving objects in video, from simple to complex, including pixel-by-pixel difference, background modeling, optical flow estimation, and several typical moving object tracking methods.

Chapter 6 introduces binocular stereo vision, including the functions of each module of stereo vision, region-based binocular stereo matching, and feature-based binocular stereo matching technology, as well as a disparity map error detection and correction method.

Chapter 7 presents two common methods for scene restoration using multiple monocular images, including the method based on photometric stereo and the method based on optical flow field to obtain structure from motion.

Chapter 8 introduces two types of methods for scene restoration using monocular single images, including methods for restoring the shape of objects from tone changes (shading) in the surface and methods for restoring the orientation of the surface from texture changes in the surface of the object.

Chapter 9 introduces the typical methods for representing the actual 3-D scene, including the methods of representing the 3-D surface, constructing and representing the 3-D iso-surface, and interpolating the 2-D parallel contour to obtain 3-D surface, as well as the method of directly representing 3-D entities.

Chapter 10 introduces different levels of matching techniques, including more specific object matching and dynamic pattern matching methods, more abstract methods of using graph isomorphism to match relationships, and method of using line drawing signatures to achieve scene model matching.

Chapter 11 combines scene knowledge and learning reasoning to introduce the models of scene interpretation, including predicate logic and fuzzy reasoning. It also discusses two widely used models in scene classification: bag-of-words/features model and probabilistic implicit semantic analysis model.

Chapter 12 introduces the understanding of spatial-temporal behavior, including the concepts of spatial-temporal technology and points of interest in spatial-temporal space, methods for learning and analyzing dynamic trajectories, and methods for classifying and recognizing actions.

Appendix A introduces visual perception and introduces the characteristics and laws of shape perception, space perception, and movement perception in more detail. The understanding of human vision also has implications for computer vision.

At the end of each chapter and appendix, there is a section of "Key points and references for each section." On the one hand, it summarizes the central content of each section; and on the other hand, it provides several suitable references for in-depth study. Except the appendix, each chapter has a certain number of self-test questions (all including hints and answers).

## 1.5  Key Points and References for Each Section

The following combines the main contents of each section to introduce some references that can be further consulted.

1. **Human Vision and Characteristics**

    The estimation of the amount of information the brain receives from the eyes can be found in reference [1]. For the discussion of subjective brightness in psychology, please refer to reference [2]. For a discussion of visual phenomena that change over time, see reference [3]. For the discussion of visual perception, see reference [4]. Visual perception has also psychological factors; see reference [5]. More examples of brightness contrast perception can be found in reference [6].

2. **Computer Vision Theory and Model**

    For the discussion of computer vision research goals, please refer to reference [7]. The long-term goal of computer vision research should be to build a universal system; see reference [8] for more discussions. For the original explanation of the visual computational theory, please refer to the reference [9]. The analysis of the essence of visual representation can be found in the reference [10]. The viewpoint that active vision and selective vision can be regarded as two forms of active vision can be found in reference [11]. The introduction of purposive vision into the vision system can be found in reference [12]. The introduction of high-level knowledge into the visual system can be found in reference [13].

3. **Three-Dimensional Vision System and Image Technology**

    For a hierarchical discussion of computer vision, see references [1, 14, 15], etc. For the layering method of image technology, please refer to references [16–18]. A complete introduction to image technology can be found in references [19–21]. The hierarchical classification of image technology in the past 26 years can be found in the series of annual review [22–49]. For concise definitions of related concepts and subjects, see reference [50].

4. **Overview of the Structure and Content of This Book**

    The main content of this book is introduced in five parts. This book mainly focuses on the principles and techniques of the high-level contents of computer vision. The specific implementation of various algorithms can be achieved with the help of different programming languages. For example, using MATLAB can refer to references [51–52]. For more detailed analysis and answers to various problems in learning, please refer to reference [53].

## Self-Test Questions

The following questions include both single-choice questions and multiple-choice questions, so each option must be judged.

### 1.1 **Human Vision and Characteristics**

    1.1.1 Compare vision and other related concepts (·).

        (a) Vision and computer vision both perceive the objective world subjectively.

(b) Vision and image generation both generate images from the abstract description of the scene.

(c) The computer vision system and the machine vision system are comparable to the human vision system.

(d) The vision process and the computer vision process are completely deterministic and predictable.

[Hint] Consider the difference between vision and other concepts.

1.1.2 Mach band effect (·).

(a) Can be explained by simultaneous contrast

(b) Shows the same fact as simultaneous contrast

(c) Depends on the brightness adaptation level of the human visual system

(d) Indicates that the actual brightness distribution on the strip will be affected by the subjective brightness curve

[Hint] The Mach band effect shows that the brightness that people perceive is not only related to the light intensity of the scene.

1.1.3 Subjective brightness (·).

(a) Is only related to scene brightness

(b) Is proportional to the illuminance of the object

(c) Is possible independent to the absolute value of the object brightness

(d) Determines the overall sensitivity of the human visual system

[Hint] Subjective brightness refers to the brightness of the observed object, which is judged by the human eyes according to the intensity of the light stimulation of the retina.

## 1.2 Computer Vision Theory and Model

1.2.1 Computer vision (·).

(a) Whose goal is to uncover all the mysteries of the visual process.

(b) The research method refers to the structural principles of the human visual system.

(c) It is a means to explore the working mechanism of human brain vision.

(d) It is realized with the help of the understanding of the human visual system.

[Hint] Analyze according to the definition of computer vision.

1.2.2 Marr's visual computational theory believes that (·).

(a) The visual process is far more complicated than human imagination

(b) The key to solve visual problems is the representation and processing of information

(c) To complete the visual task, all the works must be combined

(d) All visual information problems can be computed with modern computers.

[Hint] See the five points of Marr's visual computational theory.

1.2.3 In the improved visual computational framework shown in Fig. 1.7, (·).

(a) The image acquisition module provides the basis for qualitative vision.
(b) The image acquisition module provides the basis for selective vision.
(c) The vision purpose module should be constructed based on the purpose of active vision.
(d) The function of the high-level knowledge module is to feed back the later result information to the early processing.

[Hint] Analyze the shortcomings of Marr's theory.

## 1.3  Three-Dimensional Vision System and Image Technology

1.3.1 According to the 3-D vision system flow chart, (·).

(a) The 3-D reconstruction must use motion information.
(b) The objective analysis of the scene is based on the interpretation of the scene.
(c) Decisions can only be made based on the interpretation and understanding of the scene.
(d) To obtain motion information, video images must be collected.

[Hint] Analyze the connection between each step.

1.3.2 For image understanding, (·).

(a) Its abstraction is high, its operand is the object, and its semantic level is high level.
(b) Its abstraction is high, its operand is the symbol, and its semantic level is middle level.
(c) Its abstraction is high, its amount of data is small, and its semantic level is high level.
(d) Its abstraction is high, its amount of data is large, and its operand is the symbol.

[Hint] Refer to Fig. 1.9.

1.3.3 Which of the following image technique(s) is/are image understanding technologies? (·).

(a) Image segmentation
(b) Scene restoration
(c) Image matching and fusion
(d) Extraction and analysis of object characteristics

[Hint] Consider the input and output of each technology.

1.4 **Overview of the Structure and Content of This Book**

1.4.1 In the following content, the five modules in this book in turn are (·).

    (a) 3-D image acquisition, video and motion, binocular stereo vision, scenery matching, scene interpretation

    (b) 3-D image acquisition, binocular stereo vision, monocular multi-image restoration, scene matching, scene interpretation

    (c) Camera calibration, moving object detection and tracking, binocular stereo vision, monocular and single image restoration, and spatial-temporal behavior understanding

    (d) Camera calibration, video and motion, monocular multi-image restoration, moving object detection and tracking, and spatial-temporal behavior understanding

[Hint] Refer to Fig. 1.10.

1.4.2 Among the following statements, the correct one/ones is/are (·).

    (a) 3-D image is a kind of depth image

    (b) Background modeling is a technique for detecting and tracking moving objects in videos

    (c) Recovering the shape of the object from the tonal change of the object surface is a method of recovering the scene by using multiple monocular images

    (d) The bag-of-words/bag of feature model is a model of spatial-temporal behavior understanding

[Hint] Consider the content discussed in each chapter separately.

1.4.3 Among the following statements, the incorrect one/ones is/are (·).

    (a) The region-based binocular stereo matching technology is a relatively abstract matching technology

    (b) It is possible to use a non-linear camera model for camera calibration

    (c) The classification of actions is a technique for detecting and tracking moving objects

    (d) The method of obtaining structure from motion based on the optical flow field is a method of recovering the scene by using multiple monocular images

[Hint] Refer to the introduction in the overview of each chapter.

# References

1. Davies E R. Computer and Machine Vision: Theory, Algorithms, Practicalities, 4th Ed. Elsevier. 2012.
2. Lu Y L, Fu C Y, Zeng S R, et al. College Physics Dictionary. Chemical Industry Press, 1991.

3. Aumont J. The Image. Translation: Pajackowska C. British Film Institute. 1994,
4. Hao B Y, Zhang H C, Chen S Y. Experimental Psychology. Beijing University Press, 1983.
5. Guo X Y, Yang Z L. Basic Experimental Psychology. Higher Education Press, 2005.
6. Qian J Y. Visual Psychology — Thinking and Communication of Visual Forms. Xue Lin Press, 2006.
7. Shapiro L, Stockman G. Computer Vision. Prentice Hall. 2001.
8. Jain A K, Dorai C. Practicing vision: integration, evaluation and applications. Pattern Recognition, 1997, 30(2): 183-196.
9. Marr D. Vision — A Computational Investigation into the Human Representation and Processing of Visual Information. W.H. Freeman. 1982.
10. Edelman S. Representation and Recognition in Vision. MIT Press. 1999.
11. Davies E R. Machine Vision: Theory, Algorithms, Practicalities. 3rd Ed. Elsevier. 2005.
12. Aloimonos Y (ed.). Special Issue on Purposive, Qualitative, Active Vision. CVGIP-IU, 1992, 56(1): 1-129.
13. Huang T, Stucki P (eds.). Special Section on 3-D Modeling in Image Analysis and Synthesis. IEEE-PAMI, 1993, 15(6): 529-616.
14. Forsyth D, Ponce J. Computer Vision: A Modern Approach. Prentice Hall. 2003.
15. Forsyth D, Ponce J. Computer Vision: A Modern Approach, 2nd Ed. Prentice Hall. 2012.
16. Zhang Y J. Image engineering and bibliography in China. Technical Digest of International Symposium on Information Science and Technology, 1996, 158-160.
17. Zhang Y-J. Statistics on image engineering literatures. Encyclopedia of Information Science and Technology, 3rd Ed. 2015, Chapter 595 (6030-6040).
18. Zhang Y-J. Development of image engineering in the last 20 years. Encyclopedia of Information Science and Technology, 4th Ed., 2018, Chapter 113 (1319-1330).
19. Zhang Y-J. Image Engineering, Vol.1: Image Processing. De Gruyter, 2017.
20. Zhang Y-J. Image Engineering, Vol.2: Image Analysis. De Gruyter, 2017.
21. Zhang Y-J. Image Engineering, Vol.3: Image Understanding. De Gruyter, 2017.
22. Zhang Y-J. Image Engineering in China: 1995. Journal of Image and Graphics, 1996, 1(1): 78-83.
23. Zhang Y-J. Image Engineering in China: 1995 (Complement). Journal of Image and Graphics, 1996, 1(2): 170-174.
24. Zhang Y-J. Image Engineering in China: 1996. Journal of Image and Graphics, 1997, 2(5): 336-344.
25. Zhang Y-J. Image Engineering in China: 1997. Journal of Image and Graphics, 1998, 3(5): 404-414.
26. Zhang Y-J. Image Engineering in China: 1998. Journal of Image and Graphics, 1999, 4A(5): 427-438.
27. Zhang Y-J. Image Engineering in China: 1999. Journal of Image and Graphics, 2000, 5A(5): 359-373.
28. Zhang Y-J. Image Engineering in China: 2000. Journal of Image and Graphics, 2001, 6A(5): 409-424.
29. Zhang Y-J. Image Engineering in China: 2001. Journal of Image and Graphics, 2002, 7A(5): 417-433.
30. Zhang Y-J. Image Engineering in China: 2002. Journal of Image and Graphics, 2003, 8A(5): 481-498.
31. Zhang Y-J. Image Engineering in China: 2003. Journal of Image and Graphics, 2004, 9A(5): 513-531.
32. Zhang Y-J. Image Engineering in China: 2004. Journal of Image and Graphics, 2005, 10A(5): 537-560.
33. Zhang Y-J. Image Engineering in China: 2005. Journal of Image and Graphics, 2006, 11(5): 601-623.
34. Zhang Y-J. Image Engineering in China: 2006. Journal of Image and Graphics, 2007, 12(5): 753-775.

35. Zhang Y-J. Image Engineering in China: 2007. Journal of Image and Graphics, 2008, 13(5): 825-852.
36. Zhang Y-J. Image Engineering in China: 2008. Journal of Image and Graphics, 2009, 14(5): 809-837.
37. Zhang Y-J. Image Engineering in China: 2009. Journal of Image and Graphics, 2010, 15(5): 689-722.
38. Zhang Y-J. Image Engineering in China: 2010. Journal of Image and Graphics, 2011, 16(5): 693-702.
39. Zhang Y-J. Image Engineering in China: 2011. Journal of Image and Graphics, 2012, 17(5): 603-612.
40. Zhang Y-J. Image Engineering in China: 2012. Journal of Image and Graphics, 2013, 18(5): 483-492.
41. Zhang Y-J. Image Engineering in China: 2013. Journal of Image and Graphics, 2014, 19(5): 649-658.
42. Zhang Y-J. Image Engineering in China: 2014. Journal of Image and Graphics, 2015, 20(5): 585-598.
43. Zhang Y-J. Image Engineering in China: 2015. Journal of Image and Graphics, 2016, 21(5): 533-543.
44. Zhang Y-J. Image Engineering in China: 2016. Journal of Image and Graphics, 2017, 22(5): 563-574.
45. Zhang Y-J. Image Engineering in China: 2017. Journal of Image and Graphics, 2018, 23(5): 617-629.
46. Zhang Y-J. Image Engineering in China: 2018. Journal of Image and Graphics, 2019, 24(5): 665-676.
47. Zhang Y-J. Image Engineering in China: 2019. Journal of Image and Graphics, 2020, 25(5): 864-878.
48. Zhang Y-J. Image Engineering in China: 2020. Journal of Image and Graphics, 2021, 26(5): 978-990.
49. Zhang Y-J. Image Engineering in China: 2021. Journal of Image and Graphics, 2022, 27(4): 1009-1022.
50. Zhang Y-J. Handbook of Image Engineering. Springer Nature, 2021.
51. Marques O. Practical Image and Video Processing Using MATLAB. Wiley Publishing, Inc. 2013.
52. Peters J F. Foundations of Computer Vision. Springer, 2017.
53. Zhang Y-J. Problem Analysis in Image Engineering. Tsinghua University Press, 2018.

# Chapter 2
# Camera Calibration

Video cameras (cameras) are the most commonly used equipment for capturing images. **Camera calibration** has the purpose to use the feature point coordinates $(X, Y, Z)$ of a given 3-D space object and its image coordinates $(x, y)$ in 2-D image space to calculate the internal and external parameters of the camera, thereby establishing the quantitative relationship between the objective scene and the captured image.

Camera calibration is a very important part of machine vision technology and photogrammetry. The essence of machine vision technology and photogrammetry is to obtain geometric information of three-dimensional objects from the image information taken by the camera. It can also be said that camera calibration is the foundation of machine vision technology and photogrammetry. The process of camera calibration is the process of obtaining the internal and external parameters of the camera through calculations. Among them, the internal parameters include the focal length of the camera, and the external parameters include the position information of the camera itself in the world coordinate system. The projection relationship between the world coordinate system and the image coordinate system is determined by these internal and external parameters of the cameras.

The sections of this chapter are arranged as follows:

Section 2.1 introduces the basic linear camera model, gives a typical calibration procedure, and discusses the internal and external parameters of the camera.

Section 2.2 discusses typical non-linear camera models, analyzes various types of distortions in detail, and summarizes the criteria and results for the classification of calibration methods.

Section 2.3 introduces the traditional camera calibration method, analyzes its characteristics, and describes an example of a typical two-stage calibration method. In addition, an improved method is analyzed.

Section 2.4 introduces the self-calibration method (including the calibration method based on active vision). In addition to analyzing the advantages and

© The Author(s), under exclusive license to Springer Nature Singapore Pte Ltd. 2023
Y.-J. Zhang, *3-D Computer Vision*, https://doi.org/10.1007/978-981-19-7580-6_2

disadvantages of this type of method, a simple calibration method is also specifically introduced.

## 2.1   Linear Camera Model

The **camera model** represents the relationship between the coordinates in the world coordinate system and the coordinates in the image coordinate system. In other words, the projection relationship between the object point and the image point is provided by the camera model.

The **linear model** is also called the **pinhole model**. In this model, it is considered that any point in the 3-D space whose image in the image coordinate system is formed according to the principle of small hole imaging.

### 2.1.1   Complete Imaging Model

General imaging models have been discussed in *2D Computer Vision: Principles, Algorithms and Applications*. A more complete imaging model in practical utilization also considers two factors.

1. Not only the world coordinate system *XYZ* and the camera coordinate system *xyz* are separated, but the camera coordinate system and the image coordinate system *x'y'* are also separated.
2. The ultimate goal of imaging is for computer processing, so it is necessary to establish a connection from the world coordinate system to the computer image coordinate system *MN*.

Here, since the image coordinate unit used in the computer is the number of discrete pixels in the memory, so the coordinates on the image plane need to be rounded and converted. It is also believed that the image coordinate system includes two parts, the image physical coordinate system and the image pixel coordinate system. The former corresponds to the coordinates on the image plane, while the latter corresponds to the coordinates in the (memory of) computer.

Taking into account these two factors discussed here, a complete imaging process involves a total of three conversions between four non-coincident coordinate systems, as shown in Fig. 2.1.

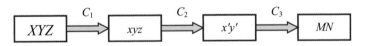

**Fig. 2.1** Conversion from 3-D world coordinates to computer image coordinates under the linear camera model

1. Conversion $C_1$ from the world coordinate system $XYZ$ to the camera coordinate system $xyz$. This conversion can be represented as

$$\begin{bmatrix} x \\ y \\ z \end{bmatrix} = R \begin{bmatrix} X \\ Y \\ Z \end{bmatrix} + T \tag{2.1}$$

where $R$ and $T$ are, respectively, $3 \times 3$ rotation matrix (actually a function of the angles between the three pairs of corresponding coordinate axes of the two coordinate systems) and $1 \times 3$ translation vector:

$$R \equiv \begin{bmatrix} r_1 & r_2 & r_3 \\ r_4 & r_5 & r_6 \\ r_7 & r_8 & r_9 \end{bmatrix} \tag{2.2}$$

$$T \equiv \begin{bmatrix} T_x & T_y & T_z \end{bmatrix}^T \tag{2.3}$$

2. Conversion $C_2$ from the camera coordinate system $xyz$ to the image plane coordinate system $x'y'$. This conversion can be represented as

$$x' = \lambda \frac{x}{z} \tag{2.4}$$

$$y' = \lambda \frac{y}{z} \tag{2.5}$$

3. Conversion $C_3$ from the image plane coordinate system $x'y'$ to the computer image coordinate system $MN$. This conversion can be represented as

$$M = \mu \frac{x' M_x}{S_x L_x} + O_m \tag{2.6}$$

$$N = \frac{y'}{S_y} + O_n \tag{2.7}$$

where $M$ and $N$ are the total numbers of rows and columns of pixels in the computer memory (computer coordinates), respectively; $O_m$ and $O_n$ are separately the number of rows and the number of columns of the center pixels in the computer memory; $S_x$ is the distance between the centers of two adjacent sensors along the $x$ direction (scanning line direction); $S_y$ is the distance between the centers of two adjacent sensors along the $y$ direction; $L_x$ is the number of sensor elements in the $X$ direction; and $M_x$ is the number of samples (number of pixels) of the computer in a row. In Eq. (2.6), $\mu$ is an uncertain image scale factor that depends on the camera. According to the working principle of the sensor, the time difference between the image acquisition hardware and the camera scanning hardware or the time inaccuracy of the camera scanning itself will introduce certain uncertain factors during progressive scanning. For example, when using a CCD, the image is scanned line by line. The distance between adjacent pixels along the $y'$ direction is also the distance between adjacent CCD photosensitive points, but along the $x'$ direction due to the time difference between the image acquisition hardware and the camera scanning hardware or the inaccuracy of the camera scanning time itself, some uncertain factors will be introduced. These uncertain factors can be described by introducing the **uncertainty image scale factor** $\mu$, which helps to establish the connection between the image plane coordinate system $x'y'$ and the computer image coordinate system $MN$ affected by the uncertainty image scale factor.

### 2.1.2  Basic Calibration Procedure

According to the general imaging model discussed in *2D Computer Vision: Principles, Algorithms and Applications*, if a series of transformations $PRTW_h$ are performed on the homogeneous coordinates $W_h$ of a space point, the world coordinate system can be overlapped with the camera coordinate system. Here, $P$ is the imaging projection transformation matrix, $R$ is the camera rotation matrix, and $T$ is the camera translation matrix. Let $A = PRT$; the elements in $A$ include camera translation, rotation, and projection parameters; and then there is a homogeneous representation of image coordinates $C_h = AW_h$. If $k = 1$ in the homogeneous representation, one can get

$$\begin{bmatrix} C_{h1} \\ C_{h2} \\ C_{h3} \\ C_{h4} \end{bmatrix} = \begin{bmatrix} a_{11} & a_{12} & a_{13} & a_{14} \\ a_{21} & a_{22} & a_{23} & a_{24} \\ a_{31} & a_{32} & a_{33} & a_{34} \\ a_{41} & a_{42} & a_{43} & a_{44} \end{bmatrix} \begin{bmatrix} X \\ Y \\ Z \\ 1 \end{bmatrix} \tag{2.8}$$

According to the definition of homogeneous coordinates, the camera coordinates (image plane coordinates) in Cartesian form are

$$x = C_{h1}/C_{h4} \tag{2.9}$$

$$y = C_{h2}/C_{h4} \tag{2.10}$$

Substitute Eqs. (2.9) and (2.10) into Eq. (2.8) and expand the matrix product to get

$$xC_{h4} = a_{11}X + a_{12}Y + a_{13}Z + a_{14} \tag{2.11}$$

$$yC_{h4} = a_{21}X + a_{22}Y + a_{23}Z + a_{24} \tag{2.12}$$

$$C_{h4} = a_{41}X + a_{42}Y + a_{43}Z + a_{44} \tag{2.13}$$

where the expansion of $C_{h3}$ is omitted because it is related to $z$.

Substituting $C_{h4}$ into Eqs. (2.11) and (2.12), then two equations with a total of 12 unknowns can be obtained:

$$(a_{11} - a_{41}x)X + (a_{12} - a_{42}x)Y + (a_{13} - a_{43}x)Z + (a_{14} - a_{44}x) = 0 \tag{2.14}$$

$$(a_{21} - a_{41}y)X + (a_{22} - a_{42}y)Y + (a_{23} - a_{43}y)Z + (a_{24} - a_{44}y) = 0 \tag{2.15}$$

It can be seen that a calibration procedure should include the following:

1. Obtaining $M \geq 6$ space points with known world coordinates $(X_i, Y_i, Z_i)$, $i = 1$, 2, ..., $M$ (more than 25 points are often taken in practical applications, and then the least squares fitting is used to reduce the error).
2. Take these points with the camera at a given position to get their corresponding image plane coordinates $(x_i, y_i)$, $i = 1, 2, ..., M$.
3. Substitute these coordinates into Eqs. (2.14) and (2.15) to solve for the unknown coefficients.

In order to realize the above-mentioned calibration procedure, it is necessary to obtain the corresponding spatial points and image points. In order to accurately determine these points, it is necessary to use a calibration object (also called a calibration target, i.e., a standard reference object), which has a fixed pattern of marking points (reference points). The most commonly used 2-D calibration objects have a series of regularly arranged square patterns (similar to a chess board), and the vertices of these squares (cross-hairs) can be used as reference points for calibration. If the calibration algorithm of co-planar reference points is used, the calibration object corresponds to one plane; if the calibration algorithm of non-coplanar reference points is adopted, the calibration object generally corresponds to two orthogonal planes.

### 2.1.3 Internal and External Parameters

The calibration parameters involved in camera calibration can be divided into external parameters (outside the camera) and internal parameters (inside the camera).

### 2.1.3.1  External Parameters

The first step of transformation in Fig. 2.1 is to transform from the 3-D world coordinate system to the 3-D coordinate system whose center is at the optical center of the camera. The transformation parameters are called **external parameters** or **camera attitude parameters**. The rotation matrix $R$ has a total of nine elements, but in fact there are only three degrees of freedom, which can be represented by the three Euler angles of the rigid body rotation. As shown in Fig. 2.2 (the line of sight is reverse to the $X$ axis), the intersection line $AB$ of the $XY$ plane and the $xy$ plane is called the pitch line, and the angle $\theta$ between $AB$ and the $x$ axis is an Euler angle called the rotation angle (also called deflection angle yaw), which is the angle of rotation around the $z$ axis; the angle $\psi$ between $AB$ and $X$ axis is another Euler angle, called precession angle (also called tilt angle), which is the angle of rotation around the $Z$ axis; the angle $\phi$ between $Z$ axis and $z$ axis is the third Euler angle, called the nutation angle (also called pitch/slant angle), which is the angle of rotation around the pitch line.

Using Euler angles, the rotation matrix can be represented as a function of $\theta$, $\phi$, and $\psi$:

$$R = \begin{bmatrix} \cos\psi\cos\theta & \sin\psi\cos\theta & -\sin\theta \\ -\sin\psi\cos\phi + \cos\psi\sin\theta\sin\phi & \cos\psi\cos\phi + \sin\psi\sin\theta\sin\phi & \cos\theta\sin\phi \\ \sin\psi\sin\phi + \cos\psi\sin\theta\cos\phi & -\cos\psi\sin\phi + \sin\psi\sin\theta\cos\phi & \cos\theta\cos\phi \end{bmatrix}$$

$$(2.16)$$

It can be seen that the rotation matrix has three degrees of freedom. In addition, the translation matrix also has three degrees of freedom (translation coefficients in three directions). In this way, the camera has six independent external parameters, namely, the three Euler angles $\theta$, $\phi$, $\psi$ in $R$ and the three elements $T_x$, $T_y$, $T_z$ in $T$.

**Fig. 2.2** Schematic diagram of Euler angles

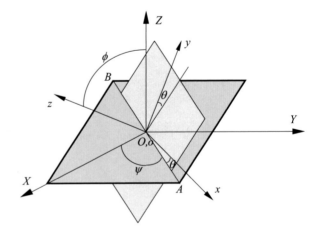

### 2.1.3.2   Internal Parameters

The last two transformations in Fig. 2.1 are to transform the 3-D coordinates in the camera coordinate system to the 2-D coordinates in the computer image coordinate system. The transformation parameters are called **internal parameters**, also called the **interior camera parameters**. There are four internal parameters in Fig. 2.1: focal length $\lambda$, uncertainty image scale factor $\mu$, and computer image coordinates $O_m$ and $O_n$ of the origin of the image plane.

   The main significance of distinguishing external parameters and internal parameters is when a camera is used to acquire multiple images at different positions and orientations, the external parameters of the camera corresponding to each image may be different, but the internal parameters will not change, so after moving the camera, it only needs to re-calibrate the external parameters but not the internal parameters.

**Example 2.1 The Internal and External Parameters in Camera Calibration**
Camera calibration is to align the camera's coordinate system with the world coordinate system. From this point of view, another way to describe the internal and external parameters of camera calibration is as follows. Decompose a complete camera calibration transformation matrix $C$ into the product of the internal parameter matrix $C_i$ and the external parameter matrix $C_e$:

$$C = C_i C_e \tag{2.17}$$

$C_i$ is a $4 \times 4$ matrix in general, but it can be simplified to a $3 \times 3$ matrix:

$$C_i = \begin{bmatrix} S_x & P_x & T_x \\ P_y & S_y & T_y \\ 0 & 0 & 1/\lambda \end{bmatrix} \tag{2.18}$$

where $S_x$ and $S_y$ are the scaling coefficients along the $X$ and $Y$ axes, respectively; $P_x$ and $P_y$ are the skew coefficients along the $X$ and $Y$ axes, respectively (originated from the non-strict orthogonality of the actual camera optical axes, which is reflected in the image as that there is not strict 90° between pixel rows and pixel columns); $T_x$ and $T_y$ are the translation coefficients along the $X$ and $Y$ axes, respectively (to help move the projection center of the camera to a suitable position); and $\lambda$ is the focal length of the lens.

   The general form of $C_e$ is also a $4 \times 4$ matrix, which can be written as

$$C_e = \begin{bmatrix} R_1 & R_1 \cdot T \\ R_2 & R_2 \cdot T \\ R_3 & R_3 \cdot T \\ \mathbf{0} & 1 \end{bmatrix} \tag{2.19}$$

where $R_1$, $R_2$, and $R_3$ are three row vectors of a $3 \times 3$ rotation matrix (only 3 degrees of freedom), and $T$ is a 3-D translation column vector, and $0$ is a $1 \times 3$ vector.

It can be seen from the above discussions that the matrix $C_i$ has seven internal parameters and the matrix $C_e$ has six external parameters. However, notice that both matrices have rotation parameters, so the rotation parameters of the internal matrix can be merged into the external matrix. Because rotation is a combination of scaling and skew, after removing the rotation from the internal matrix, $P_x$ and $P_y$ become the same ($P_x = P_y = P$). When considering the linear camera model, $P = 0$. So there are only five parameters in the internal matrix, namely, $\lambda$, $S_x$, $S_y$, $T_x$, and $T_y$. In this way, the two matrices have a total of 11 parameters to be calibrated, which can be calibrated according to the basic calibration procedure. In special cases, if the camera is very accurate, then $S_x = S_y = S = 1$. At this time, there are only three internal parameters. Furthermore, if the cameras are aligned, then $T_x = T_y = 0$. This leaves only one internal parameter $\lambda$.

## 2.2  Non-Linear Camera Model

In actual situations, a camera usually uses a lens (often containing multiple lenses) for imaging. Due to the levels of the processing technology of the lens and the manufacturing technology of the camera, the projection relationship of the camera cannot be simply described as a pinhole model. In other words, due to the influence of various factors such as lens processing and installation, the projection relationship of the camera is no longer a linear projection relationship, that is, the linear model cannot accurately describe the imaging geometric relationship of the camera.

The real optical system does not work exactly according to the idealized pinhole imaging principle, but there is **lens distortion**. Due to the influence of various distortion factors, the pixel coordinates of the 3-D space object point projected to the 2-D image plane will deviate from the ideal image point position without distortion. The optical distortion error between the actual image point formed by the spatial object point on the camera imaging plane and the ideal image is more obvious in the region close to the boundary of the lens. Especially if one uses a wide-angle lens, there are often a lot of distortions in the image plane away from the center. This will cause deviations in the measured coordinates and reduce the accuracy of the obtained world coordinates. Therefore, a non-linear camera model that takes into account these distortions must be used for camera calibration.

### 2.2.1  Type of Distortion

Due to the influence of various distortion factors, when projecting a 3-D space object point onto a 2-D image plane, the actually obtained image point coordinates $(x_a, y_a)$

**Fig. 2.3** Schematic diagram of radial and tangential distortion

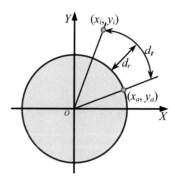

and the undistorted ideal image point coordinates $(x_i, y_i)$ will be different (there are deviations), which can be expressed as

$$x_a = x_i + d_x \tag{2.20}$$

$$y_a = y_i + d_y \tag{2.21}$$

where $d_x$ and $d_y$ are the total non-linear distortion deviation values in the $X$ and $Y$ directions, respectively. There are two common basic distortion types: **radial distortion** and **tangential distortion**. The influence of these two basic distortions is shown in Fig. 2.3, where $d_r$ represents the deviation caused by radial distortion and $d_t$ represents the deviation caused by tangential distortion. Other distortions are mostly a combination of these two basic distortions. The most typical combined distortion is **eccentric distortion** or **centrifugal distortion** and **thin prism distortion**; they all contain both radial distortion and tangential distortion.

### 2.2.1.1 Radial Distortion

**Radial distortion** is mainly caused by irregular lens shape (surface curvature error). The deviation caused by it is often symmetrical about the main optical axis of the camera lens, and it is more obvious at the distance from the optical axis along the lens radius. Generally, the positive radial distortion is called **pincushion distortion**, and the negative radial distortion is called **barrel distortion**, as shown in Fig. 2.4. The mathematical model is

$$d_{xr} = x_i \left( k_1 r^2 + k_2 r^4 + \cdots \right) \tag{2.22}$$

$$d_{yr} = y_i \left( k_1 r^2 + k_2 r^4 + \cdots \right) \tag{2.23}$$

where $r = (x_i^2 + y_i^2)^{1/2}$ is the distance from the image point to the image center and $k_1, k_2$, etc. are the radial distortion coefficients.

**Fig. 2.4** Pincushion
distortion and barrel
distortion

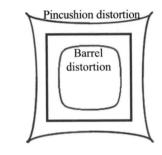

**Fig. 2.5** Tangential
distortion

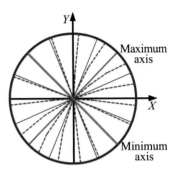

### 2.2.1.2   Tangential Distortion

**Tangential distortion** is mainly caused by the non-collinear optical centers of the lens group, which produces the actual image point to move tangentially on the image plane. Tangential distortion has a certain orientation in space, so there is a maximum axis of distortion in a certain direction, and a minimum axis in the direction perpendicular to that direction, as shown in Fig. 2.5. The solid line represents the absence of distortion, and the dashed line represents the result caused by tangential distortion. Generally, the influence of tangential distortion is relatively small, and independent modeling is relatively small.

### 2.2.1.3   Eccentric Distortion

The **eccentric distortion** is caused by the inconsistency between the optical center and the geometric center of the optical system, that is, the optical center of the lens device is not strictly collinear. The mathematical model can be represented by

$$d_{xt} = l_1\left(2x_i^2 + r^2\right) + 2l_2 x_i y_i + \cdots \tag{2.24}$$

$$d_{yt} = 2l_1 x_i y_i + l_2\left(2y_i^2 + r^2\right) + \cdots \tag{2.25}$$

where $r = (x_i^2 + y_i^2)^{1/2}$ is the distance from the image point to the image center and $l_1$, $l_2$, etc. are the eccentric distortion coefficients.

#### 2.2.1.4  Thin Prism Distortion

The **thin prism distortion** is caused by improper lens design and assembly. This kind of distortion is equivalent to adding a thin prism to the optical system, which causes not only radial deviation but also tangential deviation. The mathematical model is

$$d_{xp} = m_1 \left( x_i^2 + y_i^2 \right) + \cdots \tag{2.26}$$

$$d_{yp} = m_2 \left( x_i^2 + y_i^2 \right) + \cdots \tag{2.27}$$

where $m_1$, $m_2$, etc. are the distortion coefficients of the thin prism.

Combining the radial distortion, eccentric distortion, and thin prism distortion, the total distortion deviation of $d_x$ and $d_y$ is

$$d_x = d_{xr} + d_{xt} + d_{xp} \tag{2.28}$$

$$d_y = d_{yr} + d_{yt} + d_{yp} \tag{2.29}$$

If ignoring terms higher than order 3, and let $n_1 = l_1 + m_1$, $n_2 = l_2 + m_2$, $n_3 = 2\,l_1$, $n_4 = 2\,l_2$, then

$$d_x = k_1 x r^2 + (n_1 + n_3) x^2 + n_4 xy + n_1 y^2 \tag{2.30}$$

$$d_y = k_1 y r^2 + n_2 x^2 + n_3 xy + (n_2 + n_4) y^2 \tag{2.31}$$

### 2.2.2  Calibration Steps

In practice, the radial distortion of the camera lens tends to have a greater impact. The radial distortion it causes is often proportional to the distance between a point in the image and the point on the optical axis of the lens. The transformation from the undistorted image plane coordinates $(x', y')$ to the actual image plane coordinates $(x^*, y^*)$ shifted by the lens radial distortion is

$$x^* = x' - R_x \tag{2.32}$$

$$y^* = y' - R_y \tag{2.33}$$

where $R_x$ and $R_y$ represent the radial distortion of the lens, referring to Eqs. (2.22) and (2.23); one can get

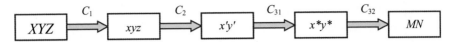

**Fig. 2.6** Conversion from 3-D world coordinates to computer image coordinates using the non-linear camera model

$$R_x = x^* \left( k_1 r^2 + k_2 r^4 + \cdots \right) \approx x^* k r^2 \tag{2.34}$$

$$R_y = y^* \left( k_1 r^2 + k_2 r^4 + \cdots \right) \approx y^* k r^2 \tag{2.35}$$

Here, only a single coefficient $k$ of lens radial distortion is introduced for simplifying approximation. On the one hand, the higher-order term of $r$ can be ignored in practice. On the other hand, it is also considered that the radial distortion is often symmetrical about the main optical axis of the camera lens.

Taking into account the conversion from the undistorted image plane coordinates $(x', y')$ to the actual image plane coordinates $(x^*, y^*)$, the transformation from 3-D world coordinates to the computer image plane coordinates is realized according to the non-linear camera model, as shown in Fig. 2.6. The original conversion $C_3$ is now decomposed into two conversions, $C_{31}$ and $C_{32}$, and Eqs. (2.6) and (2.7) can still be used to define $C_{32}$ (it needs only to use $x^*$ and $y^*$ to replace $x'$ and $y'$).

Although Eqs. (2.32) and (2.33) only consider radial distortion, the forms of Eqs. (2.30) and (2.31) can actually represent various distortions. In this sense, the flow chart of Fig. 2.6 can be applied to situations with various distortions, as long as the corresponding $Z_{31}$ is selected according to the type of distortion. Comparing Fig. 2.6 with Fig. 2.1, the non-linearity is reflected in the conversion from $x'y'$ to $x^*y^*$.

### 2.2.3   Classification of Calibration Methods

There are many ways to achieve camera calibration, and there are different classification methods according to different criteria. For example, according to the characteristics of the camera model, it can be divided into linear methods and non-linear methods; according to whether calibration objects are required, it can be divided into traditional camera calibration methods, camera self-calibration methods, and active vision-based calibration methods (someone also combines the latter two). In addition, when using the calibration object, according to the dimension of calibration objects, it can be divided into the methods of using the 2-D plane target and the methods of using the 3-D solid target; according to the results of solving the parameters, it can be divided into explicit methods and implicit methods; according to whether the internal parameters of the camera can be changed, it can be divided into methods with variable internal parameters and methods with invariable internal parameters; according to the camera motion mode, it can be divided into the methods with limited motion mode and the methods with non-limited motion mode;

according to the number of cameras used by the vision system, it can be divided into the methods using a single camera and the methods using multi-cameras. Table 2.1 provides a classification table of calibration methods, listing some classification criteria, categories, and typical methods.

In Table 2.1, non-linear methods are generally complex, slow, and require a good initial value; besides, non-linear search cannot completely guarantee that the parameters converge to the global optimal solution. The implicit parameter method uses the elements of transformation matrix as calibration parameters and uses a transformation matrix to represent the correspondence between spatial object points and image plane points. Because the parameter itself does not have a clear physical meaning, it is called the implicit parameter method. Since the implicit parameter method only requires solving linear equations, this method can provide higher efficiency when the accuracy requirements are not very high. Direct linear methods (DLT) take linear model as the object and uses a $3 \times 4$ matrix to represent the correspondence between 3-D space object points and 2-D space image points, ignoring the intermediate imaging process (or, in other words, combining the factors in the process for consideration). The most common multi-camera method is the dual-camera method. Compared with single-camera calibration, dual-camera calibration not only needs to know the internal and external parameters of each camera itself but also needs to measure the relative position and orientation between the two cameras through calibration.

## 2.3   Traditional Calibration Methods

Traditional camera calibration needs to use a known calibration object (calibration board with known 2-D data, or calibration block with known 3-D data), that is, the size and shape of the calibration object (position and distribution of calibration points), and then determine the internal and external parameters of the camera by establishing the correspondence between the points on the calibration object and the corresponding points on the captured images. Its advantages are clear theory, simple solution, and high calibration accuracy, but the calibration process is relatively complicated, and the accuracy of the calibration object should be high.

### 2.3.1   Basic Steps and Parameters

The calibration can be carried out along the conversion direction from 3-D world coordinates to computer image coordinates. The typical process is shown in Fig. 2.7. The conversion from the world coordinate system to the computer image coordinate system has four steps, and each step has parameters to be calibrated:

**Table 2.1** Camera calibration method classification table

| Classification criteria | Types | Typical methods |
|---|---|---|
| Characteristics of the camera model | Linear | Two-stage calibration method |
| | Non-linear | LM optimization method <br> Newton Raphson (NR) optimization method <br> Non-linear optimization method for parameter calibration <br> The method assuming only the condition of radial distortion |
| Whether calibration objects are required | Traditional calibration | Methods of using optimization algorithms <br> Methods of using camera transformation matrix <br> A two-step method considering distortion compensation <br> Biplane method using camera imaging model <br> Direct linear transformation (DLT) method <br> Method using radial alignment constraint (RAC) |
| | Camera self-calibration | The method of solving Kruppa equation directly <br> Layered stepwise approach <br> Method using absolute conic <br> Method based on quadric surface |
| | Active vision-based calibration | Linear method based on two sets of three orthogonal motions <br> Method based on four-group and five-group plane orthogonal motion <br> Orthogonal movement method based on planar homography matrix <br> Orthogonal motion method based on epi-pole |
| Dimension of calibration targets | 2-D plane target | Black and white checkerboard calibration target (take grid intersection as calibration point) <br> Arrange dots in a grid (take the center of the dot as the calibration point) |
| | 3-D solid target | 3-D objects of known size and shape |
| Results of solving the parameters | Implicit calibration | Consider calibration parameters with direct physical meaning (such as distortion parameters) |
| | Explicit calibration | Direct linear transformation (DLT) method to calibrate geometric parameters |
| Internal parameters of the camera can be changed | Variable internal parameters | During the calibration process, the optical parameters of the camera (such as focal length) can be changed |
| | Invariable internal parameters | During the calibration process, the optical parameters of the camera cannot be changed |
| Camera motion mode | Limited motion mode | The method in which camera only has a pure rotation |
| | | Method for camera to perform orthogonal translation movement |
| | Non-limited motion mode | There is no limit to the movement of the camera during calibration |

(continued)

**Table 2.1** (continued)

| Classification criteria | Types | Typical methods |
|---|---|---|
| Number of cameras used by the vision system | Using a single camera | Calibrate only a single camera |
| | Using multi-cameras | Use 1-D calibration objects for multiple cameras (more than 3 collinear points with known distances), and use the maximum likelihood criterion to refine the linear algorithm |

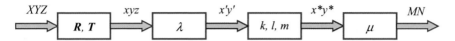

**Fig. 2.7** Perform camera calibration along the coordinate conversion direction

Step 1: The parameters to be calibrated are the rotation matrix $R$ and the translation vector $T$.

Step 2: The parameter to be calibrated is the focal length of the lens $\lambda$.

Step 3: The parameters to be calibrated are the lens radial distortion coefficient $k$, eccentric distortion coefficient $l$, and thin lens distortion coefficient $m$.

Step 4: The parameter to be calibrated is the uncertainty image scale factor $\mu$.

## *2.3.2 Two-Stage Calibration Method*

The two-stage calibration method is a typical traditional calibration method. It gets its name because the calibration is divided into two stages: the first stage is to calculate the external parameters of the camera (but not considering the translation along the camera's optical axis, $T_z$, at this time), and the second stage is to calculate other parameters of the camera. Because it uses the **radial alignment constraint** (RAC), it is also called the RAC method. Most of the equations in its calculation process are linear equations, so the process of solving parameters is relatively simple. This method has been widely used in industrial vision systems. The average accuracy of 3-D measurement can reach 1/4000, and the accuracy of depth direction can reach 1/8000.

Calibration can be divided into two cases/situations. If $\mu$ is known, only one image containing a set of coplanar reference points is needed for calibration. At this time, the first stage is to calculate $R$ and $T_x$ and $T_y$, and the second stage is to calculate $\lambda$, $k$, $T_z$. Here, because $k$ is the radial distortion of the lens, $k$ is not considered in the calculation of $R$. Similarly, the calculation of $T_x$ and $T_y$ may not consider $k$, but the calculation of $T_z$ needs to consider $k$ (the change effect of $T_z$ on the image is similar to the change effect of $k$), so it is placed in the second stage. In addition, if $\mu$ is unknown, an image containing a set of non-coplanar reference points should be used for calibration. At this time, the first stage is to calculate $R$ and $T_x$, $T_y$, and $\mu$, and the second stage is still to calculate $\lambda$, $k$, $T_z$.

The specific calibration method is to first calculate a set of parameters $s_i$ ($i = 1$, 2, 3, 4, 5), or $s = [s_1 \; s_2 \; s_3 \; s_4 \; s_5]^T$, and further calculate the external parameters of the camera with this set of parameters. Given $M$ ($M \geq 5$) points whose world coordinates $(X_i, Y_i, Z_i)$ and their corresponding image plane coordinates $(x_i, y_i)$ are known, $i = 1$, 2, ..., $M$, one can construct a matrix $A$, in which row $a_i$ can be represented as follows:

$$a_i = [y_i X_i \quad y_i Y_i \quad -x_i X_i \quad -x_i Y_i \quad y_i] \tag{2.36}$$

Let $s_i$ have the following relations with rotation parameters $r_1$, $r_2$, $r_4$, $r_5$ and translation parameters $T_x$, $T_y$:

$$s_1 = \frac{r_1}{T_y} \quad s_2 = \frac{r_2}{T_y} \quad s_3 = \frac{r_4}{T_y} \quad s_4 = \frac{r_5}{T_y} \quad s_5 = \frac{T_x}{T_y} \tag{2.37}$$

Suppose the vector $u = [x_1 \; x_2 \; \ldots \; x_M]^T$, and then from the following linear equations

$$As = u \tag{2.38}$$

$s$ can be solved. Next, the rotation and translation parameters can be calculated according to the subsequent steps.

1. Set $S = s_1^2 + s_2^2 + s_3^2 + s_4^2$; calculate

$$T_y^2 = \begin{cases} \dfrac{S - \sqrt{\left[S^2 - 4(s_1 s_4 - s_2 s_3)^2\right]}}{4(s_1 s_4 - s_2 s_3)^2} & (s_1 s_4 - s_2 s_3) \neq 0 \\[4mm] \dfrac{1}{s_1^2 + s_2^2} & s_1^2 + s_2^2 \neq 0 \\[4mm] \dfrac{1}{s_3^2 + s_4^2} & s_3^2 + s_4^2 \neq 0 \end{cases} \tag{2.39}$$

2. Set $T_y = \left(T_y^2\right)^{1/2}$, that is, take the positive square root and calculate

$$r_1 = s_1 T_y \quad r_2 = s_2 T_y \quad r_4 = s_3 T_y \quad r_5 = s_4 T_y \quad T_x = s_5 T_y \tag{2.40}$$

3. Choose a point whose world coordinates are $(X, Y, Z)$ and require its image plane coordinates $(x, y)$ to be far away from the image center, and calculate

$$p_X = r_1 X + r_2 Y + T_x \tag{2.41}$$

$$p_Y = r_4 X + r_5 Y + T_y \tag{2.42}$$

This is equivalent to applying the calculated rotation parameters to the $X$ and $Y$ of the point $(X, Y, Z)$. If the signs of $p_X$ and $x$ are the same, and the signs of $p_Y$ and $y$ are the same, it means that $T_y$ has the correct sign. Otherwise, it should negative for $T_y$.

4. Calculate other rotation parameters as follows:

$$r_3 = \sqrt{1 - r_1^2 - r_2^2} r_6 = \sqrt{1 - r_4^2 - r_5^2} r_7 = \frac{1 - r_1^2 - r_2 r_4}{r_3} r_8 = \frac{1 - r_2 r_4 - r_5^2}{r_6} r_9$$

$$= \sqrt{1 - r_3 r_7 - r_6 r_8}$$

$$\tag{2.43}$$

Note: If the sign of $r_1 r_4 + r_2 r_5$ is positive, then should negative for $r_6$, and the signs of $r_7$ and $r_8$ should be adjusted after the focal length $\lambda$ is calculated.

5. Establish another set of linear equations to calculate the focal length $\lambda$ and the translation parameter $T_z$ in the $z$ direction. A matrix $B$ can be constructed first, in which row $b_i$ can be represented as follows:

$$b_i = \lfloor r_4 X_i + r_5 Y_i + T_y \quad y_i \rfloor \tag{2.44}$$

In this equation, $\lfloor \cdot \rfloor$ means rounding down.

Let the row $v_i$ of the vector $v$ be represented as

$$v_i = (r_7 X_i + r_8 Y_i) y_i \tag{2.45}$$

Then, from the linear equations

$$Bt = v \tag{2.46}$$

$t = [\lambda \ T_z]^\mathrm{T}$ can be solved. Note that what was obtained here is only an estimate of $t$.

6. If $\lambda < 0$, to use the right-handed coordinate system, it needs to negative for $r_3$, $r_6$, $r_7$, $r_8$, $\lambda$, and $T_z$.

7. Use the estimation of $t$ to calculate the radial distortion $k$ of the lens, and improve the values of $\lambda$ and $T_z$. Using the perspective projection equation including distortion, the following non-linear equation can be obtained:

$$\left\{ y_i (1 + k r^2) = \lambda \frac{r_4 X_i + r_5 Y_i + r_6 Z_i + T_y}{r_7 X_i + r_8 Y_i + r_9 Z_i + T_z} \right\} \qquad i = 1, 2, \cdots, M \tag{2.47}$$

**Table 2.2** World coordinate values and image plane coordinate values of five reference points

| $i$ | $X_i$ | $Y_i$ | $Z_i$ | $x_i$ | $y_i$ |
|---|---|---|---|---|---|
| 1 | 0.00 | 5.00 | 0.00 | −0.58 | 0.00 |
| 2 | 10.00 | 7.50 | 0.00 | 1.73 | 1.00 |
| 3 | 10.00 | 5.00 | 0.00 | 1.73 | 0.00 |
| 4 | 5.00 | 10.00 | 0.00 | 0.00 | 1.00 |
| 5 | 5.00 | 0.00 | 0.00 | 0.00 | −1.00 |

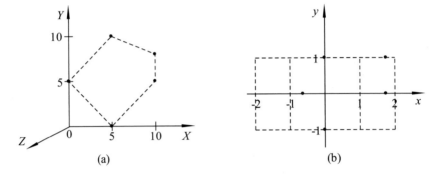

(a)                                          (b)

**Fig. 2.8** The positions of five reference points in the world coordinate system and image plane coordinate system

Solve the above equation by non-linear regression method to get the values of $k$, $\lambda$, and $T_z$.

## Example 2.2 Calibration Example of Camera External Parameters

Table 2.2 shows five reference points whose world coordinates and their corresponding image plane coordinates are known.

Figure 2.8a shows the positions of the above five reference points in the world coordinate system, and their positions in the image plane coordinate system are shown in Fig. 2.8b.

From the data given in Table 2.2 and Eq. (2.36), one can get the matrix $A$ and vector $u$ as follows:

$$A = \begin{bmatrix} 0.00 & 0.00 & 0.00 & 2.89 & 0.00 \\ 10.00 & 7.50 & -17.32 & -12.99 & 1.00 \\ 0.00 & 0.00 & -17.32 & -8.66 & 0.00 \\ 5.00 & 10.00 & 0.00 & 0.00 & 1.00 \\ -5.00 & 0.00 & 0.00 & 0.00 & -1.00 \end{bmatrix}$$

$$u = \begin{bmatrix} -0.58 & 1.73 & 1.73 & 0.00 & 0.00 \end{bmatrix}^T$$

From Eq. (2.38), one can get

$$s = \begin{bmatrix} -0.17 & 0.00 & 0.00 & -0.20 & 0.87 \end{bmatrix}^T$$

The other calculation steps are as follows:

1. Because $S = s_1^2 + s_2^2 + s_3^2 + s_4^2 = 0.07$, so from Eq. (2.39), it has the following:

$$T_y^2 = \frac{S - \left[ S^2 - 4(s_1 s_4 - s_2 s_3)^2 \right]^{1/2}}{2(s_1 s_4 - s_2 s_3)^2} = 25$$

2. Taking $T_y = 5$, then $r_1 = s_1 T_y = -0.87$, $r_2 = s_2 T_y = 0$, $r_4 = s_3 T_y = 0$, $r_5 = s_4 T_y = -1.0$, $T_x = s_5 T_y = 4.33$ can be obtained, respectively.
3. Select the point with the world coordinates (10.0, 7.5, 0.0) that is the farthest from the image center, and its image plane coordinates are (1.73, 1.0). By calculation, it gets $p_X = r_1 X + r_2 Y + T_x = -4.33$, $p_Y = r_4 X + r_5 Y + T_y = -2.5$.
    Since the signs of $p_X$ and $p_Y$ are inconsistent with the signs of $x$ and $y$, take the negative of $T_y$, and go back to step (2) to get $r_1 = s_1 T_y = 0.87$, $r_2 = s_2 T_y = 0$, $r_4 = s_3 T_y = 0$, $r_5 = s_4 T_y = 1.0$, $T_x = s_5 T_y = -4.33$.
4. Continue to calculate several other parameters; one can successively get $r_3 = (1 - r_1^2 - r_2^2)^{1/2} = 0.5$, $r_6 = (1 - r_4^2 - r_5^2)^{1/2} = 0.0$, $r_7 = \frac{1 - r_1^2 - r_2 r_4}{r_3} = 0.5$, $r_8 = \frac{1 - r_2 r_4 - r_5^2}{r_6} = 0.0$, $r_9 = (1 - r_3 r_7 - r_6 r_8)^{1/2} = 0.87$ in turn. Because $r_1 r_4 + r_2 r_5 = 0$, it is not positive, so it does not need to negative for $r_6$.
5. Establish the second set of linear equations, and get the following matrices and vectors from Eqs. (2.44) and (2.45):

$$B = \begin{bmatrix} 0.00 & 0.00 \\ 2.50 & -1.00 \\ 0.00 & 0.00 \\ 5.00 & -1.00 \\ -5.00 & 1.00 \end{bmatrix}$$

$$v = \begin{bmatrix} 0.00 & 5.00 & 0.00 & 2.50 & -2.50 \end{bmatrix}^T$$

Solving these linear equations, by Eq. (2.46), one can get $t = \begin{bmatrix} l & T_z \end{bmatrix}^T = \begin{bmatrix} -1.0 & -7.5 \end{bmatrix}^T$.

6. Since $\lambda$ is negative, it indicates that it is not a right-handed coordinate system. To reverse the $Z$ coordinate axis, it needs to negative for $r_3$, $r_6$, $r_7$, $r_8$, $\lambda$, and $T_z$. Finally, it gets $\lambda = 1$, and the following results:

$$\boldsymbol{R} = \begin{bmatrix} 0.87 & 0.00 & -0.50 \\ 0.00 & 1.00 & 0.00 \\ -0.50 & 0.00 & 0.87 \end{bmatrix}$$

$$\boldsymbol{T} = \begin{bmatrix} -4.33 & -5.00 & 7.50 \end{bmatrix}^{\mathrm{T}}$$

7. The radial distortion $k$ of the lens is not considered in this example, so the above result is the final result.

### 2.3.3   Precision Improvement

The above two-stage calibration method only considers the radial distortion factor of the camera lens. If the tangential distortion of the lens is further considered on this basis, it is possible to further improve the accuracy of camera calibration.

According to Eqs. (2.28) and (2.29), considering the total distortion deviation $d_x$ and $d_y$ of radial distortion and tangential distortion are

$$d_x = d_{xr} + d_{xt} \tag{2.48}$$

$$d_y = d_{yr} + d_{yt} \tag{2.49}$$

Considering the fourth-order term for radial distortion and the second-order term for tangential distortion, there are

$$d_x = x_i \left( k_1 r^2 + k_2 r^4 \right) + l_1 \left( 3x_i^2 + y_i^2 \right) + 2l_2 x_i y_i \tag{2.50}$$

$$d_y = y_i \left( k_1 r^2 + k_2 r^4 \right) + 2l_1 x_i y_i + l_2 \left( x_i^2 + 3y_i^2 \right) \tag{2.51}$$

The camera calibration can be carried out in two steps as follows.

1. First, set the initial values of lens distortion parameters $k_1$, $k_2$, $l_1$, and $l_2$ to be 0, and calculate the values of $\boldsymbol{R}$, $\boldsymbol{T}$, and $\lambda$.

   Refer to Eqs. (2.4) and (2.5), and refer to the derivation of Eq. (2.47); one can get

$$x = \lambda \frac{X}{Z} = \lambda \frac{r_1 X + r_2 Y + r_3 Z + T_x}{r_7 X + r_8 Y + r_9 Z + T_z} \tag{2.52}$$

$$y = \lambda \frac{Y}{Z} = \lambda \frac{r_4 X + r_5 Y + r_6 Z + T_y}{r_7 X + r_8 Y + r_9 Z + T_z} \tag{2.53}$$

From Eqs. (2.52) and (2.53)

$$\frac{x}{y} = \frac{r_1 X + r_2 Y + r_3 Z + T_x}{r_4 X + r_5 Y + r_6 Z + T_y} \tag{2.54}$$

Equation (2.54) holds for all reference points, that is, an equation can be established by using the 3-D world coordinates and 2-D image coordinates of each reference point. There are eight unknowns in Eq. (2.54), so if there are eight reference points, an equation set with eight equations can be constructed, and then the values of $r_1$, $r_2$, $r_3$, $r_4$, $r_5$, $r_6$, $T_x$, and $T_y$ can be calculated. Because $\boldsymbol{R}$ is an orthogonal matrix, the values of $r_7$, $r_8$, and $r_9$ can be calculated according to its orthogonality. Substituting these calculated values into Eqs. (2.52) and (2.53), and then taking the 3-D world coordinates and 2-D image coordinates of any two reference points, the values of $T_z$ and $\lambda$ can be calculated.

2. Calculate the values of lens distortion parameters $k_1$, $k_2$, $l_1$, and $l_2$.

According to Eqs. (2.20) and (2.21) and Eqs. (2.48) to Eq. (2.51), one can get

$$\lambda \frac{X}{Z} = x = x_i + x_i \left( k_1 r^2 + k_2 r^4 \right) + l_1 \left( 3x_i^2 + y_i^2 \right) + 2l_2 x_i y_i \tag{2.55}$$

$$\lambda \frac{Y}{Z} = y = y_i + y_i \left( k_1 r^2 + k_2 r^4 \right) + 2l_1 x_i y_i + l_2 \left( x_i^2 + 3y_i^2 \right) \tag{2.56}$$

With the help of $\boldsymbol{R}$ and $\boldsymbol{T}$ that have been obtained, $(X, Y, Z)$ can be calculated using Eq. (2.54) and then substituting into Eqs. (2.55) and (2.56) to obtain

$$\lambda \frac{X_j}{Z_j} = x_{ij} + x_{ij} \left( k_1 r^2 + k_2 r^4 \right) + l_1 \left( 3x_{ij}^2 + y_{ij}^2 \right) + 2l_2 x_{ij} y_{ij} \tag{2.57}$$

$$\lambda \frac{Y_j}{Z_j} = y_{ij} + y_{ij} \left( k_1 r^2 + k_2 r^4 \right) + 2l_1 x_{ij} y_{ij} + l_2 \left( x_{ij}^2 + 3y_{ij}^2 \right) \tag{2.58}$$

where $j = 1, 2, \ldots, N$, $N$ is the number of reference points. Using $2N$ linear equations and solving with the least square method, the values of four distortion parameters $k_1$, $k_2$, $l_1$, and $l_2$ can be obtained.

## 2.4  Self-Calibration Methods

The camera **self-calibration** method was proposed in the early 1990s. Camera self-calibration can obtain camera parameters without resorting to high-precision calibration objects. Real-time and online camera model parameters can be calculated from the geometric constraints obtained from the image sequence. This is especially suitable for cameras that often need to move. Since all self-calibration methods are only related to the internal parameters of the camera and have nothing to do with the external environment and the movement of the camera, the self-calibration method is more flexible than the traditional calibration method. However, the accuracy of the

**Fig. 2.9** The geometric relationship between the images made by camera translation

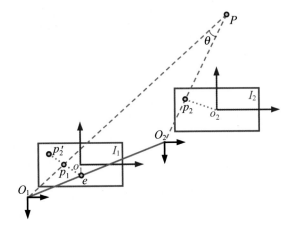

general self-calibration method is not very high, and the robustness is also not very high.

The basic idea of the self-calibration method is to first establish a constraint equation about the camera's internal parameter matrix through the absolute conic, called the Kruppa equation, and then to solve the Kruppa equation to determine the matrix $C$ ($C = K^T K^{-1}$, $K$ is the internal parameter matrix). Finally, the matrix $K$ is obtained by Cholesky decomposition.

The self-calibration method can also be realized by means of active vision technology. However, some researchers have separately proposed calibration methods based on active vision technology as a single category. The so-called active vision system means that the system can control the camera to obtain multiple images in motion and then use its motion trajectory and the corresponding relationship between the obtained images to calibrate the camera parameters. The **active vision-based calibration** technology is generally used when the camera's motion parameters in the world coordinate system are known. It can usually be solved linearly and the obtained results have high robustness.

In practice, the method based on active vision generally installs the camera accurately on a controllable platform, actively controls the platform to perform special movements to obtain multiple images, and then uses the image and camera motion parameters to determine the camera parameters. However, if the camera movement is unknown or the camera movement cannot be controlled, this method cannot be used. In addition, the method requires high precision of the motion platform, and the cost is high.

The following describes a typical self-calibration method, which is also often referred to as a method based on active vision. As shown in Fig. 2.9, the camera's optical center is translated from $O_1$ to $O_2$, and the two images captured are $I_1$ and $I_2$ (the origins of the coordinates are $O_1$ and $O_2$), respectively. A point $P$ in space is imaged as point $p_1$ on $I_1$ and as point $p_2$ on $I_2$, and $p_1$ and $p_2$ form a pair of corresponding points. If a point $p_2'$ is marked on $I_1$ according to the coordinate values of point $p_2$ on $I_2$, the connecting line between $p_2'$ and $p_1$ is called the connecting line of the corresponding point on $I_1$. It can be proved that when the camera performs pure translational motion, the lines of the corresponding points of all spatial points on $I_1$ intersect at the same point $e$, and it is the direction of the camera movement $\overrightarrow{O_1e}$ (here $e$ is on the line between $O_1$ and $O_2$, and $O_1O_2$ is the trajectory of translational motion).

According to the analysis of Fig. 2.9, by determining the intersection of the corresponding points, the translational movement direction of the camera in the camera coordinate system can be obtained. In this way, control the camera to perform translational movement in three directions ($i = 1, 2, 3$) during the calibration, and calculate the corresponding intersection point $e_i$ with the corresponding points before and after each movement, so as to obtain the three translational movement direction $\overrightarrow{O_1e_i}$.

With reference to Eqs. (2.6) and (2.7), consider the ideal situation of uncertain image scale factor $\mu$ being one, and take each sensor in the $X$ direction to sample 1 pixel in each row. Then Eqs. (2.6) and (2.7) become

$$M = \frac{x'}{S_x} + O_m \tag{2.59}$$

$$N = \frac{y'}{S_y} + O_n \tag{2.60}$$

Equations (2.59) and (2.60) establish the conversion relationship between the image plane coordinate system $x'y'$ represented in physical units (such as millimeters) and the computer image coordinate system $MN$ represented in pixels. According to Fig. 2.8, the coordinates of the intersection point $e_i$ ($i = 1, 2, 3$) on $I_1$ are $(x_i, y_i)$, respectively, and then from Eqs. (2.59) and (2.60), the coordinates of $e_i$ in the camera coordinate system are

$$\mathbf{e}_i = \left[ (x_i - O_m)S_x \quad (y_i - O_n)S_y \quad \lambda \right]^{\mathrm{T}} \tag{2.61}$$

If the camera is translated 3 times, and the directions of these three movements are orthogonal, $e_iTe_j = 0$ ($i \neq j$) can be obtained, and then

$$(x_1 - O_m)(x_2 - O_m)S_x^2 + (y_1 - O_n)(y_2 - O_n)S_y^2 + \lambda^2 = 0 \tag{2.62}$$

$$(x_1 - O_m)(x_3 - O_m)S_x^2 + (y_1 - O_n)(y_3 - O_n)S_y^2 + \lambda^2 = 0 \tag{2.63}$$

$$(x_2 - O_m)(x_3 - O_m)S_x^2 + (y_2 - O_n)(y_3 - O_n)S_y^2 + \lambda^2 = 0 \tag{2.64}$$

Equations (2.62), (2.6.3), and (2.64) are further rewritten as

$$(x_1 - O_m)(x_2 - O_m) + (y_1 - O_n)(y_2 - O_n)\left(\frac{S_y}{S_x}\right)^2 + \left(\frac{\lambda}{S_x}\right)^2 = 0 \qquad (2.65)$$

$$(x_1 - O_m)(x_3 - O_m) + (y_1 - O_n)(y_3 - O_n)\left(\frac{S_y}{S_x}\right)^2 + \left(\frac{\lambda}{S_x}\right)^2 = 0 \qquad (2.66)$$

$$(x_2 - O_m)(x_3 - O_m) + (y_2 - O_n)(y_3 - O_n)\left(\frac{S_y}{S_x}\right)^2 + \left(\frac{\lambda}{S_x}\right)^2 = 0 \qquad (2.67)$$

and two intermediate variables are defined

$$Q_1 = \left(\frac{S_y}{S_x}\right)^2 \qquad (2.68)$$

$$Q_2 = \left(\frac{\lambda}{S_x}\right)^2 \qquad (2.69)$$

In this way, Eqs. (2.65), (2.66), and (2.67) become three equations with four unknown quantities of $O_m$, $O_n$, $Q_1$, and $Q_2$. These equations are non-linear. If one subtracts Eqs. (2.66) and (2.67) from Eq. (2.65), one can get two linear equations:

$$x_1(x_2 - x_3) = (x_2 - x_3)O_m + (y_2 - y_3)O_nQ_1 - y_1(y_2 - y_3)Q_1 \qquad (2.70)$$

$$x_2(x_1 - x_3) = (x_1 - x_3)O_m + (y_1 - y_3)O_nQ_1 - y_2(y_1 - y_3)Q_1 \qquad (2.71)$$

Let $O_nQ_1$ in Eqs. (2.70) and (2.71) be represented by intermediate variable $Q_3$:

$$Q_3 = O_nQ_1 \qquad (2.72)$$

Then, Eqs. (2.70) and (2.71) become two linear equations about three unknowns, $O_m$, $Q_1$, and $Q_3$. Since the two equations have three unknowns, the solutions of Eqs. (2.70) and (2.71) are generally not unique. In order to obtain a unique solution, the camera can be moved three times along the other three orthogonal directions to obtain three other intersection points $e_i$ ($i = 4, 5, 6$). If these three translational motions have different directions from the previous three translational motions, two equations similar to Eqs. (2.70) and (2.71) can be obtained. In this way, a total of four equations are obtained, and any three equations can be selected, or the least square method can be used to solve $O_m$, $Q_1$, and $Q_3$ from these equations. Next, solve for $O_n$ from Eq. (2.72), and then substitute $O_m$, $O_n$, and $Q_1$ into Eq. (2.67) to solve for $Q_2$. In this way, all the internal parameters of the camera can be obtained by controlling the camera to perform two sets of three orthogonal translational movements.

## 2.5   Key Points and References for Each Section

The following combines the main contents of each section to introduce some references that can be further consulted.

1. **Linear Camera Model**
    The linear camera model is an idealized model based on pin-hole imaging, which can be approximated for many occasions, and many books are also introduced, such as [1].
2. **Non-linear Camera Model**
    There are many kinds of non-linear camera model, and the basic elements can be found in [2].
3. **Traditional Calibration Methods**
    The two-stage calibration method is a typical traditional calibration method; see [3, 4].
4. **Self-Calibration Methods**
    The early self-calibration method can be found in [5]. The proof of the nature of the camera when it does pure translation can be found in [6].

## Self-Test Questions

The following questions include both single-choice questions and multiple-choice questions, so each option must be judged.

2.1 **Linear Camera Model**

   2.1.1 The camera calibration method introduced in Sect. 2.1 needs to obtain more than 6 spatial points with known world coordinates because (·)

   (a) There are 12 unknowns in the camera calibration equations.
   (b) The rotation and translation of the camera need three parameters to describe
   (c) The world coordinates are 3-D, and the image plane coordinates are 2-D
   (d) The transformation matrix from real- world coordinates to image plane coordinates is a 3 × 3 matrix

   [Hint] Note that some parameters are related.

   2.1.2 In camera calibration, (·).

   (a) The relationship between the camera's internal parameters and external parameters can be established.
   (b) The obtained parameters can also be determined by the measurement of the camera.

(c) It is needed to determine both the internal parameters of the camera and the external parameters of the camera.

(d) It is to determine the transformation type from a given world point $W(X, Y, Z)$ to its image plane coordinates $(x, y)$.

[Hint] Consider the purpose and specific steps of camera calibration.

2.1.3 In camera calibration, (·).

(a) The internal parameters must be determined first and then the external parameters.

(b) The external parameters must be determined first and then the internal parameters.

(c) The internal parameters and external parameters must be determined at the same time.

(d) The internal parameters and external parameters can be determined at the same time.

[Hint] Pay attention to the exact meaning and subtle differences of different text descriptions.

## 2.2 **Non-linear Camera Model**

2.2.1 Due to lens distortion, (·).

(a) The projection from 3-D space to 2-D image plane cannot be described by a linear model.

(b) The distortion error generated will be more obvious near the optical axis.

(c) The distortion error generated in the image plane will be more obvious at the place which is far from the center.

(d) The object point in the 3-D space can be determined according to the pixel coordinates of the 2-D image plane.

[Hint] Distortion causes the projection relationship to no longer be a linear projection relationship.

2.2.2 For radial distortion, (·).

(a) The deviation caused is often symmetrical about the main optical axis of the camera lens.

(b) The positive one is called barrel distortion.

(c) The negative one is called pincushion distortion.

(d) The barrel distortion caused in the image plane is more obvious at a place away from the optical axis.

[Hint] The radial distortion is mainly caused by the curvature error of the lens surface.

2.2.3 In lens distortion, (·).

(a) The distortion of the thin prism only causes radial deviation.
(b) The eccentric distortion originates from the discrepancy between the optical center and geometric center of the optical system.
(c) The tangential distortion mainly comes from the non-collinear optical centers of the lens group.
(d) The centrifugal distortion includes both radial distortion and tangential distortion.

[Hint] Some distortions are combined distortions.

2.2.4 According to the non-linear camera model, in the conversion from 3-D world coordinates to computer image coordinates, (·).

(a) The non-linearity comes from the lens radial distortion coefficient $k$.
(b) The non-linearity comes from the distance between a point in the image and the optical axis point of the lens.
(c) The non-linearity comes from the image plane coordinates $(x', y')$ being affected by the lens radial distortion.
(d) The non-linearity comes from the actual image plane coordinates $(x^*, y^*)$ being affected by the lens radial distortion.

[Hint] Not every step of the non-linear camera model is non-linear.

## 2.3 Traditional Calibration Methods

2.3.1 According to Fig. 2.7, (·).

(a) The calibration process is consistent with the imaging process.
(b) There are coefficients to be calibrated for each step of the coordinate system conversion.
(c) There are more internal parameters to be calibrated than external parameters.
(d) There are always four steps in the conversion from the world coordinate system to the computer image coordinate system.

[Hint] Pay attention to the meaning of each step of conversion and content.

2.3.2 In the two-stage calibration method, (·).

(a) Calculate $R$ and $T$ in Step 1, and calculate other parameters in Step 2.
(b) Calculate all external parameters in Step 1, and calculate all internal parameters in Step 2.
(c) The $k$ corresponding to radial distortion is always calculated in Step 2.
(d) Uncertain image scale factor $\mu$ is always calculated in Step 1.

[Hint] Uncertain image scale factor $\mu$ may also be known in advance.

2.3.3 When improving the accuracy of the two-stage calibration method, the tangential distortion of the lens is also considered, so ($\cdot$).

(a) Eight reference points are needed for calibration
(b) Ten reference points are rdequired for calibration
(c) There can be up to 12 parameters to be calibrated
(d) There can be up to 15 parameters to be calibrated

[Hint] The numbers of distortion parameters considered here are 4.

## 2.4  Self-Calibration Methods

2.4.1 Self-calibration method ($\cdot$).

(a) No needs to resort to known calibration materials
(b) Always needs to collect multiple images for calibration
(c) Can only calibrate the internal parameters of the camera
(d) Is not very highly robust when it is implemented with active vision technology

[Hint] Analyze the basic principles of self-calibration.

2.4.2 Under the ideal situation of uncertain image scale factor $\mu = 1$, ($\cdot$).

(a) The camera model is linear.
(b) If the number of sensor elements in the $X$ direction is increased, the number of rows of pixels will also increase.
(c) If the number of samples along the $X$ direction made by the computer in a row is increased, the number of rows of pixels will also increase.
(d) The image plane coordinates represented in physical units (such as millimeters) are also the computer image coordinates in pixels.

[Hint] Note that the uncertain image scale factor is introduced in the transformation from the image plane coordinate system $x'y'$ to the computer image coordinate system $MN$.

2.4.3 To calibrate the camera according to the self-calibration method introduced in Sect. 2.4, ($\cdot$).

(a) The camera needs to do three pure translation movements.
(b) The camera needs to do four pure translation movements.
(c) The camera needs to do five pure translation movements.
(d) The camera needs to do six pure translation movements.

[Hint] Analyze the number of equations that can be obtained when the method is calibrated and the number of unknowns to be calculated.

# References

1. Forsyth D, Ponce J. Computer Vision: A Modern Approach. Prentice Hall. 2003.
2. Weng J Y, Cohen P, Hernion M. Camera calibration with distortion models and accuracy evaluation. IEEE-PAMI, 1992, 14(10): 965-980.
3. Tsai R Y. A versatile camera calibration technique for high-accuracy 3D machine vision metrology using off-the shelf TV camera and lenses. Journal of Robotics and Automation, 1987, 3(4): 323-344.
4. Zhang Y-J. Image Engineering, Vol.3: Image Understanding. De Gruyter, 2017.
5. Faugeras O. Three-dimensional Computer Vision: A Geometric Viewpoint. MIT Press. 1993.
6. Ma S D, Zhang Z Y. Computer Vision — Computational theory and algorithm foundation. Science Press, 1998.

# Chapter 3
# Three-Dimensional Image Acquisition

The general imaging method obtains a 2-D image from a 3-D physical space, where the information on the plane perpendicular to the optical axis of the camera is often retained in the image, but the depth information along the optical axis of the camera is lost. For 3-D computer vision, it often needs to obtain 3-D information of the objective world or higher-dimensional comprehensive information. For this purpose, **3-D image acquisition** is required. This includes not only collecting 3-D images directly but also collecting (implicitly) images containing 3-D information and extracting the 3-D information in subsequent processing.

Specifically, there are a variety of methods to obtain (or restore) depth information, including stereo vision technology that refers to the human binocular vision system to observe the world, using specific equipment and devices to directly obtain distance information, moving the focus plane layer by layer to obtain 3-D information, etc.

The sections of this chapter are arranged as follows:

Section 3.1 introduces the generalized high-dimensional image $f(x, y, z, t, \lambda)$ with five variables and gives several typical examples.

Section 3.2 introduces the comparison of depth images and grayscale images and further the comparison of more general intrinsic images and non-intrinsic image images. In addition, various depth imaging methods are also listed.

Section 3.3 introduces several typical direct methods for depth imaging, including time-of-flight method, structured light method, Moiré contour stripes method, and laser radar (LADAR) that can simultaneously acquire depth and intensity images.

Section 3.4 introduces several typical modes of using binocular (dual cameras) to collect images for stereo imaging, including binocular lateral mode, binocular convergence mode, and binocular axial mode.

© The Author(s), under exclusive license to Springer Nature Singapore Pte Ltd. 2023
Y.-J. Zhang, *3-D Computer Vision*, https://doi.org/10.1007/978-981-19-7580-6_3

## 3.1   High-Dimensional Image

The objective world is high-dimensional, and correspondingly collected images can also be high-dimensional. Here, high dimension can refer to the high dimension of the space where the image is located or the high dimension of the image's attributes. Compared with the most basic 2-D static gray image $f(x, y)$, the generalized **high-dimensional image** should be a vector function $f(x, y, z, t, \lambda)$ with five variables, where $f$ represents the objective properties reflected by the image; $x, y, z$ are spatial variables; $t$ is a time variable; and $\lambda$ is a spectrum variable (wavelength). This section introduces first the types of high-dimensional images and some corresponding image acquisition methods.

With the advancement of electronic technology and computer technology, many image acquisition methods and equipment have been applied, making the image continuously expand from $f(x, y)$ to $f(x, y, z, t, \lambda)$. Some typical examples are given below.

1. Consider $f(x, y)$ as an image reflecting the surface radiation of the scene: If the scene can be divided into multiple slices (multiple sections) along the acquisition direction, and each slice can be imaged separately, a complete scenery with 3-D information (including the interior of the scene) can be obtained by combining these slice images. That is, the 3-D image $f(x, y, z)$ is collected. For example, imaging methods such as CT and MRI all obtain 3-D images $f(x, y, z)$ by moving the imaging plane to scan the objects layer by layer.

2. Consider $f(x, y)$ as a still image acquired at a given moment: Here, the process of image acquisition is regarded as an instantaneous process; if multiple images are continuously acquired along the time axis, complete information (including dynamic information) over a period of time can be obtained. Video (and other images acquired in sequence) gives another type of 3-D image $f(x, y, t)$.

3. Consider $f(x, y)$ as an image obtained only in response to a certain wavelength of electromagnetic radiation (or the average value of radiation in a certain band): In fact, the images obtained by using different wavelength radiation can reflect different nature of the scene (corresponding to the reflection and absorption characteristics of the surface of the scene at different wavelengths). The acquisition of images collected in the same time and space by using various wavelengths of radiation can fully reflect the spectrum information of the scene, each of which can be a 3-D image $f(x, y, \lambda)$ or a 4-D image $f(x, y, t, \lambda)$. A typical example is a multispectral image; each image corresponds to a different band of frequency, but all these images correspond to the same time and space.

4. Consider $f(x, y)$ as an image that only considers a single property at a given spatial location: In reality, a scene at a certain location in space can have multiple properties, or the image at point $(x, y)$ can also have multiple attribute values at the same time, which can be represented by vector $f$. For example, a color image can be regarded as an image with three values of red, green, and blue at each image point, $f(x, y) = [f_r(x, y), f_g(x, y), f_b(x, y)]$. In addition, the above-mentioned image collection obtained by using various wavelengths of radiation in the same

time and space can also be regarded as vector images $f(x, y) = [f_{\lambda 1}(x, y), f_{\lambda 2}(x, y),$ ...] or $f(x, y) = [f_{t1\lambda 1}(x, y), f_{t1\lambda 2}(x, y), ..., f_{t2\lambda 1}(x, y), f_{t2\lambda 2}(x, y), ...]$.

5. Consider $f(x, y)$ as an image collected by projecting a 3-D scene onto a 2-D plane: In this process, the depth (or distance) information is lost (information loss). For example, it is possible to obtain complete information (including depth information) of the scene by combining two images collected from different viewpoints of the same scene (stereo vision; see Chap. 6). An image whose image property is depth is called a **depth image**, which can be expressed as $z = f(x, y)$. From the depth image, the 3-D image $f(x, y, z)$ can be further obtained.

The above-mentioned various expansion methods for image $f(x, y)$ can also be combined, so that various high-dimensional images $f(x, y, z, t, \lambda)$ can be obtained.

## 3.2  Depth Image

Computer vision technology is based on images of objective scenes, and it is very important to obtain complete information of the objective world. When the 3-D scene is projected to the 2-D plane and the image is collected, the depth (or distance) information will be lost (information loss). In order to obtain the complete information of the scene, the depth information needs to be restored.

### 3.2.1  Depth Image and Grayscale Image

The **depth image** $z = f(x, y)$ not only reflects the depth information $z$ of the scene but also reflects the $(x, y)$ plane information at each depth. The geometric shape and spatial relationship of the objects in scene can be easily obtained from the depth image.

**Example 3.1 The Difference Between Depth Image and Grayscale Image**
Consider a section on the object in Fig. 3.1, and the grayscale image and the depth image can be collected separately for this section. For the grayscale image, its attribute value corresponds to the grayscale (intensity) at $(x, y)$. For the depth image, its attribute value corresponds to the distance (depth) between $(x, y)$ and the imaging device. Comparing the gray image and the depth image, there are two different characteristics as follows:

1. The pixel value of the same outer plane on the corresponding object in the depth image changes at a certain rate (the plane is inclined relative to the image plane). This value changes with the shape and orientation of the object but has nothing to do with the external lighting conditions. The corresponding pixel value in grayscale image depends not only on the illuminance of the surface (this is not

**Fig. 3.1** The difference
between depth image and
gray image

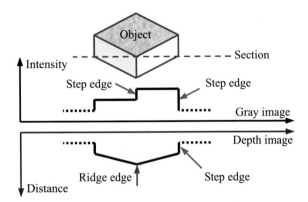

only related to the shape and orientation of the object but also related to the external lighting conditions) but also on the reflection coefficient of the surface.

2. There are two types of boundary lines in depth images: one is the (distance) **step edge** between the object and the background (the depth is discontinuous); the other is the **ridge edge** at the intersection of the regions inside the object (corresponding to the extreme value, the depth is still continuous). For the grayscale image, there are step edges in both places (as shown by the two steps of the intensity curve in Fig. 3.1).

### 3.2.2   *Intrinsic Image and Non-Intrinsic Image*

Further analysis and comparison of gray image and depth image show that they are typical representatives of the two types of images. These two types of images are **intrinsic images** and non-intrinsic images, which are distinguished according to the nature of the objective scene described by the image.

The image is the result of the scene captured by the observer or acquiring device. The scene and the objects in the scene have some properties that have nothing to do with the nature of the observer and the acquiring device themselves, and these properties exist objectively, for example, the surface reflectivity, transparency, surface orientation, movement speed of the object, and the distance and the relative orientation between the different objects in the scene. These properties are called **intrinsic properties** (of the scene), and the images representing the physical quantities of these intrinsic properties are called intrinsic images. There are many types of intrinsic images, and each intrinsic image may only represent an intrinsic property of the scene, without the influence of other properties. If the intrinsic image can be obtained, it is very useful for correctly interpreting the scene represented by the image. For example, a depth image is one of the most commonly used intrinsic images, in which each pixel value represents the distance (depth, also known as the elevation of the scene) between the scene point represented by the pixel and the camera. Actually, these pixel values directly reflect the shape (an intrinsic property) of the visible surface of the scene. Another example is the image representation method with motion vector field introduced in Chap. 4. If the values of those motion vectors are directly converted into amplitude values, the intrinsic images that represent the moving speed of the object are obtained.

The physical quantity represented by the non-intrinsic image is not only related to the scene itself but also related to the nature of the observer/sensor or the conditions of image acquisition or the surrounding environment. A typical representative of non-intrinsic images is the commonly used intensity image (luminance image or illuminance image), which is generally represented as a grayscale image. The intensity image is an image that reflects the amplitude of radiation received by the observation site. Its intensity value is often the combined result of multiple factors such as the intensity of the radiation source, the orientation of the radiation mode, the reflection properties of the surface of the scene, and the location and performance of the sensor (more discussions can be found in Chap. 7).

In computer vision, many images acquired are non-intrinsic images, while to perceive the world, the intrinsic properties of the scene are needed. In other words, intrinsic images need to be obtained so that the scene can be characterized and explained further. In order to recover the intrinsic nature and structure of the scene from non-intrinsic images, various image (pre)processing methods are often utilized. For example, in the imaging process of grayscale images, a lot of physical information about the scene is mixed and integrated in the pixel gray values, so the imaging process can be regarded as a degenerate transformation. However, the physical information about the scene is not completely lost after being mixed in the grayscale image. Various preprocessing techniques (such as filtering, edge detection, distance transformation, etc.) can be used to eliminate the degradation in the imaging process with the help of redundant information in the image (it is to "reverse" the transformation of the physical imaging process), thereby converting the image into an intrinsic image reflecting the spatial nature of the scene.

From the perspective of image acquisition, there are two methods to obtain intrinsic images: one is to first collect non-intrinsic images containing intrinsic information and then use image technology to restore intrinsic properties; the other is to directly collect intrinsic images with intrinsic information. To take the collection of depth images as an example, one can use specific equipment to directly collect depth images (such as the direct depth imaging in Sect. 3.3), or one can collect grayscale images containing stereo information and then obtain depth information from them (such as binocular stereo imaging in Sect. 3.4). For the former method, one needs to use some specific image acquisition equipment (imaging devices). For the latter method, one needs to consider the use of some specific image acquisition modes (imaging modes) and the use of some targeted image technology.

### 3.2.3   Depth Imaging Modes

To obtain a depth image with intrinsic properties, one can proceed from two aspects. On the one hand, it is necessary to use an imaging device with such capabilities; on the other hand, certain acquisition modes and methods can also be used.

There are many ways of depth imaging, which are mainly determined by the mutual position and movement of the light source, sensor, and object/scene. Table 3.1 summarizes the characteristics of light source, sensor, and object/scene in some depth imaging methods.

The most basic imaging method is monocular imaging, which uses a sensor to obtain an image of the scene at a fixed position. Although as discussed in Chap. 2 of *2D Computer Vision: Principles, Algorithms and Applications*, the Z coordinate of a 3-D point cannot be uniquely determined by the image point $(x, y)$. That is, the depth information of the scene is not directly reflected in the image, but this information is actually hidden in the geometric distortion, shading (shadow), texture changes, surface contours, and other factors in imaging (Chaps. 7 and 8 will introduce how to recover depth information from such an image).

If one uses two sensors to take images of the same scene, each at one location (or use one sensor to take images of the same scene at two locations one after the other, or use one sensor to obtain two images with the help of an optical imaging system), it is binocular imaging (see Sect. 2.4 and Chap. 6). At this time, the parallax generated between the two images (similar to the human eyes) can be used to support calculating the distance between the sensor and the scene. If more than two sensors are used to take images of the same scene at different locations (or one sensor is used

**Table 3.1**   Characteristics of common imaging methods

| Imaging mode | Source | Sensor | Object/ scene | See also |
|---|---|---|---|---|
| Monocular imaging | Fixed | Fixed | Fixed | *2D Computer Vision: Principles, Algorithms and Applications* |
| Binocular imaging | Fixed | Two positions | Fixed | Chapter 6 |
| Multi-ocular imaging | Fixed | Multi-positions | Fixed | Chapter 6 |
| Video/sequence imaging | Fixed/ moving | Fixed/ moving | Moving/ fixed | Chapter 4 |
| Light shift (photo-metric stereo) imaging | Translation | Fixed | Fixed | Chapter 7 |
| Active vision imaging | Fixed | Moving | Fixed | Chapter 2 |
| Active vision (self-motion) imaging | Fixed | Moving | Moving | Chapter 2 |
| Structured light imaging | Fixed/ rotation | Fixed/ rotation | Rotation/ fixed | Chapter 2 |

to take images of the same scene at multiple positions successively), it is multi-ocular imaging. Monocular, binocular or multi-ocular methods can not only obtain still images but also obtain sequence images by continuous shooting. Monocular imaging is simpler than binocular imaging, but it is more complicated to obtain depth information from it. Conversely, binocular imaging increases the complexity of acquisition equipment but can reduce the complexity of acquiring depth information.

In the above discussion, it is considered that the light source is fixed in several imaging methods. If the sensor is fixed relative to the scene and the light source moves around the scene, this imaging method is called photometric stereo imaging (also known as light shift imaging). Because the surface of the same scene can have different brightness under different lighting conditions, the surface orientation of the object can be obtained from multiple such images (but absolute depth information cannot be obtained). If one keeps the light source fixed and let the sensor move to track the scene, or allows the sensor and the scene to move at the same time will constitute active vision imaging (referring to the initiative of human vision, i.e., people will move their body or head to change the perspective according to the requirements of observation and selectively pay special attention to part of the scene). This is also known as active vision self-motion imaging. In addition, if a controllable light source is used to illuminate the scene, the structured light imaging method is used to explain the surface shape of the scene through the collected projection mode (see Sect. 3.3). In this way, it can be that the light source and the sensor are fixed while the scene is rotated, or the scene is fixed, while the light source and the sensor are rotated around the scene together.

## 3.3   Direct Depth Imaging

With the help of some special imaging equipment, depth images can be directly collected. Commonly used methods include time-of-flight method (flying spot ranging method), structured light method, Moiré fringe method (Moiré contour stripes), holographic interferometry, geometric optical focusing method, laser radar method (including scanning imaging and non-scanning imaging), Fresnel diffraction technology, etc. The possible ranging accuracy and maximum working distance of several commonly used direct depth image acquisition methods can be seen in Table 3.2.

**Table 3.2**  Comparison of several direct depth image acquisition methods

| Direct depth imaging methods | Time of flight | Structured light | Moiré stripes | Holographic interferometry[a] |
|---|---|---|---|---|
| Possible ranging accuracy | 0.1 mm | 1 μm | 1 μm | 0.1 μm |
| Maximum working distance | 100 km | 100 m | 10 m | 100 μm |

[a]Holographic interferometry is just listed for reference; it will not be detailed in this book

### 3.3.1  Time-of-Flight Method

Using the principle of radar ranging, the distance information can be obtained by measuring the time required for the light wave from the light source to return to the sensor after being reflected by the measured object. In general, the light source and the sensor are placed in the same position, so the relationship between the propagation time $t$ and the measured distance $d$ is

$$d = \frac{1}{2}ct \qquad (3.1)$$

where $c$ is the speed of light ($3 \times 10^8$ m/s in a vacuum).

The acquisition method of **time-of-flight**-based depth image is a typical method of obtaining distance information by measuring the propagation time of light waves. Because point light sources are generally used, it is also called the flying point method. To obtain a 2-D image, one needs to scan the beam in 2-D or make the measured object move in 2-D. The key to this method of ranging is to accurately measure time, because the speed of light is $3 \times 10^8$ m/s, so if the spatial distance resolution is required to be 0.001 m (i.e., it can distinguish two points or two lines separated by 0.001 m in space), then the time resolution needs to reach $6.6 \times 10^{-12}$ s.

#### 3.3.1.1  Pulse Time Interval Measurement Method

This method uses the **pulse interval** to measure time, specifically by measuring the time difference of the pulse waves. The basic block diagram is shown in Fig. 3.2. The specific frequency laser light emitted by the pulsed laser source is shot forward through the optical lens and beam scanning system and is reflected after touching the object. The reflected light is received by another optical lens and enters the time difference measurement module after photoelectric conversion. The module also receives the laser light directly from the pulsed laser source and measures the time difference between the transmitted pulse and the received pulse. According to the time difference, the measured distance can be calculated by Eq. (3.1). It should be

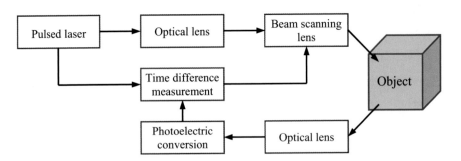

**Fig. 3.2** Block diagram of the principle of pulse time interval measurement method

noted that the starting pulse and echo pulse of the laser cannot overlap within the working distance.

Using the above-mentioned principle, the distance measurement can also be performed by replacing the pulsed laser source with ultrasound. Ultrasound can work not only in natural light but also in water. Because the propagation speed of sound waves is slow, the requirement to the accuracy of time measurement is relatively low; however, because the medium absorbs sound relatively large, the requirement for the sensitivity of the receiver is relatively high. In addition, due to the large divergence of sound waves, very high-resolution distance information cannot be obtained.

### 3.3.1.2 Phase Measurement Method of Amplitude Modulation

The time difference can also be measured by measuring the phase difference. The basic block diagram of a typical method can be seen in Fig. 3.3. The laser light emitted by the continuous laser source is under **amplitude modulation** by the light intensity with a certain frequency, and it is emitted in two ways. One way is shot forward through the optical scanning lens and reflected after touching the object; here the reflected light is filtered to get the phase; the other way enters the phase difference measurement module to compare the phase with the reflected light. Because the phase takes $2\pi$ as the period, the phase difference range measured is between 0 and $2\pi$, so the depth measurement value $d$ is

$$d = \frac{1}{2}\left\{\frac{c}{2\pi f_{\mathrm{mod}}}\theta + k\frac{c}{f_{\mathrm{mod}}}\right\} = \frac{1}{2}\left\{\frac{r}{2\pi}\theta + kr\right\} \tag{3.2}$$

where $c$ is the speed of light, $f_{\mathrm{mod}}$ is the modulation frequency, $\theta$ is the phase difference (the unit is radians), and $k$ is an integer.

Limiting the depth measurement range (limiting the value of $k$) can overcome the possible ambiguity of the depth measurement value. The $r$ introduced in Eq. (3.2) can be called the measurement scale. The smaller the $r$, the higher the accuracy of

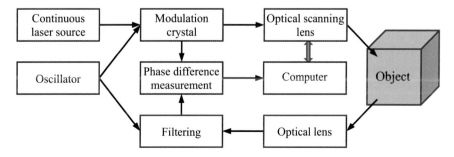

**Fig. 3.3** Block diagram of the phase measurement method of amplitude modulation

distance measurement. In order to obtain a smaller $r$, a higher modulation frequency $f_{mod}$ should be used.

### 3.3.1.3   Coherent Measurement Method of Frequency Modulation

The laser light emitted by the continuous laser source is under **frequency modulation** by a linear waveform with a certain frequency. Suppose the laser frequency is $F$, the modulating wave frequency is $f_{mod}$, and the modulated laser frequency changes linearly and periodically between $F \pm \Delta F/2$ (where $\Delta F$ is the frequency change after the laser frequency is modulated). One part of the modulated laser light is used as the reference light, and the other part is projected to the object to be measured. After the light contacts the object, it is reflected and then received by the receiver. Two optical signals coherently produce a beat signal $f_B$, which is equal to the product of the slope of the laser frequency change and the propagation time:

$$f_B = \frac{\Delta F}{1/(2f_{mod})} t \tag{3.3}$$

Substitute Eq. (3.1) into Eq. (3.3) and solve for $d$ to get

$$d = \frac{c}{f_{mod} \Delta F} f_B \tag{3.4}$$

With the help of the phase change of the emitted light wave and the return light wave

$$\Delta\theta = 2\pi\Delta Ft = 4\pi\Delta Fd/c \tag{3.5}$$

it can further get

$$d = \frac{c}{2\Delta F} \left( \frac{\Delta\theta}{2\pi} \right) \tag{3.6}$$

Comparing Eqs. (3.4) and (3.6), the number of coherent fringes $N$ (also the number of zero crossings of the beat signal in the half cycle of the modulation frequency) can be obtained:

$$N = \frac{\Delta\theta}{2\pi} = \frac{f_B}{2f_{mod}} \tag{3.7}$$

In practice, the actual distance (by counting the actual coherent fringe number) can be calculated by using Eq. (3.8) according to the accurate reference distance $d_{ref}$ and the measured reference coherent fringe number $N_{ref}$:

$$d = \frac{d_{ref}}{N_{ref}} N \qquad (3.8)$$

## 3.3.2   Structured Light Method

**Structured light** method is a commonly used method of active sensing and direct acquisition of depth images. Its basic idea is to use geometric information in lighting to help extract geometric information of a scene. The imaging system with structured light ranging is mainly composed of a camera and a light source, which are arranged in a triangle with the observed object. The light source produces a series of point or line lasers to illuminate the surface of the object, and the light-sensitive camera records the illuminated part and then obtains the depth information through triangulation calculation, so it is also called active triangulation ranging method. The distance measurement accuracy of active structured light method can reach the micron level, and the measurable depth field range can reach hundreds to tens of thousands of times the accuracy.

There are many specific ways to use structured light imaging, including light stripe method, grid method, circular light stripe method, cross line method, thick light stripe method, spatial coding mask method, color coded stripe method, density ratio method, etc. Due to the different geometric structures of the projected beams they use, the camera shooting methods and depth distance calculation methods are also different, but the common point is that they both use the geometric structure relationship between the camera and the light source.

In the basic light stripe method, a single light plane is used to illuminate each part of the scene in turn, so that a light stripe appears on the scene, and only this light stripe part can be detected by the camera. In this way, a 2-D entity (light plane) image is obtained every time, and then by calculating the intersection of the camera's line of sight and the light plane, the third dimension (distance) information of the spatial point corresponding to the visible image point on the light stripe can be obtained.

### 3.3.2.1   Structured Light Imaging

When using structured light for imaging, the camera and light source must be calibrated first. Figure 3.4 shows the geometric relationship of a structured light system. Here is the *XZ* plane perpendicular to the light source, where the lens is located (the *Y* axis goes from the inside of the paper to the outside, and the light source is a strip along the *Y* axis). The laser emitted through the narrow slit is irradiated from the origin *O* of the world coordinate system to the spatial point *W* (on the surface of the object) to produce a linear projection. The optical axis of the camera intersects the laser beam, so that the camera can collect the linear projection to obtain the distance information of point *W* on the surface of the object.

**Fig. 3.4** Schematic
diagram of structured light
imaging

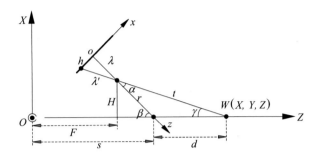

In Fig. 3.4, $F$ and $H$ determine the position of the lens center in the world coordinate system, $\alpha$ is the angle between the optical axis and the projection line, $\beta$ is the angle between the $z$ and $Z$ axes, $\gamma$ is the angle between the projection line and the $Z$ axis, $\lambda$ is the focal length of the camera, $h$ is the imaging height (the distance that the image deviates from the optical axis of the camera), and $r$ is the distance from the center of the lens to the intersection of the $z$ and $Z$ axes. It can be seen from the figure that the distance $Z$ between the light source and the object is the sum of $s$ and $d$, where $s$ is determined by the system and $d$ can be obtained by the following formula:

$$d = r\frac{\sin \alpha}{\sin \gamma} = \frac{r \sin \alpha}{\cos \alpha \sin \beta - \sin \alpha \cos \beta} = \frac{r \tan \alpha}{\sin \beta(1 - \tan \alpha \cot \beta)} \qquad (3.9)$$

Substituting $\tan \alpha = h/\lambda$, then $Z$ can be represented as

$$Z = s + d = s + \frac{r \csc \beta \times (h/\lambda)}{1 - \cot \beta \times (h/\lambda)} \qquad (3.10)$$

Equation (3.10) relates $Z$ and $h$ (the rest are all system parameters) and provides a way to obtain the object distance based on the imaging height. It can be seen that the imaging height contains 3-D depth information or the depth is a function of the imaging height.

### 3.3.2.2   Imaging Width

Structured light imaging can give not only the distance $Z$ of the spatial point but also the thickness of the object along the $Y$ direction. At this time, the imaging width can be analyzed by using the top view plane observed from the bottom of the camera upward, as shown in Fig. 3.5.

Figure 3.5 shows a schematic diagram of the plane determined by the $Y$ axis and the lens center, where $w$ is the imaging width:

**Fig. 3.5** Schematic diagram of top view during structured light imaging

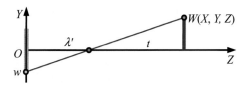

$$w = \lambda' \frac{Y}{t} \tag{3.11}$$

where $t$ is the distance from the center of the lens to the vertical projection of point $W$ on the $Z$ axis (see Fig. 3.4)

$$t = \sqrt{(Z-f)^2 + H^2} \tag{3.12}$$

and $\lambda'$ is the distance from the center of the lens to the imaging plane along the $z$-axis (see Fig. 3.4)

$$\lambda' = \sqrt{h^2 + \lambda^2} \tag{3.13}$$

Substitute Eq. (3.12) and Eq. (3.13) into Eq. (3.11) to obtain

$$Y = \frac{wt}{\lambda'} = w\sqrt{\frac{(Z-F)^2 + H^2}{h^2 + \lambda^2}} \tag{3.14}$$

In this way, the object thickness coordinate $Y$ is related to the imaging height, system parameters, and object distance.

### 3.3.3 Moiré Contour Stripes Method

Moiré stripes can be formed when two gratings have a certain inclination and overlap. The distribution of **Moiré contour stripes** obtained by a certain method can include distance information on the surface of the scene.

#### 3.3.3.1 Basic Principles

When the projection light is used to project the grating onto the surface of the scene, the undulation of the surface will change the distribution of the projected image. If the deformed projection image is reflected from the surface of the scene and then passed through another grating, the Moiré contour stripes can be obtained. According to the principle of optical signal transmission, the above process can be described as the result of optical signal undergoing secondary spatial modulation. If both gratings are linear sinusoidal perspective gratings, and the parameter that defines the period change of the grating is defined as l, then the observed output light signal is

$$f(l) = f_1\{1 + m_1 \cos [w_1 l + \theta_1(l)]\} * f_2\{1 + m_2 \cos [w_2 l + \theta_2(l)]\} \qquad (3.15)$$

where $f_i$ is the light intensity; $m_i$ is the modulation coefficient; $\theta_i$ is the phase change caused by the fluctuation of the scene surface; and $w_i$ is the spatial frequency determined by the grating period. In Eq. (3.15), the first term on the right corresponds to the modulation function of the first grating through which the optical signal passes, and the second term on the right corresponds to the modulation function of the second grating through which the optical signal passes.

There are four periodic variables of spatial frequency in the output signal $f(l)$ of Eq. (3.15), which are, respectively, $w_1$, $w_2$, $w_1 + w_2$, and $w_1 - w_2$. Since the receiving process of the detector has a low-pass filtering effect on the spatial frequency, the light intensity of the Moiré fringe can be represented as

$$T(l) = f_1 f_2 [1 + m_1 m_2 \cos (w_1 - w_2) l + \theta_1(l) - \theta_2(l)] \qquad (3.16)$$

If the periods of the two gratings are the same, there is

$$T(l) = f_1 f_2 \{1 + [1 + \theta_1(l) - \theta_2(l)]\} \qquad (3.17)$$

It can be seen that the distance information from the surface of the scene is directly reflected in the phase change of the Moiré stripe.

### 3.3.3.2   Basic Method

Figure 3.6 shows a schematic diagram of distance measurement using the Moiré stripe method. The distance between the light source and the viewpoint D is the same

**Fig. 3.6** Schematic diagram of distance measurement using Moiré stripe method

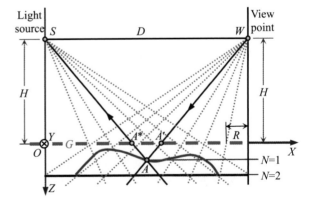

as that of the grating $G$; all are $H$. The grating is a transmissive line grating with alternating black and white (period $R$). According to the coordinate system in the figure, the grating surface is on the $XOY$ plane; the measured height is along the $Z$ axis, which is represented by the $Z$ coordinate.

Consider a point $A$ with coordinates $(x, y)$ on the measured surface. The illuminance of the light source through the grating is the product of the light source intensity and the transmittance of the grating at point $A^*$. The light intensity distribution at this point is

$$T_1(x, y) = C_1 \left[ \frac{1}{2} + \frac{2}{\pi} \sum_{n=1}^{\infty} \frac{1}{n} \sin \left( \frac{2\pi n}{R} \frac{xH}{z+H} \right) \right] \tag{3.18}$$

where $n$ is an odd number and $C_1$ is a constant related to intensity. Passing $T$ through the grating $G$ again is equivalent to another transmission modulation at point $A'$, and the light intensity distribution at $A'$ is

$$T_2(x, y) = C_2 \left[ \frac{1}{2} + \frac{2}{\pi} \sum_{m=1}^{\infty} \frac{1}{m} \sin \left( \frac{2\pi m}{R} \frac{xH + Dz}{z+H} \right) \right] \tag{3.19}$$

where $m$ is an odd number and $C_2$ is a constant related to intensity. The final light intensity received at the viewpoint is the product of the two distributions:

$$T(x, y) = T_1(x, y) T_2(x, y) \tag{3.20}$$

Expand the Eq. (3.20) with a polynomial; after the low-pass filtering of the receiving system, a partial sum containing only the variable $z$ is obtained:

$$T(z) = B + S \sum_{n=1}^{\infty} \left( \frac{1}{n} \right)^2 \cos \left( \frac{2\pi n}{R} \frac{Dz}{z+H} \right) \tag{3.21}$$

where $n$ is an odd number, $B$ is the background intensity of the Moiré stripe, and $S$ is the contrast of the stripe. Eq. (3.21) gives the mathematical description of Moiré contour stripes. Generally, only the fundamental frequency term of $n = 1$ can approximately describe the distribution of Moiré stripes, that is, Eq. (3.21) is simplified to

$$T(z) = B + S \cos \left( \frac{2\pi}{R} \frac{Dz}{z+H} \right) \tag{3.22}$$

From Eq. (3.22), it can be seen:

1. The position of the bright stripe is at the place where the phase term is equal to an integer multiple of $2\pi$, namely

$$Z_N = \frac{NRH}{D - NR} \quad N \in I \tag{3.23}$$

2. The height differences between any two bright stripes are not equal, so the number of stripes cannot be used to determine the height; only the height difference between two adjacent bright stripes can be calculated.
3. If the distribution of the phase term $\theta$ can be obtained, the height distribution of the surface of the measured object can be obtained:

$$Z = \frac{RH\theta}{2\pi D - R\theta} \tag{3.24}$$

### 3.3.3.3 Improvement Methods

The above-mentioned basic method needs to use a grating of the same size as the object to be measured ($G$ in Fig. 3.6), which brings inconvenience to use and manufacture. An improved method is to install the grating in the projection system of the light source and use the magnification capability of the optical system to obtain the effect of a large grating. Specifically, two gratings are used, which are, respectively, placed close to the light source and the viewpoint. The light source transmits the light beam through the grating, and the viewpoint is imaged behind the grating. In this way, the size of the grating only needs to be the size of the camera lens.

The practical schematic diagram of distance measurement using the above projection principle is shown in Fig. 3.7. Two imaging systems with the same parameters are used, their optical axes are parallel, and take geometrical imaging of two gratings with the same spacing at the same imaging distance, and make the projection images of the two gratings coincident.

Suppose that the Moiré stripe is observed behind the grating $G_2$ and $G_1$ is used as the projection grating, and the projection center $O_1$ of the projection system $L_1$ and the convergence center $O_2$ of the receiving system $L_2$ are, respectively, equivalent to the light source point $S$ and the viewpoint $W$ in the basic method. In this way, as long as $MR$ is used to replace $R$ in Eqs. (3.22) and (3.24) ($M = H/H_0$ is the imaging magnification of the two optical paths), the distribution of Moiré stripes can be described as above, and the height distribution of the surface of the measured object be calculated.

In practical applications, the grating in front of the projection system $L_1$ can be omitted, and computer software is used to complete its function. At this time, the projection grating image containing the depth information of the measured object surface is directly received by the camera.

From Eq. (3.24), it can be seen that if the distribution of the phase term $\theta$ can be obtained, the distribution of the height $Z$ of the measured object surface can be

**Fig. 3.7** Schematic diagram of Moiré stripe method ranging with projection principle

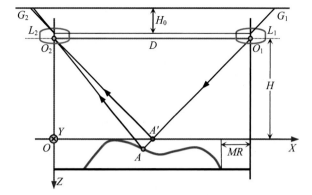

obtained. The phase distribution can be obtained by using multiple Moiré images with a certain phase shift. This method is often referred to as the phase shift method. Taking three images as an example, after obtaining the first image, move the projection grating horizontally by a distance of $R/3$ to obtain the second image, and then move the projection grating horizontally by a distance of $R/3$ to obtain the third image. Refer to Eq. (3.22); these three images can be expressed as

$$
\begin{cases}
T_1(z) = A'' + C'' \cos \theta \\
T_2(z) = A'' + C'' \cos (\theta + 2\pi/3) \\
T_3(z) = A'' + C'' \cos (\theta + 4\pi/3)
\end{cases}
\tag{3.25}
$$

The joint solution is

$$
\theta = \arctan \left[ \frac{\sqrt{3}(T_3 - T_2)}{2T_1(T_2 + T_3)} \right]
\tag{3.26}
$$

In this way, $\theta$ can be calculated point by point.

### 3.3.4  Simultaneous Acquisition of Depth and Brightness Images

Some imaging systems can simultaneously obtain depth information and brightness information in the scene. An example is **LIDAR** using lasers. The schematic diagram is shown in Fig. 3.8. A device placed on a platform capable of **nod** and **pan** movements transmits and receives amplitude-modulated laser waves (see the time-of-flight method in this section). For each point on the surface of the 3-D object, compare the transmission wave at this point and the wave received from this point to obtain information. The spatial coordinates $X$ and $Y$ of this point are related to the

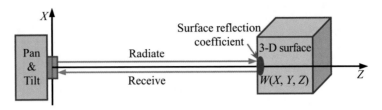

**Fig. 3.8** Simultaneous acquisition of depth and brightness images

nod and horizontal movement of the platform, and its depth $Z$ is closely related to the phase difference, and the reflection characteristics of this point to a given wavelength of laser light can be determined by the wave amplitude difference. In this way, LIDAR can obtain two registered images at the same time: one is the depth image, and the other is the brightness image. Note that the depth range of the depth image is related to the modulation period of the laser wave. If the modulation period is $\lambda$, the same depth will be calculated every $\lambda/2$, so the depth measurement range needs to be limited. LIDAR works similarly to radar. Both can measure the distance between the sensor and a specific point in the scene, except that the radar reflects electromagnetic waves.

Compared with CCD acquisition equipment, the acquisition speed of LIDAR is relatively slow due to the need to calculate the phase for each 3-D surface point. In addition, because the requirements for mechanical devices are relatively high (the laser beam needs to be guided), the cost of LIDAR is also relatively high. But it is worthwhile to use LIDAR on mining robots or robots that probe other parts of the solar system.

## 3.4   Stereo Vision Imaging

**Stereo vision** is one of human visual functions, which mainly refers to the use of binocular observation to obtain depth information. In computer vision, the use of binocular imaging can obtain two images of the same scene with different viewpoints (similar to human eyes), which can further obtain depth information. The **binocular imaging model** can be regarded as a combination of two monocular imaging models. In actual imaging, this can be achieved by using two monocular systems to collect at the same time, or one monocular system can be used to collect in two poses one after another (in this case, there is generally no movement of the subject and light source). In computer vision, multiple cameras can also be used to form a multi-ocular imaging system, but the basic principle is similar to binocular imaging. Only the case of binocular imaging is discussed below.

Depending on the relative poses of the two cameras, binocular imaging can have multiple modes. Here are some typical situations.

### 3.4.1 Binocular Horizontal Mode

Figure 3.9 shows a schematic diagram of **binocular horizontal mode** imaging. The focal lengths of the two lenses (each maybe composited with multiple lenses) are both $\lambda$, and the line between their centers is called the baseline $B$ of the system. The corresponding axes of the two camera coordinate systems are completely parallel ($X$ axis coincides), and the two image planes are parallel to the $XY$ plane of the world coordinate system. The $Z$ coordinate of a 3-D space point $W$ is the same for both camera coordinate systems.

#### 3.4.1.1 Disparity and Depth

It can be seen from Fig. 3.9 that the same 3-D space point is imaged on two image planes respectively, and the position difference between the two image points (with their respective coordinate reference points) is called **disparity**/parallax. Let's discuss the relationship between disparity and depth (object distance) in the binocular horizontal mode with the help of Fig. 3.10. Here is a schematic diagram of the plane ($XZ$ plane) where the two lenses connect. Among them, the world coordinate system coincides with the first camera coordinate system and only has a translation amount $B$ along the $X$ axis direction with the second camera coordinate system.

Consider the geometric relationship between the coordinate $X$ of the point $W$ in the 3-D space with the coordinate $^x1$ of the projected point on the first image plane. It has

$$\frac{|X|}{Z - \lambda} = \frac{x_1}{\lambda} \tag{3.27}$$

Then consider the geometric relationship between the coordinate $X$ of the 3-D space point $W$ with the coordinate $^x2$ of the projected point on the second image plane. It has

**Fig. 3.9** Schematic diagram of binocular horizontal mode imaging

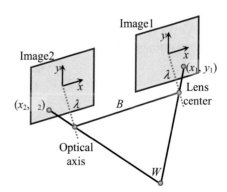

**Fig. 3.10** Disparity in
parallel binocular imaging

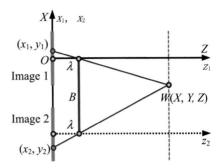

$$\frac{B-|X|}{Z-\lambda}=\frac{|x_2|-B}{\lambda} \qquad (3.28)$$

Combine the two equations, eliminate $X$, and get the disparity

$$d=x_1+|x_2|-B=\frac{\lambda B}{Z-\lambda} \qquad (3.29)$$

Solve $Z$ from it as

$$Z=\lambda\left(1+\frac{B}{d}\right) \qquad (3.30)$$

Equation (3.30) directly connects the distance $Z$ between the object and the image plane (i.e., the depth in the 3-D information) with the disparity $d$. Conversely, it also shows that the magnitude of the disparity is related to the depth, that is, the disparity contains the spatial information of the 3-D object. According to Eq. (3.30), when the baseline and focal length are known, it is very simple to calculate the $Z$ coordinate of space point $W$ after determining the disparity $d$. In addition, after the $Z$ coordinate is determined, the world coordinates $X$ and $Y$ of point $W$ can be calculated with $(x_1, y_1)$ or $(x_2, y_2)$ referring to Eqs. (3.27) or (3.28).

**Example 3.2 Measurement Error of Relative Depth**
Equation (3.30) gives the representation of the relationship between absolute depth and disparity. With the help of differentiation, the relationship between the depth change and the disparity change is

$$\frac{\Delta Z}{\Delta d}=\frac{-B\lambda}{d^2} \qquad (3.31)$$

Multiply both sides by $1/Z$; then

**Fig. 3.11** Schematic
diagram of geometric
structure for calculating
measurement error

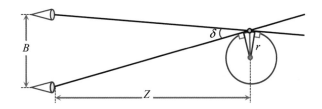

$$\frac{(1/Z)\Delta Z}{\Delta d} = \frac{-1}{d} = \frac{-Z}{B\lambda} \tag{3.32}$$

and so,

$$\left|\frac{\Delta Z}{Z}\right| = \frac{|\Delta d|Z}{B\lambda} = \left(\frac{\Delta d}{d}\right)\left(\frac{d}{\lambda}\right)\left(\frac{Z}{B}\right) \tag{3.33}$$

If both the disparity and the disparity change are measured in pixels, it can be known that the measurement error of the relative depth in the scene will be:

1. Proportional to the pixel size.
2. Proportional to the depth $Z$.
3. Inversely proportional to the baseline length $B$ between the cameras.

In addition, it can be obtained by Eq. (3.32)

$$\frac{\Delta Z}{Z} = \frac{-\Delta d}{d} \tag{3.34}$$

It can be seen that the measurement error of relative depth and the measurement error of relative disparity are the same in value.

**Example 3.3 Measurement Errors of Two Cameras**
Suppose two cameras are used to observe a cylindrical object with a circular cross-section and a local radius $r$, as shown in Fig. 3.11. There is a certain distance between the intersection point of the two cameras' sight lines and the boundary point of the circular section, which is the error $\delta$. Now it is needed to obtain the formula for calculating this error $\delta$.

To simplify the calculation, it is assumed that the boundary point is at the orthogonal bisector connecting the projection centers of the two cameras. The simplified geometric structure is shown in Fig. 3.12a, and the detailed diagram of the error is shown in Fig. 3.12b.

From Fig. 3.12, it can get $d = r\sec(\theta/2) - r$ and $\tan(\theta/2) = B/2Z$; replace $\theta$ to get

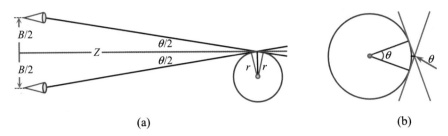

(a)                                                                                    (b)

**Fig. 3.12** Schematic diagram of the simplified geometric structure for calculating measurement error

**Fig. 3.13** Angle scanning camera for stereoscopic imaging

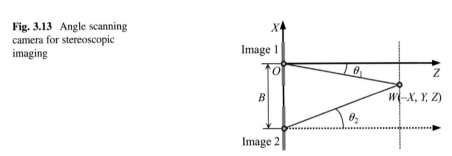

$$\delta = \sqrt{r\left[1 + (B/2Z)^2\right]} - r \approx \frac{rB^2}{8Z^2}$$

This is the equation for calculating the error $\delta$. It can be seen that the error is proportional to $r$ and $Z^{-2}$.

### 3.4.1.2   Angular Scanning Imaging

In binocular horizontal mode imaging, in order to determine the information of a 3-D space point, the point needs to be in the common field of view of the two cameras. If the two cameras are rotated (around the $X$ axis), it can increase the common field of view and collect panoramic images. This can be called **stereoscopic imaging** with an **angle scanning camera**, that is, a **binocular angular scanning mode**, where the coordinates of the imaging point are determined by the azimuth angle and elevation angle of the camera. In Fig. 3.13, $\theta_1$ and $\theta_2$, respectively, give the azimuth angles (corresponding to the panning around the $Y$ axis outward from the paper surface), and the elevation angle $\phi$ is the angle between the $XZ$ plane and the plane defined by the two optical centers and point $W$.

Generally, the azimuth angle of the lens can be used to indicate the spatial distance between objects. Using the coordinate system shown in Fig. 3.13, there are

$$\tan \theta_1 = \frac{|X|}{Z} \tag{3.35}$$

$$\tan \theta_2 = \frac{B - |X|}{Z} \tag{3.36}$$

Combining Eqs. (3.35) and (3.36) to eliminate $X$, the $Z$ coordinate of point $W$ is

$$Z = \frac{B}{\tan \theta_1 + \tan \theta_2} \tag{3.37}$$

Equation (3.37) actually connects directly the distance $Z$ between the object and the image plane (i.e., the depth in the 3-D information) with the tangent of the two azimuth angles. Comparing Eq. (3.37) with Eq. (3.30), it can be seen that the effects of disparity and focal length are both implicit in the azimuth angle. According to the $Z$ coordinate of the space point $W$, the $X$ and $Y$ coordinates can be obtained, respectively, as

$$X = Z \tan \theta_1 \tag{3.38}$$

$$Y = Z \tan \phi \tag{3.39}$$

### 3.4.2 Binocular Convergence Horizontal Mode

In order to obtain a larger **field of view** (FOV) overlap, one can place two cameras side by side, but let the two optical axes converge. This **binocular convergence horizontal mode** can be regarded as the extension of binocular horizontal mode (at this time, the **vergence** between the binoculars is not zero).

#### 3.4.2.1 Disparity and Depth

Consider only the situation shown in Fig. 3.14, which is obtained by rotating the two monocular systems in Fig. 3.10 around their respective centers. Figure 3.14 shows the plane ($XZ$ plane) where the two lenses connect. The distance between the centers of the two lenses (i.e., the baseline) is $B$. The two optical axes intersect at point $(0, 0, Z)$ in the $XZ$ plane, and the angle of intersection is $2\theta$. Now let's look at how to find the coordinates $(X, Y, Z)$ of point $W$ in 3-D space if two image plane coordinate points $(^x{}_1, {}^y{}_1)$ and $(^x{}_2, {}^y{}_2)$ are known.

First, it can be seen from the triangle enclosed by the two world coordinate axes and the camera optical axis:

**Fig. 3.14** Disparity in
convergent horizontal
binocular imaging

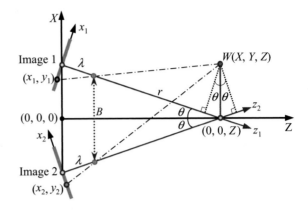

$$Z = \frac{B}{2} \frac{\cos \theta}{\sin \theta} + \lambda \cos \theta \tag{3.40}$$

Now draw perpendicular lines respectively from point $W$ to the optical axes of the two cameras, because the angles between the two perpendicular lines and the $X$ axis are both $\theta$, so according to the relationship of similar triangles, it can get

$$\frac{|x_1|}{\lambda} = \frac{X \cos \theta}{r - X \sin \theta} \tag{3.41}$$

$$\frac{|x_2|}{\lambda} = \frac{X \cos \theta}{r + X \sin \theta} \tag{3.42}$$

where $r$ is the distance from (any) lens center to the convergence point of the two optical axes.

Combine Eqs. (3.41) and (3.42), as well as eliminate $r$ and $X$ to get (refer to Fig. 3.14)

$$\lambda \cos \theta = \frac{2|x_1| \cdot |x_2| \sin \theta}{|x_1| - |x_2|} = \frac{2|x_1| \cdot |x_2| \sin \theta}{d} \tag{3.43}$$

Substitute Eq. (3.43) into Eq. (3.40) to get

$$Z = \frac{B \cos \theta}{2 \sin \theta} = \frac{2|x_1| \cdot |x_2| \sin \theta}{d} \tag{3.44}$$

Both Eqs. (3.44) and (3.30) directly relate the distance $Z$ between the object and the image plane with the disparity $d$. In addition, it can be obtained from Fig. 3.14

$$r = \frac{B}{2 \sin \theta} \tag{3.45}$$

Substitute it into Eq. (3.41) or Eq. (3.42) to get the $X$ coordinate of point $W$

$$|X| = \frac{B}{2 \sin \theta} \frac{|x_1|}{\lambda \cos \theta + |x_1| \sin \theta} = \frac{B}{2 \sin \theta} \frac{|x_2|}{\lambda \cos \theta - |x_2| \sin \theta} \tag{3.46}$$

### 3.4.2.2  Image Rectification

The case of binocular convergence can also be converted to the case of binocular parallelism. **Image rectification** is the process of geometrically transforming the image obtained by the camera with the optical axis converging to get the image obtained by the camera with the optical axis parallel. Consider the images before and after rectifications in Fig. 3.15. The light from the point $W$ intersects the left image at $(x, y)$ and $(X, Y)$ before and after rectifications, respectively. Each point on the image before rectification can be connected to the center of the lens and extended to intersect the image after rectification. Therefore, for each point on the image before rectification, one can determine its corresponding point on the image after rectification. The coordinates of the points before and after rectifications are related by projection transformation ($^a_1$ to $^a_8$ are the coefficients of the projection transformation matrix):

$$x = \frac{a_1 X + a_2 Y + a_3}{a_4 X + a_5 Y + 1} \tag{3.47}$$

$$y = \frac{a_6 X + a_7 Y + a_8}{a_4 X + a_5 Y + 1} \tag{3.48}$$

The eight coefficients in Eqs. (3.47) and (3.48) can be determined by using four sets of corresponding points on the images before and after rectifications. Here one can consider using the horizontal epipolar line (the intersection of the plane formed by the baseline and a point in the scene with the imaging plane; see Sect. 6.2). For this reason, one needs to select two epipolar lines in the image before rectification

**Fig. 3.15** Using projection transformation to rectify the image obtained by two cameras with the optical axis converging

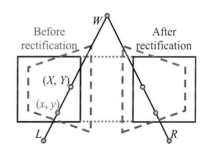

**Fig. 3.16** Schematic
diagram of images before
and after rectification

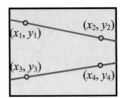 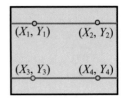

and map them to the two horizontal lines in the image after rectification, as shown in
Fig. 3.16. The corresponding relationship is

$$X_1 = x_1 \quad X_2 = x_2 \quad X_3 = x_3 \quad X_4 = x_4 \tag{3.49}$$

$$Y_1 = Y_2 = \frac{y_1 + y_2}{2} \quad Y_3 = Y_4 = \frac{y_3 + y_4}{2} \tag{3.50}$$

The above corresponding relationship can maintain the width of the image before
and after rectifications, but the scale will change in the vertical direction (in order to
map the non-horizontal epipolar line to the horizontal epipolar line). In order to
obtain the rectified image, each point $(X, Y)$ on the rectified image needs to use
Eqs. (3.47) and (3.48) to find their corresponding point $(x, y)$ on the image before
rectification. Also, assign the gray value at point $(x, y)$ to point $(X, Y)$.

The above process is also repeated for the right image. In order to ensure that the
corresponding epipolar lines on the rectified left and right images represent the same
scan line, it is necessary to map the corresponding epipolar lines on the image before
rectification to the same scan line on the image after rectification, so the $Y$ coordinate
in Eq. (3.50) should be used when rectifying both the left image and right image.

### 3.4.3 Binocular Axial Mode

When using binocular horizontal mode or binocular convergence horizontal mode, it
needs to make calculation according to the triangle method, so the baseline cannot be
too short; otherwise it will affect the accuracy of depth calculation. But when the
baseline is longer, the problems caused by the misalignment of the field of view will
be more serious. In order to avoid the difficulty of baseline selection, it is considered
adopting **binocular axial mode**, also called **binocular longitudinal mode**, that is,
two cameras are arranged in sequence along the optical axis. This situation can also
be seen as moving the camera along the optical axis and collecting the second image
closer to the subject than the first image, as shown in Fig. 3.17. In Fig. 3.17, only the
$XZ$ plane is drawn, and the $Y$ axis is outward from the inside of the paper. The origins
of the two camera coordinate systems for the first image and the second image are
only different in the $Z$ direction by $B$, and $B$ is also the distance between the optical
centers of the two cameras (baseline in this mode).

According to the geometric relationship in Fig. 3.17, there are

**Fig. 3.17** Binocular axial
mode imaging

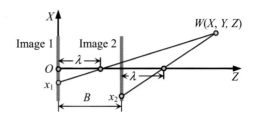

$$\frac{X}{Z-\lambda}=\frac{|x_1|}{\lambda} \tag{3.51}$$

$$\frac{X}{Z-\lambda-B}=\frac{|x_2|}{\lambda} \tag{3.52}$$

Combining Eqs. (3.51) and (3.52) can obtain (only consider $X$, similar to $Y$)

$$X=\frac{B}{\lambda}\frac{|x_1|\bullet|x_2|}{|x_2|-|x_1|}=\frac{B}{\lambda}\frac{|x_1|\bullet|x_2|}{d} \tag{3.53}$$

$$Z=\lambda+\frac{B|x_2|}{|x_2|-|x_1|}=\lambda+\frac{B|x_2|}{d} \tag{3.54}$$

Compared with the binocular horizontal mode, the common field of view of the two cameras in the binocular axial mode is the field of view of the front camera (the camera that acquired the second image in Fig. 3.17), so the boundary of the common field of view is easy to determine, and the problem that the 3-D space point is only seen by one camera, caused by occlusion, can be basically eliminated. However, since the binoculars basically use the same orientation to observe the scene at this time, the benefit of lengthening the baseline to increasing the depth calculation accuracy cannot be fully reflected. In addition, the precisions of the disparity and depth calculation are related to the distance between the 3-D space point and the optical axis of the camera (e.g., in Eq. (3.54), the depth $Z$ as well as the distance $|^x{}_2|$ between the projection of the 3-D space point and optical axis). This is different from the binocular horizontal mode.

**Example 3.4 Measurement of Relative Height**
The relative height of the ground objects can be obtained by taking two images of the object in the air by the camera carried by the aircraft. In Fig. 3.18, $W$ represents the distance the camera moves, $H$ is the height of the camera, $h$ is the relative height difference between the two measurement points $A$ and $B$, and $(d_1 - d_2)$ corresponds to the disparity between $A$ and $B$ in the two images. When $d_1$ and $d_2$ are much smaller than $W$, and $h$ is much smaller than $H$, then the calculation of $h$ can be simplified as follows:

**Fig. 3.18** Using stereo
vision to measure relative
height

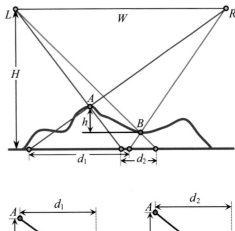

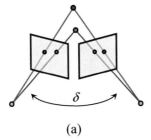

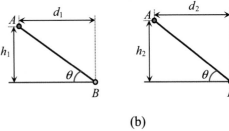

(a)                                                                          (b)

**Fig. 3.19** Object is rotated to obtain two images for measuring the relative height

$$h = \frac{H}{W}(d_1 - d_2) \tag{3.55}$$

If the above conditions are not met, the $x$ and $y$ coordinates in the image need to be corrected as follows:

$$x' = x\frac{H - h}{H} \tag{3.56}$$

$$y' = y\frac{H - h}{H} \tag{3.57}$$

When the object is relatively close, one can rotate the object to obtain two images. A schematic diagram is given in Fig. 3.19a, where $\delta$ represents a given rotation angle. At this time, the horizontal distances between the two object points $A$ and $B$, $d_1$ and $d_2$, are different in the two images, as shown in Fig. 3.19b. The connection angle $\theta$ and the height difference h between them can be calculated as follows:

$$\theta = \tan^{-1}\left(\frac{\cos\delta - d_2/d_1}{\sin\delta}\right) \tag{3.58}$$

$$h = |h_1 - h_2| = \left| \frac{d_1 \cos \delta - d_2}{\sin \delta} - \frac{d_1 - d_2 \cos \delta}{\sin \delta} \right| = (d_1 + d_2) \frac{1 - \cos \delta}{\sin \delta} \quad (3.59)$$

## 3.5 Key Points and References for Each Section

The following combines the main contents of each section to introduce some references that can be further consulted.

1. **High-Dimensional Image**

   Here high-dimensional images generally refer to all kinds of images that are not enough to describe with only $f(x, y)$. In practical applications, there are many other than the few examples listed in this section. For example, in the diagnosis of cardiovascular disease, the image $f(x, y, z, t)$ needs to be used to measure the thickness of the aortic vessel wall and blood flow velocity; see [1].

2. **Depth Image**

   The image can reflect many kinds of information of the objective world. The depth image reflects the information that is generally lost during the projection from the 3-D scene to the 2-D image. It has received extensive attention in 3-D computer vision; see reference [2, 3]. For the early discussion of intrinsic images and extrinsic images, please refer to reference [4]. The description of step edges and roof-like edges can be found in the book *2D Computer Vision: Principles, Algorithms and Applications*. Some typical multi-ocular imaging methods based on stereo vision can be found in [5].

3. **Direct Depth Imaging**

   The derivation from Eq. (3.20) to Eq. (3.21) can be found in [6]. More discussions about laser LIDAR can be found in [7], where there are more applications of laser LIDAR.

4. **Stereo Vision Imaging**

   Stereo vision imaging can use not only binoculars but also various forms of multi-ocular; see [5]. More discussion on image rectification can be found in [8]. Using four sets of corresponding points on the image to determine the eight coefficients in Eqs. (3.47) and (3.48) can be found in the book *2D Computer Vision: Principles, Algorithms and Applications*.

## Self-Test Questions

The following questions include both single-choice questions and multiple-choice questions, so each option must be judged.

### 3.1 High-Dimensional Image

3.1.1 Which of the following function(s) represent(s) high-dimensional images? (·).

(a) $f(x, z)$
(b) $f(x, t)$
(c) $f(x, \lambda)$
(d) $f(t, \lambda)$

[Hint] High dimension can refer to both the high dimension of the space where the image is located or the high dimension of the attributes of the image.

3.1.2 Which of the following function(s) represent(s) high-dimensional images? (·).

(a) $f(x, z)$
(b) $f(x, y, z)$
(c) $f(t, \lambda)$
(d) $f(z, t, \lambda)$

[Hint] The basic image is the 2-D grayscale image.

3.1.3 Which of the following image(s) is/are high-dimensional image(s)? (·).

(a) Video image
(b) Depth image
(c) Moving image
(d) Multispectral image

[Hint] Consider both the dimension of image space and the dimension of attributes.

## 3.2 Depth Image

3.2.1 For depth images, (·).

(a) The pixel value of the same outer plane on the corresponding object has nothing to do with the external lighting conditions.
(b) The pixel value of the same outer plane on the corresponding object has nothing to do with the orientation of the plane.
(c) The pixel value of the same outer plane on the corresponding object has nothing to do with the size of the plane.
(d) The pixel value of the same outer plane on the corresponding object has nothing to do with the reflection coefficient of the plane.

[Hint] The attribute value of the depth image corresponds to the distance.

3.2.2 The boundary line in the depth image (·).

(a) Always corresponds to the discontinuity of brightness
(b) Always corresponds to the discontinuity of depth
(c) Is possible to correspond to the depth continuity
(d) Is possible to correspond to the depth discontinuity

[Hint] Analyze two situations of the boundary line in the depth image.

3.2.3 Among the following images, the image(s) belonging to the intrinsic images is/are (·).

(a) Grayscale image
(b) Depth image
(c) Orientation image
(d) Reflective image

[Hint] The intrinsic image reflects an intrinsic characteristic of the scene, not the mixed influence of multiple characteristics.

3.2.4 In binocular stereo imaging, the positions of the light source, sensors, and scene are as follows: (·).

(a) Fixed, fixed, self-moving
(b) Moving, fixed, fixed
(c) Fixed, two positions, fixed
(d) Fixed, two positions, rotating

[Hint] Consider the characteristics of binocular stereo imaging.

## 3.3 Direct Depth Imaging

3.3.1 In the time-of-flight-based depth image acquisition, the pulse wave is measured for (·).

(a) Difference in amplitude
(b) Difference in phase
(c) Difference in time
(d) Difference in frequency

[Hint] Analyze the principle of the time-of-flight-based depth image acquisition.

3.3.2 In the method for obtaining the depth image of the phase difference of the amplitude modulation wave, the equation $d = \frac{c}{2\pi f_{mod}} \theta + \frac{c}{f_{mod}}$ is used to calculate the depth, where $f_{mod}$, $\theta$, c are, respectively (·).

(a) Phase difference, speed of light, modulation frequency
(b) Phase difference, modulation frequency, speed of light
(c) Modulation frequency, speed of light, phase difference
(d) Modulation frequency, phase difference, speed of light

[Hint] It can be judged according to the equation derived from the principle of using the phase difference to obtain the depth image.

3.3.3 The imaging system with structured light ranging is mainly composed of the following two parts: (·).

(a) Camera, light source
(b) Cameras, scene
(c) Scene, light source
(d) Sensors, cameras

[Hint] Structured light imaging should use the geometric information in the illumination to help extract the geometric information of the scene, thereby imaging.

## 3.4 Stereo Vision Imaging

3.4.1 In the equation of binocular imaging $Z = \lambda(1\text{-}B/D)$, $Z$, $B$, $D$ represent (·).

(a) Disparity, baseline, object image distance
(b) Object image distance, baseline, disparity
(c) Baseline, disparity, object image distance
(d) Object image distance, disparity, baseline

[Hint] It can also be analyzed according to the imaging principle.

3.4.2 When using binocular horizontal mode for imaging, given the baseline length, (·).

(a) The small disparity corresponds to the long distance between the object and the image plane.
(b) The large disparity corresponds to the long distance between the object and the image plane.
(c) The disparity value has a linear relationship with the distance between the object and the image plane.
(d) The disparity value has a non-linear relationship with the distance between the object and the image plane.

[Hint] Refer to the binocular imaging equation.

3.4.3 Using two cameras with the same given focal length to perform stereo imaging, (·).

(a) The common field of view when using the binocular horizontal mode has nothing to do with the baseline.
(b) The common field of view when using binocular axial mode has nothing to do with the baseline.
(c) The common field of view when using the binocular convergence horizontal mode is only related to the baseline.
(d) The common field of view when using the binocular angle scanning mode is only related to the baseline.

[Hint] Analyze what factors other than the baseline may affect the common field of view in the four modes.

# References

1. Liu K, Zhang Y-J, Li R. A method to calculate the wall shear stress of aortas based on image segmentation with magnetic resonance imaging. Science Technology and Engineering, 2013,13 (25): 7395-7400.
2. Faugeras O. Three-dimensional Computer Vision: A Geometric Viewpoint. MIT Press. 1993.
3. Forsyth D, Ponce J. Computer Vision: A Modern Approach, 2nd Ed. Prentice Hall. 2012.
4. Ballard D H, Brown C M. Computer Vision. Prentice-Hall. 1982.
5. Zhang Y-J. Image Engineering, Vol.3: Image Understanding. De Gruyter, 2017.
6. Liu X L. Optical vision sensor. Beijing Science Technology Press, 1998.
7. Shapiro L, Stockman G. Computer Vision. Prentice Hall. 2001.
8. Goshtasby A A. 2-D and 3-D Image Registration – for Medical, Remote Sensing, and Industrial Applications. Wiley-Interscience. 2005.

# Chapter 4
# Video Image and Motion Information

Video or video image represents a special kind of sequence image, which describes the radiation intensity of the scene obtained by three separate sensors when a 3-D scene is projected onto a 2-D image plane over a period of time. At present, video is generally regarded as a sequence of images with regular intervals in color, changing more than 25 frames per second (with continuous motion).

Digital video can be acquired by means of a digital camera using a CCD sensor or the like. The output of a digital camera is divided into discrete frames in time, and each frame is divided into discrete rows and columns in space similar to a still image, so it is 3-D. The basic unit of each frame of image is still represented by pixels. If time is considered, the basic unit of video is similar to voxel. This chapter mainly discusses digital video images, which are called **video images** or videos unless they cause confusion.

From the perspective of learning image technology, video can be seen as an extension of (still) images. In fact, a still image is a video with a given time (constant). In addition to some concepts and definitions of the original image, some new concepts and definitions are needed to represent the video. The most obvious difference between video and image is that it contains motion information in the scene, which is also a main purpose of using video. In view of the characteristics of videos containing motion information, the original image processing technology also needs to be extended accordingly.

The sections of this chapter are arranged as follows:

Section 4.1 introduces first the basic content of the video, including the representation, modeling, display, and format of the video and also introduces the color model and resolution in the color TV system.

Section 4.2 discusses first the classification of the motion information in the video compared to the still image. Then, the characteristics and representation methods of foreground motion and background motion are introduced respectively.

Section 4.3 discusses the detection of motion information. The motion detection methods using image difference, the principle of motion detection in the frequency domain, and the detection of the direction of motion are respectively introduced.

Section 4.4 starts from the video preprocessing and discusses the filtering methods that combine the characteristics of the video and consider the motion information, including motion detection filtering and motion compensation filtering.

## 4.1   Video Basic

To discuss video image processing, the discussions on the representation of the video, as well as the format and display of the video, are provided.

### 4.1.1   Video Expression and Model

**Video** can be seen as an extension of (still) images along the time axis. Video is a sequence of images taken at regular intervals, so the video has an extension in time relative to the image. When discussing video, it is generally considered that the video image is in color, so the expansion from grayscale to color should also be considered. Because human vision has different sensitivity to brightness and color components, different resolutions are often used for them when capturing and representing videos.

#### 4.1.1.1   Video Representation Function

If the function $f(x, y)$ is used to represent the image, considering the expansion of the video in time, the function $f(x, y, t)$ can be used to represent the video, which describes the projection to the image plane XY at a given time $t$ by the 3-D scene with certain properties of (such as radiation intensity). In other words, the video represents a certain physical property that changes in space and time or a certain physical property that is projected onto the image plane $(x, y)$ at time $t$. Further, if the color image is represented by the function $f(x, y)$, considering the extension of the video from grayscale to color, the video can be represented by the function $f(x, y, t)$, which describes the color nature of the video at the specific time and space. The actual video always has a limited time and space range, and the property value is also limited. The spatial range depends on the observation region of the camera, the time range depends on the duration of the scene being captured, and the color properties depend on the characteristics of the scene.

Ideally, since various color models are 3-D, color video should be represented by three functions (they constitute a vector function), and each function describes a color component. Video in this format is called **component video** and is only used in professional video equipment. This is because the quality of component video is higher, but its data volume is also relatively large. Various **composite video** formats are often used in practice, in which three color signals are multiplexed into one single signal. The fact that the chrominance signal has a much smaller bandwidth than the luminance component is taken into account when constructing composite video. By modulating each chrominance component to a frequency located at the high end of the luminance component, and adding the chrominance component to the original luminance signal, a composite video containing luminance and chrominance information can be produced. The composite video format has a small amount of data but poor quality. In order to balance the amount of data and quality, the S-video format can be used, which includes one luminance component and one chrominance component compounded by two original chrominance signals. The bandwidth of the composite signal is smaller than the sum of the bandwidth of the two component signals, so it can be transmitted or stored more efficiently. However, since the chrominance and luminance components will crosstalk, artifacts may appear.

### 4.1.1.2 Video Color Model

A commonly used **color model** in video is the **$YC_BC_R$ color model**, where $Y$ represents the luminance component and $C_B$ and $C_R$ represent chrominance components. The brightness component can be obtained by using the RGB component of the color:

$$Y = rR + gG + bB \tag{4.1}$$

where $r$, $g$, $b$ are proportional coefficients. The chrominance component $C_B$ represents the difference between the blue part and the luminance value, and the chrominance component $C_R$ represents the difference between the red part and the luminance value (so $C_B$ and $C_R$ are also called color difference components):

$$C_B = B - Y$$
$$C_R = R - Y \tag{4.2}$$

In addition, one can define the chrominance component $C_G = G - Y$, but $C_G$ can be obtained by $C_B$ and $C_R$, so it is not used alone. The inverse transformation from $Y$, $C_B$, $C_R$ to $R$, $G$, $B$ can be represented as

$$\begin{bmatrix} R \\ G \\ B \end{bmatrix} = \begin{bmatrix} 1.0 & -0.00001 & 1.40200 \\ 1.0 & -0.34413 & -0.71414 \\ 1.0 & 1.77200 & 0.00004 \end{bmatrix} \begin{bmatrix} Y \\ C_B \\ C_R \end{bmatrix} \tag{4.3}$$

In the practical **$YC_BC_R$** color coordinate system, the value range of $Y$ is [16, 235]; the value ranges of $C_B$ and $C_R$ are both [16, 240]. The maximum value of $C_B$ corresponds to blue ($C_B = 240$ or $R = G = 0$, $B = 255$), and the minimum value of $C_B$ corresponds to yellow ($C_B = 16$ or $R = G = 255$, $B = 0$). The maximum value of $C_R$ corresponds to red ($C_R = 240$ or $R = 255$, $G = B = 0$), and the minimum value of $C_R$ corresponds to blue-green ($C_B = 16$ or $R = 0$, $G = B = 255$).

#### 4.1.1.3   Video Space Sampling Rate

The **spatial sampling rate** of color video refers to the sampling rate of the luminance component $Y$. Generally, the sampling rate of the chrominance components $C_B$ and $C_R$ is usually only one-half of the luminance component. The advantage of this is that the number of pixels per line can be halved (i.e., the sampling rate is halved), but the number of lines per frame remains unchanged. This format is called 4:2:2, that is, every four $Y$ sampling points correspond to two $C_B$ sampling points and two $C_R$ sampling points. The data volume of this format is lower than the 4:1:1 format, that is, every four $Y$ sampling points correspond to one $C_B$ sampling point and one $C_R$ sampling point. However, in this format, the horizontal and vertical resolutions are asymmetrical. Another format with the same amount of data as the 4:1:1 format is the 4:2:0 format. It still corresponds to one $C_B$ sampling point and one $C_R$R sampling point for every four $Y$ sampling points, but one-half of the sampling rates in the horizontal and vertical directions are taken for both $C_B$ and $C_R$. Finally, for applications requiring high resolution, a 4:4:4 format is also defined, that is, the sampling rate for the chrominance components $C_B$ and $C_R$ is the same as the sampling rate for the luminance component $Y$. The corresponding relationship between the luminance and chrominance sampling points in the above four formats is shown in Fig. 4.1.

### 4.1.2   Video Display and Format

Video can be displayed according to different forms and formats.

#### 4.1.2.1   Video Display

The aspect ratios of the monitor that displays video are mainly 4:3 and 16:9. In addition, there can be two raster scan modes when displaying: progressive scan and interlaced scan. The **progressive scan** takes the frame as the unit and progresses line

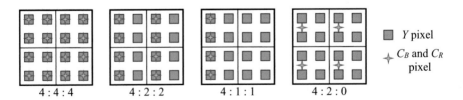

**Fig. 4.1** Examples of four sampling formats (two adjacent rows belong to two different fields)

by line from the upper left corner to the lower right corner when displaying. **Interlaced scan** takes the field as the unit (a frame is divided into two fields: the top field and the bottom field; the top field contains all odd lines, and the bottom field contains all even lines), and the vertical resolution is half of the frame's resolution. In interlaced scanning, the top field and the bottom field alternate, and the visual persistence characteristics of the human visual system are used to make people perceive as a picture. The progressive scan has high definition, but the data volume is large; the interlaced scan only needs half the data volume, but it is a little blur. Various standard TV systems, such as NTSC, PAL, SECAM, and many high-definition TV systems, use interlaced scanning.

The video needs to have a certain frame rate when displaying, that is, the frequency of two adjacent frames. According to the persistence characteristics of human eyes, the frame rate needs to be higher than 25 frames per second. If it is lower, flicker and discontinuity will appear.

### 4.1.2.2 Video Bit Rate

The amount of video data is determined together by the time resolution, spatial resolution, and amplitude resolution of the video. Suppose the frame rate of the video is $L$ (i.e., the time sampling interval is $1/L$), the spatial resolution is $M \times N$, and the amplitude resolution is $G$ ($G = 2^k$, $k = 8$ for black and white video and $k = 24$ for color video), and then the number of bits $b$ required to store 1 second of video image (also called **video bit rate**, unit is $b/s$) is

$$b = L \times M \times N \times k \tag{4.4}$$

The amount of video data can also be defined by the number of lines $f_y$, the number of samples per line $f_x$, and the frame rate $f_t$. Thus, the horizontal sampling interval is $\Delta_x = $ pixel width$/f_x$, the vertical sampling interval is $\Delta_y = $ pixel height$/f_y$, and the time sampling interval is $\Delta_t = 1/f_t$. If $k$ is used to represent the number of bits used for a pixel value in a video, it is 8 for monochrome video and 24 for color video, so the video bit rate can also be expressed as

$$b = f_x \times f_y \times f_t \times k \tag{4.5}$$

### 4.1.2.3 Video Format

Due to historical reasons and different application fields, there are many different formats of actual video. Some commonly used **video formats** are shown in Table 4.1. In the frame rate column, P represents progressive, and I represents interlaced (see the next sub-section for common TV formats).

**Table 4.1** Some video formats in practical applications

| Application and format | Name | Y size/ (pixel) | Sampling format | Frame rate | Original bit rate/ Mbps |
|---|---|---|---|---|---|
| Terrestrial, cable, satellite HDTV, MPEG-2, 20–45 Mbps | SMPTE 296 M | 1280 × 720 | 4:2:0 | 24P/ 30P/ 60P | 265/332/ 664 |
| | SMPTE 296 M | 1920 × 1080 | 4:2:0 | 24P/ 30P/ 60I | 597/746/ 746 |
| Video production, MPEG-2, 15–50 Mbps | BT.601 | 720 × 480/ 576 | 4:4:4 | 60I/ 50I | 249 |
| | BT.601 | 720 × 480/ 576 | 4:2:0 | 60I/ 50I | 166 |
| High-quality video publishing (DVD, SDTV) MPEG-2, 4–8 Mbps | BT.601 | 720 × 480/ 576 | 4:2:0 | 60I/ 50I | 124 |
| Medium-quality video release (VCD, WWW) MPEG-1, 1.5 Mbps | SIF | 352 × 240/ 288 | 4:2:0 | 30P/ 25P | 30 |
| ISDN/internet video conference, H.261/H.263, 128–384 kbps | CIF | 352 × 288 | 4:2:0 | 30P | 37 |
| Wired/wireless modem video phone, H.263, 20–64 kbps | QCIF | 176 × 144 | 4:2:0 | 30P | 9.1 |

**Example 4.1 BT.601 Standard Format**

The BT.601 standard (formerly known as CCIR601) formulated by the Radio Department of the International Telecommunication Union (ITU-R) provides two video formats with an aspect ratio of 4:3 and 16:9. In the 4:3 format, the sampling frequency is set to 13.5 MHz. The one corresponding to the NTSC standard is called the 525/60 system, and the one corresponding to the PAL/SECAM standard is called the 625/50 system. There are 525 lines in the 525/60 system, and the number of pixels in each line is 858. There are 625 lines in the 625/50 system, and the number of pixels in each line is 864. In practice, considering the need for some lines for blanking, the effective number of lines in the 525/60 system is 480, the effective number of lines in the 625/50 system is 576, and the effective number of pixels per line in both systems is 720. The rest are the retrace points that fall in the invalid region, as shown in Fig. 4.2a, b, respectively.

## 4.1.3   Color TV System

Color TV is a special kind of video. Commonly used **color TV formats** include NTSC (developed by the United States and used in countries such as the United States and Japan), PAL (developed by Germany and used in countries such as

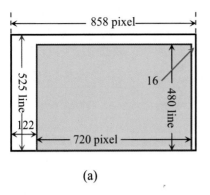
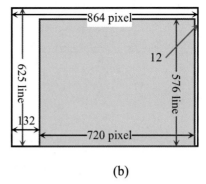

(a)                                    (b)

**Fig. 4.2** The 4:3 format in the BT.601 standard

Germany and China), and SECAM (developed by France and used in countries such as France and Russia).

The color models used in color television systems are also based on different combinations of RGB, although some concepts of color models for visual perception are used, too.

The **YUV model** is used in the PAL and SECAM systems, where $Y$ represents the brightness component and $U$ and $V$ are, respectively, proportional to the color difference $B$-$Y$ and $R$-$Y$, which are called chrominance components (or color difference components). $Y$, $U$, and $V$ can be obtained from the normalized $R'$, $G'$, and $B'$ in the PAL system (after gamma correction) through the following calculations ($R' = G' = B' = 1$ corresponds to the reference white):

$$\begin{bmatrix} Y \\ U \\ V \end{bmatrix} = \begin{bmatrix} 0.299 & 0.587 & 0.114 \\ -0.147 & -0.289 & 0.436 \\ 0.615 & -0.515 & -0.100 \end{bmatrix} \begin{bmatrix} R' \\ G' \\ B' \end{bmatrix} \tag{4.6}$$

The inverse transformation of $R'$, $G'$, and $B'$ from $Y$, $U$, and $V$ is

$$\begin{bmatrix} R' \\ G' \\ B' \end{bmatrix} = \begin{bmatrix} 1.000 & 0.000 & 1.140 \\ 1.000 & -0.395 & -0.581 \\ 1.000 & 2.032 & 0.001 \end{bmatrix} \begin{bmatrix} Y \\ U \\ V \end{bmatrix} \tag{4.7}$$

The **YIQ model** is used in the NTSC system, where $Y$ still represents the brightness component, and $I$ and $Q$ are the results of the $U$ and $V$ components rotated by 33°, respectively. After being rotated, $I$ corresponds to the color between orange and cyan, and $Q$ corresponds to the color between green and purple. Because the human eye is not as sensitive to the color change between green and purple as the color change between orange and cyan, the number of bits required for the $Q$ component during quantization can be less than that for the $I$ component, and the bandwidth required for the $Q$ component during transmission can be narrower than

**Table 4.2**  Spatial sampling rate of ordinary TV system

| TV formats | Luminance component | | Chrominance component | | |
| | Line number | Pixel/line | Line number | Pixel/line | $Y{:}U{:}V$ |
| --- | --- | --- | --- | --- | --- |
| NTSC | 480 | 720 | 240 | 360 | 4:2:2 |
| PAL | 576 | 720 | 288 | 360 | 4:2:2 |
| SECAM | 576 | 720 | 288 | 360 | 4:2:2 |

the $I$ component. $Y$, $I$, and $Q$ can be obtained from the normalized $R'$, $G'$, and $B'$ in the NTSC system (after gamma correction) through the following calculations ($R' = G' = B' = 1$ corresponds to the reference white):

$$
\begin{bmatrix} Y \\ I \\ Q \end{bmatrix} = \begin{bmatrix} 0.299 & 0.587 & 0.114 \\ 0.596 & -0.275 & -0.321 \\ 0.212 & -0.523 & 0.311 \end{bmatrix} \begin{bmatrix} R' \\ G' \\ B' \end{bmatrix}
\tag{4.8}
$$

The inverse transformation of $R'$, $G'$, and $B'$ obtained from $Y$, $I$, and $Q$ is

$$
\begin{bmatrix} R' \\ G' \\ B' \end{bmatrix} = \begin{bmatrix} 1.000 & 0.956 & 0.620 \\ 1.000 & -0.272 & -0.647 \\ 1.000 & -1.108 & 1.700 \end{bmatrix} \begin{bmatrix} Y \\ I \\ Q \end{bmatrix}
\tag{4.9}
$$

It should be pointed out that the reference white in the PAL system is slightly different from the reference white in the NTSC system. With the help of $R'$, $G'$, and $B'$ in the NTSC system, one can also get

$$
\begin{bmatrix} Y \\ C_B \\ C_R \end{bmatrix} = \begin{bmatrix} 0.257 & 0.504 & 0.098 \\ -0.148 & -0.291 & 0.439 \\ 0.439 & -0.368 & -0.071 \end{bmatrix} \begin{bmatrix} R' \\ G' \\ B' \end{bmatrix} + \begin{bmatrix} 16 \\ 128 \\ 128 \end{bmatrix}
\tag{4.10}
$$

Because the human eye has a low ability to distinguish chrominance signals, the spatial sampling rate of chrominance signals in ordinary TV systems is lower than that of luminance signals, which can reduce the amount of video data without affecting the visual effect. The spatial sampling rate of various TV systems is shown in Table 4.2.

## 4.2  Motion Classification and Representation

Video images can record various movements of different scenes. The motion information is unique to the video, and the classification and representation of the motion situation have its own characteristics.

### 4.2.1 Motion Classification

In the research and application of images, people often divide images into foreground (object/target) and background. Similarly, in the research and application of video, each frame can be divided into two parts: foreground and background. In this way, it is necessary to distinguish between foreground motion and background motion in the video. **Foreground motion** refers to the object's own motion in the scene, which leads to the change of some pixels of the image, so it is also called **local motion**, while **background motion** is mainly caused by the motion of the camera itself that is shooting and induces the overall movement of all pixels in the entire frame image, so it is also called **global motion** or **camera motion**.

Each of the above two types of motions has its own characteristics. Global motion generally has the characteristics of strong integrity and relatively regularity. In many cases, the global motion can be represented with only some features or a set of models with several parameters. Local movement is often more complicated, especially when there are more moving objects (components); each object can do different movements. The movement of the object only shows a certain consistency in a small range of space, and it needs a more sophisticated method to accurately represent it.

In an image, there may be four combinations of motion or stillness of the foreground and background, that is, both are moving or both are still, and one of them is still and the other is moving. Since a model can often be established for global motion, in the case having both motions, local motion can be regarded as a part that does not conform to the global motion model.

### 4.2.2 Motion Vector Field Representation

Since motion may include both global motion and local motion, the global model cannot be used to represent the entire motion field (although only a few model parameters may be enough at this time). In extreme cases, one can consider describing the motion of each pixel separately, but this requires calculating a vector at each pixel location (the motion has both magnitude and direction), and the result does not necessarily meet the physical constraints of the actual object. A **motion vector field representation** method that comprehensively compromises accuracy and complexity is to divide the entire image into many fixed-size blocks. The choice of block size needs to be determined according to the requirements of the application. If the block size is relatively small, the motion in the block can be represented by a single model and obtain a higher accuracy, but the total calculation amount will be relatively large. If the block size is relatively large, the overall complexity of motion detection will be relatively small, and each block has a comprehensive motion with average motion details. For example, in the international standard H.264/AVC for image coding, blocks from $4 \times 4$ to $16 \times 16$ are used.

**Fig. 4.3** Global motion vector superimposed on the original image

For the motion of the image block, both the size and the direction must be considered, so it needs to be represented by a vector. In order to represent the instantaneous motion vector field, in practice, each motion vector is often represented by a line segment (with a starting point) without an arrow (the length of the line segment is proportional to the vector size, that is, the motion speed) and superimposed on the original image. The arrow is not used here just to make the representation concise and to reduce the impact of the arrow superimposed on the image. Since the starting point is determined, the direction without arrows is still clear.

**Example 4.2 The Representation Example of Motion Vector Field**

Figure 4.3 shows a scene of a football match. The calculation of the motion vector field uses the method of dividing first the image into blocks (evenly distributed) and then calculating the comprehensive motion vector of each image. In this way, a motion vector is obtained from each block of image, which is represented by a line segment projected from the starting point (the starting point is in the center of the block). These line segments are superimposed on the scene image to obtain the representation image of the motion vector field.

Figure 4.3 only shows the global motion situation. It can be seen from the direction and size of most of the motion vector line segments in the figure that the speed of the lower right part of the figure is faster. This is because the camera has a step-by-step zoom (zoom out the lens, the direction of the motion vector is mostly away from the goal) centered on the upper left where the goalkeeper is and starts from the goal.

### 4.2.3 Motion Histogram Representation

The local motion mainly corresponds to the movement of the object in the scene. The movement of the object is often more irregular than the movement of the camera. Although the motion of each point on the same rigid object is often consistent, there can be relative motion between different objects, so the local motion vector field is often more complicated than the global motion vector field.

The global motion caused by the camera often lasts longer than the interval of the object motion change. Using this relationship, a global motion vector field can be used to represent the video over a period of time. In order to represent the complex and variability of object motion, it is necessary to obtain a continuous short period of dense local motion vector field. The problem that this brings is that the amount of data will be quite large, and a more compact way is needed to represent the local motion vector field.

#### 4.2.3.1 Histogram of Motion Vector Direction

The **motion vector direction histogram** (MDH) is a compact way to represent motion. The basic idea of this method is to only retain the motion direction information to reduce the amount of data. The basis is that people first distinguish different motions according to the motion direction, and the magnitude of the motion amplitude requires more attention to distinguish, so the motion direction can be regarded as the most basic motion information. MDH extracts the distribution of the motion direction in the field through the statistics of the data in the motion vector field to represent the main motion of the object in the video. In actual representation, the direction range from 0° to 360° can be divided into several intervals, and the data of each point on the motion vector field is classified into the interval closest to its motion direction. The final statistical result is the histogram of the motion vector direction. An example of MDH is shown in Fig. 4.4.

In the specific calculation, considering that there may be many static or basically static points in the local motion vector field, the motion direction calculated at these positions is usually random and may not necessarily represent the actual motion direction of the point. In order to avoid incorrect data affecting the histogram distribution, before counting the motion vector direction histogram, a minimum

**Fig. 4.4** Example of histogram of motion vector direction

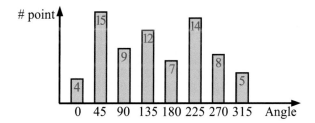

amplitude threshold can be selected for the vector size, and pixels smaller than the minimum amplitude threshold are not included in the motion vector direction histogram.

### 4.2.3.2   Histogram of Movement Area Types

The **motion region type histogram** (MRTH) is another compact way of representing motion. When the object is moving, the object can be segmented according to the local motion vector field, and each motion region with different affine parameter models can be obtained. These affine parameters can be regarded as a group of motion characteristics representing the motion region, so that the information of various motions in the motion vector field can be represented by means of the representation of the region parameter model. Specifically, it classifies motion models and counts the number of pixels in each motion region that meets different motion models. An example of MRTH is shown in Fig. 4.5. Using an affine parameter model for each motion region can not only conform to the local motion that people understand subjectively but also reduce the amount of data required to describe motion information.

The classification of the motion model is to divide the motion models into various types according to the motion vector describing the motion affine parameter model. For example, an affine motion model has six parameters, and its classification is a division of the 6-D parameter space. This division can use a vector quantization method. Specifically, according to the parameter model of each motion region, the vector quantizer is used to find the corresponding motion model type, and then the area value of the motion region that meets the motion model type is counted. The statistical histogram obtained in this way indicates the coverage area of each motion type. Different local motion types can represent not only different translational motions but also different rotational motions, different motion amplitudes, etc. Therefore, compared with the motion vector direction histogram, the motion region type histogram has a stronger description ability.

**Fig. 4.5** Histogram of motion region types

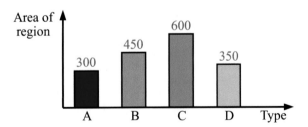

### 4.2.4 Motion Track Description

The trajectory of the object gives the position information of the object during the motion. The trajectory of a moving object can be used when performing high-level explanations of actions and behaviors under certain circumstances or conditions. The international standard MPEG-7 recommends a special descriptor to describe the trajectory of the moving object. This kind of **motion trajectory descriptor** consists of a series of key points and a set of functions that interpolate between these key points. According to requirements, key points can be represented by coordinate values in 2-D or 3-D coordinate space, and the interpolation function corresponds to each coordinate axis, $x(t)$ corresponds to the horizontal trajectory, $y(t)$ corresponds to the vertical trajectory, and $z(t)$ corresponds to the trajectory in the depth direction. Figure 4.6 shows a schematic diagram of $x(t)$. In the figure, there are four key points $t_0$, $t_1$, $t_2$, and $t_3$. In addition, there are three different interpolation functions between these pairs of key points.

The general form of the interpolation function is a second-order polynomial:

$$f(t) = f_p(t) + v_p(t - t_p) + a_p(t - t_p)^2/2 \qquad (4.11)$$

In Eq. (4.11), $p$ represents a point on the time axis; $v_p$ represents motion speed; $a_p$ represents motion acceleration. The interpolation functions corresponding to the three segments of the trajectory in Fig. 4.6 are zero-order function, first-order function, and double-order function, respectively. Segment $A$ is $x(t) = x(t_0)$, segment $B$ is $x(t) = x(t_1) + v(t_1)(t - t_1)$, and segment $C$ is $x(t) = x(t_2) + v(t_2)(t - t_2) + 0.5 \times a(t_2)(t - t_2)^2$.

According to the coordinates of the key points in the trajectory and the forms of the interpolation functions, the motion of the object along a specific direction can be determined. Summing up the motion trajectories in three directions, it can determine the motion of the object in space over time. Note that interpolation functions between the two key points in the horizontal trajectory, vertical trajectory, and depth trajectory can be functions of different orders. This kind of descriptor is compact and extensible, and according to the number of key points, the granularity of the descriptor can be determined. It can both describe delicate motions with close time intervals and roughly describe motions in a large time range. In the most

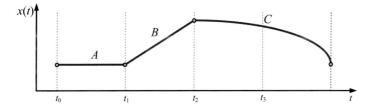

**Fig. 4.6** Schematic diagram of key points and interpolation functions in trajectory description

extreme case, one can keep only the key points without the interpolation function, because only the key point sequence can already provide a basic description of the trajectory.

## 4.3   Motion Information Detection

Compared with still images, motion changes are unique to video. Detecting the motion information in the video image (i.e., determining whether there is motion, which pixels and regions are in motion, and the speed and direction of the motion) is the basis of many video image processing and analysis tasks.

In video motion detection, it is necessary to distinguish foreground motion and background motion. This section discusses only the global motion detection, and the local motion detection will be discussed in Chap. 5.

### *4.3.1   Motion Detection Based on Camera Model*

Because the overall motion of the scene caused by **camera motion** is relatively regular, it can be detected with the help of the camera motion model. This model is mainly used to establish the connection between the pixel space coordinates before and after the camera motions in adjacent frames. When estimating model parameters, first select enough observation points from adjacent frames, then use a certain matching algorithm to obtain the observed motion vectors of these points, and finally use parameter fitting methods to estimate model parameters.

#### 4.3.1.1   Camera Motion Type

There are many types of camera motion, which can be introduced with the help of Fig. 4.7. Assuming that the camera is placed at the origin of the 3-D space coordinate system, the optical axis of the lens is along the $Z$ axis, and the spatial point $P(X, Y, Z)$ is imaged at the image plane point $p(x, y)$. The camera can have translational motions along three coordinate axes, respectively. Among them, the motion along the $X$ axis is called translation or **tracking** motion, the motion along the $Y$ axis is called **lifting** motion, and the motion along the $Z$ axis is called **dollying** motion. The camera can also have a **rotation** around three coordinate axes, respectively. The rotation around the $X$ axis is called **tilting** motion, the motion around the $Y$ axis is called **panning** motion, and the movement around the $Z$ axis is called rotation motion (around the optical axis). Finally, changes in the focal length of the camera lens will also cause changes in the field of view, which is called **zooming** motion or scaling motion. The zooming motion can be divided into two types, namely, **zoom in (forward zooming)**, which is used to align/focus the camera on the object of interest, and

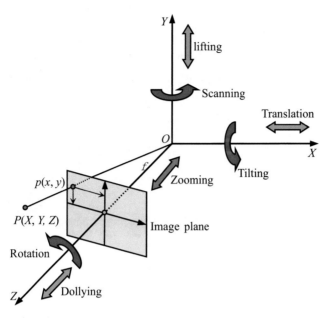

**Fig. 4.7** Types of camera motion

**zoom out** (**backward zooming**), which is used to give a panoramic expansion process of a scene gradually from fine to coarse.

To sum up, there are six types of camera motions: (1) scanning, that is, the camera rotates horizontally; (2) tilting, that is, the camera rotates vertically; (3) zooming, that is, the camera changes the focal length; (4) tracking, that is, the camera moves horizontally (laterally); (5) lifting, that is, the camera moves perpendicularly (vertical); and (6) dollying, that is, the camera moves back and forth (horizontally). These six types of motion can be combined to form three types of operations: (1) translation operation; (2) rotation operation; and (3) zoom operation.

To describe the spatial coordinate changes caused by these types of camera motions, an affine transformation model needs to be established. For general applications, the linear **six-parameter affine model** is often used:

$$\begin{cases} u = k_0 x + k_1 y + k_2 \\ v = k_3 x + k_4 y + k_5 \end{cases} \tag{4.12}$$

The affine model is a linear polynomial parameter model, which is easier to handle mathematically. In order to improve the description ability of the global motion model, some extensions can be made on the basis of the six-parameter affine model. For example, by adding the quadratic term $xy$ to the polynomial of the model, an **eight-parameter bilinear model** can be obtained:

**Fig. 4.8** The motion vector values obtained by the block matching algorithm directly

$$\begin{cases} u = k_0 xy + k_1 x + k_2 y + k_3 \\ v = k_4 xy + k_5 x + k_6 y + k_7 \end{cases} \qquad (4.13)$$

The global motion vector detection based on the bilinear model can be performed as follows. To estimate the eight parameters of the bilinear model, a set of (more than 4) motion vector observations is required (in this way, 8 equations can be obtained). When obtaining the motion vector observation values, considering that the motion vector value in the global motion is often relatively large, the entire frame image can be divided into small square blocks (such as 16 × 16), and then the **block matching** method is used to obtain the motion vector, and the result is displayed using the motion vector field representation in Sect. 4.2.

**Example 4.3 Motion Information Detection Based on Bilinear Model**
Figure 4.8 shows an image obtained by actual motion detection based on the bilinear model, in which the motion vector (starting at the center of the block) obtained by the block matching algorithm is superimposed on the original image to represent the motion of each block.

As can be seen from Fig. 4.8, because there are some local object motions in the original image, and the amplitude of these motions is relatively large, so in the location where there is local motion (e.g., near the location of each football player in the figure), the motion vectors obtained by block matching method are much larger than the global motion vectors. In addition, the block matching method may generate random error data in the low-texture regions of the image. For example, in the background of the picture (close to the stand), there are also some larger motion vectors. For these reasons, the relatively regular global motion amplitude in the figure is relatively small (but its direction and relative size distribution have some similarities with Fig. 4.3).

#### 4.3.1.2 Motion Camera

Depth information can also be obtained from the video. When a camera is used to collect a series of images in multiple poses one after another, the same 3-D space point will correspond to the coordinate points on the image plane of different frames, resulting in **parallax**. Here, the camera's motion trajectory can be regarded as a baseline. If one uses two frames of images acquired one after another and match the features in them, it is possible to obtain depth information. This method is also called **motion stereo**.

When the camera moves (this is also equivalent to the case in active vision), the distance that the object point moves laterally depends not only on $X$ but also on $Y$. To simplify the problem, the radial distance $R$ ($R^2 = X^2 + Y^2$) from the object point to the optical axis of the camera can be used for representation.

To calculate the parallax from the camera motion, refer to Fig. 4.9 (Fig. 4.9b is a section of Fig. 4.9a). The radial distances of the image points in the two images are.

$$R_1 = \frac{R\lambda}{Z_1} \quad R_2 = \frac{R\lambda}{Z_2} \tag{4.14}$$

In this way, the parallax is

$$d = R_2 - R_1 = R\lambda \left( \frac{1}{Z_2} - \frac{1}{Z_1} \right) \tag{4.15}$$

Let the baseline $B = Z_1 - Z_2$, and assuming $B << Z_1$, $B << Z_2$, then it can get (take $Z^2 = Z_1 Z_2$)

$$d = \frac{RB\lambda}{Z^2} \tag{4.16}$$

Let $R_0 \approx (R_1 + R_2)/2$, by using $R/Z = R_0/\lambda$, to get

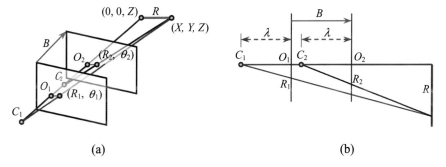

(a)                                              (b)

**Fig. 4.9** Calculate the parallax from the camera motion

$$d = \frac{BR_0}{Z} \qquad (4.17)$$

The final depth of the object point can be derived as

$$Z = \frac{BR_0}{d} = \frac{BR_0}{(R_2 - R_1)} \qquad (4.18)$$

Equation (4.17) can be compared with Eq. (3.29); here the parallax depends on the (average) radial distance $R_0$ between the image point and the optical axis of the camera, while there it is independent of the radial distance. Comparing Eq. (4.18) with Eq. (3.30), the depth information of the object point on the optical axis cannot be given here; for other object points, the accuracy of the depth information depends on the radial distance.

Now look at the ranging accuracy. It can be seen from Eq. (3.30) that depth information is related to parallax, and parallax is related to imaging coordinates. Suppose $x_1$ produces a deviation $e$, that is, $x_{1e} = x_1 + e$, then $d_{1e} = x_1 + e + |x_2| - B = d + e$, so the distance deviation is

$$\Delta Z = Z - Z_{1e} = \lambda \left(1 + \frac{B}{d}\right) - \lambda \left(1 + \frac{B}{d_{1e}}\right) = \frac{\lambda Be}{d(d + e)} \qquad (4.19)$$

Substituting Eq. (3.29) into Eq. (4.19) to get

$$\Delta Z = \frac{e(Z - \lambda)^2}{\lambda B + e(Z - \lambda)} \approx \frac{eZ^2}{\lambda B + eZ} \qquad (4.20)$$

The last step is a simplification by considering $Z \gg \lambda$ in the general case. It can be seen from Eq. (4.10) that the accuracy of distance measurement is related to the focal length of the camera, the baseline length between the cameras, and the object distance. The longer the focal length and the longer the baseline, the higher the accuracy; the larger the object distance, the lower the accuracy. In practice, the equivalent baseline taken with cameras is generally very short, because the objects in the series of images are taken from almost the same angle of view.

## 4.3.2    Frequency Domain Motion Detection

The aforementioned modeling method detects the comprehensive changes of various motions in the image space. With the help of Fourier transform, the detection of motion can also be switched to the frequency domain. The advantage of **frequency domain motion detection** is that it can handle translation, rotation, and scale changes separately.

### 4.3.2.1 Detection of Translation

Suppose that the position of the pixel at time $t_k$ is $(x, y)$ and the position of the pixel at time $t_{k+1}$ moves to $(x + dx, y + dy)$. It is generally assumed that the gray level of the pixel itself remains unchanged during this period of time; then

$$f(x + dx, y + dy, t_{k+1}) = f(x, y, t_k) \tag{4.21}$$

According to the properties of Fourier transform, there are

$$F_k(u, v) = f(x, y, t_k) \tag{4.22}$$

$$F_{k+1}(u, v) = f(x + dx, y + dy, t_{k+1}) \tag{4.23}$$

It can be obtained with the help of translation properties:

$$F_{k+1}(u, v) = F_k(u, v) \exp[j2\pi(udx + vdy)] \tag{4.24}$$

Equation (4.24) shows that the phase angle difference of the Fourier transform of the two images taken at time $t_k$ and time $t_{k+1}$ is

$$d\theta(u, v) = 2\pi(udx, vdy) \tag{4.25}$$

Taking into account the separability of Fourier transform, it can be obtained from Eq. (4.25):

$$dx = \frac{d\theta_x(u)}{2\pi u} \tag{4.26}$$

$$dy = \frac{d\theta_y(v)}{2\pi v} \tag{4.27}$$

In Eq. (4.26) and (4.27), $d\theta_x(u)$ and $d\theta_y(v)$ are the difference between the phase angle of the Fourier transform projected on the $X$ axis and the $Y$ axis by $f(x, y, t_k)$ and $f(x, y, t_{k+1})$, respectively. Due to the non-uniqueness of the phase angle, the following methods can be used when calculating $d\theta_x(u)$ and $d\theta_y(v)$. Suppose the variation range of $dx$ satisfies

$$\left| \frac{dx}{L_x} \right| < \frac{1}{2K} \tag{4.28}$$

where $K$ is a positive constant and $L_x$ is the number of pixels in the $X$ direction. Substitute $u = K/L_x$ into Eq. (4.9), take the absolute value of $d\theta_x(u)$, and get from Eq. (4.28):

$$\left| d\theta_x \left( \frac{K}{L_x} \right) \right| = 2\pi \frac{K}{L_x} |dx| < \pi \tag{4.29}$$

Under the restriction of Eq. (4.29), the phase angles of the Fourier transform projected on the X axis and the Y axis by $f(x, y, t_k)$ and $f(x, y, t_{k+1})$ are, respectively, added with an integer multiple of $2\pi$ to produce the unique value of $d\theta_x(u)$.

### 4.3.2.2 Detection of Rotation

The detection of rotational motion can be carried out with the help of the power spectrum obtained after Fourier transform, because the straight line pattern in the image (such as a straight edge) corresponds to the straight line pattern past the origin of the spectrum in the power spectrum after Fourier transform, and the two straight line patterns correspond to before and after the rotation intersect.

Specifically, the Fourier transform of $f(x, y, t_k)$ and $f(x, y, t_{k+1})$ can be performed, respectively, and their power spectra can be calculated:

$$P_k(u, v) = |F_k(u, v)|^2 \tag{4.30}$$

$$P_{k+1}(u, v) = |F_{k+1}(u, v)|^2 \tag{4.31}$$

Further, it is required to search for corresponding straight line patterns passing through the origin in $P_k(u, v)$ and $P_{k+1}(u, v)$, respectively, such as $L_k$ and $L_{k+1}$. Project $L_k$ onto $P_{k+1}(u, v)$, the angle between this projection, and $L_k$ is the angle of rotation of the object.

### 4.3.2.3 Detection of Scale Changes

The detection of scale changes can also be carried out by means of the power spectrum obtained after Fourier transform. The scale change of the image space corresponds to the change of the frequency in the Fourier transform domain. When the size of the object in the image space becomes larger, the low-frequency components of the power spectrum in the frequency domain will increase. When the size of the object in the image space becomes smaller, the high-frequency components of the power spectrum in the frequency domain will increase.

Specifically, first obtain the power spectrum of $f(x, y, t_k)$ and $f(x, y, t_{k+1})$ after Fourier transform, and then in $P_k(u, v)$ and $P_{k+1}(u, v)$, search for the linear patterns $L_k$ and $L_{k+1}$ in the same direction, respectively. $L_k$ is projected onto $P_{k+1}(u, v)$ to obtain $L_k'$. Now measure the length of $L_k'$ and $L_{k+1}$, which are $|L_k'|$ and $|L_{k+1}|$, respectively. The scale change can use the following equation to represent:

$$S = \left| \frac{L'_k}{L_{k+1}} \right| \tag{4.32}$$

If $S < 1$, it means that from time $t_k$ to $t_{k+1}$, the object's image size has increased by $S$ times. If $S > 1$, it means that from time $t_k$ to $t_{k+1}$, the object's image size has reduced to $1/S$.

### 4.3.3   Detection of Movement Direction

In many applications, certain specific **motion patterns** need to be determined. In this case, image-based information and motion-based information can be combined. Motion information can be obtained by determining a specific difference between images that are acquired sequentially. Generally, in order to improve the accuracy and use the spatial distribution information, the image is often divided into blocks, and then two moving image blocks with a time difference (one collected at time $t$ and one collected at time $t + dt$) are considered. The direction of motion can use the following four kinds of calculation for difference image:

$$\begin{aligned}
U &= |f_t - f_{t+dt\uparrow}| \\
D &= |f_t - f_{t+dt\downarrow}| \\
L &= |f_t - f_{t+dt\leftarrow}| \\
R &= |f_t - f_{t+dt\rightarrow}|
\end{aligned} \tag{4.33}$$

where the arrow represents the direction of image motion, such as $\downarrow$ represents the image frame $I_{t+dt}$ moves downward relative to the previous frame $I_t$.

The amplitude of motion can be obtained by summing the area of the image block. This sum can be quickly calculated with the help of the integral image below.

**Integral image** is a matrix representation method that maintains the global information of the image. In the integral image, the value $I(x, y)$ at the position $(x, y)$ represents the sum of all the pixel values at the upper left of the position in the original image $f(x, y)$:

$$f(x, y) = \sum_{p \leq x, q \leq y} f(p, q) \tag{4.34}$$

The construction of the integral image can be carried out by scanning the image only once by means of a loop:

1. Let $s(x, y)$ represent the cumulative sum of a row of pixels, $s(x, -1) = 0$.
2. Let $I(x, y)$ be an integral image, $I(-1, y) = 0$.

**Fig. 4.10** Schematic diagram of integral image calculation

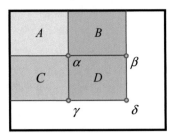

**Fig. 4.11** Haar rectangle features in integral image calculation

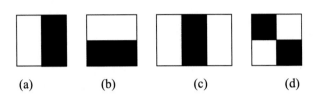

     (a)            (b)            (c)            (d)

3. Scan the entire image line by line, and calculate the cumulative sum $s(x, y)$ of the row of the pixel and the integral image $I(x, y)$ for each pixel $(x, y)$ by means of a loop:

$$s(x, y) = s(x, y - 1) + f(x, y) \tag{4.35}$$

$$I(x, y) = I(x - 1, y) + s(x, y) \tag{4.36}$$

4. When the pixel in the lower right corner is reached after a line-by-line scan of the entire image, the integral image $I(x, y)$ is constructed.

As shown in Fig. 4.10, using the integral image, the sum of any rectangle can be calculated with the help of four reference arrays. For rectangle $D$, the calculation formula is as follows:

$$D_{sum} = I(\delta) + I(\alpha) - [I(\beta) + I(\gamma)] \tag{4.37}$$

where $I(\alpha)$ is the value of the integral image at point $\alpha$, that is, the sum of pixel values in rectangle $A$; $I(\beta)$ is the sum of pixel values in rectangles $A$ and $B$; $I(\gamma)$ is the sum of pixel values in rectangles $A$ and $C$; and $I(\delta)$ is the sum of pixel values in rectangles $A$, $B$, $C$, and $D$. Therefore, the calculation that reflects the difference between two rectangles requires eight reference arrays. In practice, a look-up table can be established, and calculations can be completed with the help of the look-up table.

The Haar rectangle feature commonly used in object detection and tracking, as shown in Fig. 4.11, can be quickly calculated by subtracting the shaded rectangle from the unshaded rectangle with the help of the integral image. For Fig. 4.11a, b, it only needs to look up the table six times; for Fig. 4.11c, it only needs to look up the table eight times; and for Fig. 4.11d, it only needs to look up the table nine times.

# 4.4   Motion-Based Filtering

In order to effectively detect the motion information in a video image, it is often necessary to preprocess the video image first to eliminate various interference effects and improve image quality. Filtering here represents a variety of preprocessing processes and methods (which can be used to enhance, restore, filter out noise, etc.). Since video images include both spatial and temporal variables, video filtering is often a spatial-temporal filtering. Compared with still image filtering, video filtering can also be considered with the help of motion information. Motion detection filtering and motion compensation filtering are common modes of video filtering.

## *4.4.1   Motion Detection-Based Filtering*

There is more time-varying motion information in video than in still images, so the filtering of video can consider the problems caused by motion on the basis of filtering still images. But from another perspective, video filtering can also be effectively performed through motion detection. In other words, **motion detection-based filtering** needs to be performed on the basis of motion detection.

### 4.4.1.1   Direct Filtering

The simplest **direct filtering** method is to use **frame averaging** technology. By averaging multiple samples at the same position in different frames, noise can be eliminated without affecting the spatial resolution of the frame image. It can be proved that in the case of additive Gaussian noise, the frame averaging technique corresponds to calculating the maximum likelihood estimation and can reduce the noise variance to $1/N$ ($N$ is the number of frames participating in the averaging). This method is effective for fixed parts of the scene.

Frame averaging essentially performs 1-D filtering along the time axis, that is, time-domain averaging, so it can be regarded as a time filtering method, and time filter is a special type of spatial-temporal filter. In principle, the use of temporal filters can avoid spatial blurring. However, similar to the space domain averaging operation that will cause spatial blur, the time domain averaging operation in the scene that has a sudden change in position with time can also cause temporal blur. Here, the motion adaptive filtering corresponding to the edge-preserving filtering in the space domain (usually performed along the edge direction) can be used, and the filtering direction is determined by the motion information between adjacent frames. The motion adaptive filter can be constructed with reference to the edge-preserving filter in the spatial domain. For example, at a specific pixel in a certain frame, it can be assumed that there are five possible motion trends next: no motion, motion in the positive direction of $X$, motion in the negative direction of $X$, motion in the positive direction of $Y$, and motion in the negative direction of $Y$. If the minimum mean square error estimation is used to determine the actual motion trend, and the changes along the time axis produced by the motion from the changes caused by the noise are distinguished, then the overall good filtering effect can be obtained by filtering only in the corresponding motion direction.

### 4.4.1.2   Using Motion Detection Information

In order to determine the parameters in the filter, the motion detection can also be used to adapt the designed filter to the specific conditions of the motion. The filter can be a **finite impulse response** (FIR) filter or an **infinite impulse response** (IIR) filter, namely

$$f_{FIR}(x, y, t) = (1 - \beta)f(x, y, t) + \beta f(x, y, t - 1) \qquad (4.38)$$

$$f_{IIR}(x, y, t) = (1 - \beta)f(x, y, t) + \beta f_{IIR}(x, y, t - 1) \qquad (4.39)$$

where

$$\beta = \max \left\{ 0, \quad \frac{1}{2} - \alpha |g(x, \quad y, \quad t) - g(x, \quad y, \quad t - 1)| \right\} \qquad (4.40)$$

It is the signal obtained by motion detection, and $\alpha$ is a scalar constant. These filters will be turned off (set $\beta$ to 0) when the motion amplitude is large (the second item on the right will be less than zero) to avoid artificial error.

It can be seen from Eq. (4.38) that the FIR filter is a linear system, and the response to the input signal eventually tends to 0 (i.e., finite). It can be seen from Eq. (4.39) that there is a feedback loop in the IIR filter, so the response to the pulse input signal is infinite. Relatively speaking, FIR filters have limited noise elimination capabilities, especially when only time domain filtering is performed and the number of frames involved in filtering is small. IIR filter has stronger noise cancellation ability, but its impulse response is infinite: when the input signal is finite, the output signal will become infinite. FIR filters are more stable and easier to optimize than IIR filters, but they are more difficult to design.

## 4.4.2   Motion Compensation-Based Filtering

The **motion compensation** filter acts on the motion trajectory and needs to use accurate information at each pixel on the motion trajectory. The basic assumption of motion compensation is that the pixel gray level remains unchanged on a determined motion trajectory.

### 4.4.2.1 Motion Trajectory and Time-Space Spectrum

The motion on the image plane corresponds to the 2-D motion or motion rate of the spatial scene point under projection. In each frame of image, the points in the scene move along a curve in the XYT space, which is called a **motion trajectory**. The motion trajectory can be described by a vector function $M(t; x, y, t_0)$, which represents, at time $t$, the horizontal and vertical coordinates of the reference point $(x, y)$ at time $t_0$. An explanatory diagram is shown in Fig. 4.12, where at time $t'$, $M(t'; x, y, t_0) = (x', y')$.

Given the trajectory $M(t; x, y, t_0)$ of a point in the scene, the velocity along the trajectory at time $t'$ and position $(x', y')$ is defined as

$$s(x', y', t') = \frac{dM}{dt}(t; x, y, t_0)\big|_{t=t'} \tag{4.41}$$

Next, consider the case where there is only a uniform global motion in the video. When there is a uniform motion of $(s_x, s_y)$ on the image plane, the grayscale change between frames can be represented as

$$f_M(x, y, t) = f_M(x - s_x t, y - s_y t, 0) \approx f_0(x - s_x t, y - s_y t) \tag{4.42}$$

Among them, $s_x$ and $s_y$ are the two components of the motion vector, the reference frame is selected at $t_0 = 0$, and $f_0(x, y)$ represents the grayscale distribution in the reference frame.

In order to derive the **spatial-temporal spectrum** of this video, first define the Fourier transform of any spatial-temporal function as

$$F_M(u, v, w) = \iiint f_M(x, y, t) \exp\left[-j2\pi(ux + vy + wt)\right]dxdydt \tag{4.43}$$

Substituting Eq. (4.42) into Eq. (4.43), it gives

**Fig. 4.12** Motion trajectory

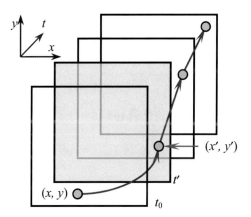

**Fig. 4.13** The definition
domain of global uniform
motion

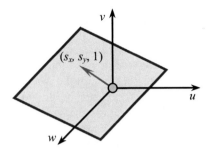

$$F_M(u, v, w) = \iiint f_0(x - s_x t, y - s_y t) \exp\left[-j2\pi(ux + vy + wt)\right] dx dy dt$$

$$= F_0(u, v) \cdot \delta(us_x + vs_y + w)$$

$$(4.44)$$

The delta function in Eq. (4.44) shows that the definition domain of spatial-temporal spectrum (support set) is a plane that satisfies Eq. (4.38) and passes through the origin (as shown in Fig. 4.13):

$$us_x + vs_y + w = 0 \tag{4.45}$$

### 4.4.2.2    Filtering Along the Motion Trajectory

The **filtering along the motion trajectory** refers to the filtering of each point on each frame along the motion trajectory. First consider the situation along an arbitrary motion trajectory. The output of the filter defined at $(x, y, t)$ is

$$g(x, y, t) = \mathcal{F}\{f_1[q; M(q; x, y, t)]\} \tag{4.46}$$

where $f_1[q; M(q; x, y, t)] = f_M[M(q; x, y, t), q]$ means that the motion trajectory along $(x, y, t)$ is a 1-D signal in the input image and F represents the 1-D filter along the motion trajectory (which can be linear or non-linear).

The linear and spatial invariant filtering along a uniform motion trajectory can be represented as

$$g(x, y, t) = \iiint h_1(q)\delta(z_1 - s_x q, z_2 - s_y q)f_M(x - z_1, y - z_2, t - q)dz_1 dz_2 dq$$

$$= \int h_1(q)f_M(x - s_x q, y - s_y q, t - q)dq = \int h_1(q)f_1(t - q; x, y, t)dq$$

$$(4.47)$$

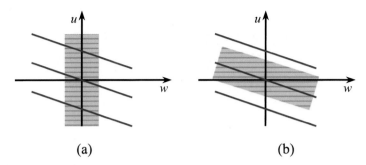

**Fig. 4.14** Definition domain of the frequency response of the motion compensation filter

In Eq. (4.47), $h_1(q)$ is the impulse response of the 1-D filter used along the motion trajectory. The impulse response of the above-mentioned spatial-temporal filter can also be represented as

$$h(x, y, t) = h_1(t)\delta(x - s_x t, y - s_y t)$$ (4.48)

Perform 3-D Fourier transform on Eq. (4.48) to get the frequency domain response of the motion compensation filter:

$$
\begin{aligned}
H(u, v, w) &= \iiint h_1(t)\delta(x - s_x t, y - s_y t)\exp\left[-j2\pi(ux + vy + wt)\right]\mathrm{d}x\mathrm{d}y\mathrm{d}t \\
&= \int h_1(t)\exp\left[-j2\pi(us_x + vs_y + w)t\right]\mathrm{d}t = H_1(us_x + vs_y + w)
\end{aligned}
$$

(4.49)

Project the definition domain of the frequency domain response of the motion compensation filter to the *uw* plane, as shown in the shaded part in Fig. 4.14, and the diagonal lines in the figure represent the motion trajectory. Figure 4.14a corresponds to $s_x = 0$, that is, pure time domain filtering without motion compensation; and Fig. 4.14b represents the situation when motion compensation is right and $s_x$ is matching to speed in the input video.

### 4.4.2.3 Motion Compensation Filter

It is assumed here that along the path of the motion trajectory $M(q; x, y, t)$, the change of the pixel gray level is mainly owing to noise. Due to different motion estimation methods, different domains of filters (such as spatial domain or temporal domain), and different filter structures (such as FIR or IIR), there are many types of **motion compensation filters**.

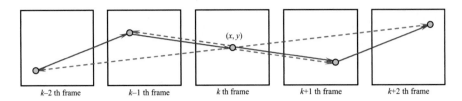

**Fig. 4.15** Motion trajectory estimation

Figure 4.15 shows a schematic diagram of motion trajectory estimation in a sampling sequence in the time-space domain, where five frames of images are taken as an example. Assuming that $N$ frames of images are used to filter the $k$-th frame of images, these $N$ frames of images can be denoted as $k - M$, ..., $k - 1$, $k, k + 1$, ..., $k + M$, where $N = 2M + 1$. First estimate the discrete motion trajectory $M(l; x, y, t)$ at $(x, y)$ of the $k$-th frame image, $l = k - M$, ..., $k - 1, k, k + 1$, ..., $k + M$. The function $M(l; x, y, t)$ is a continuous vector function, which gives the pixel coordinates in the $l$-th frame of image corresponding to the pixel at $(x, y)$ in the $k$-th frame of image. The solid arrows in Fig. 4.15 indicate the trajectory of motion. When estimating the trajectory, refer to the $k$-th frame of image to estimate the offset vector, as shown by the dotted arrow.

Considering that the noise is zero mean and additive spatial-temporal noise, the noisy video image that needs to be filtered at this time is

$$g(x, y, t) = f(x, y, t) + n(x, y, t) \tag{4.50}$$

If the noise is white in space and time, its frequency spectrum is evenly distributed. According to Eq. (4.45), the definition domain of video is a plane, and designing an appropriate motion compensation filter can effectively eliminate all noise energy outside the plane without blurring. Equivalently, in the spatial-temporal domain, white noise with zero mean can be completely filtered out as long as it follows the correct trajectory.

After the definition domain of the motion compensation filter is determined, various filtering methods can be used for filtering. Two basic methods are described below.

### 4.4.2.4   Spatial-Temporal Adaptive Linear Minimum Mean Square Error Filtering

The spatial-temporal adaptive **linear minimum mean square error** (LMMSE) filtering can be performed as follows. The pixel estimate at $(x, y, t)$ is

$$f_e(x, y, t) = \frac{\sigma_f^2(x, y, t)}{\sigma_f^2(x, y, t) + \sigma_n^2(x, y, t)} \left[ g(x, y, t) - \mu_g(x, y, t) \right] + \mu_f(x, y, t) \quad (4.51)$$

In Eq. (4.51), $\mu_f(x, y, t)$ and $\sigma_f^2(x, y, t)$ correspond to the mean value and the variance of the noise-free image, respectively; $\mu_g(x, y, t)$ represents the mean value of the noisy image; and $\sigma_n^2(x, y, t)$ represents the variance of the noise. Considering stationary noise, it can also be obtained:

$$f_e(x, y, t) = \frac{\sigma_f^2(x, y, t)}{\sigma_f^2(x, y, t) + \sigma_n^2(x, y, t)} g(x, y, t)$$

$$+ \frac{\sigma_n^2(x, y, t)}{\sigma_f^2(x, y, t) + \sigma_n^2(x, y, t)} \mu_g(x, y, t) \quad (4.52)$$

From Eq. (4.52), the adaptive ability of the filter can be seen. When the variance of the spatial-temporal signal is much smaller than the noise variance, $\sigma_f^2(x, y, t) \approx 0$, the above estimation approximates the spatial-temporal mean value, $\mu_g = \mu_f$. On the other extreme, when the variance of the spatial-temporal signal is much greater than the variance of the noise, $\sigma_f^2(x, y, t) >> \sigma_n^2(x, y, t)$, the above estimation will approximate the value of the noisy image to avoid blurry.

#### 4.4.2.5 Adaptive Weighted Average Filtering

**Adaptive weighted average** (AWA) filtering calculates a weighted average of image values along the motion trajectory in space and time. The weight is determined by optimizing a criterion function, and its value depends on the accuracy of the motion estimation and the spatial uniformity of the region around the motion trajectory. When the motion estimation is sufficiently accurate, the weights tend to be consistent, and the AWA filter performs direct spatial-temporal averaging. When the difference between the value of a pixel in the space and the value of the pixel to be filtered is greater than a given threshold, the weight for this pixel is reduced, and the effects of other pixels are strengthened. Therefore, the AWA filter is particularly suitable for filtering when different scenes are contained in the same image region caused by rapid zooming or viewing angle changes of camera. In this case, the effect is better than that of the spatial-temporal adaptive linear minimum mean square error filter.

The AWA filter can be defined as follows:

$$\widehat{f}(x, y, t) = \sum_{(r, c, k) \in (x, y, t)} w(r, c, k) g(r, c, k) \quad (4.53)$$

where

$$w(r, c, k) = \frac{K(x, y, t)}{1 + \alpha \max \left\{ \varepsilon^2, \ [g(x, \ y, \ t) - g(r, \ c, \ k)]^2 \right\}} \tag{4.54}$$

is the weight, $K(x, y, t)$ is the normalization constant:

$$K(r, c, k) = \left\{ \sum_{(r, \ c, \ k) \in (x, \ y, \ t)} \frac{1}{1 + \alpha \max \left\{ \varepsilon^2, \ [g(x, \ y, \ t) - g(r, \ c, \ k)]^2 \right\}} \right\}^{-1} \tag{4.55}$$

In Eqs. (4.53) and (4.54), both $\alpha$ ($\alpha > 0$) and $\varepsilon$ are filter parameters, and they are determined according to the following principles:

1. When the grayscale difference of pixels in the spatial-temporal region is mainly caused by noise, it is best to convert the weighted average to a direct average, which can be achieved by appropriately selecting $\varepsilon^2$. In fact, when the square of the difference is less than $\varepsilon^2$, all weights take the same value $K/(1 + \alpha\varepsilon^2) = 1/L$, and $\widehat{f}(x, y, t)$ degenerates into a direct average. Therefore, the value of $\varepsilon^2$ can be set to twice the noise variance.
2. When the difference between $g(x, y, t)$ and $g(r, c, k)$ is greater than $\varepsilon^2$, then the contribution of $g(r, c, k)$ is weighted by $w(r, c, k) < w(x, y, t) = K/(1 + \alpha\varepsilon^2)$. The parameter $\alpha$ acts as a "penalty" term, which determines the sensitivity of the weight to the squared difference $[g(x, y, t) - g(r, c, k)]^2$. Generally, it can be set to 1. At this time, the pixels whose grayscale difference between each frame is greater than $\pm\varepsilon$ will participate in the average.

## 4.5  Key Points and References for Each Section

The following combines the main contents of each section to introduce some references that can be further consulted.

1. **Video Basic**
   For more introduction to the basic concepts of video, please refer to [1, 2].
2. **Motion Classification and Representation**
   For the applications of the histogram of the motion vector direction and the histogram of the motion region type, please refer to [3]. The motion trajectory descriptor recommended by the international standard (MPEG-7) can be found in [4, 5].
3. **Motion Information Detection**
   The original introduction to the integral image can be found in [6].

4. **Motion-Based Filtering**

The principle of eliminating noise with the help of frame averaging can be found in the book *2D Computer Vision: Principles, Algorithms and Applications.*

# Self-Test Questions

The following questions include both single-choice questions and multiple-choice questions, so each option must be judged.

### 4.1 Video Basic

4.1.1 Video has many different representation forms; among the three formats introduced, ($\cdot$).

(a) The data volume of the component video format is the smallest.
(b) The data volume of the S-video format is the smallest.
(c) The quality of S-video format is the worst.
(d) The quality of the composite video format is the worst.

[Hint] The three formats are sorted by data volume and quality, respectively.

4.1.2 In the practical $\mathbf{YC_BC_R}$ color coordinate system, ($\cdot$).

(a) The maximum value of $C_B$ can only be obtained at one point.
(b) The minimum value of $C_R$ can only be obtained at one point.
(c) The value range of $Y$ is smaller than the value ranges of $C_B$ and $C_R$.
(d) The value range of $Y$ is larger than the value ranges of $C_B$ and $C_R$.

[Hint] Refer to the representation of RGB color space.

4.1.3 The video bit rate (b/s) of NTSC color TV system is ($\cdot$).

(a) 249 M
(b) 373 M
(c) 498 M
(d) 746 M

[Hint] Calculate according to Eq. (4.4).

### 4.2 Motion Classification and Representation

4.2.1 Between the foreground motion and background motion, ($\cdot$).

(a) The foreground motion is more complicated.
(b) Background motion is more difficult to detect than foreground motion.
(c) The foreground motion is related to the motion of the camera.
(d) Background motion generally has the characteristics of strong integrity.

**Fig. 4.16** Original figure

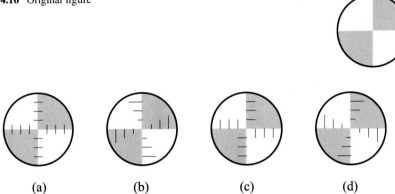

**Fig. 4.17** Figures superimposed with optical flow vectors

[Hint] Foreground motion is also called local motion; background motion is also called global motion or camera motion.

4.2.2 By observing the image obtained through superimposing the calculated motion vector on the original image, (·).

(a) The image can be divided into blocks.
(b) The spatial position of the motion can be determined.
(c) It can understand the magnitude and direction of the motion.
(d) It can distinguish background motion and foreground motion.

[Hint] The vector has magnitude and direction, and the vector superimposed on the original image describes the motion speed of the image block.

4.2.3 When the figure in Fig. 4.16 rotates clockwise around the center, the figure superimposed with the optical flow field vector is the closest to (·).

(a) Fig. 4.17a
(b) Fig. 4.17b
(c) Fig. 4.17c
(d) Fig. 4.17d

[Hint] When drawing the line segment representing the vector, pay attention to the starting point and length, where the length is proportional to the linear velocity of motion.

## 4.3 Motion Information Detection

4.3.1 The six motion types of the camera can be combined to form three types of operations, among which the translation operations include (·).

(a) Scanning, tilting, zooming
(b) Tilting, zooming, tracking

(c) Zooming, tracking, lifting

(d) Tracking, lifting, dollying

[Hint] Analyze the camera motion conditions represented by various motion types in detail.

4.3.2 Suppose the motion vector of a point in the image is [3, 5], then the values of the coefficients in its six-parameter motion model are ($\cdot$).

(a) $k_0 = 0, k_1 = 0, k_2 = 3, k_3 = 0, k_4 = 0, k_5 = 5$

(b) $k_0 = 0, k_1 = 3, k_2 = 0, k_3 = 0, k_4 = 0, k_5 = 5$

(c) $k_0 = 0, k_1 = 0, k_2 = 3, k_3 = 0, k_4 = 5, k_5 = 0$

(d) $k_0 = 0, k_1 = 3, k_2 = 0, k_3 = 0, k_4 = 5, k_5 = 0$

[Hint] Substitute into Eq. (4.12) to calculate.

4.3.3 For detecting the change of object scale in the frequency domain, ($\cdot$).

(a) It needs to calculate the Fourier transform phase angle of the object image.

(b) It needs to calculate the Fourier transform power spectrum of the object image.

(c) If the scale change value is greater than 1, it indicates that the object size has increased.

(d) If the scale change value is smaller than 1, it indicates that the object size has reduced.

[Hint] Analyze the meaning of each parameter in Eq. (4.32).

## 4.4 Motion-Based Filtering

4.4.1 Motion adaptive filtering ($\cdot$).

(a) Is a filtering method based on motion detection

(b) Is a filtering method based on motion compensation

(c) Uses the motion information between adjacent frames to determine the filtering direction

(d) Detects the changes in noise intensity along the time axis

[Hint] Analyze the characteristics of motion adaptive filtering in detail.

4.4.2 Which of the following statement(s) is/are correct? ($\cdot$).

(a) It is difficult to design an infinite impulse response filter.

(b) The infinite impulse response filter updates its response iteratively.

(c) The finite impulse response filter uses feedback to limit the output signal length.

(d) The output signal of the finite impulse response filter is finite when the input signal is infinite.

[Hint] Analyze according to Eqs. (4.38) and (4.39).

4.4.3 In the filtering based on motion compensation, (·).

   (a) Suppose the gray scale of moving pixels is constant.
   (b) Consider that all points in the scene are projected onto the XY plane.
   (c) Suppose that the trajectory of the point is a straight line along the time axis.
   (d) Need to apply the motion compensation filter to the motion trajectory.

[Hint] Analyze the characteristics of motion compensation filtering.

# References

1. Tekalp A M. Digital Video Processing. UK London: Prentice Hall. 1995.
2. Poynton C A. A Technical Introduction to Digital Video. USA New York: John Wiley & Sons Inc. 1996.
3. Yu T L, Zhang Y J. A local motion information based video retrieval method. Journal of Tsinghua University (Sci & Tech), 2002, 42(7): 925-928.
4. Jeannin S, Jasinschi R, She A, *et al*. Motion descriptors for content-based video representation. Signal Processing: Image Communication, 2000, 16(1-2): 59-85.
5. ISO/IEC. JTC1/SC29/WG11. MPEG-7 requirements, Doc. N4035, 2001.
6. Viola P, Jones M. Rapid object detection using a boosted cascade of simple features. Proc. CVPR, 2001, 511-518.

# Chapter 5
# Moving Object Detection and Tracking

In order to analyze the change information in the image or to detect the moving object, it is necessary to use an **image sequence** (also called a dynamic image). An image sequence is composed of a series of 2-D (spatial) images that are continuous in time or a special type of 3-D image, which can be represented as $f(x, y, t)$. Compared with the still image $f(x, y)$, the time variable $t$ is added here. When $t$ takes a certain value, one frame of image in the sequence is obtained. Generally, video is considered to be a sequence of images with regular changes in $t$ (generally collected 25 to 30 times per second).

Unlike a single image, the continuously collected image sequence can reflect the movement of the scene and the change of the scene. On the other hand, objective things are always in constant motion and change, motion is absolute, and stillness is relative. An image is a special case of an image sequence. The changes of the scene and the movement of the scene are more obvious and clear in the sequence images.

The analysis of the motion in the image sequence is not only based on the analysis of the object in the still image but also needs to be expanded in technology, changed in means, and expanded in purpose.

The sections of this chapter are arranged as follows:

Section 5.1 introduces the basic method of using pixel-by-pixel difference to detect change information. The cumulative difference image can better overcome the influence of random noise.

Section 5.2 discusses some basic background modeling methods and compares their effects, including single Gaussian model-based methods, video initialization-based methods, Gaussian mixture model-based methods, and codebook-based methods.

Section 5.3 introduces the derivation of the optical flow equation and the least square method of optical flow estimation. On this basis, the optical flow in motion is analyzed, and a dense optical flow algorithm based on the brightness gradient is given.

Section 5.4 introduces several typical moving object tracking methods, including Kalman filter, particle filter, and mean shift and kernel tracking technology.

## 5.1  Differential Image

The movement change of the scenery in the scene will lead to the change of the object in the video image, and this change generally corresponds to a local region. The simplest method for moving object detection is to find changes in local regions.

In video, the difference between the two images before and after can be directly obtained by comparing pixel by pixel. This image is called a **difference image**. Assuming that there is basically no change in the lighting conditions between multiple frames, then the value in the difference image is not zero, indicating that the pixel at that position may have moved (i.e., the pixel at this position in the next frame of image has moved, and the pixel of the next position now occupies this position, causing the grayscale difference to change). It should be noted that the pixel with value zero in the difference image may also have moved (i.e., the new pixel moved over has the same grayscale as the original pixel). In other words, generally, the difference between two adjacent images in time can highlight the changes in the position and shape of the moving object in the image.

### 5.1.1  Calculation of Difference Image

Refer to Fig. 5.1a, assuming that the gray level of the object is brighter than the gray level of the background. With the help of difference calculation, one can get the positive value region before the motion and the negative value region after the motion. In this way, the motion information of the object can be obtained, and the shape of some parts of the object can also be obtained. If the difference between a series of images is calculated, and the regions with positive or negative values in the difference image are logically combined, then the shape of the entire object can be

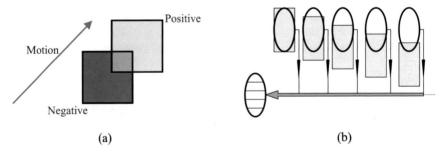

(a)                                                              (b)

**Fig. 5.1**  Using difference images to extract objects

determined. Figure 5.1b shows an example. The rectangular region is gradually moved downward, and the different parts of the elliptical object are drawn in turn, and the results of different time are combined to produce a complete elliptical object.

If a series of images are acquired with relative motion between the image acquisition device and the scene being photographed, the motion information existing in it can be used to help determine the changed pixels in the image. Suppose two images $f(x, y, t_i)$ and $f(x, y, t_j)$ are collected at time $t_i$ and $t_j$, then the difference image can be obtained accordingly:

$$d_{ij}(x, y) = \begin{cases} 1 & |f(x, y, t_i) - f(x, y, t_j)| > T_g \\ 0 & \text{otherwise} \end{cases} \tag{5.1}$$

where $T_g$ is the gray level threshold. The pixels with 0 in the difference image correspond to the places where there is no change (due to motion) between the two moments before and after. The pixel of 1 in the difference image corresponds to the change between the two images, which is often caused by the motion of the object. However, the pixel of 1 in the difference image may also originate from different situations. For example, $f(x, y, t_i)$ is a pixel of a moving object and $f(x, y, t_j)$ is a background pixel or vice versa. It may also be that $f(x, y, t_i)$ is a pixel of a moving object and $f(x, y, t_j)$ is a pixel of another moving object or even a pixel of the same moving object but at different positions (may have different gray levels).

The threshold $T_g$ in Eq. (5.1) is used to determine whether there is a significant difference in the gray levels of the images at two different moments. Another method for judging the significance of gray level differences is to use the following likelihood ratio:

$$\frac{\left[ \frac{\sigma_i + \sigma_j}{2} + \left( \frac{\mu_i - \mu_j}{2} \right)^2 \right]^2}{\sigma_i \cdot \sigma_j} > T_s \tag{5.2}$$

where each $\mu$ and $\sigma$ are the mean and variance of the two images collected at time $t_i$ and $t_j$, respectively, and $T_s$ is the significance threshold.

In the actual situation, due to the influence of random noise, the difference between two images is not zero where there is no pixel shift. In order to distinguish the effect of noise from the movement of pixels, a larger threshold can be used for the difference image, that is, when the difference is greater than a certain threshold, it is considered that the pixel has moved. In addition, the pixels that are 1 due to noise in the difference image are generally isolated, so they can also be removed based on connectivity analysis. But doing so will sometimes eliminate slow motion objects and/or smaller objects.

## *5.1.2   Calculation of Accumulative Difference Image*

To overcome the above-mentioned random noise problem, one can consider using multiple images to calculate the difference image. If the change in a certain location only occasionally occurs, it can be judged as noise. Suppose there are a series of images $f(x, y, t_1), f(x, y, t_2), \ldots, f(x, y, t_n)$, and take the first image $f(x, y, t_1)$ as the reference image. The **accumulative difference image** (ADI) can be obtained by comparing the reference image with each subsequent image. Here, it is supposed that the value of each position in the image is the sum of the number of changes in each comparison.

Refer to Fig. 5.2. Fig. 5.2a shows the image collected at the time $t_1$. There is a square object in the image. Let it move 1 pixel horizontally to the right per unit time. Figure 5.2b, c are the following images collected at time $t_2$ and time $t_3$, respectively; Fig. 5.2d, e show the accumulative difference ($d$) of the images corresponding to time $t_2$ and time $t_3$, respectively. The accumulative difference in Fig. 5.2d is also the ordinary difference discussed earlier (because it is only accumulated once at this time). The square marked 1 on the left represents the gray level difference (one unit) between the object trailing edge of Fig. 5.2a and the backgrounds of Fig. 5.2b; the square marked with 1 on the right corresponds to the gray level difference between the background of Fig. 5.2a and the front edge of the object in Fig. 5.2b (also one unit). Figure 5.2e can be obtained by adding the gray level difference (a unit) between Fig. 5.2a, c to Fig. 5.2d (two accumulations), where the gray level difference between positions 0 and 1 is 2 units and the gray level difference between positions 2 and 3 is also 2 units.

Referring to the above example, it can be seen that the accumulative difference image ADI has three functions:

1. The gradient relationship between adjacent pixel values in ADI can be used to estimate the speed vector of the object motion, where the direction of the gradient is the direction of the speed and the magnitude of the gradient is proportional to the speed.

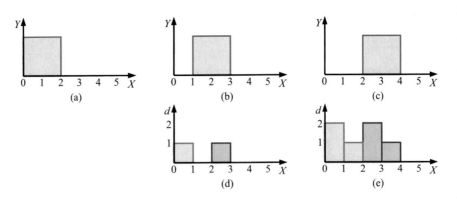

**Fig. 5.2** Determining the motion of the object with the accumulative difference image

2. The number of pixels in ADI can help determine the size and moving distance of the moving object.
3. ADI contains all the historical data of the object motion, which is helpful for detecting slow motion and the motion of smaller objects.

In practical applications, three types of ADI images can be further distinguished: absolute ADI, denoted as $A_k(x, y)$; positive ADI, denoted as $P_k(x, y)$; and negative ADI, denoted as $N_k(x, y)$. Assuming that the gray level of the moving object is greater than the gray level of background, then for $k > 1$, the following three definitions of ADI can be obtained (take $f(x, y, t_1)$ as the reference image):

$$A_k(x, y) = \begin{cases} A_{k-1}(x, y) + 1 & |f(x, y, t_1) - f(x, y, t_k)| > T_g \\ A_{k-1}(x, y) & \text{otherwise} \end{cases} \tag{5.3}$$

$$P_k(x, y) = \begin{cases} P_{k-1}(x, y) + 1 & [f(x, y, t_1) - f(x, y, t_k)] > T_g \\ P_{k-1}(x, y) & \text{otherwise} \end{cases} \tag{5.4}$$

$$N_k(x, y) = \begin{cases} N_{k-1}(x, y) + 1 & [f(x, y, t_1) - f(x, y, t_k)] < -T_g \\ N_{k-1}(x, y) & \text{otherwise} \end{cases} \tag{5.5}$$

The values of the above three ADI images are the result of counting the pixels, and they are all zero initially. The following information can be obtained from them:

1. The area of the non-zero region in the positive ADI image is equal to the area of the moving object.
2. The position of the corresponding moving object in the positive ADI image is the position of the moving object in the reference image.
3. When the moving object in the positive ADI image does not coincide with the moving object in the reference image, the positive ADI image stops counting.
4. The absolute ADI image contains all object regions in the positive ADI image and the negative ADI image.
5. The moving direction and speed of the moving object can be determined according to the absolute ADI image and the negative ADI image.

## 5.2 Background Modeling

Background modeling is a kind of idea for motion detection, which can be realized by different technologies, and it is applied in many moving object detection.

## 5.2.1  Basic Principle

The calculation of the difference image introduced in Sect. 5.1 is a simple and fast motion detection method, but the effect is not good enough in many practical situations. This is because when calculating the difference image, all environmental fluctuations (background clutter), lighting changes, camera shake, etc. and the effects of the object motion are mixed together and all detected at the same time (especially when the first frame is always used as the reference frame, the problem is more serious), so only in very strictly controlled situations (such as when the environment and background are unchanged) can the real object motion be separated.

A more reasonable motion detection idea is not to regard the background as completely unchanged but to calculate and maintain a dynamic (satisfying a certain model) background frame. This is the basic idea of **background modeling**. Background modeling is a training-testing process. Firstly, a background model is trained using some of the first frame images in the video image sequence, and then this model is used to test the subsequent frames, and motion is detected based on the difference between the current frame image and the background model.

A simple background modeling method is to use the average or median value of the previous $N$ frames in the detection of the current frame to determine and update the value of each pixel in the period of $N$ frames. A specific algorithm mainly includes the following steps:

1. Obtain the first $N$ frames of images, and determine the median value of these $N$ frames at each pixel as the current background value.  ·
2. Obtain the $N + 1$-th frame, and calculate the difference between this frame and current background at each pixel position (the difference can be threshold to eliminate or reduce noise).
3. Use a combination of smoothing or morphological operations to eliminate very small regions in the difference image and fill holes in large regions. The reserved region represents the moving object in the scene.
4. Update the median value with the $N + 1$-th frame.
5. Return to Step (2), and consider the next frame of the current frame.

This basic method of using the median to maintain the background is relatively simple and has a small amount of calculation, but the effect is not very good when there are multiple objects in the scene at the same time or when the object motion is slow.

## 5.2.2  Typical Practical Methods

Several typical basic methods for background modeling are introduced below. They all divide the motion foreground extraction into two steps: model training and actual detection. A mathematical model is established for the background through training, and the built model is used to eliminate the background in the detection to obtain the foreground.

### 5.2.2.1 Method Based on Single Gaussian Model

The method based on the **single Gaussian model** believes that the value of the pixel in the video sequence obeys the Gaussian distribution. Specifically, for each fixed pixel position, the mean $\mu$ and variance $\sigma$ of the pixel value at that position in the $N$-frame training image sequence are calculated, and thus a single Gaussian background model is uniquely determined. In motion detection, the background subtraction method is used to calculate the difference between the value f of the pixel in the current frame image and the background model, and then the difference with the threshold $T$ (usually three times the variance $\sigma$) is compared, that is, according to $|f - \mu| \leq 3\sigma$ the pixel as foreground or background can be determined.

This model is relatively simple, but the disadvantage is that it is more sensitive to changes in lighting intensity. Sometimes when both the mean and variance change, the model will not be valid. It generally requires that the lighting intensity has no obvious change in a long time, and the shadow of the moving foreground in the background during the detection period is small. In addition, when there is a moving foreground in the scene, since there is only one model, the moving foreground cannot be separated from the static background, which may cause a larger false alarm rate.

### 5.2.2.2 Method Based on Video Initialization

In the training sequence, the background is generally required to be static. If there is still moving foreground in the training sequence, problems may occur. At this time, if the background value on each pixel can be extracted first, the static background and the moving foreground can be separated, and then the background modeling can be performed, so it is possible to overcome the aforementioned problems. This process can also be seen as initializing the training video before modeling the background, so as to filter out the influence of the motion foreground on the background modeling.

The **video initialization** can be specifically performed as follows. For $N$ frames of training images with moving foreground, first set a minimum length threshold $T_l$, and intercept the sequence of length $N$ at each pixel position to obtain several sub-sequences $\{L_k\}$, $K = 1, 2, \ldots$, with relatively stable pixel values and with length greater than $T_l$. From this, a longer sequence with a smaller variance is selected as the background sequence.

Through this initialization step, the situation where the background is static but there is a moving foreground in the training sequence can be transformed into a situation where the background is static and there is no moving foreground in the training sequence. When the background modeling problem with moving fore-ground under the static background is transformed into the background modeling problem without moving foreground under the static background, the aforemen-tioned method based on the single Gaussian model can still be used for background modeling.

### 5.2.2.3   Method Based on Gaussian Mixture Model

If there is motion for the background in the training sequence, the method based on the single Gaussian model will not work well. At this time, a more robust and effective method is to model each pixel with a mixed Gaussian distribution, that is, introduce a **Gaussian mixture model** (GMM) to model multiple states of the background separately, and update the model parameters of state according to which state the data belongs to, in order to solve the background modeling problem under the motion background.

The basic method based on Gaussian mixture model is to read each frame of training images in turn, and iteratively model every pixel in every occasion. Suppose a pixel can be (mixed) modeled with multiple Gaussian distribution weights at a certain moment. Set an initial standard deviation at the beginning of training. When a new image is read in, its pixel values are used to update the original background model. Compare each pixel value with the Gaussian function value at this time. If it falls within 2.5 times the variance around the mean, it is considered a match, that is, the pixel is considered to be compatible with the model, and its pixel value can be used to update the mean and variance of Gaussian mixture model. If the number of current pixel models is less than expected, a new model is established for this pixel. If there are multiple matches, one can choose the best.

If no match is found, the Gaussian distribution corresponding to the lowest weight is replaced with a new Gaussian distribution with a new mean. Compared with other Gaussian distributions, the new Gaussian distribution has higher variance and lower weight at this time and may become part of the local background. If the models have been judged and they do not meet the conditions, replace the model with the smallest weight with the new model. The mean of the new model is the value of the pixel, and then an initial standard deviation is set. This is done until all training images have been trained.

### 5.2.2.4   Method Based on Codebook

In the **codebook**-based method, each pixel is represented by a codebook. A codebook can contain one or more code words, and each code word represents a state. The codebook was originally generated by learning a set of training frame images. There is no restriction on the content of the training frame image, which can include moving foreground or moving background. Next, use a time domain filter to filter out the code words representing the moving foreground in the codebook, and retain the code words representing the background; then use a spatial filter to restore the code words (representing the rare background) filtered by error with the time domain filter to the codebook, to reduce the false alarms of sporadic foreground in the background region. Such a codebook represents a compressed form of the background model of a video sequence. The background model can be constructed based on the codebook.

## *5.2.3  Effect Examples*

Some test results of the above four background modeling methods are introduced as follows. In addition to the visual effect, the average value of the detection rate (the ratio of the number of detected foreground pixels to the number of real foreground pixels) and the false alarm rate (the ratio of the number of detected pixels that do not belong to the foreground to the number of all detected foreground pixels) is used for quantitative comparison.

### 5.2.3.1  No Moving Foreground in Static Background

Consider the simplest case first. In the training sequence, the background is static and there is no moving foreground. Figure 5.3 shows a set of images of experimental results. In the image sequence used, there is only a static background in the initial scene, and a person who enters the scene later is to be detected. Figure 5.3a is a scene after the entering of a person, Fig. 5.3b shows the corresponding reference result, and Fig. 5.3c shows the detection result obtained by the method based on the single Gaussian model. It can be seen from Fig. 5.3c that there are many pixels in the middle of the human body and the hair part (all in the lower gray value and relatively consistent region) that are not detected, and there are some sporadic false detection points on the background.

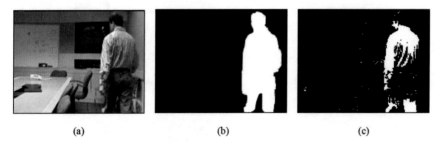

(a)                              (b)                              (c)

**Fig. 5.3**  The detection result when there is no moving foreground on a static background

### 5.2.3.2    There Is a Moving Foreground in a Static Background

Consider a slightly more complicated situation. In the training sequence, the background is static, but there is a moving foreground. Figure 5.4 shows a set of images of experimental results. In the sequence used, there is a person in the initial scene, and then he leaves, and the person who has left the scene is to be detected. Figure 5.4a is a scene when the person has not left. Figure 5.4b shows the corresponding reference result, and Fig. 5.4c shows the result obtained by the method based on video initialization. Figure 5.4d shows the results obtained with the codebook-based method.

Comparing the two methods, the codebook-based method has a higher detection rate and a lower false alarm rate than the video initialization method. This is because the codebook-based method establishes multiple code words for each pixel, thereby improving the detection rate; at the same time, the spatial filter used in the detection process reduces the false alarm rate.

### 5.2.3.3    There Is a Moving Foreground in the Moving Background

Consider a more complicated situation. The background in the training sequence is moving, and there is also a moving foreground. Figure 5.5 shows a set of images of experimental results. In the sequence used, the tree is shaking in the initial scene, and a person entering the scene is to be detected. Figure 5.5a is a scene after the entering of a person. Figure 5.5b shows the corresponding reference results. Figure 5.5c shows the results obtained by the Gaussian mixture model method. Figure 5.5d gives the result obtained with the codebook-based method.

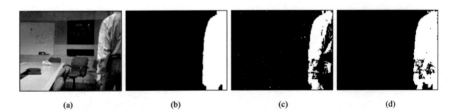

(a)                    (b)                    (c)                    (d)

**Fig. 5.4**  The result when there is a moving foreground on a static background

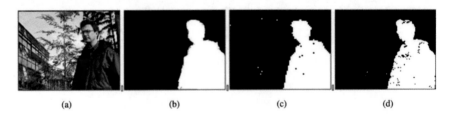

(a)                    (b)                    (c)                    (d)

**Fig. 5.5**  The result when there is a moving foreground on the moving background

Comparing the two methods, both the method based on the Gaussian mixture model and the method based on the codebook have more designing efforts for moving background, and therefore both have a higher detection rate (the detection rate of the former is slightly higher than the latter). Since the former has no processing steps corresponding to the latter's spatial filter, the false alarm rate of the former is slightly higher than that of the latter.

## 5.3   Optical Flow Field and Motion

The motion of the scenery in the scene will cause the scenery in the video image obtained during the motion to be in different relative positions. This difference in position can be called **parallax**, which corresponds to the displacement vector (including size and direction) reflecting the scenery motion on the video image. If the parallax is divided by the time difference, the velocity vector (also called the instantaneous displacement vector) can be obtained. All velocity vectors (may be different each other) in each frame of image form a vector field, which can also be called an **optical flow field** in many cases.

### 5.3.1   Optical Flow Equation

Suppose a specific image point is at $(x, y)$ at time $t$, and the image point moves to $(x + dx, y + dy)$ at time $t + dt$. If the time interval $dt$ is small, it can be expected (or assumed) that the gray level of the image point remains unchanged; in other words, there is

$$f(x, y, t) = f(x + dx, y + dy, t + dt) \tag{5.6}$$

Expand the right side of the above equation with Taylor series, set $dt \rightarrow 0$, take the limit, and omit the higher-order terms to get

$$-\frac{\partial f}{\partial t} = \frac{\partial f}{\partial x}\frac{dx}{dt} + \frac{\partial f}{\partial y}\frac{dy}{dt} = \frac{\partial f}{\partial x}u + \frac{\partial f}{\partial y}v = 0 \tag{5.7}$$

where $u$ and $v$ are the moving speed of the image point in the $X$ and $Y$ directions, respectively, and they form a speed vector with three components:

$$f_x = \frac{\partial f}{\partial x}, \quad f_y = \frac{\partial f}{\partial y}, \quad f_t = \frac{\partial f}{\partial t} \tag{5.8}$$

From Eq. (5.8), the optical flow equation obtained is

$$[f_x, f_y] \bullet [u, v]^{\mathrm{T}} = -f_t \tag{5.9}$$

The **optical flow equation** shows that the gray time change rate of a certain point in a moving image is the product of the grayscale space change rate of the point and the spatial motion speed of the point.

In practice, the grayscale time change rate can be estimated by the first-order difference average along the time direction:

$$f_t \approx \frac{1}{4}[f(x, y, t+1) + f(x+1, y, t+1) + f(x, y+1, t+1) + f(x+1, y+1, t+1)]$$
$$- \frac{1}{4}[f(x, y, t) + f(x+1, y, t) + f(x, y+1, t) + f(x+1, y+1, t)] \tag{5.10}$$

The grayscale spatial change rate can be estimated by the average value of the first-order difference along the $X$ and $Y$ directions:

$$f_x \approx \frac{1}{4}[f(x+1, y, t) + f(x+1, y+1, t) + f(x+1, y, t+1) + f(x+1, y+1, t+1)]$$
$$- \frac{1}{4}[f(x, y, t) + f(x, y+1, t) + f(x, y, t+1) + f(x, y+1, t+1)] \tag{5.11}$$

$$f_y \approx \frac{1}{4}[f(x, y+1, t) + f(x+1, y+1, t) + f(x, y+1, t+1) + f(x+1, y+1, t+1)]$$
$$- \frac{1}{4}[f(x, y, t) + f(x+1, y, t) + f(x, y, t+1) + f(x+1, y, t+1)] \tag{5.12}$$

### 5.3.2  Optical Flow Estimation with Least Square Method

After substituting Eqs. (5.10) to (5.12) into Eq. (5.9), the least square method can be used to estimate the optical flow components $u$ and $v$. Take $N$ pixels at different positions on the same object with the same $u$ and $v$ on two consecutive images $f(x, y, t)$ and $f(x, y, t+1)$; use $\widehat{f}_t^{(k)}$, $\widehat{f}_x^{(k)}$, and $\widehat{f}_y^{(k)}$ to denote the estimations of $f_t, f_x$, and $f_y$ at the $k$-th position ($k = 1, 2, \ldots, N$), respectively:

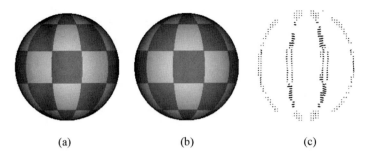

**Fig. 5.6**   Optical flow detection example

$$
f_t = \begin{bmatrix} -\widehat{f}_t^{(1)} \\ -\widehat{f}_t^{(2)} \\ \vdots \\ -\widehat{f}_t^{(N)} \end{bmatrix} \qquad
F_{xy} = \begin{bmatrix} \widehat{f}_x^{(1)} & \widehat{f}_y^{(1)} \\ \widehat{f}_x^{(2)} & \widehat{f}_y^{(2)} \\ \vdots & \vdots \\ \widehat{f}_x^{(N)} & \widehat{f}_y^{(N)} \end{bmatrix} \tag{5.13}
$$

Then the least square estimations of $u$ and $v$ are

$$
[u, v]^\mathrm{T} = \left( F_{xy}^\mathrm{T} F_{xy} \right)^{-1} F_{xy}^\mathrm{T} f_t \tag{5.14}
$$

**Example 5.1 Optical Flow Detection Example**
Figure 5.6 shows a set of examples of optical flow detection and results. Figure 5.6a
is a side image of a sphere with a pattern, and Fig. 5.6b is a side image obtained by
rotating the sphere (around the vertical axis) a small angle to the right. The motion of
the sphere in the 3-D space reflected on the 2-D image is basically a translational
motion, so in the optical flow detected in Fig. 5.6c, the parts with larger optical flow
are distributed along the meridian, reflecting the result of horizontal motion of the
vertical edge.

## 5.3.3   Optical Flow in Motion Analysis

The image difference can be used to obtain the motion trajectory. The optical flow
cannot be used to obtain the motion trajectory, but information useful for image
interpretation can be obtained. Optical flow analysis can be used to solve a variety of
motion problems: camera stationary object moving, camera moving object stationary, and both are moving.

The motion in the dynamic image can be regarded as a combination of the
following four basic motions. The detection and recognition of them by optical

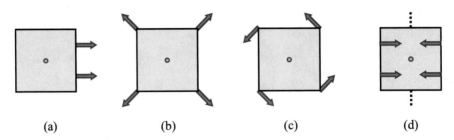

**Fig. 5.7** Recognition of motion forms

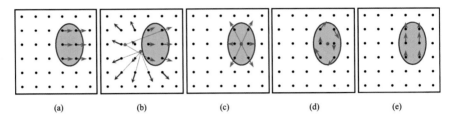

**Fig. 5.8** Explanation of the optical flow field

flow can be carried out based on their characteristics with the help of some simple operators.

1. Translation with a constant distance from the camera (may be along different directions): a group of parallel motion vectors are formed; see Fig. 5.7a.
2. The translation along the line of sight in the depth direction relative to the camera (symmetric in each direction): a set of vectors with the same **focus of expansion** (FOE) are formed; see Fig. 5.7b.
3. Equidistant rotation around the line of sight: a group of concentric motion vectors are produced; see Fig. 5.7c.
4. The rotation of the flat object orthogonal to the line of sight: constitute one or more groups of vectors starting from the straight line; see Fig. 5.7d.

**Example 5.2 Explanation of the Optical Flow Field**
The optical flow field reflects the motion in the scene. Figure 5.8 shows some examples of optical flow fields and their explanations (the length of the arrow corresponds to the speed of motion). In Fig. 5.8a, only one object moves toward the right; Fig. 5.8b corresponds to the camera moving forward (into the paper). At this time, the fixed object in the scene appears to be starting and diverging outward from the focus of expansion. In addition, there is a horizontal moving object that has its own focus of expansion. Figure 5.8c corresponds to an object moving in the direction of a fixed camera, and the focus of expansion is inside its contour (if the object moves away from the camera, it appears to leave each **focus of contraction** (FOC), which is opposite to the focus of expansion). Figure 5.8d corresponds to the situation where an object rotates around the line of sight of the camera, while

Fig. 5.8e corresponds to the situation where an object rotates around a horizontal axis orthogonal to the line of sight; the feature points on the object appear to move up and down (its contour may oscillate).

A lot of information can be obtained by analyzing motion using optical flow, such as the following:

### 5.3.3.1 Mutual Velocity

The optical flow representation can be used to determine the **mutual velocity** $T$ between the camera and the object. Let the mutual velocities in the $X$, $Y$, and $Z$ directions of the world coordinate system be $T_X = u$, $T_Y = v$, $T_Z = w$, where $Z$ gives information about the depth ($Z > 0$ represents a point in front of the image plane). If the coordinates of an object point at $t_0 = 0$ are $(X_0, Y_0, Z_0)$, then the coordinate of the image of that point (set the focal length of the optical system to one and the object moving velocity is constant) at time $t$ is

$$(x, y) = \left( \frac{X_0 + ut}{Z_0 + wt}, \quad \frac{Y_0 + vt}{Z_0 + wt} \right) \tag{5.15}$$

### 5.3.3.2 Focus of Expansion

Next, use optical flow to determine the focus of expansion of the 2-D image. Assuming that the motion is toward the camera, when $t \to -\infty$, the motion starting at an infinite distance from the camera can be obtained. This motion proceeds along a straight line toward the camera, and the starting point on the image plane is

$$(x, y)_{\text{FOE}} = \left( \frac{u}{w}, \quad \frac{v}{w} \right) \tag{5.16}$$

Note that this same equation can also be used for $t \to \infty$; at this time the motion is in the opposite direction. Any change in the direction of motion will cause changes in the speed $u$, $v$, $w$ and the position of the focus of expansion on the image.

### 5.3.3.3 Collision Distance

Assume that the origin of the image coordinates moves along the direction $S = (u/w, v/w, 1)$, and the trajectory in the world coordinate system is a straight line, namely

$$(X, Y, Z) = t \quad S = t\left(\frac{u}{w}, \frac{v}{w}, 1\right) \tag{5.17}$$

where $t$ represents time. Let $X$ represent $(X, Y, Z)$; the position of the camera closest to the world point $X$ is

$$X_c = \frac{S(S \cdot X)}{S \cdot S} \tag{5.18}$$

When the camera is moving, the minimum distance from the world point $X$ is

$$d_{min} = \sqrt{(X \cdot X) - \frac{(S \cdot X)^2}{S \cdot S}} \tag{5.19}$$

In this way, a collision occurs when the distance between a point camera and a point object is less than $d_{min}$.

### 5.3.4  Dense Optical Flow Algorithm

In order to accurately calculate the local motion vector field, a **luminance gradient-based dense optical flow algorithm** (also known as Horn-Schunck algorithm) can be used, which gradually approximates the motion vector of each pixel between adjacent frame images through an iterative method.

#### 5.3.4.1  Solving the Optical Flow Equation

The dense optical flow algorithm is based on the optical flow equation. It can be seen from the optical flow equation of (5.9) that there is one equation but two unknown quantities $(u, v)$ for each pixel, so the optical flow equation is an ill-conditioned problem; it needs to add extra constraints to transform the problem into a solvable problem. Here, the optical flow equation solving problem can be transformed into an optimization problem by introducing optical flow error and velocity field gradient error. First, define the optical flow error $e_{of}$ as the part of the motion vector field that does not meet the optical flow equation, namely

$$e_{of} = \frac{\partial f}{\partial x} u + \frac{\partial f}{\partial y} v + \frac{\partial f}{\partial t} \tag{5.20}$$

Obtaining the motion vector field is to minimize the sum of squares of $e_{of}$ in the entire frame image, that is, to minimize $e_{of}$ is to make the calculated motion vector meet the constraints of the optical flow equation as much as possible. In addition, define the velocity field gradient error $e_s^2$ as

$$e_s^2 = \left(\frac{\partial u}{\partial x}\right)^2 + \left(\frac{\partial u}{\partial y}\right)^2 + \left(\frac{\partial v}{\partial x}\right)^2 + \left(\frac{\partial v}{\partial y}\right)^2 \tag{5.21}$$

The error $e_s^2$ describes the smoothness of the optical flow field. The smaller the $e_s^2$, the closer the optical flow field is to smooth. Therefore, the meaning of minimizing $e_s^2$ is to make the entire motion vector field as smooth as possible. The dense optical flow algorithm considers two constraints at the same time, hoping to find the optical flow field $(u, v)$ that minimizes the weighted sum of the two errors in the entire frame, namely

$$\min_{\substack{u(x, y) \\ v(x, y)}} = \int_A \left[e_{of}^2(u, v) + w^2 e_s^2(u, v)\right] dxdy \tag{5.22}$$

where $A$ represents the image region and $w$ is the relative weight of optical flow error and smoothing error, used to strengthen or weaken the influence of smoothness constraints in the calculation.

When the motion in the scene is violent and the motion vector amplitude is large, the optical flow error will also be relatively large, resulting in a large error in the optimized result according to Eq. (5.22). An improvement at this time is to use the displacement frame difference term

$$f(x + \bar{u}_n, y + \bar{v}_n, t + 1) - f(x, y, t) \tag{5.23}$$

to substitute the optical flow error term $e_{of}$ and use the average gradient term

$$f_x = \frac{1}{2} \left[\frac{\partial f}{\partial x}(x + \bar{u}_n, y + \bar{v}_n, t + 1) + \frac{\partial f}{\partial x}(x, y, t)\right] \tag{5.24}$$

$$f_y = \frac{1}{2} \left[\frac{\partial f}{\partial y}(x + \bar{u}_n, y + \bar{v}_n, t + 1) + \frac{\partial f}{\partial y}(x, y, t)\right] \tag{5.25}$$

to substitute the partial derivatives $\partial f/\partial x$ and $\partial f/\partial y$, respectively; in this way, it can better approximate larger motion vectors.

Using the displacement frame difference term and average gradient term defined by Eqs. (5.23) to (5.25), the increment of the motion vector, $[\Delta u(x, y, t)_{n+1}, \Delta v(x, y, t)_{n+1}]$, calculated in the $n + 1$th iteration can be represented by the following two equations:

$$\Delta u(x, y, t)_{n+1} = -f_x \frac{[f(x + \bar{u}_n, y + \bar{v}_n, t + 1) - f(x, y, t)]}{w^2 + f_x^2 + f_y^2} \tag{5.26}$$

$$\Delta v(x, y, t)_{n+1} = -f_y \frac{[f(x + \bar{u}_n, \ y + \bar{v}_n, \ t + 1) - f(x, y, t)]}{w^2 + f_x^2 + f_y^2} \tag{5.27}$$

Finally, because the dense optical flow algorithm uses the global smoothness constraint, the motion vector at the boundary of the moving object will be smoothed into a gradual transition, which will blur the motion boundary. The following discusses how to use global motion information for motion compensation to obtain motion vectors caused by local objects.

### 5.3.4.2  Global Motion Compensation

Based on the global motion parameters caused by the camera motion, the global motion vector can be recovered according to the estimated motion parameters, so that the global motion vector is first compensated in the dense optical flow algorithm, and then the motion vector caused by local object is gradually approached with iteration.

In the actual calculation process, the global motion vector of each pixel is first calculated from the estimated **global motion vector** and then combined with the current **local motion vector** as the initial value input for the next iteration. The specific steps are as follows:

1. Set the initial local motion vector $(u_l, v_l)_0$ of all points in the image to 0.
2. Calculate the global motion vector $(u_g, v_g)$ of each point according to the global motion model.
3. Calculate the actual motion vector of each pixel

$$(\bar{u}_n, \bar{v}_n) = (\bar{u}_g, \bar{v}_g) + (\bar{u}_l, \bar{v}_l)_n \tag{5.28}$$

where $(\bar{u}_l, \bar{v}_l)_n$ is the average value of the local motion vector in the pixel neighborhood after the $n$-th iteration.

4. Calculate the correction value $(\Delta u, \Delta v)_{n+1}$ of the motion vector at this point according to Eqs. (5.26) and (5.27).
5. If the magnitude of $(\Delta u, \Delta v)_{n+1}$ is greater than a certain threshold $T$, then let

$$(\bar{u}_l, \bar{v}_l)_{n+1} = (\bar{u}_l, \bar{v}_l)_n + (\Delta u, \Delta v)_{n+1} \tag{5.29}$$

and go to step (3); otherwise, end the calculation.

Figure 5.9 shows the comparison between the calculation results of the direct **block matching** method (see Example 4.3) and the improved dense optical flow iteration algorithm with global motion compensation. For the same original image, Fig. 5.9a superimposes the motion vector field calculated by the block matching method on it, and Fig. 5.9b superimposes the motion vector estimated for the global

(a)                    (b)                    (c)

**Fig. 5.9** Comparison of calculation results of block matching method and improved dense optical flow iterative algorithm

motion (the global smoothness constraint causes the motion boundary to be inconspicuous and the motion vector amplitude is small); Fig. 5.9c superimposes the local motion vector calculated by the dense optical flow iterative algorithm with global motion compensation. It can be seen from these figures that the effect of global motion in the results of the block matching method has been successfully compensated, and the erroneous motion vectors in the low-texture background region have also been eliminated, so that the motion vectors in the final result are concentrated on the players and the ball that are moving upward are more in line with the local motion content in the scene.

## 5.4 Moving Object Tracking

To track the moving object in the video is to detect and locate the same object in each frame of the video image. The following difficulties are often encountered in practical applications:

1. The object and the background are similar, and it is not easy to capture the difference between the two.
2. The appearance of the object itself changes with time. On the one hand, some objects are nonrigid, and their appearance will inevitably change with time; on the other hand, external conditions such as light will change over time, whether it is a rigid body or a nonrigid body.
3. During the tracking process, due to the change of the spatial position between the background and the object, the tracked object may be blocked, and the (complete) object information will not be obtained. In addition, tracking must take into account the accuracy of object positioning and the real-time nature of the application.

**Moving object tracking** often combines the location and representation of the object (this is mainly a bottom-up process that needs to overcome the effects of object appearance, orientation, lighting, and scale changes) and trajectory filtering and data fusion (this is a top-down process that requires consideration of the object's motion characteristics, the use of various prior knowledge and motion models, and the promotion and evaluation of motion assumptions).

Moving object tracking can use many different methods, including contour-based tracking, region-based tracking, mask-based tracking, feature-based tracking, and motion information-based tracking. Tracking based on motion information is also divided into tracking using the continuity of motion information and tracking using the method of predicting the object location in the next frame to reduce the search range. Several commonly used techniques are introduced below, among which both Kalman filtering and particle filtering are methods to reduce the search range.

### 5.4.1  Kalman Filter

When tracking an object in the current frame, it is often desirable to be able to predict its position in the subsequent frame, so that the previous information can be utilized in maximum and the minimum search in the subsequent frame can be performed. In addition, prediction is also helpful to solve the problems caused by short-term occlusion. To this end, it is necessary to continuously update the position and speed of the tracked object point:

$$x_i = x_{i-1} + v_{i-1} \tag{5.30}$$

$$v_i = x_i - x_{i-1} \tag{5.31}$$

Here one needs to obtain three quantities: the original position, the optimal estimate of the corresponding variable (model parameter) before the observation (with sup-script mark $-$), and the optimal estimate of the corresponding variable after the observation (with sup-script mark $+$). In addition, noise needs to be considered. If $m$ is used to represent the noise of position measurement and $n$ is used to represent the noise of velocity estimation, the above two equations become

$$x_i^- = x_{i-1}^+ + v_{i-1} + m_{i-1} \tag{5.32}$$

$$v_i^- = v_{i-1}^+ + n_{i-1} \tag{5.33}$$

When the velocity is constant and the noise is Gaussian noise, the optimal solution is

$$x_i^- = x_{i-1}^+ \tag{5.34}$$

$$\sigma_i^- = \sigma_{i-1}^+ \tag{5.35}$$

They are called **prediction equations**, and

$$x_i^+ = \frac{x_i/\sigma_i^2 + \left(x_i^-\right)/\left(\sigma_i^-\right)^2}{1/\sigma_i^2 + 1/\left(\sigma_i^-\right)^2} \tag{5.36}$$

$$\sigma_i^+ = \left[\frac{1}{1/\sigma_i^2 + 1/\left(\sigma_i^-\right)^2}\right]^{1/2} \tag{5.37}$$

They are called **correction equations**, where $\sigma^\pm$ is the standard deviation obtained by estimating $x^\pm$ with the corresponding model and $\sigma$ is the standard deviation of the original measurement $x$. Here is a brief explanation why the variances in Eq. (5.37) are not combined in the usual way of addition. If there are multiple error sources all acting on the same data, these variances need to be added up. If each error source contributes the same amount of error, the variance needs to be multiplied by the number of error sources $M$. In the opposite case, if there are more data and the error source does not change, the variance needs to be divided by the total number of data points $N$. So there is a natural ratio $M/N$ to control the total error. Here, a small-scale correlation variance is used to describe the results, so the variances are combined in a special way.

It can be seen from the above equation that repeated measurements can improve the estimation of the position parameters and reduce the errors based on them in each iteration. Since the noise is modeled as the position, the positions earlier than $i-1$ can be ignored. In fact, many position values can be averaged to improve the accuracy of the final estimation, which will be reflected in the values of $x_i^-$, $\sigma_i^-$, $x_i^+$, and $\sigma_i^+$.

The above algorithm is called the **Kalman filter**, which is the best estimate for a linear system with zero mean Gaussian noise. However, since the Kalman filter is based on averaging, large errors will occur if there are outliers in the data. This problem occurs in most motion applications, so each estimate needs to be tested to determine if it is too far from the actual. Furthermore, this result can be generalized to multi-variable and variable speed (even variable acceleration) situations. At this time, define a state vector including position, velocity, and acceleration, and use linear approximation to proceed.

## 5.4.2 Particle Filter

The Kalman filter requires that the state equation is linear and the state distribution is Gaussian. These requirements are not always met in practice. **Particle filter** is an effective algorithm for solving non-linear problems. The basic idea is to use random samples (these samples are called "particles") propagated in the state space to approximate the posterior probability distribution (PPD) of the system state, thereby obtaining the estimated value of system state. The particle filter itself represents a sampling method by which a specific distribution can be approximated through a time structure. Particle filters are also often referred to as sequential Monte Carlo methods, guided filtering, etc. In the research of image technology, it is also called **CONditional DENSity propagATION** (CONDENSATION).

Suppose a system has a state $X_t = \{x_1, x_2, \ldots, x_t\}$, where the subscript represents time. At time $t$, there is a probability density function that represents the possible situation of $x_t$, which can be represented by a group of particles (a group of sampling states), and the appearance of particles is controlled by its probability density function. In addition, there are a series of observations related to the probability of state $X_t$, $Z_t = \{z_1, z_2, \ldots, z_t\}$, and a Markov hypothesis that the probability of $x_t$ depends on the previous state $x_{t-1}$, which can be expressed as $P(x_t|x_{t-1})$.

Conditional density diffusion is an iterative process. At each step, a set of $N$ samples $s_i$ with weight $w_i$ are maintained, namely

$$S_t = \{(s_{ti}, \ w_{ti})\} \quad i = 1, 2, \cdots, N \quad \sum_i w_i = 1 \tag{5.38}$$

These samples and weights together represent the probability density function of the state $X_t$ given the observation $Z_t$. Unlike the Kalman filter, the distribution does not need to meet the constraints of single-mode, Gaussian distribution, etc. and can be multi-mode. Now it is necessary to derive $S_t$ from $S_{t-1}$.

The specific steps of particle filtering are as follows:

1. Suppose a set of weighted samples $S_{t-1} = \{s_{(t-1)i}, w_{(t-1)i}\}$ at a known time $t-1$. Let the cumulative probability of weight be

$$c_0 = 0$$
$$c_i = c_{i-1} + w_{(t-1)i} \quad i = 1, 2, \cdots, N \tag{5.39}$$

2. Randomly select a number $r$ in the uniform distribution between [0 1], and determine $j = \arg[\min_i(c_i > r)]$ to calculate the $n$-th sample in $S_t$. Diffusing the $j$-th sample in $S_{t-1}$ is called **importance sampling**, that is, adding the most weight to the most likely sample.
3. Use the Markov property of $x_t$ to derive $s_{tn}$.
4. Obtain $w_{tn} = p(z_t|x_t = s_{tn})$ by observing $Z_t$.
5. Return to step (2) and iterate $N$ times.
6. Normalize $\{w_{ti}\}$ so that $\sum_i w_i = 1$.
7. Output the best estimate of $x_t$:

$$x_t = \sum_{i=1}^{N} w_{ti} s_{ti} \tag{5.40}$$

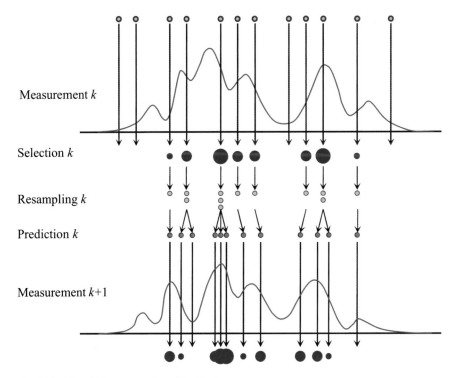

**Fig. 5.10** The whole process of particle filtering

### Example 5.3 Particle Filter Iteration Example

Consider the 1-D case, where $x_t$ and $s_t$ are only scalar real numbers. Suppose that at time $t$, $x_t$ has a displacement $v_t$ and is affected by zero-mean Gaussian noise $e$, that is, $x_{t+1} = x_t + v_t + e_t$, $e_t \sim N(0, \sigma_1^2)$. Further assume that $z_t$ is Gaussian distribution centered on $x$, and the variance is $\sigma_2^2$. Particle filtering needs to make $N$ "guess" on $x_1$, and get $S_1 = \{s_{11}, s_{12}, \ldots, s_{1N}\}$.

Now let's generate $S_2$. Choose a $s_j$ from $S_1$ (without considering the value of $w_{1i}$); let $s_{21} = s_j + v_1 + e$, where $e \sim N(0, \sigma_1^2)$. Repeat the above process $N$ times to generate particles at $t = 2$. At this time, $w_{2i} = \exp\left[(s_{2i} - z_2)^2/\sigma_2^2\right]$. Renormalize $w_{2i}$ and the iteration ends. The estimate of $x_2$ thus obtained is $\sum_i^N w_{2i} s_{2i}$.

A more detailed description of the particle filter is as follows. The particle filter is a recursive (iterative) Bayesian method that uses a set of samples of the posterior probability density function at each step. With a large number of samples (particles), it will be close to the optimal Bayesian estimation. The following is discussed with the help of the schematic process shown in Fig. 5.10.

Consider the observations $z_1$ to $z_k$ of an object in consecutive frames, corresponding to the obtained object states $x_1$ to $x_k$. At each step, the most likely state of the object needs to be estimated. Bayes' rule gives the posterior probability density:

$$p(\mathbf{x}_{k+1}|\mathbf{z}_{1:k+1}) = \frac{p(\mathbf{z}_{k+1}|\mathbf{x}_{k+1})p(\mathbf{x}_{k+1}|\mathbf{z}_{1:k})}{p(\mathbf{z}_{k+1}|\mathbf{z}_{1:k})} \tag{5.41}$$

where the normalization constant is

$$p(\mathbf{z}_{k+1}|\mathbf{z}_{1:k}) = \int p(\mathbf{z}_{k+1}|\mathbf{x}_{k+1})p(\mathbf{x}_{k+1}|\mathbf{z}_{1:k})\mathrm{d}\mathbf{x}_{k+1} \tag{5.42}$$

The prior probability density can be obtained from the last time:

$$p(\mathbf{x}_{k+1}|\mathbf{z}_{1:k}) = \int p(\mathbf{x}_{k+1}|\mathbf{x}_k)p(\mathbf{x}_k|\mathbf{z}_{1:k})\mathrm{d}\mathbf{x}_k \tag{5.43}$$

Using the Markov hypothesis common in Bayesian analysis, it can get

$$p(\mathbf{x}_{k+1}|\mathbf{x}_k, \qquad \mathbf{z}_{1:k}) = p(\mathbf{x}_{k+1}|\mathbf{x}_k) \tag{5.44}$$

That is, the transition probability required to update $x_k \rightarrow x_{k+1}$ depends only on $z_{1:k}$ indirectly.

For the above equations, especially Eqs. (5.41) and (5.43), there is no universal solution, but the constraint solution is possible. For the Kalman filter, it is assumed that all posterior probability densities are Gaussian. If the Gaussian constraint does not hold, a particle filter should be used.

To use this method, write the posterior probability density as the sum of the delta function samples:

$$p(\mathbf{x}_k| \qquad \mathbf{z}_{1:k}) \approx \sum_{i=1}^{N} w_k^i \delta(\mathbf{x}_k - \mathbf{x}_k^i) \tag{5.45}$$

Among them, the weight is normalized by the following equation:

$$\sum_{i=1}^{N} w_k^i = 1 \tag{5.46}$$

Substituting Eq. (5.41) into Eq. (5.43), it can get

$$p(\mathbf{x}_{k+1}|\mathbf{z}_{1:k+1}) \propto p(\mathbf{z}_{k+1}|\mathbf{x}_{k+1}) \sum_{i=1}^{N} w_k^i p(\mathbf{x}_{k+1}|\mathbf{x}_k^i) \tag{5.47}$$

**Fig. 5.11** Use cumulative discrete probability distribution for systematic resampling

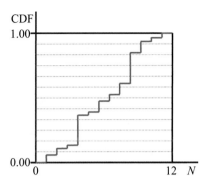

Although the above equation gives a discrete weighted approximation to the true posterior probability density, it is very difficult to directly sample from the posterior probability density. Therefore, this problem needs to use Sequence Importance Sampling (SIS), with the help of a suitable "suggested" density function $q(x_{0:k}|z_{1:k})$ to solve. The importance density function is best decomposable:

$$q(\mathbf{x}_{0:k+1}|\mathbf{z}_{1:k+1}) = q(\mathbf{x}_{k+1}|\mathbf{x}_{0:k}\,\mathbf{z}_{1:k+1})q(\mathbf{x}_{0:k}|\mathbf{z}_{1:k}) \tag{5.48}$$

Next, the weight update equation can be calculated:

$$w_{k+1}^i = w_k^i \frac{p(\mathbf{z}_{k+1}|\mathbf{x}_{k+1}^i)p(\mathbf{x}_{k+1}^i|\mathbf{x}_k^i)}{q(\mathbf{x}_{k+1}^i|\mathbf{x}_{0:k}^i,\,\mathbf{z}_{1:k+1})} = w_k^i \frac{p(\mathbf{z}_{k+1}|\mathbf{x}_{k+1}^i)p(\mathbf{x}_{k+1}^i|\mathbf{x}_k^i)}{q(\mathbf{x}_{k+1}^i|\mathbf{x}_k^i,\,\mathbf{z}_{k+1})} \tag{5.49}$$

where the path $x_{0:k}^i$ and the observation $z_{1:k}$ are eliminated, which is necessary to enable the particle filter to iteratively track in a controllable manner.

Using only the sequence importance sampling will make all but one particle become very small after a few iterations. A simple way to solve this problem is to resample to remove small weights and redouble to increase the large weights. A basic algorithm for resampling is "systematic resampling," which includes the use of cumulative discrete probability (CDF, in which the original delta function sampling is combined into a series of steps) distribution and cutting between [0 1] to find suitable indicators for the new sample. As shown in Fig. 5.11, this results in the elimination of small samples and doubles the large samples. The graph uses regularly spaced horizontal lines to indicate the cuts needed to find a suitable index $(N)$ for the new sample. These cuts tend to ignore the small steps in the CDF and strengthen large samples by doubling.

The above result is called Sampling Importance Resampling (SIR), which is important for generating a stable sample set. Using this special method, the importance density is selected as the prior probability density:

$$q\left(\mathbf{x}_{k+1}|\mathbf{x}_k^i, \mathbf{z}_{k+1}\right) = p\left(\mathbf{x}_{k+1}|\mathbf{x}_k^i\right) \tag{5.50}$$

and substituting it back into Eq. (5.49), a greatly simplified weight update equation is obtained:

$$w_{k+1}^i = w_k^i p\left(\mathbf{z}_{k+1}|\mathbf{x}_{k+1}^i\right) \tag{5.51}$$

Furthermore, since the resampling is performed at every time, all previous weights $w_k^i$ take the value $1/N$. The above equation is simplified to

$$w_{k+1}^i \propto p\left(\mathbf{z}_{k+1}|\mathbf{x}_{k+1}^i\right) \tag{5.52}$$

### 5.4.3  Mean Shift and Kernel Tracking

The **mean shift** represents the mean vector of the shift. The mean shift is a non-parametric technique that can be used to analyze complex multi-modal feature spaces and determine feature clusters. It assumes that the distribution of clusters in its central part is dense, and it iteratively calculates the mean value of the density kernel (corresponding to the centroid or the center of gravity of the cluster, which is also the most frequent value in a given window) to achieve the goal.

The principle and steps of the mean shift method are introduced below with the help of Fig. 5.12, where the dots in each figure represent the feature points in the 2-D feature space (actually maybe higher dimensional). First, randomly select an initial region of interest (initial window) and determine its centroid (as shown in Fig. 5.12a). It can also be regarded as drawing a ball with this point as the center (drawing a circle in 2-D). The radius of the ball or circle should be able to contain a certain number of data points, but not all data points can be included. Next, search for a region of interest with a greater density of surrounding points, and determine its centroid (equivalent to moving the center of the ball to a new position, which is the average position of all points in this radius), and then move the window to this

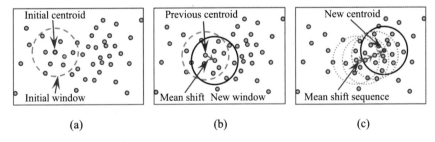

(a)                                      (b)                                      (c)

**Fig. 5.12** Schematic diagram of the principle of the mean shift method

position that is determined by the centroid, where the displacement vector between the original centroid and the new centroid corresponds to mean shift (as shown in Fig. 5.12b). Repeat the above process to continuously move the mean (the result is that the ball/circle will gradually approach the region with greater density) until convergence (as shown in Fig. 5.12c). The position of the last centroid here determines the maximum value of the local density, that is, the most frequent value of the local probability density function.

Mean shift technique can also be used for moving object tracking. At this time, the region of interest corresponds to the tracking window, and a feature model is required for the tracked object. The basic idea of using the mean shift technique for object tracking is to continuously move the object model in the tracking window to search for the position with the largest correlation value. This is equivalent to moving the window to coincide (converge) with the centroid when determining the cluster center.

In order to track the object continuously from the previous frame to the current frame, the object model determined in the previous frame can be placed at the center position $x_c$ of the local coordinate system of the tracking window, and the candidate object in the current frame is at the position $y$. The feature description of the candidate object can be described by the probability density function $p(y)$ estimated from the current frame data. The probability density functions of the object model $Q$ and the candidate object $P(y)$ are, respectively, defined as

$$Q = \{q_v\} \quad \sum_{v=1}^{m} q_v = 1 \tag{5.53}$$

$$P(y) = \{p_v(y)\} \quad \sum_{v=1}^{m} p_v = 1 \tag{5.54}$$

in which $v = 1, \ldots, m$, where $m$ is the number of features. Let $S(y)$ be the similarity function between $P(y)$ and $Q$, namely

$$S(y) = S\{P(y), Q\} \tag{5.55}$$

For an object tracking task, the similarity function $S(y)$ is the likelihood that an object to be tracked in the previous frame is at the position $y$ in the current frame. Therefore, the local extremum of $S(y)$ corresponds to the position of the object in the current frame.

In order to define the similarity function, an isotropic kernel can be used, where the description of the feature space is represented by the kernel weight, and then $S(y)$ is a smooth function of $y$. If $n$ is the total number of pixels in the tracking window and $x_i$ is the position of the $i$th pixel, the probability of the candidate object feature vector $Q_v$ in the candidate window is estimated as

$$\widehat{Q}_v = C_q \sum_{i}^{n} K(x_i - x_c) \delta[b(x_i) - q_v] \tag{5.56}$$

Among them, $b(x_i)$ is the value of the object feature function at the pixel point $x_i$; the role of the $\delta$ function is to determine whether the value of $x_i$ is the quantization result of the feature vector $Q_v$; $K(x)$ is a convex and monotonically decreasing kernel function; $C_q$ is the normalization constant

$$C_q = 1 \; / \sum_{i=1}^{n} K(x_i - x_c) \tag{5.57}$$

Similarly, the probability of the feature model vector $P_v$ of the candidate object $P(y)$ is estimated as

$$\widehat{P}_v = C_p \sum_{i}^{n} K(x_i - y)\delta[b(x_i) - p_v] \tag{5.58}$$

Among them, $C_p$ is the normalization constant (which can be calculated in advance for a given kernel function), and

$$C_p = 1 \; / \sum_{i=1}^{n} K(\mathbf{x}_i - \mathbf{y}) \tag{5.59}$$

The Bhattacharyya coefficient is usually used to estimate the degree of similarity between the object mask and the density of the candidate region. The more similar the distribution between the two densities, the greater the degree of similarity. The object center position is

$$\mathbf{y} = \frac{\sum_{i=1}^{n} x_i w_i K(\mathbf{y} - x_i)}{\sum_{i=1}^{n} w_i K(\mathbf{y} - x_i)} \tag{5.60}$$

where $w_i$ is the weighting coefficient. Note that the analytical solution of $\mathbf{y}$ cannot be obtained from Eq. (5.60), so iterative solution is required. This iterative process corresponds to a process of finding the maximum value in the neighborhood. The characteristics of the **kernel tracking** method are high operating efficiency and easy to modularize, especially for objects with regular movement and low speed, and new object center positions can always be obtained successively, so as to achieve object tracking.

### Example 5.4 Feature Selection During Tracking
In the tracking of the object, in addition to the tracking strategy and method, the choice of object features is also very important. An example is given below, which uses the color histogram and the **edge orientation histogram** (EOH) to perform tracking under the mean shift tracking framework, as shown in Fig. 5.13. Figure 5.13a is a frame of image in a video sequence, where the color of the object to be tracked is similar to the background. At this time, the color histogram does not work well (as shown in Fig. 5.13b). Using the edge orientation histogram can keep up with the object (as shown in Fig. 5.13c). Figure 5.13d is an image in another video sequence, in which the edge orientation of the object to be tracked is not obvious. At this time, the color histogram can follow the object (as shown in Fig. 5.13e), while

(a)    (b)    (c)

(d)    (e)    (f)

**Fig. 5.13** An example of tracking using a feature alone

**Fig. 5.14** An example of combining two types of feature in tracking

the use of edge orientation histogram is not effective (as shown in Fig. 5.13f). It can be seen that the use of a feature alone will lead to the result of tracking failure under certain circumstances.

The color histogram mainly reflects the information inside the object, and the edge orientation histogram mainly reflects the information of the object contour. Combining the two features, it is possible to obtain a more general effect. Figure 5.14 shows an example, where the four images correspond to the four frames of the video sequence in time order. Here is a car to be tracked. Due to the changes in the size of the object, changes in the viewing angle, and partial occlusion of the object in the video sequence, the color or outline of the car alters to a certain degree over time. By combining the color histogram and the edge orientation histogram, the joint effect is better than any of the two.

## 5.5   Key Points and References for Each Section

The following combines the main contents of each section to introduce some references that can be further consulted.

1. **Differential Image**

   Difference operation is a basic arithmetic operation; please refer to the document *2D Computer Vision: Principles, Algorithms and Applications*.

2. **Background Modeling**

   Background modeling can be seen as a method to reduce the amount of modeling calculations with the help of adaptive sub-sampling; see [1].

3. **Optical Flow Field and Motion**

   For further distinction and discussion of optical flow field and motion field, see Sect. 7.3. More discussion of Horn-Schunck algorithm can be found in [2]. In the dense optical flow algorithm, the global motion is compensated first, and then the local motion is calculated; see [3].

4. **Moving Object Tracking**

   In Kalman filtering, the use of prediction methods to solve the problem of short-term occlusion can be found in [4]. For the specific steps of particle filtering, please refer to [5]. The discussion of isotropic kernel in the mean shift technique can also be found in the [6]. More examples of selecting object features in tracking can be found in [7].

## Self-Test Questions

The following questions include both single-choice questions and multiple-choice questions, so each option must be judged.

5.1. **Differential Image**

   5.1.1 Point out the following correct description: (·).

   (a) If the value of a place in the difference image is not zero, the pixel at that place has moved.

   (b) If the value of a place in the difference image is zero, the pixel at that place has not moved.

   (c) If the pixel in a place does not move, the value at the place of the difference image is zero.

   (d) If a pixel in a place has moved, the value at the place of the difference image is not zero.

   [Hint] When the value at a place of the difference image is not zero, the pixel must have moved there, but the reverse is not necessarily true.

5.1.2 Consider a non-zero pixel in the difference image, (·).

(a) It must be an object pixel.
(b) It must be a background pixel.
(c) It may originate from an object pixel and a background pixel.
(d) It is possibly from a background pixel and an object pixel.

[Hint] There may be many reasons why the pixel value of difference image is not zero.

5.1.3 Accumulative difference image (·).

(a) Is the sum of two or more difference images
(b) Is the difference between two or more difference images
(c) Has the pixel region that is not zero with equal size to the object region
(d) Has the pixel region that is not zero with bigger size than the object region

[Hint] Consider the definition of accumulative difference image.

5.1.4 According to the accumulative difference image, it can estimate (·).

(a) The gray level of the object
(b) The size of the object
(c) The motion direction of the object
(d) The motion magnitude of the object

[Hint] The accumulative difference image counts the number of changes in position and motion situations.

## 5.2. Background Modeling

5.2.1 The reasons for the difference in pixel values between the previous and next image frames in the video sequence include (·).

(a) The camera moves when shooting
(b) There are sceneries moving in the scene
(c) The illumination has changed during the shooting
(d) The transmittance of the atmosphere has changed

[Hint] Analyze from the point of view of imaging brightness.

5.2.2 In background modeling, (·).

(a) It is assumed that the background and foreground cannot move at the same time.
(b) The same strategy is used to calculate the difference image.
(c) It is supposed that the background is fixed and the foreground is moving.
(d) It is considered that the background changes dynamically according to a certain model.

[Hint] Analyze according to the background modeling principle.

**Fig. 5.15** A flat object and
its motion vectors

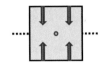

5.2.3 Various basic background modeling methods have their own characteristics: (·).

(a) The single Gaussian model can be used as long as there are no
moving objects in the background.
(b) The method based on video initialization needs to first separate the
moving foreground from the static background.
(c) The number of Gaussian distributions in the Gaussian mixture model
should be the same as the number of moving objects in the scene.
(d) The codebook produced by the codebook-based method can represent both the motion foreground and the motion background.

[Hint] Consider the ideas related to various background modeling methods,
respectively.

5.3. **Optical Flow Field and Motion**

5.3.1 The optical flow equation shows: (·).

(a) The motion of the scenery corresponds to the displacement vector on
the image
(b) All displacement vectors in the image constitute an optical flow field
(c) The gray time change rate of a certain point in the moving image is
proportional to the gray space change rate of that point
(d) The gray time change rate of a certain point in the moving image is
proportional to the spatial motion speed of that point

[Hint] The optical flow field is an instantaneous displacement vector field

5.3.2 The motion vector in Fig. 5.15 represents (·)

(a) The translation of the flat object along the vertical direction
(b) The translation of the flat object along the depth direction
(c) The rotation of the flat object orthogonal to the line of sight
(d) The flat object rotates clockwise around the line of sight

[Hint] The arrow indicates the direction of the object movement.

5.3.3 Why is it an ill-conditioned problem to solve the optical flow equation?
(·).

(a) Because the optical flow equation solving problem is an optimization
problem
(b) Because there are two unknowns in one optical flow eq.

(c) Because the optical flow equation corresponds to a smooth motion vector field

(d) Because the optical flow error has a larger amplitude in intense motion

[Hint] Consider the solution from the definition of the optical flow equation.

## 5.4. **Moving Object Tracking**

5.4.1 When tracking a moving object, (·).

(a) It needs to obtain the complete trajectory of the moving object.
(b) If the object is a nonrigid body, it cannot be tracked.
(c) If the object is blocked, the viewing angle must be changed.
(d) It can consider either the object contour or the object region.

[Hint] Having difficulty does not mean that it cannot be done.

5.4.2 Kalman filter (·).

(a) Is a tracking method based on motion information
(b) Is a tracking method based on object contour
(c) Can be used when the object is blocked
(d) Can solve the problem of nonlinear state

[Hint] Consider the characteristics of Kalman filter.

5.4.3 Particle filter (·).

(a) Needs to assume that the state distribution is Gaussian
(b) Can obtain the optimal result through iteration
(c) Is a tracking method based on the object region
(d) Uses random samples called "particles" to represent each tracking object

[Hint] Consider the characteristics of particle filters.

# References

1. Paulus C, Zhang Y J. Spatially adaptive subsampling for motion detection. Tsinghua Science and Technology, 2009, 14(4): 423-433.
2. Ohm J R, Bunjamin F, Liebsch W, et al. A set of visual feature descriptors and their combination in a low-level description scheme. SP: IC, 2000, 16(1-2): 157-179.
3. Yu T L, Zhang Y J. A local emotion information based video retrieval method. Journal of Tsinghua University (Sci & Tech), 2002, 42(7): 925-928.

4. Davies E R. Machine Vision: Theory, Algorithms, Practicalities. 3rd Ed. Elsevier. 2005.
5. Sonka M, Hlavac V, Boyle R. Image Processing, Analysis, and Machine Vision. 3rd Ed. Thomson. 2008.
6. Comaniciu D, Ramesh V, Meer P. Real-time tracking of non-rigid objects using mean shift. Proc. CVPR, 2000, 2: 142-149.
7. Liu W J, Zhang Y J. Real time object tracking using fused color and edge cues. Proc. 9th ISSPIA, 2007, 1-4.

# Chapter 6
# Binocular Stereo Vision

The human visual system is a natural stereoscopic vision system that acquires 3-D information through binocular imaging.

In computer vision, stereo vision mainly studies how to use (multi-image) imaging technology to obtain distance (depth) information of objects in a scene from (multiple) images, and its pioneering work began as early as the mid-1960s. **Stereo vision** observes the same scene from two or more viewpoints, collects a set of images from different perspectives, and then obtains the **disparity** between corresponding pixels in different images through the principle of triangulation (i.e., the difference between the positions of the two corresponding points on the image when the same 3-D point is projected on two 2-D images), from which the depth information is obtained, and then the shape of the object in the scene and the spatial position between them are calculated. The working process of stereo vision has many similarities with the perception process of the human visual system.

Artificial stereo vision using electronic equipment and computers can be realized with binocular images, trinocular images, or multi-eye images. This chapter only considers binocular stereo vision.

The sections of this chapter are arranged as follows:

Section 6.1 introduces the workflow of stereo vision and analyzes the six functional modules involved in the process of stereo vision one by one.

Section 6.2 discusses the method of matching binocular images based on regions. First, the principle of mask matching is introduced, and then the focus is on the detailed analysis of various constraints in stereo matching.

Section 6.3 discusses the method of matching binocular images based on features. Based on the introduction of the basic steps and methods, the widely used Scale Invariant Feature Transformation (SIFT) is described in detail, and dynamic programming based on ordering constraints is also discussed.

Section 6.4 introduces a method for detecting and correcting the errors of the parallax map/image, which is characterized by being more versatile and fast.

© The Author(s), under exclusive license to Springer Nature Singapore Pte Ltd. 2023
Y.-J. Zhang, *3-D Computer Vision*, https://doi.org/10.1007/978-981-19-7580-6_6

## 6.1   Stereo Vision Process and Modules

Stereo vision needs to reconstruct the objective scene in the computer, and the process is shown in Fig. 6.1. The complete stereo vision system that performs this process can be divided into six functional modules, that is, six tasks are required to complete the stereo vision task.

### *6.1.1   Camera Calibration*

**Camera calibration** has been introduced in Chap. 2. Its purpose is to determine the internal and external parameters of the camera based on an effective imaging model, so as to correctly establish the corresponding relationship between the object point in the spatial coordinate system and its image point on the image plane. In stereo vision, multiple cameras are often used, and each camera must be calibrated separately. When deriving 3-D information from 2-D image coordinates, if the camera is fixed, only one time of calibration is required. If the camera is moving, it may require multiple calibrations.

### *6.1.2   Image Acquisition*

**Image acquisition** involves two aspects of spatial coordinates and image attributes, as introduced in Chap. 3, where there is a special introduction to the acquisition of high-dimensional images containing 3-D information, including various direct imaging methods and imaging methods in stereo vision. Many direct imaging methods use specific equipment to obtain 3-D spatial information under specific environments or conditions. The video images introduced in Chap. 4 also contain spatial-temporal 3-D information.

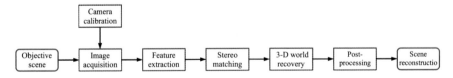

**Fig. 6.1** Stereo vision process and modules

### 6.1.3   Feature Extraction

Stereo vision helps to obtain 3-D information (especially depth information) by using the parallax between different observation points on the same scene. How to determine the corresponding relationship of the same scene in different images would be a key step/phase. One of the methods to solve this problem is to select appropriate image features to match multiple images. The **feature** here is a general concept, representing the abstract representation and description of a pixel or a set of pixels (e.g., in Sect. 6.2, the pixel gray value of the sub-image is mainly considered, and in Sect. 6.3, the grayscale distribution in the pixel neighborhood is mainly considered). At present, there is no universally applicable theory for obtaining image features. The commonly used matching features from small to large include point-like features, line-like features, planar (regional) features, and body-like (volumetric) features. Generally speaking, large-scale features contain richer image information, and the requirement for feature number is small, which is easy to obtain fast matching; but their extraction and description are relatively complicated, and the positioning accuracy is also poor. On the other hand, the small-scale features themselves have high positioning accuracy and simple representation and description; however, they are often large in number and contain less information. Therefore, strong constraint criteria and corresponding matching strategies need to be adopted when matching.

### 6.1.4   Stereo Matching

**Stereo matching** refers to the establishment of correspondence between features based on the calculation of selected features, thereby establishing the relationship between image points of the same spatial point in different images and obtaining corresponding parallax images. Stereo matching is the most important and difficult step in stereo vision. The most difficult problem of using Eqs. (3.30), (3.37), or (4.18) to calculate distance $Z$ is to find corresponding points in different images of the same scene, that is, it is to solve the problem of finding the corresponding points of the object in the two images. If the corresponding point is defined by brightness, the actual corresponding point may have different brightness on the two images due to the different observation positions of the eyes. If the corresponding point is defined by a geometric shape, the geometric shape of the object itself is just what needs to obtain. Relatively speaking, using binocular axial mode is less affected by this problem than using binocular horizontal mode. This is because of the three points, namely, the origin $(0, 0)$, as well as $(x_1, y_1)$ and $(x_2, y_2)$, are all arranged in a straight line, and the points $(x_1, y_1)$ and points $(x_2, y_2)$ are on the same side of the point $(0, 0)$, which is easier to search.

Currently, the practical technologies are mainly divided into two categories, namely, **grayscale correlation** and **feature matching**. The former type is based on the gray value of the regional pixels, which also considers the neighborhood properties of each point to be matched. The latter type is a method based on feature points, that is, first select points with unique or special properties in the image as matching points. The features used by the latter method are mainly the coordinates of inflection point and corner point in the image, the edge line segment, the contour of the object, and so on. The above two methods are similar to the region-based and edge-based methods in image segmentation. Sections 6.2 and 6.3 will, respectively, introduce some matching methods based on regional gray level correlation and feature points.

### 6.1.5   3-D Information Recovery

After the parallax image is obtained through stereo matching, the depth image can be further calculated, and the 3-D world/information in the scene can be restored (this is also often referred to as **3-D reconstruction**). The factors that affect the accuracy of distance measurement mainly include digital quantization effects, camera calibration errors, exactness of feature detection, as well as matching and positioning. Generally speaking, the accuracy of distance measurement is directly proportional to the exactness of matching and positioning and is proportional to the length of the camera baseline (line between different camera positions). Increasing the length of the baseline can improve the depth measurement accuracy, but at the same time, it will increase the difference between the corresponding images, and the possibility of the scene being blocked is greater, thereby increasing the difficulty of matching. Therefore, in order to design an accurate stereo vision system, various factors must be considered comprehensively to ensure that each aspect has high accuracy, so that the 3-D information can be accurately restored.

By the way, accuracy is an important indicator in 3-D information recovery, but some models try to circumvent this problem. For example, in the network-symbol model, it is not necessary to accurately reconstruct or calculate the 3-D model but to transform the image into an understandable relational format similar to the knowledge model. In this way, there is no need to limit the accuracy of 3-D information recovery. Using the network-symbol model, it is no longer necessary to perform object recognition based on the field of view but based on the derived structure, and it is less affected by local changes and the appearance of the object.

### 6.1.6   Post-Processing

The 3-D information obtained through the above steps is often incomplete or has certain errors due to various reasons and requires further post-processing. There are three main types of commonly used post-processing:

### 6.1.6.1   Depth Interpolation

The primary purpose of stereo vision is to restore the complete information of the visual surface of the scene, and the feature-based stereo matching algorithm can only directly restore the parallax values at the feature points in the image because the features are often discrete. Therefore, a parallax surface interpolation and reconstruction step is added in the post-processing, that is, the discrete data is interpolated to obtain the parallax values that are not at the feature points. There are many **interpolation** methods, such as nearest neighbor interpolation, bilinear interpolation, and spline interpolation. There are also model-based interpolation reconstruction algorithms. During the interpolation process, the main concern is how to effectively protect the discontinuous information on the surface of the scene.

### 6.1.6.2   Error Correction

Stereo matching is performed between images affected by geometric distortion and noise interference. In addition, due to the existence of periodic patterns and smooth regions in the image, as well as the occlusion effect and the lack of strictness of the constraint principle, errors will occur in the parallax image. The detection and correction of errors are therefore also an important post-processing content. It is often necessary to select appropriate techniques and methods according to the specific reasons and methods of error. Section 6.4 will introduce an **error correction** algorithm.

### 6.1.6.3   Precision Improvement

The calculation of parallax and the restoration of depth information are the basis of subsequent work. Therefore, the precision of parallax calculation is often highly demanded in specific applications. In order to further improve the precision, after obtaining the usual pixel-level parallax of general stereo vision, the precision can be further improved to achieve **subpixel-level disparity** accuracy.

## 6.2   Region-Based Stereo Matching

Determining the relationship of the corresponding points in the binocular image is a key step to obtain the depth image. The following discussion only takes the **binocular horizontal mode** as an example. If the unique geometric relationships among various modes are considered, the results obtained with the binocular horizontal mode can also be extended to other modes.

The most intuitive way to determine the relationship between corresponding points is to use point-to-point correspondence matching. However, the direct use of the grayscale of a single pixel for matching will be affected by factors such as many points in the image with the same gray values and interfering noise in the image. In addition, when a spatial 3-D scene is projected onto a 2-D image, not only the same scene may have different appearances in images from different viewpoints, but also many changing factors in the scene, such as various lighting conditions, noise interference, scene geometry and distortion, surface physical appearances, and camera characteristics, are all integrated into a single image gray value. It is very difficult to determine the above factors separately from this gray value. So far this problem has not been well solved.

### 6.2.1  Template Matching

The region-based method needs to consider the nature of the neighborhood of the point, and the neighborhood is often determined with the help of **templates** (also called mask, sub-images, or windows). When a point in the left image of a given binocular image pair needs to be searched for a matching point in the corresponding right image, the neighborhood centered on the point in the left image can be extracted as a mask, and the mask can be translated on the right image, and calculate the correlation with each position, to determine whether it matches according to the correlation value. If it matches, it is considered that the center point of the matching position in the right image and that point in the left image form a corresponding point pair. Here, the place of maximum correlation value can be selected as the matching position, or a threshold value can be given first, and the points satisfying the correlation value greater than the threshold value can be extracted first and then selected according to some other factors.

The generally used matching method is called **template matching**, and its essence is to use a mask (smaller image) to match a part (sub-image) of a larger image. The result of the matching is to determine whether there is a small image in the large image, and if so, the position of the small image in the large image is further determined. In template matching, the template is often square, but it can also be rectangular or other shapes. Now consider finding the matching position of a template image $w(x, y)$ of size $J \times K$ and a large image $f(x, y)$ of $M \times N$; set $J \leq M$ and $K \leq N$. In the simplest case, the correlation function between $f(x, y)$ and $w(x, y)$ can be written as

$$c(s, t) = \sum_x \sum_y f(x, y) w(x - s, y - t) \tag{6.1}$$

where $s = 0, 1, 2, \ldots, M - 1$; $t = 0, 1, 2, \ldots, N - 1$.

The summation in Eq. (6.1) is performed on the image region where $f(x, y)$ and $w(x, y)$ overlap. Figure 6.2 shows a schematic diagram of related calculations,

**Fig. 6.2** Template
matching schematic

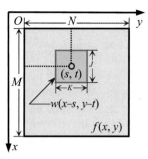

assuming that the origin of $f(x, y)$ is at the upper left corner of the image and the
origin of $w(x, y)$ is at the center of the template. For any given position $(s, t)$ in $f(x, y)$,
a specific value of $c(s, t)$ can be calculated according to Eq. (6.1). When $s$ and
$t$ change, $w(x, y)$ moves in the image region and gives all the values of the function
$c(s, t)$. The maximum value of $c(s, t)$ indicates the position that best matches $w(x, y)$.
Note that for $s$ and $t$ values close to the boundary of $f(x, y)$, the matching accuracy
will be affected by the image boundary, and the error is proportional to the size of
$w(x, y)$.

In addition to determining the matching position according to the maximum
correlation criterion, the minimum mean square error function can also be used:

$$M_{me}(s, t) = \frac{1}{MN} \sum_x \sum_y [f(x, y)w(x - s, y - t)]^2 \tag{6.2}$$

In VLSI hardware, the square operation is more difficult to implement, so the
absolute value can be used instead of the square value to get the minimum average
difference function:

$$M_{ad}(s, t) = \frac{1}{MN} \sum_x \sum_y |f(x, y)w(x - s, y - t)| \tag{6.3}$$

The correlation function defined by Eq. (6.1) has a drawback, that is, it is more
sensitive to changes in the amplitude of $f(x, y)$ and $w(x, y)$. For example, when the
value of $f(x, y)$ is doubled, the value of $c(s, t)$ will also be doubled. To overcome this
problem, the following correlation coefficient can be defined:

$$C(s, t) = \frac{\sum_x \sum_y [f(x, y) - \bar{f}(x, y)][w(x - s, y - t) - \bar{w}]}{\left\{ \sum_x \sum_y [f(x, y) - \bar{f}(x, y)]^2 \sum_x \sum_y [w(x - s, y - t) - \bar{w}]^2 \right\}^{1/2}} \tag{6.4}$$

where $s = 0, 1, 2, \ldots, M - 1; t = 0, 1, 2, \ldots, N - 1$, $\bar{w}$ is the mean value of $w$ (it needs
to be calculated once), and $\bar{f}(x, y)$ represents the mean value of the region
corresponding to the current position of $w$ in $f(x, y)$.

The summation in Eq. (6.4) is performed on the common coordinates of $f(x, y)$ and $w(x, y)$. Because the correlation coefficient has been scaled to the interval $[-1, 1]$, the change in its value is independent of the amplitude change of $f(x, y)$ and $w(x, y)$.

Another method is to calculate the gray level difference between the template and the sub-image and establish the correspondence between the two sets of pixels that meet the **mean square difference** (MSD). The advantage of this type of method is that the matching result is not easily affected by the grayscale detection accuracy and density of the template, so it can get a high positioning accuracy and a dense parallax surface. The disadvantage of this type of method is that it relies on the statistical characteristics of the image gray level, so it is more sensitive to the surface structure of the scene and the reflection of light. Therefore, there are certain difficulties for the surface of the space scene that lacks sufficient texture details, and the imaging distortion is large (such as the baseline length is too large). Some derivation of gray levels can also be used in actual matching, but experiments have shown that in matching comparisons using gray level, gray level difference and direction, gray level Laplacian value, and gray level curvature as matching parameters, the gray level is still the best in matching.

As a basic matching technique, template matching has been applied in many aspects, especially when the image is only shifted. Using the calculation of the correlation coefficient above, the correlation function can be normalized to overcome the problems caused by the amplitude change. But it is more difficult to normalize the image size and rotation. The normalization of the size requires spatial scale transformation, and this process requires a lot of calculations. Normalizing the rotation is more difficult. If the rotation angle of $f(x, y)$ is known, it is possible to just rotate $w(x, y)$ by the same angle to align $w(x, y)$ with $f(x, y)$. But without knowing the rotation angle of $f(x, y)$, to find the best match, one needs to rotate $w(x, y)$ at all possible angles. In practice, this method is not feasible, so it is seldom to directly use region-related methods (such as template matching) under arbitrary rotation or without constraints on rotation.

The method of image matching using templates representing matching primitives must solve the problem that the amount of calculation will increase exponentially with the number of primitives. If the number of primitives in the image is $n$ and the number of primitives in the template is $m$, there are $O(n^m)$ possible correspondences between the primitives of the template and the image, where the number of combinations is $C(n, m)$ or $C_m^n$.

**Example 6.1 Template Matching Using Geometric Hashing**
To achieve efficient template matching, **geometric hashing** can also be used. Its basis is that three points can define a 2-D plane. That is, if you choose three non-collinear points $P_1$, $P_2$, $P_3$, you can use the linear combination of these three points to represent any point:

$$Q = P_1 + s(P_2 - P_1) + t(P_3 - P_1) \qquad (6.5)$$

Equation (6.5) will not change under the affine transformation, that is, the value of $(s, t)$ is only related to the three non-collinear points and has nothing to do with the affine transformation itself. In this way, the value of $(s, t)$ can be regarded as the affine coordinates of point $Q$. This feature is also applicable to line segments: three non-parallel line segments can be used to define an affine benchmark.

Geometric hashing requires the construction of a hash table, which can help the matching algorithm to quickly determine the potential position of a template in the image. The hash table can be constructed as follows: For any three non-collinear points (reference point group) in the template, calculate the affine coordinates $(s, t)$ of other points. The affine coordinates $(s, t)$ of these points will be used as the index of the hash table. For each point, the hash table retains the index (serial number) of the current reference point group. If you want to search for multiple templates in an image, you need to keep more template indexes.

To search for a template, randomly select a set of reference points in the image, and calculate the affine coordinates $(s, t)$ of other points. Using this affine coordinate $(s, t)$ as the index of the hash table, the index of the reference point group can be obtained. In this way, a vote for the occurrence of this reference point group in the image is obtained. If the randomly selected points do not correspond to the reference point group on the template, there is no need to accept voting. However, if the randomly selected point corresponds to the reference point group on the template, the vote is accepted. If many votes are accepted, it means that this template is likely to be in the image, and the benchmark set of indicators can be obtained. Because the selected set of reference points will have a certain probability of being inappropriate, the algorithm needs to iterate to increase the probability of finding the correct match. In fact, it is only necessary to find a correct set of reference points to determine the matching template. Therefore, if $k$ points of the $N$ template points are found in the image, the probability that the reference point group is correctly selected at least once in $m$ attempts is

$$p = 1 - \left[1 - (k/N)^3\right]^m \tag{6.6}$$

In the image, if the ratio of the number of points in the template to the number of image points $k/N$ is 0.2, and the expected probability of the template matching is 99% (i.e., $p = 0.99$), then the number of attempts $m$ is 574.

## 6.2.2 Stereo Matching

Using the principle of template matching, the similarity of regional gray levels can be used to search for the corresponding points of two images. Specifically, in the stereo image pair, first select a window centered on a certain pixel in the left image, construct a template based on the grayscale distribution in the window, and then use the template to search in the right image to find the most matching window position, and then the pixel in the center of the matching window corresponds to the pixel to be matched in the left image.

In the above search process, if there is no prior knowledge or any restriction on the position of the template in the right image, the search range may cover the entire right image. It is time-consuming to search in this way for each pixel in the left image. In order to reduce the search range, it is better to consider using some constraints, such as the following three constraints.

1. Compatibility constraints. **Compatibility constraint** means that black dots can only match black dots. More generally speaking, only the features of the same type of physical properties in the two images can be matched. It is also called **photometric compatibility constraint**.
2. Uniqueness constraint. The **uniqueness constraint** means that a single black point in one image can only be matched with a single black point in another image.
3. Continuity constraints. The **continuous constraint** means that the parallax change near the matching point is smooth (gradual) in most points except the occluded region or the discontinuous region in the entire image, which is also called the **disparity smoothness constraint**.

When discussing stereo matching, in addition to the above three constraints, you can also consider the epipolar constraints introduced below and the sequential constraints introduced in Sect. 6.3.

### 6.2.2.1 Epipolar Line Constraint

The **epipolar line constraint** can help reduce the search range (from 2-D to 1-D) during the search process and speed up the search process.

First, introduce the two important concepts of **epipole** and **epipolar line** with the help of the binocular lateral convergence mode diagram in Fig. 6.3. In Fig. 6.3, the left eye center is at the origin of the coordinate system, the $X$ axis connects the left and right eye centers, the $Z$ axis points to the observation direction, the distance between the left and right eyes is $B$ (also often called the system baseline), the optical

**Fig. 6.3** Schematic diagram of epipoles and epipolar lines

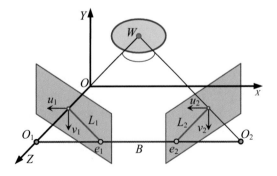

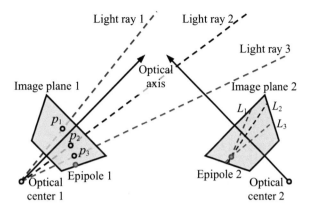

**Fig. 6.4** Correspondence between epipoles and epipolar lines

axis of the left and right image planes is all in the *XZ* plane, and the angle of intersection is $\theta$. Consider the connection between the left and right image planes. $O_1$ and $O_2$ are the optical centers of the left and right image planes, and the connecting line between them is called the optical center line. The intersection points $^e{}_1$ and $^e{}_2$ of the optical center line with the left and right image planes are called the poles of the left and right image planes (the pole coordinates are $e_1$ and $e_2$, respectively). The optical center line and the spatial point *W* are in the same plane. This plane is called the **polar plane**. The intersection lines $L_1$ and $L_2$ of the polar plane and the left and right image planes are, respectively, called the polar lines of the projection points of the spatial point *W* on the left and right image planes. The polar line defines the position of the corresponding point of the binocular image, and the right image plane projection point $p_2$ (coordinates $p_2$) corresponding to the projection point $p_1$ (coordinates $p_1$) of the space point *W* on the left image plane must be on the polar line $L_2$. On the contrary, the projection point of the left image plane corresponding to the projection point of the spatial point *W* on the right image plane must be on the epipolar line $L_1$.

### Example 6.2 Correspondence Between Epipoles and Epipolar Lines

There are two sets of optical systems in the binocular stereo vision system, as shown in Fig. 6.4. Consider a set of points $(p_1, p_2, ...)$ on the image plane 1, and each point corresponds to a ray in the 3-D space. Each ray projects a line $(L_1, L_2, ...)$ on the image plane 2. Because all light rays converge to the optical center of the first camera, these lines must intersect at a point on the image plane 2. This point is the image of the optical center of the first camera in the second camera, which is called the epipole. Similarly, the image of the optical center of the second camera in the first camera is also an epipole. These projection lines are epipolar lines.

### Example 6.3 Epipolar Line Mode

The epipoles are not always in the observed image, because the epipolar lines may intersect outside the field of view. There are two common situations shown in Fig. 6.5. First, in the binocular horizontal mode, the two cameras are facing the same direction, there is a certain distance between their optical axes, and the

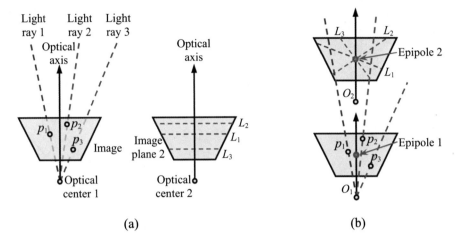

**Fig. 6.5** Epipolar line mode example

coordinate axes of the image plane are correspondingly parallel, then the epipolar lines will form a parallel pattern, and the intersection (epipole) will be at infinity, as shown in Fig. 6.5a. Second, in the binocular axial mode, the optical axes of the two cameras are in a line, and the image plane coordinate axes are correspondingly parallel, then the epipoles are in the middle of the corresponding images, and the epipolar lines will form a radiation pattern, as shown in Fig. 6.5b. Both cases indicate that the epipolar mode provides information about the relative position and orientation of the cameras.

The epipolar line defines the positions of the corresponding points on the binocular image. The projection point of the right image plane that corresponds to the projection point of the space point $W$ on the left image plane must be on the epipolar line $L_2$; on the contrary, the projection point of the left image plane that corresponds to the projection point of the space point $W$ on the right image plane must be on the epipolar line $L_1$. This is the **epipolar line constraint**.

In binocular vision, when an ideal parallel optical axis model is used (i.e., the lines of sight of every camera are parallel), the epipolar line coincides with the image scan line, and the stereo vision system at this time is called the parallel stereo vision system. In parallel stereo vision systems, epipolar line constraints can also be used to reduce the search range of stereo matching. In an ideal situation, the use of epipolar constraints can change the search for the entire image into a search for a line in the image. But it should be pointed out that the epipolar line constraint is only a local constraint. For a space point, there may be more than one projection point on the epipolar line.

**Example 6.4 Epipolar Line Constraint Diagram**
As shown in Fig. 6.6, use a camera (left) to observe a point $W$ in space. The imaged point $p_1$ should be on the line connecting the optical center of the camera and point $W$. However, all points on the line will be imaged at point $p_1$, so the position/distance

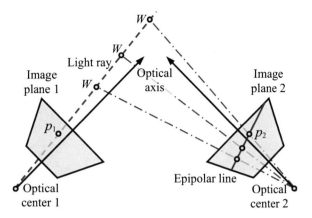

**Fig. 6.6** Epipolar line constraint illustration

of a specific point $W$ cannot be completely determined from point $p_1$. Now use the second camera to observe the same spatial point $W$, and the imaged point $p_2$ should also be on the line connecting the optical center of the camera and point $W$. All points like $W$ on this line are projected onto a straight line on the image plane 2, and this straight line is called an **epipolar line**.

From the geometric relationship in Fig. 6.6, it can be seen that for any point $p_1$ on image plane 1, the image plane 2 and all its corresponding points are (constrained) on the same straight line, which is the epipolar line constraint mentioned above.

### 6.2.2.2 Essential Matrix and Fundamental Matrix

The connection between the projected coordinate points of the space point $W$ on the two images can be described by an **essential matrix $E$** with five degrees of freedom, which can be decomposed into an orthogonal rotation matrix $R$ followed by a translation matrix $T$ ($E = RT$). If the projection point coordinates in the left image are represented by $p_1$, and the projection point coordinates in the right image are represented by $p_2$, then

$$p_2^T E p_1 = 0 \tag{6.7}$$

The epipolar lines passing through $p_1$ and $p_2$ on the corresponding image satisfy $L_2 = E^p{}_1$ and $L_1 = E^{Tp}{}_2$, respectively. On the corresponding image, the epipoles passing through $p_1$ and $p_2$ satisfy $Ee_1 = 0$ and $E^T e_2 = 0$, respectively.

### Example 6.5 Derivation of Essential Matrix

The essential matrix indicates the relationship between the projection point coordinates of the same space point $W$ (coordinates $W$) on the two images. In Fig. 6.7, suppose you can observe the projection positions $p_1$ and $p_2$ of the point $W$ on the image, and you also know the rotation matrix $R$ and the translation matrix $T$ between the two cameras; then you can get three 3-D vectors $O_1O_2$, $O_1W$, and $O_2W$. The three

**Fig. 6.7** The derivation of
the essential matrix

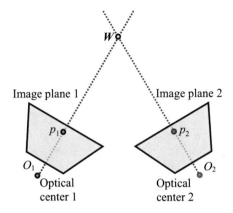

3-D vectors must be coplanar. Because in mathematics, the criterion that three 3-D vectors $\boldsymbol{a}$, $\boldsymbol{b}$, and $\boldsymbol{c}$ are coplanar can be written as $\boldsymbol{a} \cdot (\boldsymbol{b} \times \boldsymbol{c}) = 0$, this criterion can be used to derive the essential matrix.

According to the perspective relationship of the second camera, it is known: vector $\boldsymbol{O}_1\boldsymbol{W} \propto \boldsymbol{R}\boldsymbol{p}_1$, vector $\boldsymbol{O}_1\boldsymbol{O}_2 \propto \boldsymbol{T}$, and vector $\boldsymbol{O}_2\boldsymbol{W} = \boldsymbol{p}_2$. Combining these relationships with the coplanar condition, you get the desired result:

$$\boldsymbol{p}_2^T(\boldsymbol{T} \times \boldsymbol{R}\boldsymbol{p}_1) = \boldsymbol{p}_2^T\boldsymbol{E}\boldsymbol{p}_1 = 0 \tag{6.8}$$

The epipolar lines passing through points $p_1$ and $p_2$ on the corresponding image satisfy $\boldsymbol{L}_2 = \boldsymbol{E}\boldsymbol{p}_1$ and $\boldsymbol{L}_1 = \boldsymbol{E}^T\boldsymbol{p}_2$, respectively. The epipoles $e_1$ and $e_2$ passing through points $p_1$ and $p_2$ on the corresponding image satisfy $\boldsymbol{E}\boldsymbol{e}_1 = 0$ and $\boldsymbol{E}^T\boldsymbol{e}_2 = 0$, respectively.

In the above discussion, it is assumed that $\boldsymbol{p}_1$ and $\boldsymbol{p}_2$ are the pixel coordinates after the camera has been corrected. If the camera has not been calibrated, the original pixel coordinates $\boldsymbol{q}_1$ and $\boldsymbol{q}_2$ need to be used. Suppose the internal parameter matrix of the camera is $\boldsymbol{G}_1$ and $\boldsymbol{G}_2$, then

$$\boldsymbol{p}_1 = \boldsymbol{G}_1^{-1}\boldsymbol{q}_1 \tag{6.9}$$

$$\boldsymbol{p}_2 = \boldsymbol{G}_2^{-1}\boldsymbol{q}_2 \tag{6.10}$$

Substituting the above two equations into Eq. (6.7), it gives $\boldsymbol{q}_2^T(\boldsymbol{G}_2^{-1})^T\boldsymbol{E}\boldsymbol{G}_1^{-1}\boldsymbol{q}_1 = 0$, which can be written as

$$\boldsymbol{q}_2^T\boldsymbol{F}\boldsymbol{q}_1 = 0 \tag{6.11}$$

where

$$F = \left(G_2^{-1}\right)^{\mathrm{T}} E G_1^{-1} \qquad (6.12)$$

It is called the **fundamental matrix** because it contains all the information for camera calibration. The fundamental matrix has 7 degrees of freedom (each epipole requires two parameters, plus three parameters to map three epipolar lines from one image to another image, because the projective transformation in the two 1-D projection spaces has 3 degrees of freedom). The essential matrix has 5 degrees of freedom, so the fundamental matrix has two more free parameters than the essential matrix. However, by comparing Eqs. (6.7) and (6.11), it shows that the roles or functions of these two matrices are similar.

The essential matrix and the fundamental matrix are related to the internal and external parameters of the camera. If the internal and external parameters of the camera are given, it can be known from the epipolar line constraint that for any point on the image plane 1, a 1-D search only needs to be performed on the image plane 2 to determine the position of the corresponding point. Further, the correspondence constraint is a function of the internal and external parameters of the camera. Given the internal parameters, the external parameters can be determined by the observed pattern of the corresponding points, and the geometric relationship between the two cameras can be established.

### 6.2.2.3   Influencing Factors in Matching

There are still some specific issues that need to be considered and resolved when using the region matching method in practice.

1. Due to the shape of the scenery or the occlusion of the scenery when shooting the scene, the scenery captured by the left camera may not be all captured by the right camera, so some templates determined with the left image may not be able to find an exact match in the right image. At this time, it is often necessary to perform interpolation based on the matching results of other matching positions to obtain the data of these unmatched points.
2. When using the pattern of a template image to represent the characteristics of a single pixel, the premise is that different template images should have different patterns, so that the matching can be distinguished, that is, it can reflect the characteristics of different pixels. But sometimes there are certain smooth regions in the image, and the template images obtained in these smooth regions have the same or similar patterns; there will be uncertainty in the matching, leading to mismatches. In order to solve this problem, it is sometimes necessary to project some random textures onto these surfaces to convert smooth regions into texture regions, thereby obtaining template images with different patterns to eliminate uncertainty.

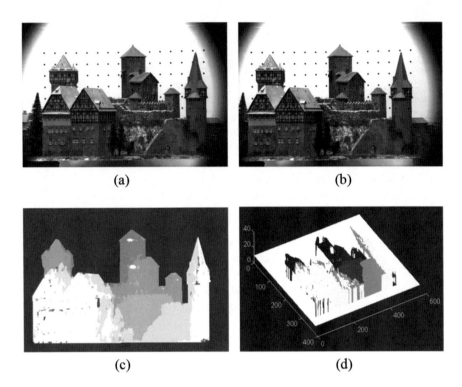

(a)                                                  (b)

(c)                                                  (d)

**Fig. 6.8**  Binocular stereo matching is affected by the smooth region of the image

## Example 6.6 Binocular Stereo Matching Is Affected by the Smooth Region of the Image

Figure 6.8 shows an example of stereo matching errors when there are smooth grayscale regions along the binocular baseline direction. Figure 6.8a, b are the left and right images of a pair of perspective views, respectively. Figure 6.8c is a parallax image obtained by using binocular stereo matching (here, for clarity, only the result of scene matching is retained), the darker gray in the image represents a longer distance (larger depth), and the lighter gray represents a closer distance (smaller depth). Figure 6.8d is a 3-D perspective view (contour map) corresponding to Fig. 6.8c. Comparing these images, it can be seen that because the gray values of some locations in the scene (such as the horizontal eaves of towers and houses, etc.) are roughly similar along the horizontal direction, it is difficult to search and match them along the epipolar line. Determining the corresponding points produced a lot of errors due to mismatching. In Fig. 6.8c, there are some white or black (patch) regions that are inconsistent with the surroundings, while reflecting in Fig. 6.8d there are some sharp glitch regions.

### 6.2.2.4  Calculation of Surface Optical Properties

Using the grayscale information of the binocular image, it is possible to further calculate some optical properties of the object surface (see Sect. 7.1). There are two factors to pay attention for the reflection characteristics of the surface: one is the scattering caused by surface roughness; the other is the specular reflection caused by the surface compactness. The two factors are combined as follows: let $N$ be the unit vector in the normal direction of the surface patch, $S$ is the unit vector in the direction of the point light source, and $V$ is the unit vector in the direction of the observer's line of sight, and the reflecting brightness obtained on the patch $I(x, y)$ is the product of the composed reflectance $\rho(x, y)$ and the composed reflectance $R[N(x, y)]$, namely

$$I(x, y) = \rho(x, y)R[N(x, y)] \tag{6.13}$$

where

$$R[N(x, y)] = (1 - \alpha)N \cdot S + \alpha(N \cdot H)^k \tag{6.14}$$

Among them, $\rho$, $\alpha$, and $k$ are coefficients related to the surface optical properties, which can be calculated from the image data.

The first term on the right side of the Eq. (6.14) considers the scattering effect, which does not vary with the angle of sight; the second term considers the specular reflection effect. Let $H$ be the unit vector in the direction of the specular reflection angle:

$$H = \frac{(S + V)}{\sqrt{2[1 + (S \cdot V)]}} \tag{6.15}$$

The second term on the right side of the Eq. (6.14) reflects the change of the line of sight vector $V$ through the vector $H$. In the coordinate system used in Fig. 6.3

$$\begin{aligned} V' &= \{0, \ 0, \ -1\} \\ V'' &= \{-\sin\theta, \ 0, \ \cos\theta\} \end{aligned} \tag{6.16}$$

## 6.3  Feature-Based Stereo Matching

The disadvantage of the region-based matching method is that it relies on the statistical characteristics of the image gray level, so it is more sensitive to the surface structure of the scenery and the light reflection. If the scenery surface lacks enough texture details on the space (such as along the epipolar direction in Example 6.6), there are certain difficulties when imaging distortion is large (e.g., the baseline length is too large). Taking into account the characteristics of the actual image, some salient **feature points** (also called control points, key points, or matching points) in the image can be determined first, and then these feature points can be used for matching. Feature points are less sensitive to changes in ambient lighting during matching, and their performance is relatively stable.

### 6.3.1 Basic Steps and Methods

The main steps of feature point matching are as follows:

1. Select feature points for matching in the image. The most commonly used feature points are some special points in the image, such as edge points, corner points, inflection points, landmark points, etc. In recent years, local feature points (local feature descriptors), such as SIFT points (see below), are also widely used.
2. Match the feature point pairs in the stereo image pair (see below; also refer to Chap. 10).
3. Calculate the parallax of the matching point pair, and obtain the depth at the matching point (similar to the region-based method in Sect. 6.2).
4. Interpolate the result of the sparse depth values to obtain a dense depth map (because the feature points are discrete, the dense parallax field cannot be directly obtained after matching).

#### 6.3.1.1  Matching with Edge Points

For an image $f(x, y)$, the feature point image can be obtained by calculating the edge points:

$$t(x, y) = \max \{H, \quad V, \quad L, \quad R\} \tag{6.17}$$

where $H, V, L, R$ are all calculated by gray gradient

$$H = [f(x, y) - f(x - 1, y)]^2 + [f(x, y) - f(x + 1, y)]^2 \tag{6.18}$$

$$V = [f(x, y) - f(x, y - 1)]^2 + [f(x, y) - f(x, y + 1)]^2 \tag{6.19}$$

$$L = [f(x, y) - f(x - 1, y + 1)]^2 + [f(x, y) - f(x + 1, y - 1)]^2 \tag{6.20}$$

$$R = [f(x, y) - f(x + 1, y + 1)]^2 + [f(x, y) - f(x - 1, y - 1)]^2 \tag{6.21}$$

Then $t(x, y)$ is divided into small regions $W$ that do not overlap each other, and the point with the largest calculated value is selected as the feature point in each small region.

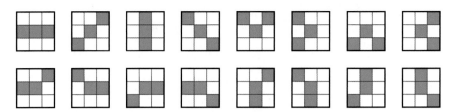

**Fig. 6.9** The diagram of 16 kinds of zero-crossing patterns

Now consider matching the image pair formed by the left image and the right image. For each feature point of the left image, all possible matching points in the right image can be formed into a possible matching point set. In this way, a label set can be obtained for each feature point of the left image, where the label $l$ is either the parallax between the left image feature point and its possible matching points or a special label representing no matching point. For each possible matching point, calculate the following equation to set the initial matching probability $P^{(0)}(l)$:

$$A(l) = \sum_{x,y \in W} \left[ f_L(x, y) - fR(x + l_x, y + l_y) \right]^2 \tag{6.22}$$

where $l = (l_x, l_y)$ is the possible parallax. $A(l)$ represents the grayscale fit between the two regions, which is inversely proportional to the initial matching probability $P^{(0)}$ $(l)$. In other words, $P^{(0)}(l)$ is related to the similarity in the neighborhood of possible matching points. Accordingly, with the aid of the relaxation iteration method, the points with close parallax in the neighborhood of possible matching points are given positive increments, and the points with distant parallax in the neighborhood of possible matching points are given negative increments to adjust $P^{(0)}(l)$ for iterative update. As the iteration progresses, the iterative matching probability $P^{(k)}(l)$ of the correct matching point will gradually increase, while the iterative matching probability $P^{(k)}(l)$ of other points will gradually decrease. After a certain number of iterations, the point with the largest matching probability $P^{(k)}(l)$ is determined as the matching point.

### 6.3.1.2 Matching with Zero-Crossing Points

When matching feature points, the **zero-crossing pattern** can also be selected to obtain matching primitives. Use the Laplacian (of Gaussian function) to perform convolution to get the zero-crossing point. Considering the connectivity of the zero-crossing points, 16 different zero-crossing patterns of $3 \times 3$ templates can be determined, as shown by the shadows in Fig. 6.9.

For each zero-crossing pattern of the left image in the binocular image, all possible matching points in the right image form a possible matching point set. In stereo matching, all the non-horizontal zero-crossing patterns in the left image can be formed into a point set with the help of the horizontal **epipolar line constraint**, and a label set is assigned to each point, and an initial matching probability is determined. Using a similar method as the matching using edge points, the final matching point can also be obtained through relaxation iteration.

### 6.3.1.3  Depth of Feature Points

Figure 6.10 (it is obtained by removing the epipolar line in Fig. 6.3 and then by moving the baseline to the $X$ axis to facilitate the description; the meaning of each letter is the same as Fig. 6.3) explains the corresponding relationship among feature points.

In the 3-D space coordinates, a feature point $W(x, y, -z)$ after orthogonal projection is on the left and right images, respectively:

$$(u', v') = (x, y) \tag{6.23}$$

$$(u'', v'') = [(x - B) \cos \theta - z \sin \theta, y] \tag{6.24}$$

The calculation of $u''$ here is based on the coordinate transformation of first translation and then rotation. Equation (6.24) can also be derived with the help of Fig. 6.11 (here a diagram parallel to the $XZ$ plane in Fig. 6.10 is provided, where $Q$ is the result of shifting point $W$ along the positive direction of $X$ by $B$):

**Fig. 6.10**  Schematic diagram of the coordinate system of binocular vision

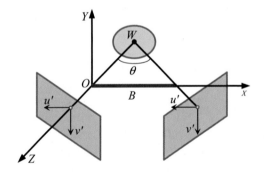

**Fig. 6.11**  The coordinate arrangement for calculating binocular stereo matching parallax

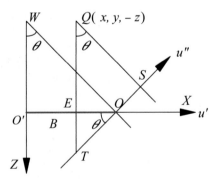

$$u'' = \overline{OS} = \overline{ST} - \overline{TO} = \left(\overline{QE} + \overline{ET}\right)\sin\theta - \frac{B-x}{\cos\theta} \qquad (6.25)$$

Note that $W$ is on the $-Z$ axis, so there is

$$u'' = -z\sin\theta + (B-x)\tan\theta\sin\theta - \frac{B-x}{\cos\theta} = (x-B)\cos\theta - z\sin\theta \qquad (6.26)$$

If $u''$ has been determined by $u'$ (i.e., the matching between the feature points has been established), the depth of the feature points projected to $u'$ and $u''$ can be inversely solved from Eq. (6.24) as

$$-z = u''\csc\theta + (B-u')\cot\theta \qquad (6.27)$$

### 6.3.1.4  Sparse Matching Points

It can be seen from the above discussion that the feature points are only some specific points on the object, and there is a certain interval between them. Only with the sparse matching points, a dense parallax field cannot be directly obtained, so it may not be possible to accurately restore the shape of the object. For example, Fig. 6.12a shows four points that are coplanar in space (equal distance from another space plane). These points are sparse matching points obtained by parallax calculation. Suppose these points are located on the outer surface of the object, but there can be infinitely many curved surfaces passing these four points; Fig. 6.12b–d give several possible examples. It can be seen that only the sparse matching points cannot uniquely restore the shape of the object, and some other conditions or interpolation of the sparse matching points needs to be combined to obtain a dense parallax map such as that obtained in region matching.

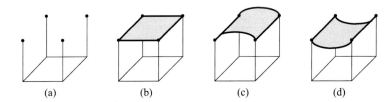

(a)             (b)             (c)             (d)

**Fig. 6.12** Only sparse matching points cannot restore the shape of the object uniquely

### 6.3.2  Scale Invariant Feature Transformation

**Scale Invariant Feature Transformation** (SIFT) can be regarded as a method of detecting **salient features** in an image. It can not only determine the position of a point with salient features in the image but also give a description vector of the point, also known as SIFT operator or descriptor. It is a kind of local descriptor, which contains three types of information: location, scale, and direction.

The basic ideas and steps of SIFT are as follows. First obtain the multi-scale representation of the image, which can be convolved with the image using a Gaussian convolution kernel (referred to as Gaussian kernel, the only linear kernel). The Gaussian convolution kernel is a Gaussian function with variable scale:

$$G(x, y, \sigma) = \frac{1}{2\pi\sigma^2} \exp\left[\frac{-(x^2 + y^2)}{2\sigma^2}\right] \tag{6.28}$$

where $\sigma$ is the scale factor. The multi-scale representation of the image after the convolution of Gaussian convolution kernel and image is represented as

$$L(x, y, \sigma) = G(x, y, \sigma) \otimes f(x, y) \tag{6.29}$$

The Gaussian function is a low-pass function, and the image will be smoothed after convolution with the image. The size of the scale factor is related to the degree of smoothness. Large $\sigma$ corresponds to a large scale, which mainly gives an overview of the image after convolution; small $\sigma$ corresponds to a small scale, and the details of the image are retained after convolution. In order to make full use of image information of different scales, a series of convolutions of Gaussian convolution kernels and image with different scale factors can be used to construct a Gaussian pyramid. In general, the scale factor coefficient between two adjacent layers of the Gaussian pyramid is $k$. If the scale factor of the first layer is $\sigma$, the scale factor of the second layer is $k\sigma$, the scale factor of the third layer is $k^2\sigma$, and so on.

SIFT then searches for **salient feature points** in the multi-scale representation of the image, using the **difference of Gaussian** (DoG) operator for this purpose. DoG is the difference between the convolution results of two Gaussian kernels of different scales, which is similar to the **Laplacian of Gaussian** (LoG) operator. If $h$ and $k$ are used to represent the coefficients of different scale factors, the DoG pyramid can be represented as

$$D(x, y, \sigma) = [G(x, y, k\sigma) - G(x, y, h\sigma)] \otimes f(x, y) = L(x, y, k\sigma) \\ - L(x, y, h\sigma) \tag{6.30}$$

The multi-scale representation space of the DoG pyramid of the image is a 3-D space (image plane and scale axis). To search for extreme values in such a 3-D space, it is necessary to compare the value of a point in the space with the values of its

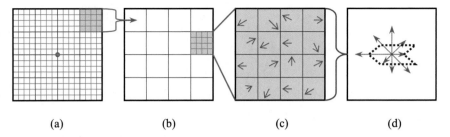

(a)                       (b)                       (c)                       (d)

**Fig. 6.13** The calculation steps of SIFT description vector

26 neighboring voxels. The result of this search determines the location and scale of the salient feature points.

Next, the gradient distribution of pixels in the neighborhood of the salient feature point is used to determine the direction parameter of each point. The modulus (amplitude) and direction of the gradient at $(x, y)$ in the image are, respectively (the scale used for each $L$ is the scale of each salient feature point)

$$m(x, y) = \sqrt{[L(x+1, \ y) - L(x-1, \ y)]^2 + [L(x, \ y+1) - L(x, \ y-1)]^2} \quad (6.31)$$

$$\theta(x, y) = \arctan \left\{ \frac{L(x, \ y+1) - L(x, \ y-1)}{L(x+1, \ y) - L(x-1, \ y)} \right\} \quad (6.32)$$

After obtaining the direction of each point, the direction of the pixels in the neighborhood can be combined to obtain the direction of the salient feature point. For details, please refer to Fig. 6.13. First (on the basis of determining the location and scale of the salient feature point), take a $16 \times 16$ window centered on the salient feature point, as shown in Fig. 6.13a. Divide the window into 16 groups of $4 \times 4$, as shown in Fig. 6.13b. Calculate the gradient of every pixel in each group to obtain the gradients of the pixels in this group, as shown in Fig. 6.13c; here the arrow direction indicates the gradient direction, and the length of the arrow is proportional to the magnitude of gradient. Use eight-direction (interval 45°) histogram to count the gradient direction of pixels in each group, and take the peak direction as the gradient direction of the group, as shown in Fig. 6.13d. In this way, for 16 groups, each group can get an 8-D direction vector, and concatenate them to get a $16 \times 8 = 128$-D vector. This vector is normalized and finally used as the description vector of each salient feature point, that is, the SIFT descriptor. In practice, the coverage region of the SIFT descriptor can be square or round, which is also called a **salient patch**.

The SIFT descriptor is invariant to image scaling, rotation, and illumination changes, and it has also certain stability for affine transformation, viewing angle changes, local shape distortion, noise interference, etc. This is because in the process of obtaining the SIFT descriptor, the influence of rotation is eliminated by the calculation and adjustment of the gradient direction, the influence of the illumination change is eliminated by the vector normalization, and the robustness is enhanced by the combination of the pixel direction information in the neighborhood. In addition,

(a)                                                    (b)

**Fig. 6.14** Example of the detection result of significant patches

the SIFT descriptor is rich in information and has good uniqueness (compared to edge points or corner points that only contain position and extreme value information, the SIFT descriptor has a 128-D description vector). Also due to its uniqueness or particularity, SIFT descriptors can often identify a large number of salient patches in an image for different applications to choose. Of course, due to the high dimension of the description vector, the computation amount of the SIFT descriptor is often relatively large. There are also many improvements to SIFT, including replacing the gradient histogram with PCA (for effective dimensionality reduction), limiting the amplitude of each direction of the histogram (some non-linear illumination changes mainly affect the amplitude), using speeded-up robust feature (SURF), etc.

**Example 6.7 SIFT Significant Patch Detection Results**
With the help of SIFT, it is possible to determine a large number (generally, hundreds of $256 \times 384$ images can be obtained) in the image scale space, covering the local regions of the image that do not change with the translation, rotation, and scaling of the image, and the impact of affecting by noise and interference is very small.

Figure 6.14 shows the two results of salient patch detection. Figure 6.14a is a ship image, and Fig. 6.14b is a beach image, in which all detected SIFT salient patches are represented by a circle overlaid on the image (a salient patch of the circle shape is used here).

### 6.3.3 Dynamic Programming Matching

The selection method of feature points is often closely related to the matching method used for them. The matching of feature points needs to establish the corresponding relationship between the feature points. For this purpose, **ordering constraints** can be adopted and **dynamic programming** methods can be used.

Take Fig. 6.15a as an example, consider three characteristic points on the visible surface of the observed object, and name them in order $A$, $B$, $C$. They are exactly the

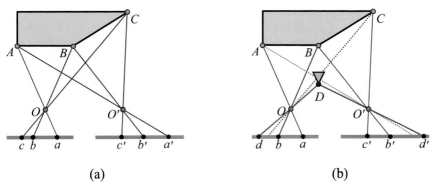

**Fig. 6.15** Sequence constraints

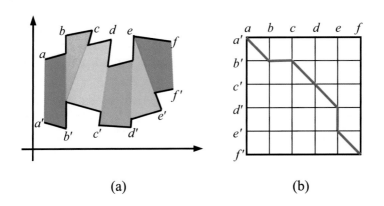

**Fig. 6.16** Matching based on dynamic programming

reverse of the order of projection on the two images (along the epipolar line); see $c$, $b$, $a$ and $c'$, $b'$, $a'$. The rule of opposite order is called sequential constraints. Sequential constraint is an ideal situation, and it is not guaranteed to always hold in actual scenarios. For example, in the situation shown in Fig. 6.15b, a small object is blocked in front of the large object behind and occludes the part of the large object and makes the original point $c$ and $a'$ invisible on the image. The order of projection on the image also does not satisfy the order constraint.

However, in most practical situations, the sequential constraint is still a reasonable constraint, so it can be used to design a stereo matching algorithm based on dynamic programming. In the following, suppose that multiple feature points on the two epipolar lines have been determined (as shown in Fig. 6.15), and the corresponding relationship between them should be established as an example for discussion. Here, the problem of matching each feature point pair can be transformed into a problem of matching the interval between adjacent feature points on the same epipolar line. Refer to the example in Fig. 6.16a, which shows two feature point sequences that are arranged on two grayscale profiles. Although due to occlusion and other reasons, the interval between some feature points degenerates into one point, the order of feature points determined by the sequential constraint is still retained.

According to Fig. 6.16a, the problem of matching each feature point pair can be described as a problem of searching for the optimal path on the **graph** corresponding to the nodes. The arc between the nodes in the graph representation can provide the matching paths between intervals. In Fig. 6.16a, the upper and lower contour lines correspond to two epipolar lines, respectively, and the quadrilateral between the two contour lines corresponds to the intervals between the feature points (zero length interval causes the quadrilateral to degenerate into a triangle). The matching relationship determined by dynamic programming is also shown in Fig. 6.15b, where each diagonal line corresponds to a quadrilateral interval and the vertical or horizontal line corresponds to the degenerated triangle.

The complexity of the above algorithm is proportional to the product of the number of feature points on the two epipolar lines.

## 6.4  Error Detection and Correction of Parallax Map

In practical applications, due to the existence of periodic patterns and smooth regions in the image, as well as the occlusion effects and the lack of strictness of the constraint principle, the parallax map will have errors. The parallax map is the basis for subsequent 3-D reconstruction work, so it is very important to perform error detection and correction processing on the basis of the parallax map.

The following introduces a more general and fast **disparity map** error detection and correction algorithm. The first characteristic of this algorithm is that it can directly process the parallax map and is independent of the specific stereo matching algorithm that generates the parallax map. In this way, it can be used as a general parallax map post-processing method to be added to various stereo matching algorithms without modifying the original stereo matching algorithm. Secondly, the computation amount of this method is only proportional to the number of mismatched pixels, so the computation amount is small.

### 6.4.1  Error Detection

With the help of the sequential constraints discussed earlier, let's first define the concept of **ordering matching constraints**. Suppose $f_L(x, y)$ and $f_R(x, y)$ are a pair of (horizontal) images and $O_L$ and $O_R$ are their imaging centers, respectively. Let $P$ and $Q$ be two points that do not coincide in space, $P_L$ and $Q_L$ the projections of $P$ and $Q$ on $f_L(x, y)$, and $P_R$ and $Q_R$ the projections of $P$ and $Q$ on $f_R(x, y)$; see Fig. 6.17.

Suppose that $X(\bullet)$ is used to represent the $X$ coordinate of the pixel. From Fig. 6.17, it can be seen that if $X(P) < X(Q)$, then $X(P_L) \leq X(Q_L)$ and $X(P_R) \leq$

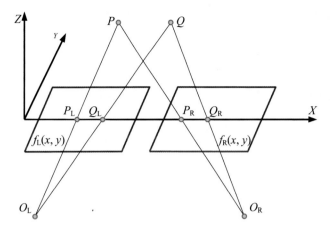

**Fig. 6.17** Schematic diagram of defining sequential matching constraints

$X(Q_R)$, and if $X(P) > X(Q)$, then $X(P_L) \geq X(Q_L)$ and $X(P_R) \geq X(Q_R)$. Therefore, if the following conditions are true ($\Rightarrow$ means implicit)

$$\begin{aligned}
X(P_L) \leq X(Q_L) &\Rightarrow X(P_R) < X(Q_R) \\
X(P_L) \geq X(Q_L) &\Rightarrow X(P_R) > X(Q_R)
\end{aligned} \tag{6.33}$$

it is said that $P_R$ and $Q_R$ meet the sequential matching constraint; otherwise it is said that there has been a crossover, that is to say, an error has occurred. It can be seen from Fig. 6.17 that the sequential matching constraint has certain restrictions on the $Z$ coordinates of points $P$ and $Q$, which is relatively easy to determine in practical applications.

According to the concept of sequential matching constraints, the crossed matching region can be detected, that is, **error detection**. Let $P_R = f_R(i, j)$ and $Q_R = f_R(k, j)$ be any two pixels in the $j$th row in $f_R(x, y)$; then their matching points in $f_L(x, y)$ can be recorded separately: $P_L = f_L(i + d(i, j), j)$ and $Q_L = f_L(k + d(k, j), j)$. Define $C(P_R, Q_R)$ as the cross-label between $P_R$ and $Q_R$. If Eq. (6.33) holds, it is recorded as $C(P_R, Q_R) = 0$; otherwise, it is recorded as $C(P_R, Q_R) = 1$. Define the crossing number $N_c$ of the corresponding pixel $P_R$ as

$$N_c(i, j) = \sum_{k=0}^{N-1} C(P_R, Q_R) \quad k \neq i \tag{6.34}$$

where $N$ is the number of pixels in the $j$th row.

## 6.4.2   Error Correction

If a region where the crossing number is not zero is called the crossing region, the mismatch in the crossing region can be corrected by the following algorithm. Assuming $\{f_R(i, j)|\ i \subseteq [p, q]\}$ is the crossing region corresponding to $P_R$, then the **total cross number** $N_{tc}$ of all pixels in this region is

$$N_{tc}(i, j) = \sum_{i=p}^{q} N_c(i, j) \tag{6.35}$$

The **error correction** of the mismatched points in the crossing region includes the following steps:

1. Find the pixel $f_R(l, j)$ with the largest crossing number; here

$$I = \max_{i \subseteq [p, q]} [N_c(i, j)] \tag{6.36}$$

2. Determine the new search range $\{f_L(i, j)|\ i \subseteq [s, t]\}$ for the matching point $f_R(k, j)$, where

$$\begin{cases} s = p - 1 + d(p - 1, j) \\ t = q + 1 + d(q + 1, j) \end{cases} \tag{6.37}$$

3. Find a new matching point that can reduce the total crossing number $N_{tc}$ from the search range (the maximum gray level correlation matching technology, e.g., can be used).
4. Use the new matching point to correct $d(k, j)$ to eliminate the mismatch of pixels corresponding to the current maximum crossing number.

The above steps can be used iteratively; after correcting one mismatched pixel, continue to correct each of the remaining error pixels. After correcting $d(k, j)$, first re-calculate $N_c(i, j)$ in the crossing region by Eq. (6.34), followed by calculating $N_{tc}$, and then perform the next round of correction processing according to the above iteration until $N_{tc} = 0$. Because the principle of correction is to make $N_{tc} = 0$, it can be called a **zero-crossing correction algorithm**. After correction, a parallax map that meets the sequential matching constraint can be obtained.

### Example 6.8 Example of Matching Error Detection and Elimination

Suppose that the calculated parallax of the interval region [153, 163] in row $j$ of the image is shown in Table 6.1 and the distribution of matching points in this region is shown in Fig. 6.18.

**Table 6.1** Parallax in the crossing region

| $i$ | 153 | 154 | 155 | 156 | 157 | 158 | 159 | 160 | 161 | 162 | 163 |
|---|---|---|---|---|---|---|---|---|---|---|---|
| $d(i, j)$ | 28 | 28 | 28 | 27 | 28 | 27 | 27 | 21 | 21 | 21 | 27 |

**Fig. 6.18** Distribution of matching points before crossing region correction

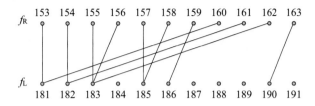

**Table 6.2** The number of horizontal crossings in the interval region [153, 163]

| $i$ | 153 | 154 | 155 | 156 | 157 | 158 | 159 | 160 | 161 | 162 | 163 |
|---|---|---|---|---|---|---|---|---|---|---|---|
| $N_c$ | 0 | 1 | 2 | 2 | 3 | 3 | 3 | 6 | 5 | 3 | 0 |

**Fig. 6.19** The distribution of matching points after crossing region correction

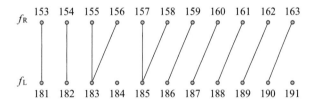

According to the correspondence between $f_L(x, y)$ and $f_R(x, y)$, it can be known that the matching points in the region [160, 162] are error mismatch points. According to Eq. (6.34), calculate the crossing number (along the horizontal direction) to get Table 6.2.

From Table 6.2, $[f_R(154, j), f_R(162, j)]$ is the crossing region. From Eq. (6.35), $N_{tc} = 28$ can be obtained; from Eq. (6.36), it can be seen that the pixel with the largest crossing number is $f_R(160, j)$; then, according to Eq. (6.37), the search range of the new matching point $f_R(160, j)$ is $\{f_L(i, j) | i \subseteq [181, 190]\}$. According to the technique of maximum gray level correlation matching, a new matching point $f_L(187, j)$ that corresponds to $f_R(160, j)$ and can reduce $N_{tc}$ is found from the search range, and the parallax value $d(160, j)$ corresponding to $f_R(160, j)$ is corrected as $d(160, j) = X[f_L(187, j)] - X[f_R(160, j)] = 27$. Then proceed to the next round of correction according to the above iterative method until $N_{tc} = 0$ in the entire region. The corrected matching point distribution is shown in Fig. 6.19. It can be seen from Fig. 6.19 that the original mismatch points in the interval region [160, 162] have been eliminated.

It should be pointed out that the above algorithm can only eliminate the mismatch points in the crossing region. Since the sequential matching constraint is only processed for the crossing region, the mismatch point in the region where the crossing number is zero cannot be detected or corrected.

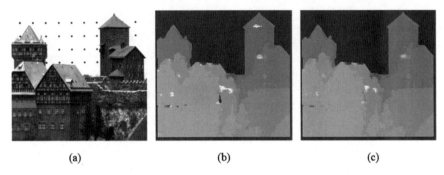

(a)                                    (b)                                    (c)

**Fig. 6.20**  A real instance of error elimination

**Example 6.9 A Real Instance of Matching Error Detection and Elimination**

Here, a pair of images in Fig. 6.8a, b are selected for matching. Figure 6.20a is a part of the original image, Fig. 6.20b is a parallax map obtained directly using the region-based stereo matching method, and the result of Fig. 6.20c is obtained after further processing with the above correction algorithm. Comparing Fig. 6.20b, c, it can be seen that there are many mismatched points (too-white and too-dark patches) in the original parallax map. After correction processing, a considerable part of the mismatched points is eliminated. The image quality has been significantly improved.

## 6.5  Key Points and References for Each Section

The following combines the main contents of each section to introduce some references that can be further consulted.

1. **Stereo Vision Process and Modules**

    In each module of stereo vision, there are many different implementation methods. For example, you can refer to [1] for further information about the network-symbol model; refer to the reference *2D Computer Vision: Principles, Algorithms and Applications* for the calculation of interpolation. The model-based interpolation reconstruction algorithm can be found in [2]; the sub-pixel level parallax accuracy can be found in [3]. This chapter only discusses binocular stereo vision, which is a direct imitation of the human visual system. In a computer vision system, it is also possible to use three or even more oculars (cameras); for example, see [4].

2. **Region-Based Stereo Matching**

    At the image boundary, the impact of using the template can be found in [3]. In stereo matching, compatibility constraints, uniqueness constraints, and continuity constraints are all commonly used constraints. For further discussion, please refer to [5]. For a more detailed introduction of essential matrix and fundamental matrix, please refer to [6]. Pixel gray values are mostly used in region-based matching, and some people have tried some derivation of gray levels, but some experiments have shown (e.g., see [7]) that among gray level, gradient magnitude and direction, Laplacian value of gray level, and gray curvature, using the grayscale parameter in matching is still the best. The imaging model used in the calculation of surface optical properties can be found in the book *2D Computer Vision: Principles, Algorithms and Applications*.

3. **Feature-Based Stereo Matching**

When matching feature points, the further discussion for selecting the zero-crossing pattern to obtain matching primitives can refer to [8]. Interpolation is required after obtaining sparse matching points, which can be found in the book *2D Computer Vision: Principles, Algorithms and Applications*. Scale Invariant Feature Transformation (SIFT) is based on the multi-scale representation of images (see [3]); for detecting salient features in images, see [9], and the 26 neighborhood concepts used can be found in [10]. For an introduction to the speeded-up robust feature (SURF), please refer to [4]. Using sequential constraints to perform dynamic programming matching can be found in [11].

4. **Error Detection and Correction of Parallax Map**

For details of the more general and fast parallax map error detection and correction algorithm introduced, please refer to [12]. A recent fast refinement algorithm for parallax results can be found in [13].

# Self-Test Questions

The following questions include both single-choice questions and multiple-choice questions, so each option must be judged.

## 6.1 **Stereo Vision Process and Modules**

6.1.1 In the stereo vision process shown in Fig. 6.1, (·).

  (a) Image acquisition should be carried out on the basis of camera calibration.
  (b) The function of the feature extraction module is to extract the features of the pixel set for matching.
  (c) The depth interpolation in post-processing is to help stereo matching.
  (d) Post-processing is needed because the 3-D information obtained is often incomplete or has certain errors.

  [Hint] Consider the sequence of the stereo vision process.

6.1.2 Consider the various modules in the stereo vision process given in Fig. 6.1, (·).

  (a) The stereo matching module is only used when it can directly make 3-D imaging.

(b) The feature extraction module can directly extract the gray value of the pixel set as a feature.

(c) The image acquisition module can directly acquire 3-D images to achieve 3-D information recovery.

(d) The function of the 3-D information recovery module is to establish the relationship between the image points of the same space points in different images.

[Hint] Consider the respective functions and connections of each module.

6.1.3 Which of the following description(s) is/are incorrect? (·).

(a) Although the positioning accuracy of large-scale features is poor, they contain a lot of information and match faster.

(b) If only a single camera is used for image acquisition, there is no need for calibration.

(c) The gray values of pixels in small regions are relatively related, so it is suitable for grayscale correlation matching.

(d) If the camera baseline is relatively short, the difference between the captured images will be relatively large.

[Hint] Analyze the meaning of each description carefully.

## 6.2 **Region-Based Stereo Matching**

6.2.1 In template matching, (·).

(a) The template used must be square.

(b) The size of the template used must be smaller than the size of the image to be matched.

(c) The matching positions determined by the correlation function and the minimum mean square error function are consistent.

(d) The matching position calculated by the correlation coefficient does not change with the gray value of the template and the matching image.

[Hint] Matching is to determine the most relevant position.

6.2.2 Among the various constraints used for matching, (·).

(a) The epipolar line constraint restricts the position of the pixel.

(b) The uniqueness constraint restricts the attributes of pixels.

(c) The continuity constraint restricts the position of pixels.

(d) The compatibility constraint restricts the attributes of pixels.

[Hint] The attribute of the pixel corresponds to $f$, while the position corresponds to $(x, y)$.

6.2.3 In the following description of epipolar line constraint, (·).

(a) The epipolar constraint can help reduce the amount of calculation by half in the matching search process.

(b) The epipolar line in one imaging plane and the extreme point in another imaging plane are corresponding.

(c) The epipolar line pattern can provide information about the relative position and orientation between two cameras.

(d) For any point on an imaging plane, all points corresponding to it on the imaging plane 2 are on the same straight line.

[Hint] Refer to Example 6.2–Example 6.4.

6.2.4 Comparing the essential matrix and the fundamental matrix, $(\cdot)$.

(a) The degree of freedom of the essential matrix is more than that of the fundamental matrix.

(b) The role or function of the fundamental matrix and the essential matrix is similar.

(c) The essential matrix is derived from uncorrected cameras.

(d) The fundamental matrix reflects the relationship between the projection point coordinates of the same space points on two images.

[Hint] Consider the different conditions in the derivation of the two matrices.

## 6.3 Feature-Based Stereo Matching

6.3.1 For feature-based stereo matching technology, $(\cdot)$.

(a) It is not very sensitive to the surface structure of the scene and light reflection.

(b) The feature point pair used is the point determined according to the local properties in the image.

(c) Each point in the stereo image pair can be used as a feature point in turn for matching.

(d) The matching result is not yet a dense parallax field.

[Hint] Consider the particularity of the features.

6.3.2 Scale Invariant Feature Transformation $(\cdot)$.

(a) Needs to use multi-scale representation of images

(b) Needs to search for extreme values in 3-D space

(c) In which the 3-D space here includes position, scale, and direction

(d) In which the Gaussian difference operator used is a smoothing operator

[Hint] Analyze the meaning of each calculation step in the scale invariant feature transformation.

6.3.3 For sequential constraints, $(\cdot)$.

(a) It indicates that the feature points on the visible surface of the object are in the same order as their projection points on the two images.

(b) It can be used to design a stereo matching algorithm based on dynamic programming.

(c) It may not be true/hold when there is occlusion between objects.

(d) When the graphical representation is performed according to the dynamic programming method, the interval between some feature points will degenerate into one point, and the order of constraint determination is invalid.

[Hint] Analyze the conditions for the establishment of sequential constraints.

### 6.4  Error Detection and Correction of Parallax Map

6.4.1  In the method of parallax map error detection and correction, (·).

(a) Only the region where the crossing number is not zero should be considered.

(b) The crossing number in a region is proportional to the size of the region.

(c) To calculate the total crossing number, twice summations are performed.

(d) The crossing number in a region is proportional to the length of the region.

[Hint] Consider the definition and connection of the crossing number and the total crossing number.

6.4.2  Analyze the following statements, which is/are correct? (·).

(a) In the crossing region, the crossing values of adjacent points differ by 1.

(b) The zero-crossing correction algorithm must make $N_{tc} = 0$, so it is named.

(c) The sequential matching constraint refers to the sequential constraint, so it indicates that the order of the space points is reversed to the order of their imaging points.

(d) The zero-crossing correction algorithm is an iterative algorithm. After each iteration, the total crossing numbers will always decrease.

[Hint] Analyze the meaning of each step in the zero-crossing correction algorithm.

6.4.3  In Example 6.8, $N_{tc} = 28$ before correction; please find a new matching point $f_L(187, j)$ that corresponds to $f_R(160, j)$ and can reduce $N_{tc}$. It can correct the parallax value $d(160, j)$, corresponding to $f_R(160, j)$, to $d(160, j) = X[f_L(187, j)] - X[f_R(160, j)] = 27$. At this time, (·).

(a) $N_{tc} = 16$

(b) $N_{tc} = 20$

  (c) $N_{tc} = 24$
  (d) $N_{tc} = 28$

[Hint] The crossing number on the left side of the correction point $f_R(160, j)$ will decrease but on the right side may increase. Need specific calculations.

6.4.4 On the basis of 6.4.3, find the $f_R(161, j)$ with the largest crossing number, and determine the new matching point corresponding to $f_R(161, j)$ that can reduce $N_{tc}$. In this way, the correction can make the total crossing number $N_{tc}$ drop to $(\cdot)$.

  (a) 20
  (b) 15
  (c) 10
  (d) 5

[Hint] The new matching point corresponding to $f_R(161, j)$ and capable of reducing $N_{tc}$ is $f_L(188, j)$.

# References

1. Kuvich G. Active vision and image/video understanding systems for intelligent manufacturing. SPIE, 2004, 5605: 74-86.
2. Maitre H, Luo W. Using models to improve stereo reconstruction. IEEE-PAMI, 1992, 14(2): 269-277.
3. Zhang Y-J. Image Engineering, Vol.1: Image Processing. De Gruyter, 2017.
4. Zhang Y-J. Image Engineering, Vol.3: Image Understanding. De Gruyter, 2017.
5. Forsyth D, Ponce J. Computer Vision: A Modern Approach, 2nd Ed. Prentice Hall. 2012.
6. Davies E R. Machine Vision: Theory, Algorithms, Practicalities. 3rd Ed. Elsevier. 2005.
7. Lew M S, Huang T S, Wong K. Learning and feature selection in stereo matching. IEEE-PAMI, 1994, 16(9): 869-881.
8. Kim Y C, Aggarwal J K. Positioning three-dimensional objects using stereo images. IEEE-RA, 1987, 1: 361-373.
9. Nixon M S, Aguado A S. Feature Extraction and Image Processing. 2nd. Ed. Academic Press. 2008.
10. Zhang Y-J. Image Engineering, Vol.2: Image Analysis. De Gruyter, 2017.
11. Forsyth D, Ponce J. Computer Vision: A Modern Approach. Prentice Hall. 2003.
12. Jia B, Zhang Y-J, Lin X G. General and fast algorithm for disparity error detection and correction. Journal of Tsinghua University (Sci & Tech), 2000, 40(1): 28-31.
13. Huang X M, Zhang Y-J. An O(1) disparity refinement method for stereo matching. Pattern Recognition, 2016, 55: 198-206.

# Chapter 7
# Monocular Multiple Image Recovery

The binocular stereo vision method introduced in Chap. 6 is an important method to imitate the principle of human stereo vision to obtain depth information. Its advantage is that the geometric relationship is very clear, but the disadvantage is that it needs to be matched to determine the corresponding points in the binocular image. Corresponding point matching is a difficult problem, especially when the scene lighting is inconsistent and there are shadows on the scene. At this time, the correspondence of the points cannot be guaranteed based on the similarity of the gray levels. In addition, the use of stereo vision methods requires that several points on the scene appear in all images for which corresponding points need to be determined. In practice, it is affected by the occlusion of the line of sight, etc., and it cannot guarantee that different cameras have the same field of view, which will cause the difficulty of corresponding point detection and affect the corresponding point matching.

To avoid complicated corresponding point matching problems, various 3-D clues from monocular images (i.e., only a single camera with a fixed position is used, but single or multiple images can be taken) are often used to recover the scene. Since one dimension is lost when the 3-D world is projected onto the 2-D image, the key to recovering the scene is to recover the lost one dimension.

From the perspective of information, the stereo vision method recovers the depth of the scene according to multiple images obtained by the camera at different positions, which can be seen as converting the redundant information between multiple images into depth information. Obtaining multiple images with redundant information can also be accomplished by collecting changing images of scene at the same location. These images can be obtained with only one (fixed) camera, so it is also called the monocular method (the stereo vision method is based on multiple-ocular multiple-image). The surface orientation of the scene can be determined from the **monocular multiple-images** obtained in this way, and the relative depth between various parts of the scene can be directly obtained from the surface orientation of the scene. In practice, the absolute depth of the scene can often be further obtained.

Y.-J. Zhang, *3-D Computer Vision*, https://doi.org/10.1007/978-981-19-7580-6_7

If the position of the light source is changed during image acquisition, a single camera at a fixed position can be used to obtain multiple images under different lighting conditions. The image brightness of the same surface varies with the shape of the scene, which can be used to help determining the shape of the 3-D scene. The multiple images at this time do not correspond to different viewpoints but correspond to different lighting, which is called shape from illumination (shape restoration by lighting). If the scene moves during the image acquisition process, an optical flow will be generated in an image sequence composed of multiple images. The magnitude and direction of the optical flow vary with the orientation of the surface of the scene, so it can be used to help determining the 3-D structure, which is called shape from motion (shape restoration by motion).

The sections of this chapter are arranged as follows:

Section 7.1 starts from the principle of photometry, first analyzes the imaging process from the light source to the scene and then to the lens, and points out that the image gray level depends on the intensity of the light source and the reflection characteristics of the scenery, as well as the geometric relationship between them.

Section 7.2 discusses the establishment of the relationship between the image gray level and the orientation of the scenery, and the orientation of the scenery is determined by the change of the image gray level.

Section 7.3 introduces how to detect the motion of the scenery and uses the optical flow equation to describe and solve the principle and several special cases of the optical flow equation.

Section 7.4 further introduces the realization of the restoration of the shape and structure of the scenery by the solution of the optical flow equation. Here, the analytical optical flow equation is solved by the transformation of the coordinate system.

## 7.1 Photometric Stereo

**Photometric stereo**, also known as **photometric stereoscopy**, is a discipline that uses the principles of photometry to obtain stereo information. It is also regarded as a way to restore the surface orientation of the scenery with a series of images collected under the same viewing angle but under different lighting conditions. Photometric stereo methods are often used in environments where lighting conditions are relatively easy to control or determine.

### 7.1.1 Light Source, Scenery, Lens

The photometric stereo method should restore the three-dimensional shape of the scenery according to the illumination (change). **Photometry** is the subject of light measurement in the process of light emission, propagation, absorption, and scattering. It mainly relates to the field of light intensity measurement in optics, that is, the part of optics that measures the quantity or spectrum of light. It is a corresponding metrology subject in the visible light band, taking into account the subjective factors of the human eye. Light is a special electromagnetic wave, so photometry is regarded as a branch of radiometry.

Photometric measurement studies the intensity of light and its measurement. It also evaluates the visual effects of radiation based on the physiological characteristics of human visual organs and certain agreed norms. The measurement methods are divided into two types: visual measurement (subjective photometry) and instrumental and physical measurement (objective photometry). The subjective photometry directly compares the brightness of the two halves of the field of view and then converts them into target detection quantities, such as luminous intensity and luminous flux. Objective photometry uses physical devices to replace the human eye for photometric comparison.

In image engineering, visible light is the most common electromagnetic radiation. The collection of visible light images from a scene requires knowledge related to photometry. The following physical quantities are commonly used in photometry to describe the emitted, transmitted, or received light energy: (i) luminous flux; (ii) luminous intensity; (iii) brightness/intensity; and (iv) illuminance.

Look at the imaging process, the **light source** illuminates the **scenery** first, and then the light reflected from the scenery reaches the **lens** (imaging sensor) to form an image, as shown in Fig. 7.1. The illumination of the scenery by the light source involves two factors. On the one hand, the light source has a certain luminance intensity. The irradiation intensity to the scene is called illuminance, and the illuminance of the scene is a function of the luminance intensity. On the other hand, the light from the light source incidents the scenery at a certain angle, and

**Fig. 7.1** From the light source through the scenery to the lens

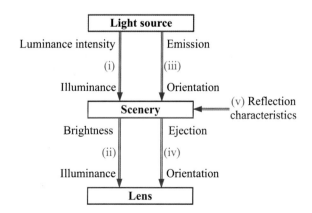

the illumination of the scenery is a function of the orientation of the scenery relative to the light source. The illumination of the lens by the reflected light from the scenery also involves two factors. On the one hand, the reflected light of the scenery has a certain brightness, so there is illuminance to the lens, and the illuminance of the lens is a function of the brightness of the scene. On the other hand, the light emitted from the scenery hits the lens, and the illuminance of the lens is a function of the orientation of the lens relative to the scene. In addition, the reflected light of the scenery is also related to the reflection characteristics of the scenery surface. The five relationships or factors here are marked with (i), (ii), (iii), (iv), and (v) in Fig. 7.1.

Further analysis shows that the process from light source to scenery and the process from scenery to lens are similar. Receiving light from a light source from a scenery is similar to receiving light from a lens, that is, the scenery for the lens is equivalent to the light source illuminating the scene and the lens relative to the scenery is equivalent to the scenery illuminated by the light source. The following is an introduction to factor (i) and factor (ii) related to the relationship between intensity/brightness and illuminance, factor (iii) and factor (iv) related to relative orientation, as well as factor (v) related to reflection characteristic.

## 7.1.2 Scene Brightness and Image Brightness

Scene brightness and image brightness are two related but different concepts. In imaging, the former is related to **radiance** and the latter is related to **irradiance**. Specifically, the former corresponds to the luminous flux emitted from the surface in the scene (as a light source), which is the power emitted per unit area of the light source surface within a unit solid angle, in $Wm^{-2} sr^{-1}$; the latter corresponds to the luminous flux illuminating the surface, it is the power per unit area hitting the surface of the scene, and the unit is $Wm^{-2}$. In optical imaging, the scene is imaged on the image plane (of the imaging system), so the brightness of the scene corresponds to the luminous flux emitted from the surface of the scene, and the brightness of the image corresponds to the luminous flux obtained from the image plane.

The brightness of the image obtained after imaging a 3-D scene depends on many factors, such as the intensity of the reflected light and the intensity of the incident light when an ideal diffuse surface is illuminated by a point light source (a light source whose line segment is small enough or far enough from the observer). The surface light reflection coefficient is proportional to the cosine of the light incident angle (the angle between the line of sight and the incident ray). In a more general case, image brightness is affected by the shape of the scene itself, its posture in space, surface reflection characteristics, the relative orientation and position of the scene and the image acquisition system, the sensitivity of the acquisition device, and the radiation intensity and distribution of the light source. That is, the image brightness does not represent the **intrinsic properties** of the scene.

### 7.1.2.1 The Relationship Between Scene Brightness and Image Brightness

Now let's discuss the relationship between the radiance of a point light source (the brightness of the scene) and the illuminance of the corresponding point on the image (the brightness of the image). As shown in Fig. 7.2, a lens with a diameter of $d$ is placed at $\lambda$ from the image plane ($\lambda$ is the focal length of the lens). Suppose the area of a certain surface element on the surface of the scene is $\delta O$ and the area of the corresponding image pixel is $\delta I$. The angle between the light ray from the scene element to the center of the lens and the optical axis is $\alpha$, and the angle with the normal $N$ of the scene surface panel is $\theta$. The distance between the scene and the lens along the optical axis is $z$ (because the direction from the lens to the image is assumed to be the positive direction, it is marked as $-z$ in the figure).

The area of the image pixel seen from the lens center is $\delta I \times \cos\alpha$, and the actual distance between the image pixel and the lens center is $\lambda/\cos\alpha$, so the **solid angle** facing the image pixel is $\delta I \times \cos\alpha/(\lambda/\cos\alpha)^2$. Similarly, it can be seen that the solid angle of the scene element seen from the center of the lens is $\delta O \times \cos\theta/(z/\cos\alpha)^2$. It can be obtained from the equality of two solid angles:

$$\frac{\delta O}{\delta I} = \frac{\cos\alpha}{\cos\theta}\left(\frac{z}{\lambda}\right)^2 \tag{7.1}$$

Let's see how much light from the surface of the scene will pass through the lens. Because the lens area is $\pi(d/2)^2$, it can be seen from Fig. 7.2 that the solid angle of the lens viewed from the scene element is

$$\Omega = \frac{\pi d^2}{4}\cos\alpha\frac{1}{(z/\cos\alpha)^2} = \frac{\pi}{4}\left(\frac{d}{z}\right)^2\cos^3\alpha \tag{7.2}$$

In this way, the power emitted from the surface element $\delta O$ of the scene and passing through the lens is

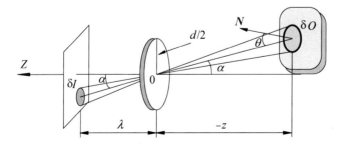

**Fig. 7.2** Scene surface elements and corresponding image pixels

$$\delta P = L \times \delta O \times \Omega \times \cos \theta = L \times \delta O \times \frac{\pi}{4} \left( \frac{d}{z} \right)^2 \cos^3 \alpha \cos \theta \qquad (7.3)$$

where $L$ is the brightness of the scene falling on the surface of the scene in the direction toward the lens. Since the light from other areas of the scene will not reach the image element $\delta I$, the illuminance obtained by this element is

$$E = \frac{\delta P}{\delta I} = L \times \frac{\delta O}{\delta I} \times \frac{\pi}{4} \left( \frac{d}{z} \right)^2 \cos^3 \alpha \cos \theta \qquad (7.4)$$

Substituting Eq. (7.1) into Eq. (7.4), we finally get

$$E = L \frac{\pi}{4} \left( \frac{d}{z} \right)^2 \cos^4 \alpha \qquad (7.5)$$

It can be seen from Eq. (7.5) that the measured element illuminance $E$ is proportional to the brightness $L$ of the scene of interest and is proportional to the area of the lens but is inversely proportional to the square of the focal length of the lens. The change in illuminance produced by camera movement is reflected in the angle $\alpha$.

### 7.1.2.2   Bidirectional Reflectance Distribution Function

When imaging the observation scene, the brightness $L$ of the scene is not only related to the luminous flux incident on the surface of the scene and the proportion of incident light reflected, but also related to the geometric factors of light reflection, that is, it is related to the direction of illumination and the direction of sight. Now look at the coordinate system shown in Fig. 7.3, where $N$ is the normal of the surface element, $OR$ is an arbitrary reference line, and the direction of a ray $I$ can be the angle $\theta$ between the ray and the normal of the surface (called the polar angle) and the angle $\phi$ (called the azimuth angle) between the orthographic projection of the ray on the surface of the scene and the reference line.

**Fig. 7.3** Polar angle $\theta$ and azimuth angle $\phi$ indicating the direction of light ray

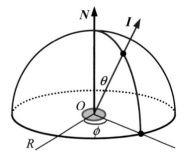

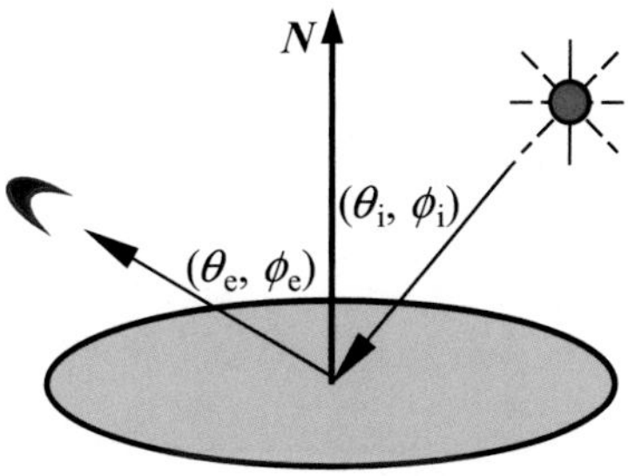

**Fig. 7.4** Schematic diagram of bidirectional reflectance distribution function

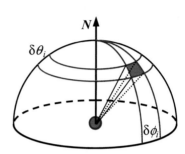

**Fig. 7.5** Schematic diagram of obtaining surface brightness under the condition of extended light source

With such a coordinate system, $(\theta_i, \phi_i)$ can be used to indicate the direction of light incident on the surface of the scene, and $(\theta_e, \phi_e)$ can be used to indicate the direction of reflection to the observer's line of sight, as shown in Fig. 7.4.

From this, we can define the **bidirectional reflectance distribution function** (BRDF), which is very important for understanding surface reflection, and denote it as $f(\theta_i, \phi_i; \theta_e, \phi_e)$ below. It represents the brightness of the surface observed by the observer in the direction $(\theta_e, \phi_e)$ when the light is incident on the surface of the scene along the direction $(\theta_i, \phi_i)$. The unit of the bidirectional reflectance distribution function is the reciprocal of the solid angle $(\mathrm{sr}^{-1})$, and its value ranges from zero to infinity (at this time, any small angle of incidence will lead to observation of radiation). Note that $f(\theta_i, \phi_i; \theta_e, \phi_e) = f(\theta_e, \phi_e; \theta_i, \phi_i)$, that is, the bidirectional reflectance distribution function is symmetric about the incident and reflection directions. Suppose $\delta E(\theta_i, \phi_i)$ is the illuminance obtained by the object when the light incidents on the surface of the object along the direction of $(\theta_i, \phi_i)$ and the brightness of the reflection (emission) observed in the direction of $(\theta_e, \phi_e)$ is $\delta L(\theta_e, \phi_e)$, and then the bidirectional reflectance distribution function is the ratio of brightness to illuminance, namely

$$f(\theta_i, \phi_i; \ \theta_e, \phi_e) = \frac{\delta L(\theta_e, \phi_e)}{\delta E(\theta_i, \phi_i)} \tag{7.6}$$

Now further consider the case of an extended light source (a light source with a certain light-emitting area). In Fig. 7.5, the width of an infinitesimal surface element on the sky (which can be considered as a radius of 1) along the polar angle is $\delta\theta_i$, and the width along the azimuth angle is $\delta\phi_i$. The solid angle corresponding to this

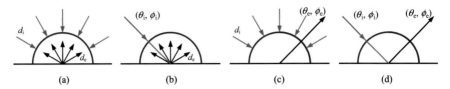

**Fig. 7.6** Four basic incident and observation modes

surface element is $\delta\omega = \sin\theta_i\delta\theta_i\delta\phi_i$ (where $\sin\theta_i$ takes into account the spherical radius after conversion). If $E_o(\theta_i,\ \phi_i)$ is the illuminance of unit solid angle along the direction of $(\theta_i,\ \phi_i)$, then the illuminance of the surface element is $E_o(\theta_i,\ \phi_i)$ $\sin\theta_i\delta\theta_i\delta\phi_i$, while the illuminance received by the entire surface is

$$E = \int_{-\pi}^{\pi} \int_{0}^{\pi/2} E_o(\theta_i,\ \phi_i) \sin\theta_i \cos\theta_i d\theta_i d\phi_i \qquad (7.7)$$

In Eq. (7.7), $\cos\theta_i$ considers the influence of the projection of the surface along the direction $(\theta_i,\ \phi_i)$ (projected onto the plane perpendicular to the normal).

In order to obtain the brightness of the entire surface, the product of the bidirectional reflectance distribution function and the surface element illuminance needs to be added up on the hemisphere that the light may enter. With the help of Eq. (7.6), it has

$$L(\theta_e,\ \phi_e) = \int_{-\pi}^{\pi} \int_{0}^{\pi/2} f(\theta_i,\ \phi_i;\ \theta_e,\ \phi_e)E_o(\theta_i,\ \phi_i) \sin\theta_i \cos\theta_i d\theta_i d\phi_i \qquad (7.8)$$

The result of Eq. (7.8) is a function of two variables ($\theta_e$ and $\phi_e$); these two variables indicate the direction of the light shining toward the observer.

### Example 7.1 Common Incident and Observation Modes

The common light incident and observation modes include the four basic forms shown in Fig. 7.6, where $\theta$ represents the incident angle and $\phi$ represents the azimuth angle. They are all combinations of diffuse incidence $d_i$ and directional $(\theta_i,\ \phi_i)$ incidence as well as diffuse reflection $d_e$ and directional $(\theta_e,\ \phi_e)$ observations. Their reflectance ratios are in order: diffuse incidence-diffuse reflection $\rho(d_i;\ d_e)$; directional incidence-diffuse reflection $\rho(\theta_i,\ \phi_i;\ d_e)$; diffuse incidence-directional observation $\rho(d_i;\ \theta_e,\ \phi_e)$; and directional incidence-directional observation $\rho(\theta_i,\ \phi_i;\ \theta_e,\ \phi_e)$.

### 7.1.3 Surface Reflection Characteristics and Brightness

The bidirectional reflectance distribution function indicates the reflection character-istics of the surface, and different surfaces have different reflectance characteristics. Only two extreme cases are considered below: an ideal scattering surface and an ideal specular reflection surface.

#### 7.1.3.1 Ideal Scattering Surface

An **ideal scattering surface** is also called a **Lambertian surface** or a **diffuse reflection surface**. It is equally bright from all viewing directions (regardless of the angle between the observation line of sight and the surface normal), and it reflects all incident light without absorption. It can be seen that $f(\theta_i, \phi_i; \theta_e, \phi_e)$ of an ideal scattering surface is a constant (not dependent on angle), and this constant can be calculated as follows. For a surface, its brightness integral in all directions should be equal to the total illuminance obtained by the surface, namely

$$L(\theta_e, \phi_e) = \int_{-\pi}^{\pi} \int_{0}^{\pi/2} f(\theta_i, \phi_i; \theta_e, \phi_e) E(\theta_i, \phi_i) \sin \theta_e \cos \theta_e d\theta_e d\phi_e$$

$$= E(\theta_i, \phi_i) \cos \theta_i \tag{7.9}$$

In Eq. (7.9), both sides are multiplied by $\cos \theta_i$ to convert to the $N$ direction. From the above equation, the BRDF of an ideal scattering surface can be solved as

$$f(\theta_i, \phi_i; \theta_e, \phi_e) = \frac{1}{\pi} \tag{7.10}$$

With the help of Eq. (7.10), it can be known that for an ideal scattering surface, the relationship between its brightness $L$ and illuminance $E$ is

$$L = \frac{E}{\pi} \tag{7.11}$$

**Example 7.2 Lambertian Surface Normal**
In practice, the common matte surface reflects light divergently, and the matte surface model under ideal conditions is the Lambertian model. The reflectivity of the Lambertian surface depends only on the incident angle $i$. Further, the change in reflectivity with angle $i$ is $\cos i$. For a given reflected light intensity $I$, it can be seen that the incident angle satisfies $\cos i = C \times I$, and $C$ is a constant, that is, the constant reflection coefficient (albedo). Therefore, the angle $i$ is also a constant. It can be concluded that the surface normal is on a directional cone surrounding the direction

**Fig. 7.7** Two directional
cones intersecting on two
lines

of the incident light, the half angle of the cone is $i$, and the axis of the cone points to the point source of illumination, that is, the cone is centered on the incident light direction.

The two directional cones that intersect on two lines can define two directions in space, as shown in Fig. 7.7. Therefore, to make the surface normal completely unambiguous, a third cone is needed. When using three light sources, each surface normal must have a common vertex with each of the three cones: the two cones have two intersection lines, and the third cone in the regular position will reduce the range to a single line, so as to give a unique explanation and estimation of the direction of the surface normal. It should be noted that if some points are hidden behind and are not hit by the light of a certain light source, there will still be ambiguity. In fact, the three light sources cannot be in one straight line, they should be relatively separated from the surface, and they should not block each other.

If the absolute reflection coefficient $R$ of the surface is unknown, a fourth cone can be considered. Using four light sources can help determine the orientation of a surface with unknown or non-ideal characteristics. But this situation is not always necessary. For example, when three rays of light are orthogonal to each other, the sum of the cosines of the angles relative to each axis must be one, which means that only two angles are independent. Therefore, using three sets of data to determine $R$ and two independent angles, a complete solution is obtained. The use of four light sources can help determine any inconsistency explanations in practical applications. This inconsistency may come from the presence of high light reflecting elements.

### 7.1.3.2 Ideal Specular Reflecting Surface

The **ideal specular reflecting surface** is totally reflective like a mirror (e.g., the bright region on the object is the result of the specular reflection of the light source on the object), so the wavelength of reflected light only depends on the light source and has nothing to do with the color of the reflecting surface. Different from an ideal scattering surface, an ideal specular reflecting surface can reflect all light incident from the direction $(\theta_i, \phi_i)$ to the direction $(\theta_e, \phi_e)$, and the incident angle is equal to the reflection angle; see Fig. 7.8. The BRDF of an ideal specular reflecting surface will be proportional (with a scale factor of $k$) to the product of the two pulses $\delta(\theta_e - \theta_i)$ and $\delta(\phi_e - \phi_i - \pi)$.

**Fig. 7.8** Schematic diagram of ideal specular reflecting surface

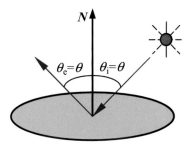

In order to find the proportional coefficient $k$, the integral of the brightness in all directions of the surface should be equal to the total illuminance obtained on the surface, namely

$$\int_{-\pi}^{\pi} \int_{0}^{\pi/2} k\delta(\theta_e - \theta_i)\delta(\phi_e - \phi_i - \pi) \sin\theta_e \cos\theta_e d\theta_e d\phi_e = k \sin\theta_i \cos\theta_i = 1 \quad (7.12)$$

From this, the BRDF of the ideal specular reflecting surface can be solved as

$$f(\theta_i, \phi_i; \ \theta_e, \phi_e) = \frac{\delta(\theta_e - \theta_i)\delta(\phi_e - \phi_i - \pi)}{\sin\theta_i \cos\theta_i} \quad (7.13)$$

When the light source is an extended light source, substituting the above equation into Eq. (7.8), the brightness of an ideal specular reflecting surface can be obtained as

$$L(\theta_e, \phi_e) = \int_{-\pi}^{\pi} \int_{0}^{\pi/2}$$

$$\times \frac{\delta(\theta_e - \theta_i)\delta(\phi_e - \phi_i - \pi)}{\sin\theta_i \cos\theta_i} E(\theta_i, \phi_i) \sin\theta_i \cos\theta_i d\theta_i d\phi_i = E(\theta_e, \phi_e - \pi) \quad (7.14)$$

That is, the polar angle does not change, but the azimuth angle is rotated by 180°.

In practice, ideal scattering surfaces and ideal specular reflecting surfaces are relatively rare. Many surfaces can be regarded as having both a part of the properties of an ideal scattering surface and a part of the properties of an ideal specular reflecting surface. In other words, the BRDF of the actual surface is the weighted sum of Eqs. (7.10) and (7.13).

## 7.2  Shape from Illumination

According to the analysis from the light source through the scene to the lens, the gray scale of the image depends not only on the illumination of the light source to the scene and the illumination of the scene to the lens but also on the surface characteristics of the scene. The illuminance is not only related to the distance between the light source and the scene plus the distance between the scene and the lens but also the direction of the light source and the scene plus the orientation of the scene and the lens. In this way, under the premise that the surface characteristics of the scene are known or certain assumptions are made, it is possible to establish the relationship between the image gray scale and the orientation of the scene and then determine the orientation of the scene according to the change of the image gray scale.

### 7.2.1  Representation of the Surface Orientation of a Scene

First consider how to represent the orientation of each point on the surface of the scene. For a smooth surface, each point on it will have a corresponding tangent plane, and the orientation of this tangent plane can be used to indicate the orientation of the surface at that point. The normal vector of the surface, that is, the (unit) vector perpendicular to the tangent plane, can indicate the orientation of the tangent plane. If we borrow the Gaussian spherical coordinate system (see Sect. 9.2) and place the end of this normal vector at the center of the ball, then the top of the vector and the sphere will intersect at a specific point. This intersection point can be used to mark the **surface orientation**. The normal vector has two degrees of freedom, so the position of the intersection on the sphere can be represented by two variables, such as using polar angle and azimuth angle or using longitude and latitude.

The selection of these variables is related to the setting of the coordinate system. Generally, for convenience, one axis of the coordinate system is often coincident with the optical axis of the imaging system, and the system origin is placed at the center of the lens, so that the other two axes are parallel to the image plane. In the right-hand system, the Z axis can be directed to the image, as shown in Fig. 7.9. In

**Fig. 7.9** Describing the surface with a distance orthogonal to the lens plane

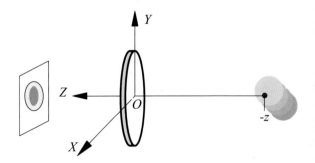

**Fig. 7.10** Use partial
differentiation to
parameterize the surface
orientation

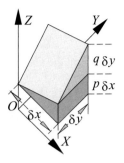

this way, the surface of the scene can be described by the distance $-z$ orthogonal to
the lens plane (i.e., parallel to the image plane).

Now write the surface normal vector in terms of $z$ and the partial derivatives of
$z$ with respect to $x$ and $y$. The surface normal is perpendicular to all the lines on the
surface tangent plane, so the outer (cross) product of any two non-parallel straight
lines on the tangent plane can provide the surface normal, which can be seen in
Fig. 7.10.

If a small step $\delta x$ is taken from a given point $(x, y)$ along the $X$ axis, according to
the Taylor expansion, the change along the $Z$ axis is $\delta z = \delta x \times \partial z / \partial x + e$, where
$e$ includes higher-order terms. In the following, $p$ and $q$ are used to represent the
partial derivatives of $z$ with respect to $x$ and $y$, and $(p, q)$ are generally called surface
gradients. In this way, the vector along the $X$ axis is $[\delta x\ 0\ p\delta x]^T$, which is parallel to
the line of vector $r_x = [1\ 0\ p]^T$ at $(x, y)$ of the tangent plane. Similarly, a straight line
parallel to the vector $r_y = [0\ 1\ q]^T$ also crosses $(x, y)$ of the tangent plane. The surface
normal can be obtained by calculating the outer product of these two straight lines.
Finally, it is determined whether to point the normal toward the observer or leave the
observer. If it points to the observer (take the reverse direction), then

$$\mathbf{N} = \mathbf{r}_x \times \mathbf{r}_y = [1\ 0\ p]^T \times [0\ 1\ q]^T = -[-p\ \ -q\ \ 1]^T \qquad (7.15)$$

Here the unit vector on the surface normal is

$$\widehat{\mathbf{N}} = \frac{\mathbf{N}}{|\mathbf{N}|} = \frac{[-p\ \ -q\ \ 1]^T}{\sqrt{1 + p^2 + q^2}} \qquad (7.16)$$

Next, calculate the angle $\theta_e$ between the surface normal of the scene and the lens
direction. Assuming that the scene is quite close to the optical axis, the unit
observation vector from the scene to the lens can be regarded as $[0\ 0\ 1]^T$, so the
result of the dot product operation of the two unit vectors can be obtained:

$$\widehat{\mathbf{N}} \cdot \widehat{\mathbf{V}} = \cos \theta_e = \frac{1}{\sqrt{1 + p^2 + q^2}} \tag{7.17}$$

When the distance between the light source and the scene is much larger than the dimension of the scene itself, the direction of the light source can be indicated by only one fixed vector, and the direction of the surface corresponding to the vector is orthogonal to the light emitted by the light source. If the normal of the surface of the scene can be represented by $[-p_s \ -q_s \ 1]^T$, when the light source and the observer are on the same side of the scene, the direction of the light source can be indicated by the gradient $(p_s, q_s)$.

## 7.2.2 Reflectance Map and Brightness Constraint Equation

Now consider linking the pixel gray scale (image brightness) with the pixel gray-scale gradient (surface orientation).

### 7.2.2.1 Reflection Map

Consider illuminating a Lambertian surface with a point light source, the illuminance is $E$, according to Eq. (7.10), and its brightness is

$$L = \frac{1}{\pi} E \cos \theta_i \quad \theta_i \geq 0 \tag{7.18}$$

where $\theta_i$ is the angle between the surface normal unit vector $[-p \ -q \ 1]^T$ and the unit vector pointing to the light source $[-p_s \ -q_s \ 1]^T$. Note that since the brightness cannot be negative, there is $0 \leq \theta_i \leq \pi/2$. Find the inner product of these two unit vectors to get

$$\cos \theta_i = \frac{1 + p_s p + q_s q}{\sqrt{1 + p^2 + q^2} \sqrt{1 + p_s^2 + q_s^2}} \tag{7.19}$$

Substituting it to Eq. (7.18), the relationship between the brightness of the scene and the surface orientation can be obtained. The relation function obtained in this way is denoted as $R(p, q)$, and the graph obtained by drawing it as a function of the gradient $(p, q)$ in the form of contours is called a **reflectance map**. The PQ plane is generally called a **gradient space**, where each point $(p, q)$ corresponds to a specific surface orientation. The point at the origin represents all planes perpendicular to the viewing direction. The reflection map depends on the nature of the object surface material and the location of the light source, or the reflectance map has integrated the surface reflection characteristics and light source distribution information.

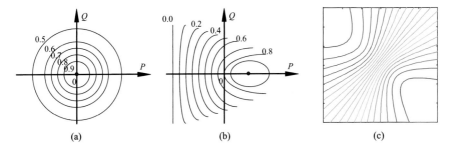

**Fig. 7.11** Examples of Lambertian surface reflectance map

The image illuminance is proportional to several constants, including the reciprocal of the focal length $\lambda$ square and the fixed brightness of the light source. In practice, the reflectance map is often normalized to facilitate unified description. For the Lambertian surface illuminated by a distant point light source, there is

$$R(p, q) = \frac{1 + p_s p + q_s q}{\sqrt{1 + p^2 + q^2}\sqrt{1 + p_s^2 + q_s^2}} \tag{7.20}$$

It can be seen from Eq. (7.20) that the relationship between the brightness of the scene and the surface orientation can be obtained from the reflectance map. For Lambertian surfaces, the contours of constant value on the reflectance map will be nested conic curves. This is because that from $R(p, q) = c$ ($c$ is a constant), the relation $(1 + p_s p + q_s q)^2 = c^2(1 + p^2 + q^2)(1 + p_s^2 + q_s^2)$ can be obtained. The maximum value of $R(p, q)$ is obtained at $(p, q) = (p_s, q_s)$.

**Example 7.3 Lambertian Surface Reflectance Map Example**
Figure 7.11 shows three examples of different Lambertian surface reflection diagrams. Figure 7.11a shows the situation when $p_s = 0$ and $q_s = 0$ (corresponding to nested concentric circles); Fig. 7.11b is the case when $p_s \neq 0$ and $q_s = 0$ (corresponding to ellipse or hyperbola); Fig. 7.11c is the case when $p_s \neq 0$ and $q_s \neq 0$ (corresponding to hyperbola).

Now consider another extreme case, called an **isotropy radiation surface**. If the surface of an object can radiate uniformly in all directions (which is not physically possible), it will feel brighter when viewed obliquely. This is because the tilt reduces the visible surface area, and it is assumed that the radiation itself does not change, so the amount of radiation per unit area will be larger. The brightness of the surface at this time depends on the reciprocal of the cosine of the radiation angle. Considering the projection of the surface of the object in the direction of the light source, it can be seen that the brightness is proportional to $\cos\theta_i/\cos\theta_e$. Because $\cos\theta_e = 1/(1 + p^2 + q^2)^{1/2}$, it has

**Fig. 7.12** Example of
surface reflectance map of
isotropy radiation

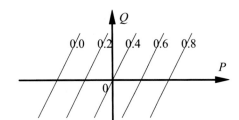

$$R(p, q) = \frac{1 + p_s p + q_s q}{\sqrt{1 + p_s^2 + q_s^2}} \qquad (7.21)$$

Contours are now parallel straight lines. This is because $R(p, q) = c$ ($c$ is a constant) gives $(1 + p_s p + q_s q) = c(1 + p_s^2 + q_s^2)^{1/2}$. These straight lines are orthogonal to the directions $(p_s, q_s)$.

**Example 7.4 Example of Surface Reflectance Map of Isotropy Radiation**
Figure 7.12 is an example of a reflection map of isotropy radiation surface, where $p_s/q_s = 1/2$, so the slope of the contour (straight line) is 2.

### 7.2.2.2   Image Brightness Constraint Equation

The reflectance map shows the dependent relationship of the surface brightness on the surface orientation. The illuminance $E(x, y)$ of a point on the image is proportional to the brightness of the corresponding point on the surface of the scene. Assuming that the surface gradient at this point is $(p, q)$, the brightness of this point can be denoted as $R(p, q)$. If the scale factor is set to a unit value through normalization, one can get

$$E(x, y) = R(p, q) \qquad (7.22)$$

This equation is called the **image brightness constraint equation**. It shows that the gray level $I(x, y)$ of the pixel at $(x, y)$ in the image $I$ depends on the reflection characteristic $R(p, q)$. The image brightness constraint equation links the brightness of any position $(x, y)$ in the image plane $XY$ with the orientation $(p, q)$ of the sampling unit represented in a gradient space $PQ$. The image brightness constraint equation plays an important role in restoring the object surface shape from the image.

Now suppose that a sphere with a Lambertian surface is illuminated by a point light source, and the observer is also at the position of point light source. Because $\theta_e = \theta_i$ and $(p_s, q_s) = (0, 0)$ at this time, from Eq. (7.20), the relationship between brightness and gradient is

**Fig. 7.13** The brightness of
the spherical surface varies
with positions

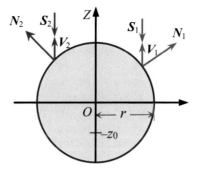

$$R(p, q) = \frac{1}{\sqrt{1 + p^2 + q^2}} \tag{7.23}$$

If the center of the sphere is on the optical axis, its surface equation is

$$z = z_0 + \sqrt{r^2 - (x^2 + y^2)} \quad x^2 + y^2 \leq r^2 \tag{7.24}$$

where $r$ is the radius of the ball and $-z_0$ is the distance between the center of the ball
and the lens (see Fig. 7.13).

According to $p = -x/(z - z_0)$ and $q = -y/(z - z_0)$, it can get $(1 + p^2 + q^2)^{1/2} = r/(z - z_0)$ and finally get

$$E(x, y) = R(p, q) = \sqrt{1 - \frac{x^2 + y^2}{r^2}} \tag{7.25}$$

It can be seen from the above equation that the brightness gradually decreases
from the maximum value at the center of the image to the zero value at the boundary
of the image. The same conclusion can be obtained by considering the light source
direction $S$, the line of sight direction $V$, and the surface direction $N$ marked in
Fig. 7.13. When people observe such a form of brightness change, they will think
that the image is obtained by imaging a round or spherical object. However, if each
part of the surface of the ball has different reflection characteristics, the resulting
image and the resulting feeling will be different. For example, when the reflection
image is represented by Eq. (7.21), and $(p_s, q_s) = (0, 0)$, a disc with uniform
brightness is obtained. For people who are accustomed to observing the reflective
properties of Lambertian surfaces, such a spherical surface will be looked
relatively flat.

### 7.2.3  Solution of Photometric Stereo

For a given image, people often hope to restore the original shape of the imaged object. The corresponding relationship from the surface orientation determined by $p$ and $q$ to the brightness determined by the reflection map $R(p, q)$ is unique, but the reverse is not necessarily true. In practice, there may be infinitely many surface orientations that can give the same brightness. These orientations corresponding to the same brightness on the reflectance map are connected by contour lines. In some cases, special points with maximum or minimum brightness can often be used to help determine the surface orientation. According to Eq. (7.20), for a Lambertian surface, only when $(p, q) = (p_s, q_s)$ will $R(p, q) = 1$, so given the surface brightness, the surface orientation can be uniquely determined. But in general, the correspondence from image brightness to surface orientation is not unique. This is because brightness has only one degree of freedom (brightness value) at each spatial position, while orientation has two degrees of freedom (two gradient values).

In this way, new information needs to be introduced in order to restore the surface orientation. In order to determine the two unknown variables $p$ and $q$, two equations are needed. Two equations can be obtained from each image point by using two images collected under different light sources (see Fig. 7.14):

$$R_1(p, q) = E_1$$
$$R_2(p, q) = E_2 \qquad (7.26)$$

If these equations are linearly independent, then there are unique solutions to $p$ and $q$. If these equations are not linear, then there are either no solutions or multiple solutions for $p$ and $q$. The corresponding relationship between brightness and surface orientation is not the only ill-conditioned problem. Collecting two images is equivalent to using additional equipment to provide additional conditions to solve the ill-conditioned problem.

**Example 7.5 Photometric Stereo Solution Calculation**
Suppose

**Fig. 7.14** Changes of lighting conditions in photometric stereoscopy

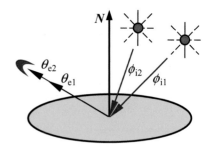

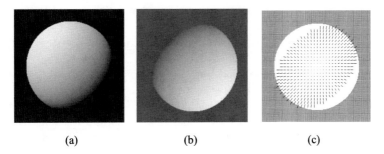

(a)               (b)               (c)

**Fig. 7.15** Calculate the surface orientation using photometric stereo

$$R_1(p, q) = \sqrt{\frac{1 + p_1 p + q_1 q}{r_1}} \quad \text{and} \quad R_2(p, q) = \sqrt{\frac{1 + p_2 p + q_2 q}{r_2}}$$

where

$$r_1 = 1 + p_1^2 + q_1^2 \quad \text{and} \quad r_2 = 1 + p_2^2 + q_2^2$$

then as long as $p_1/q_1 \neq p_2/q_2$, it can be solved from the above equations:

$$p = \frac{(E_1^2 r_1 - 1)q_2 - (E_2^2 r_2 - 1)q_1}{p_1 q_2 - q_1 p_2} \quad \text{and} \quad p = \frac{(E_2^2 r_2 - 1)p_1 - (E_1^2 r_1 - 1)p_2}{p_1 q_2 - q_1 p_2}$$

It can be seen from the above discussions that given two corresponding images collected under different illumination conditions, a unique solution can be obtained for the surface orientation of each point on the imaging object.

**Example 7.6 Photometric Stereo Solution Example**
Figure 7.15a, b are two corresponding images collected for the same sphere ball under different lighting conditions (two same light sources are at two different positions). Figure 7.15c is the result of drawing the orientation vector of each point after calculating the surface orientation using the above method. It can be seen that the orientation close to the center of the ball is relatively more perpendicular to the paper, while the orientation close to the edge of the ball is relatively parallel to the paper. Note that where there is no light, or where only one image is illuminated, the surface orientation cannot be determined.

In many practical situations, three different lighting sources are often used, which not only linearize the equations but, more importantly, improve the accuracy and the range of surface orientation that can be solved. In addition, this newly added third image can also help restore the surface reflection coefficient.

Surface reflection properties can often be described by the product of two factors (coefficients): one is a geometric term, which represents the dependence on the light reflection angle; the other is the proportion of incident light reflected by the surface, called the reflection coefficient.

Under normal circumstances, the reflection characteristics of various parts of the object surface are not consistent. In the simplest case, brightness is simply the product of the reflection coefficient and some orientation functions. The value of the reflection coefficient here is between 0 and 1. There is a Lambertian-like surface (the same brightness from all directions but not all incident lights are reflected), its brightness can be expressed as $\rho\cos\theta_i$, and $\rho$ is the surface reflection coefficient (it may change depending on the position). In order to restore the reflection coefficient and the gradient $(p, q)$, three types of information are needed, which can be obtained from the measurement of three images.

First introduce the unit vectors in the three light source directions:

$$S_j = \frac{[-p_j \quad -q_j \quad 1]^T}{\sqrt{1 + p_j^2 + q_j^2}} \quad j=1, 2, 3 \tag{7.27}$$

Then the illuminance can be represented as

$$E_j = \rho(S_j \cdot N) \quad j=1, 2, 3 \tag{7.28}$$

where

$$N = \frac{[-p \quad -q \quad 1]^T}{\sqrt{1 + p^2 + q^2}} \tag{7.29}$$

is the unit vector of the surface normal. In this way, three equations can be obtained for the unit vectors $N$ and $^\rho$:

$$\begin{aligned} E_1 &= \rho(S_1 \cdot N) \\ E_2 &= \rho(S_2 \cdot N) \\ E_3 &= \rho(S_3 \cdot N) \end{aligned} \tag{7.30}$$

Combine these equations to get

$$E = \rho S \cdot N \tag{7.31}$$

The rows of the matrix $S$ are the light source direction vectors $S_1, S_2, S_3$, and the elements of the vector $E$ are the three brightness measurement values.

Suppose $S$ is non-singular; then it can get from Eq. (7.31):

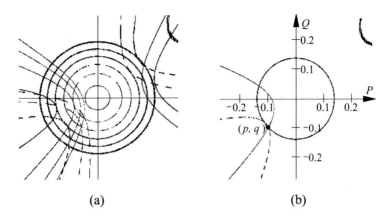

(a)          (b)

**Fig. 7.16** Use three images to restore the reflection coefficient

$$\rho\mathbf{N} = \mathbf{S}^{-1} \cdot \mathbf{E} = \frac{1}{[\mathbf{S}_1 \cdot (\mathbf{S}_2 \times \mathbf{S}_3)]} [E_1(\mathbf{S}_2 \times \mathbf{S}_3) + E_2(\mathbf{S}_3 \times \mathbf{S}_1) + E_3(\mathbf{S}_1 \times \mathbf{S}_2)] \quad (7.32)$$

The direction of the surface normal is the product of a constant and the linear combination of three vectors, each of which is perpendicular to the direction of the two light sources. If each vector is multiplied by the brightness obtained when the third light source is used, the unique reflection coefficient can be determined by determining the values of the vectors.

**Example 7.7 Recovering the Reflection Coefficient with Three Images**
Suppose a light source is placed at three positions in space $(-3.4, -0.8, -1.0)$, $(0.0, 0.0, -1.0)$, $(-4.7, -3.9, -1.0)$ to collect three images. According to the image brightness constraint equation, three sets of equations can be obtained to calculate the surface orientation and reflection coefficient $\rho$. Figure 7.16a shows these three sets of reflection characteristic curves. It can be seen from Fig. 7.16b that when the reflection coefficient $\rho = 0.8$, the three reflection characteristic curves intersect at the same point $p = -0.1$ and $q = -0.1$; in other cases, there will be no intersection.

## 7.3 Optical Flow Equation

In Sect. 4.3, the method of using the motion camera to obtain scenery depth information is introduced. Essentially, the relative movement between the camera and the scene is used there. In fact, it is equivalent if the camera is fixed but the scenery moves. The movement of the scenery will lead to the change of the scenery's pose, and the change of the scenery's pose may reveal different surface of the scene. Therefore, the use of sequence images or videos to detect the movement of the scene can also reveal the structure of each part of the scene.

The detection of motion can be based on changes in image brightness over time, which can be represented by optical flow (see Sect. 5.3). However, it should be noted that although the movement of the camera or the movement of the scenery will cause the brightness change of each image frame in the video, the change of the lighting conditions in the video may also cause the brightness of the image to change with time, so the brightness on the image plane changes with time does not always correspond to the movement of the scenery (unless the lighting conditions are known).

### 7.3.1 Optical Flow and Motion Field

Motion can be described by a **motion field**, which is composed of the motion (velocity) vector of each point in the image. When the object moves in front of the camera or the camera moves in a fixed environment, it is possible to obtain corresponding image changes. These changes can be used to restore (obtain) the relative movement between the camera and the object and the mutual interaction among multiple objects in the scene.

**Example 7.8 Calculation of Motion Field**
The motion field assigns a motion vector to each point in the image. Suppose that at a certain moment, a point $P_i$ in the image corresponds to a point $P_o$ on the object surface (see Fig. 7.17), and the two points can be connected by the projection equation. Let the movement speed of the object point $P_o$ relative to the camera be $V_o$, and then this movement will cause the corresponding image point $P_i$ to produce a movement with a speed $V_i$. These two speeds are

$$\mathbf{V}_o = \frac{d\mathbf{r}_o}{dt} \quad \mathbf{V}_i = \frac{d\mathbf{r}_i}{dt} \tag{7.33}$$

where $\mathbf{r}_o$ and $\mathbf{r}_i$ are connected by the following equation:

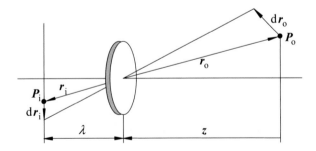

**Fig. 7.17** Object points and image points connected by projection equation

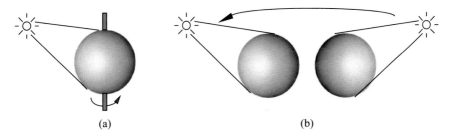

**Fig. 7.18** Optical flow is not equivalent to motion field

$$\frac{1}{\lambda}\mathbf{r}_i = \frac{1}{\mathbf{r}_o \cdot \mathbf{z}}\mathbf{r}_o \tag{7.34}$$

In Eq. (7.34), $\lambda$ is the focal length of the lens, and $z$ is the distance from the center of the lens to the object. Derivation of Eq. (7.34) can get the velocity vector assigned to each pixel, and these velocity vectors constitute the motion field.

Visual psychology believes that when relative movement occurs between a person and an object being observed, the movement of the parts with optical features on the surface of the object being observed provides information about movement and structure. When there is relative motion between the camera and the object, the motion of the brightness mode observed is called **optical flow** or **image flow**, or the movement of the object with optical features is projected onto the retinal plane (i.e., image plane) to form optical flow. Optical flow represents the change of the image; it contains the information of the object's movement, which can be used to determine the observer's movement relative to the object. Optical flow has three elements:

1. Motion (velocity field), which is a necessary condition for the formation of optical flow.
2. Parts with optical characteristics (such as grayscale pixels), which can carry information.
3. Imaging projection (from the scene to the image plane), so the optical flow can be observed.

Although there is a close relationship between optical flow and motion field, they do not completely correspond. The motion of the object in the scene causes the motion of the brightness mode in the image, and the visible motion of the brightness mode generates optical flow. In an ideal situation, the optical flow corresponds to the motion field, but in practice there are also times when it does not correspond. In other words, motion produces optical flow, so there must be motion if there is optical flow, but there is not necessarily optical flow if there is motion.

**Example 7.9 The Difference Between Optical Flow and Motion Field**
First, consider that when the light source is fixed, a ball with uniform reflection characteristics rotates in front of the camera, as shown in Fig. 7.18a. At this time, there are spatial variations in brightness everywhere in the spherical image, but this

**Fig. 7.19** The problem of corresponding points in two images at different moments

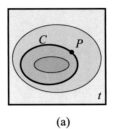
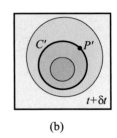

(a)                                    (b)

kind of spatial variation does not change with the rotation of the spherical surface, so the image (gray scale) does not change with time. In this case, although the motion field is not zero, the optical flow is zero everywhere. Next, consider the situation where a fixed ball is illuminated by a moving light source; see Fig. 7.18b. The gray scale everywhere in the image will change with the movement of the light source due to changes in the lighting conditions. In this case, although the optical flow is not zero, the motion field of the sphere is zero everywhere. This movement is also called apparent movement (optical flow is the apparent movement of the brightness mode). The above two situations can also be regarded as optical illusions.

It can be seen from the above example that optical flow is not equivalent to a motion field. However, in most cases, the optical flow and the motion field still have a certain corresponding relationship, so in many cases, the relative motion can be estimated from the image change according to the corresponding relationship between the optical flow and the motion field. But it should be noted that there is also a problem of determining the corresponding points between different images.

### Example 7.10 The Problem of Determining the Corresponding Points Between Images

Refer to Fig. 7.19, where each closed curve represents an equal brightness curve. Consider that there is an image point $P$ with brightness $E$ at time $t$, as shown in Fig. 7.19a. At time $t + \delta t$, which image point does $P$ correspond to? In other words, to solve this problem, it is needed to know how the brightness mode changes. Generally, there are many points near $P$ with the same brightness $E$. If the brightness changes continuously in this part of the region, then $P$ should be on an iso-brightness curve $C$. At time $t + \delta t$, there will be some iso-brightness curves $C'$ with the same brightness near the original $C$, as shown in Fig. 7.19b. However, at this time, it is difficult to say which point $P'$ on $C'$ corresponds to the original point $P$ on the original curve $C$, because the shapes of the two iso-luminance curves $C$ and $C'$ may be completely different. Therefore, although it can be determined that the curve $C$ corresponds to the curve $C'$, it cannot be specifically determined that the point $P$ corresponds to the point $P'$.

It can be seen from the above that only relying on the local information in the changing image cannot uniquely determine the optical flow. Further consider Example 7.9; if there is a region in the image with uniform brightness that does not change with time, then the optical flow of this region is likely to be zero everywhere, but in fact, the uniform region can also be assigned any vector movement mode (arbitrary optical flow).

Optical flow can represent changes in an image. Optical flow contains not only the information about the movement of the observed object but also the structural information of the scene related to it. Through the analysis of optical flow, the purpose of determining the 3-D structure of the scene and the relative motion between the observer and the moving object can be achieved. Motion analysis can use optical flow to describe image changes and infer object structure and motion. The first step is to represent the changes in the image with 2-D optical flow (or the speed of the corresponding reference point), and the second step is to calculate the result based on optical flow, that is, calculate the 3-D structure of the moving object and its motion relative to the observer.

### 7.3.2   Solving Optical Flow Equation

Optical flow can be seen as the instantaneous velocity field generated by the motion of pixels with gray scale on the image plane. Based on this, a basic optical flow constraint equation can be established, also called **optical flow equation** (see Sect. 5.3) or **image flow equation**. Let $f(x, y, t)$ be the gray scale of image point $(x, y)$ at time $t$, $u(x, y)$ and $v(x, y)$ represent the horizontal and vertical moving speeds of image point $(x, y)$, and then the optical flow equation can be represented as

$$f_x u + f_y v + f_t = 0 \tag{7.35}$$

where $f_x, f_y$, and $f_t$ represent the gradient of the pixel gray value in the image along the $X$, $Y$, and $T$ directions, respectively, which can be measured from the image.

Equation (7.35) can also be written as

$$(f_x, f_y) \cdot (u, v) = -f_t \tag{7.36}$$

This equation shows that if a fixed observer is watching a moving scene, the (first-order) time change rate of a certain point on the image obtained is the product of the scene's brightness change rate and the point's movement speed. According to Eq. (7.36), it can be seen that the component of the optical flow in the direction of the brightness gradient $(f_x, f_y)^T$ is $f_t/(f_x^2 + f_y^2)^{1/2}$. However, it can still not determine the optical flow component that it is perpendicular to the above direction (i.e., iso-brightness line direction).

### 7.3.2.1  Optical Flow Calculation: Rigid Body Motion

The calculation of optical flow is to solve the optical flow equation, that is, to find the optical flow component according to the gradient of the gray value of the image point. The optical flow equation limits the relationship between the three directional gradients and the optical flow components. It can be seen from Eq. (7.35) that this is a linear constraint equation about the velocity components $u$ and $v$. If the velocity components are used as the axes to establish a velocity space (see Fig. 7.20 for its coordinate system), then the $u$ and $v$ values satisfying the constraint Eq. (7.35) are on a straight line. It can be obtained from Fig. 7.20:

$$u_0 = -\frac{f_t}{f_x} \quad v_0 = -\frac{f_t}{f_y} \quad \theta = \arctan\left(\frac{f_x}{f_y}\right) \tag{7.37}$$

Note that each point on the line is the solution of the optical flow equation (i.e., the optical flow equation has infinite solutions). In other words, only one optical flow equation is not enough to uniquely determine the two quantities $u$ and $v$. In fact, using only one equation to solve two variables is an ill-conditioned problem, and other constraints must be added to solve it.

In many cases, the object under consideration can be regarded as a rigid body without deformation. In a **rigid body motion**, the adjacent points on it have the same optical flow velocity. This condition can be used to help solve the optical flow equation. According to the condition that adjacent points on the object have the same optical flow velocity, it can be known that the spatial change rate of optical flow velocity is zero, that is

$$(\nabla u)^2 = \left(\frac{\partial u}{\partial x} + \frac{\partial u}{\partial y}\right)^2 = 0 \tag{7.38}$$

$$(\nabla v)^2 = \left(\frac{\partial v}{\partial x} + \frac{\partial v}{\partial y}\right)^2 = 0 \tag{7.39}$$

These two conditions can be combined with the optical flow equation to calculate the optical flow by solving the minimization problem. Assume

**Fig. 7.20** The $u$ and $v$ values satisfying the optical flow constraint equation are on a straight line

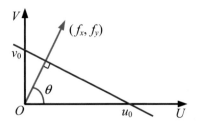

$$\varepsilon(x, y) = \sum_x \sum_y \left\{ \left( f_x u + f_y v + f_t \right)^2 + \lambda^2 \left[ (\nabla u)^2 + (\nabla v)^2 \right] \right\} \tag{7.40}$$

The value of $\lambda$ should consider the noise condition in the image. If the noise is strong, it means that the confidence of the image data itself is low and it needs to rely more on the optical flow constraint, so $\lambda$ needs to take a larger value; otherwise, $\lambda$ needs to take a smaller value.

In order to minimize the total error in Eq. (7.40), take the derivatives of $\varepsilon$ with respect to $u$ and $v$, and then take the derivatives to zero:

$$f_x^2 u + f_x f_y v = -\lambda^2 \nabla u - f_x f_t \tag{7.41}$$

$$f_y^2 v + f_x f_y u = -\lambda^2 \nabla v - f_y f_t \tag{7.42}$$

The above two equations are also called Euler equations. If $\bar{u}$ and $\bar{v}$ denote the mean values (which can be calculated with the image local smoothing operator) in the $u$ neighborhood and $v$ neighborhood, respectively, and let $\nabla u = u - \bar{u}$ and $\nabla v = v - \bar{v}$, then Eqs. (7.41) and (7.42) can be changed to

$$\left( f_x^2 + \lambda^2 \right) u + f_x f_y v = \lambda^2 \bar{u} - f_x f_t \tag{7.43}$$

$$\left( f_y^2 + \lambda^2 \right) v + f_x f_y u = \lambda^2 \bar{v} - f_y f_t \tag{7.44}$$

It can be obtained from Eqs. (7.43) and (7.44):

$$u = \bar{u} - \frac{f_x \left[ f_x \bar{u} + f_y \bar{v} + f_t \right]}{\lambda^2 + f_x^2 + f_y^2} \tag{7.45}$$

$$v = \bar{v} - \frac{f_y \left[ f_x \bar{u} + f_y \bar{v} + f_t \right]}{\lambda^2 + f_x^2 + f_y^2} \tag{7.46}$$

Equations (7.45) and (7.46) provide the basis for solving $u(x, y)$ and $v(x, y)$ by iterative method. In practice, the following relaxation iterative equations are often used to solve

$$u^{(n+1)} = \bar{u}^{(n)} - \frac{f_x \left[ f_x \bar{u}^{(n)} + f_y \bar{v}^{(n)} + f_t \right]}{\lambda^2 + f_x^2 + f_y^2} \tag{7.47}$$

$$v^{(n+1)} = \bar{v}^{(n)} - \frac{f_y \left[ f_x \bar{u}^{(n)} + f_y \bar{v}^{(n)} + f_t \right]}{\lambda^2 + f_x^2 + f_y^2} \tag{7.48}$$

Here one can take the initial value $u^{(0)} = 0$, $v^{(0)} = 0$ (straight line passing through the origin). Equations (7.47) and (7.48) have a simple geometric interpretation, that

**Fig. 7.21** The geometric
interpretation of using
iterative method to solve
optical flow

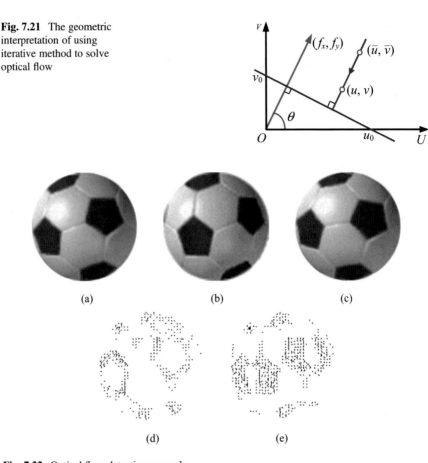

(a)                    (b)                    (c)

(d)                    (e)

**Fig. 7.22** Optical flow detection example

is, the new iteration value at a point $(u, v)$ is the average value in the neighborhood of
the point minus an adjustment amount; the quantity of adjustment is in the direction
of the brightness gradient; see Fig. 7.21. Therefore, the iterative process is a process
of moving a straight line along the brightness gradient, and the straight line is always
perpendicular to the direction of the brightness gradient.

### Example 7.11 Optical Flow Detection Example

Figure 7.22 shows an example of optical flow detection. Figure 7.22a is an image of
a football, and Fig. 7.22b, c are images obtained by rotating Fig. 7.22a around the
vertical axis and clockwise around the line of sight, respectively. Figure 7.22d, e are
the optical flows detected under these two rotation conditions.

From the optical flow maps obtained above, it can be seen that the optical flow
value is relatively large at the junction of the black and white blocks on the surface of
the football, because the gray level changes more drastically in these places, while
inside the black and white blocks, the optical flow value is very small or 0, because

when the football rotates, the gray level of these points basically does not change (similar to movement without optical flow). However, because the surface of the football is not completely smooth, there is also a certain optical flow in the interior of the black and white blocks corresponding to the certain surface regions of football.

### 7.3.2.2   Optical Flow Calculation: Smooth Motion

Further analysis of Eqs. (7.43) and (7.44) reveals that the optical flow in the region where the brightness gradient is completely zero cannot be determined in fact, while for the optical flow in the region where the brightness gradient changes quickly, the calculated error may be large. Another commonly used method for solving optical flow is to consider the **smooth motion** condition that the motion field changes generally slowly and stable in most parts of the image. At this time, consider minimizing a measure that deviates from smoothness. The commonly used measure is the integral of the square of the magnitude of the optical flow velocity gradient:

$$e_s = \iint \left[ \left( u_x^2 + u_y^2 \right) + \left( v_x^2 + v_y^2 \right) \right] dxdy \tag{7.49}$$

Also consider minimizing the error of the optical flow constraint equation

$$e_c = \iint \left[ f_x u + f_y v + f_t \right]^2 dxdy \tag{7.50}$$

Therefore, it is needed to minimize $e_s + \lambda e_c$, where $\lambda$ is the weighting quantity. If the brightness measurement is accurate, $\lambda$ should be the larger; on the contrary, if the image noise is large, $\lambda$ can be smaller.

### 7.3.2.3   Optical Flow Calculation: Gray Level Mutation

There will be discontinuities in the optical flow at the edges where the objects overlap. To extend the above-mentioned optical flow detection method from one region to another, the discontinuity needs to be determined. This brings up a similar problem to the chicken or the egg. If there is an accurate optical flow estimation, it is easy to find the place where the optical flow changes rapidly and divide the image into different regions; conversely, if the image can be well divided into different regions, an accurate estimation of the optical flow can be obtained. The solution to this contradiction is to combine the region segmentation into the iterative solution process of optical flow. Specifically, after each iteration, look for places where the optical flow changes rapidly, and mark these places to avoid the smooth solution obtained in the next iteration from crossing these discontinuities. In practical applications, the threshold is generally high to avoid dividing the image too early and too

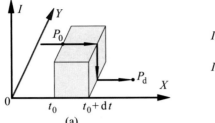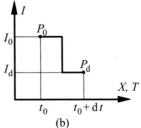

**Fig. 7.23** The situation when the gray level changes

finely, and then the threshold is gradually lowered as the estimation of the optical flow gets better.

More generally speaking, the optical flow constraint equation is applicable not only to continuous grayscale regions but also to regions with sudden grayscale changes. In other words, a condition for the application of the optical flow constraint equation is that there can be (limited) abrupt discontinuities in the image, but the changes around the discontinuities should be uniform.

Refer to Fig. 7.23a, $XY$ is the image plane, $I$ is the grayscale axis, and the object moves along the $X$ direction with speed $(u, v)$. At time $t_0$, the gray level at point $P_0$ is $I_0$, and the gray level at point $P_d$ is $I_d$; at time $t_0 + dt$, the gray level at $P_0$ moves to $P_d$ to form an optical flow. In this way, there is a **grayscale mutation** between $P_0$ and $P_d$, and the gray level gradient is $\nabla f = (f_x, f_y)$. Now look at Fig. 7.23b; if one looks at the grayscale change from the path, because the gray level at $P_d$ is the gray level at $P_0$ plus the gray level difference between $P_0$ and $P_d$, there is

$$I_d = \int_{P_0}^{P_d} \nabla f \cdot d\mathbf{l} + I_0 \qquad (7.51)$$

If one looks at the gray level change from the time course, because the observer sees the gray level change from $I_d$ to $I_0$ in $P_d$, there is

$$I_0 = \int_{t_0}^{t_0+dt} f_t dt + I_d \qquad (7.52)$$

Since the gray level changes should be the same in these two cases, the combination of Eqs. (7.51) and (7.52) can provide

$$\int_{P_0}^{P_d} \nabla f \cdot dl = - \int_{t_0}^{t_0+dt} f_t dt \qquad (7.53)$$

Substituting $dl = [u \ v]^T dt$ into it, and considering that the line integration limit and the time integration limit should correspond to each other, one can get

$$f_x u + f_y v + f_t = 0 \qquad (7.54)$$

This shows that the previous uninterrupted method can still be used to solve the problem.

It can be proved that the optical flow constraint equation is also applicable to the discontinuity of the velocity field due to the transition between the background and the object under certain conditions, provided that the image has sufficient sampling density. For example, in order to obtain the necessary information from the texture image sequence, the sampling rate of the space should be smaller than the scale of the image texture. The sampling distance in time should also be smaller than the scale of the velocity field change, or even much smaller, so that the displacement is smaller than the scale of the image texture. Another condition for the application of the optical flow constraint equation is that the grayscale change at each point in the image plane should be completely caused by the movement of a specific pattern in the image, and should not include the effects of changes in reflection properties. This condition can also be expressed as the optical flow velocity field is generated by the change of the position of a pattern in the image at different times, but the pattern itself does not change.

### 7.3.2.4   Optical Flow Calculation: Based on High-Order Gradient

The previous solution to the optical flow Eq. (7.35) only uses the first-order gradient of the image gray scale. There is a view that the optical flow constraint equation itself already contains the smoothness constraint on the optical flow field, so in order to solve the optical flow constraint equation, it is necessary to consider the continuity of the image itself on the gray scale (i.e., consider the **high-order gradient** of the image gray scale) to constrain the grayscale field.

The terms in the optical flow constraint equation are expanded with Taylor series at $(x, y, t)$, and the second order is taken to obtain

$$f_x = \frac{\partial f(x+dx, y+dy, t)}{\partial x} = \frac{\partial f(x, y, t)}{\partial x} + \frac{\partial^2 f(x, y, t)}{\partial x^2} dx$$
$$+ \frac{\partial^2 f(x, y, t)}{\partial x \partial y} dy \qquad (7.55)$$

$$f_y = \frac{\partial f(x+dx, y+dy, t)}{\partial y} = \frac{\partial f(x, y, t)}{\partial y} + \frac{\partial^2 f(x, y, t)}{\partial y \partial x} dx$$
$$+ \frac{\partial^2 f(x, y, t)}{\partial y^2} dy \qquad (7.56)$$

$$f_t = \frac{\partial f(x+dx, y+dy, t)}{\partial t} = \frac{\partial f(x, y, t)}{\partial t} + \frac{\partial^2 f(x, y, t)}{\partial t \partial x} dx$$
$$+ \frac{\partial^2 f(x, y, t)}{\partial t \partial y} dy \qquad (7.57)$$

$$u(x+dx, y+dy, t) = u(x, y, t) + u_x(x, y, t)dx + u_y(x, y, t)dy \qquad (7.58)$$
$$v(x+dx, y+dy, t) = v(x, y, t) + v_x(x, y, t)dx + v_y(x, y, t)dy \qquad (7.59)$$

Substituting Eq. (7.55) to Eq. (7.59) into the optical flow constraint equation, and obtaining

$$\left(f_x u + f_y v + f_t\right) + \left(f_{xx} u + f_{yy} v + f_x u_x + f_y v_x + f_{tx}\right)dx +$$
$$\left(f_{xy} u + f_{yy} v + f_x u_y + f_y v_y + f_{ty}\right)dy + \left(f_{xx} u_x + f_{yx} v_x\right)dx^2 + \qquad (7.60)$$
$$\left(f_{xy} u_x + f_{xx} u_y + f_{yy} v_x + f_{xy} v_y\right)dxdy + \left(f_{xy} u_y + f_{yy} v_y\right)dy^2 = 0$$

Because these terms are independent, six equations can be obtained, respectively, namely

$$f_x u + f_y v + f_t = 0 \qquad (7.61)$$

$$f_{xx} u + f_{yx} v + f_x u_x + f_y v_x + f_{tx} = 0 \qquad (7.62)$$

$$f_{xy} u + f_{yy} v + f_x u_y + f_y v_y + f_{ty} = 0 \qquad (7.63)$$

$$f_{xx} u_x + f_{yx} v_x = 0 \qquad (7.64)$$

$$f_{xy} u_x + f_{xx} u_y + f_{yy} v_x + f_{yy} v_y + f_{xy} v_y = 0 \qquad (7.65)$$

$$f_{xx} u_y + f_{yy} v_y = 0 \qquad (7.66)$$

It is more complicated to directly solve the six two-order equations from Eq. (7.61) to Eq. (7.66). With the help of the condition that the spatial rate of change of the optical flow field is zero (see the previous discussion on Eqs. (7.38) and (7.39)), it can be assumed that $u_x$, $u_y$, $v_x$, and $v_y$ are approximately zero, so that the above six equations are only the simplified equations of the first three equations, namely

$$f_x u + f_y v + f_t = 0 \tag{7.67}$$

$$f_{xx} u + f_{yx} v + f_{tx} = 0 \tag{7.68}$$

$$f_{xy} u + f_{yy} v + f_{ty} = 0 \tag{7.69}$$

To solve two unknowns from these three equations, the least square method can be used.

When solving the optical flow constraint equation with the help of gradients, it is assumed that the image is differentiable, that is, the motion of the object between image frames should be small enough (less than one pixel/frame). If it is too large, the aforementioned assumption will not hold, and the optical flow constraint equation cannot be solved accurately. One of the methods that can be taken at this time is to reduce the resolution of the image, which is equivalent to low-pass filtering the image, which has the effect of reducing the optical flow speed.

## 7.4 Shape from Motion

Optical flow contains information about the structure of the scene, so the orientation of the surface can be obtained from the optical flow of the surface of the object, that is, the shape of the surface of the object can be determined. This is called restoring shape from motion and abbreviated as **shape from motion**.

The orientation of every point in the objective world and the surface of the object can be represented by an orthogonal coordinate system $XYZ$ centered on the observer. Consider a monocular observer located at the origin of the coordinates, and suppose the observer has a spherical retina, so that the objective world can be considered to be projected onto a unit image sphere. The image sphere can be represented by a spherical coordinate system containing longitude $\phi$ and latitude $\theta$ and a distance $r$ from the origin. It can also represent all points in the objective world in a Cartesian coordinate system, as shown in Fig. 7.24.

The transformation from spherical coordinates to Cartesian coordinates is given by the following three equations:

$$x = r \sin \theta \cos \phi \tag{7.70}$$

$$y = r \sin \theta \sin \phi \tag{7.71}$$

$$z = r \cos \theta \tag{7.72}$$

The transformation from Cartesian coordinates to spherical coordinates is given by the following three equations:

**Fig. 7.24** Spherical
coordinate system and
Cartesian coordinate system

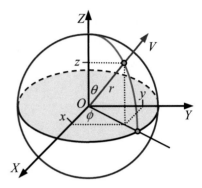

$$r = \sqrt{x^2 + y^2 + z^2} \tag{7.73}$$

$$\theta = \arccos\left(\frac{z}{r}\right) \tag{7.74}$$

$$\phi = \arccos\left(\frac{y}{x}\right) \tag{7.75}$$

With the help of coordinate transformation, the optical flow of an arbitrary moving point can be determined as follows. Let $(u, v, w) = (dx/dt, dy/dt, dz/dt)$ be the speed of the point in the $XYZ$ coordinate system, and then $(\delta, \varepsilon) = (d\phi/dt, d\theta/dt)$ is the angular velocity of the point along the $\phi$ and $\theta$ directions in the image spherical coordinate system

$$\delta = \frac{v \cos\phi - u \sin\phi}{r \sin\theta} \tag{7.76}$$

$$\varepsilon = \frac{(ur \sin\theta \cos\phi + vr \sin\theta \sin\phi + wr \cos\theta)\cos\theta - rw}{r^2 \sin\theta} \tag{7.77}$$

Equations (7.76) and (7.77) constitute the general representations of optical flow in the $\phi$ and $\theta$ directions.

Now consider the calculation of optical flow in a simple case. Suppose the scene is stationary and the observer moves along the $Z$ axis (positive direction) at a speed $S$. At this time, $u = 0$, $v = 0$, $w = -S$; substituting them into Eqs. (7.76) and (7.77) can obtain, respectively

$$\delta = 0 \tag{7.78}$$

$$\varepsilon = \frac{S \sin\theta}{r} \tag{7.79}$$

Equations (7.78) and (7.79) constitute the simplified optical flow equations, which are the basis for solving surface orientation and edge detection. According to the solution of the optical flow equation, it can be judged whether each point in the

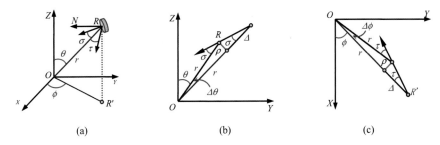

**Fig. 7.25** Schematic diagram of finding the surface direction

optical flow field is a boundary point, a surface point, or a space point. Among them, the type of boundary and the orientation of the surface can also be determined in the two cases of boundary point and surface point.

Here it is only introduced how to use optical flow to find the surface orientation. First look at Fig. 7.25a, let $R$ be a point on a given element on the surface of the object, and the monocular observer with the focus at $O$ observes this element along the line of sight $OR$. Suppose the normal vector of the element is $N$, and $N$ can be decomposed into two mutually perpendicular directions: one is in the $ZOR$ plane, and the angle with $OR$ is $\sigma$ (as shown in Fig. 7.25b); the other one is in a plane perpendicular to the $ZOR$ plane (parallel to the $XY$ plane), and the angle with $OR'$ is $\tau$ (as shown in Fig. 7.25c, where the $Z$ axis is pointed out in the paper). In Fig. 7.25b, $\phi$ is a constant, and in Fig. 7.25c, $\theta$ is a constant. In Fig. 7.25b, the $ZOR$ plane constitutes a "depth profile" along the line of sight, while in Fig. 7.25c, the "depth profile" is parallel to the $XY$ plane.

Now discuss how to determine $\sigma$ and $\tau$. Consider first the $\sigma$ in the $ZR$ plane; see Fig. 7.25b. If the vector angle $\theta$ is given a small increment $\Delta\theta$, the change of the vector radius $r$ is $\Delta r$. Making an auxiliary line $\rho$ passing $R$, it can be seen that on the one hand, $\rho/r = \tan(\Delta\theta) \approx \Delta\theta$ and, on the other hand, $\rho/\Delta r = \tan\sigma$. Putting them together to eliminate $\rho$, then

$$r\Delta\theta = \Delta r \tan\sigma \qquad (7.80)$$

Consider now the $\tau$ in the vertical plane to the $RZ$ plane; see Fig. 7.25c. If the vector angle $\phi$ is given a small increment $\Delta\phi$, the length of the vector radius $r$ changes to $\Delta r$. Now making an auxiliary line $\rho$, it can be seen that on the one hand, $\rho/r = \tan\Delta\phi \approx \Delta\phi$ and, on the other hand, $\rho/\Delta r = \tan\tau$. Putting them together to eliminate $\rho$, then

$$r\Delta\phi = \Delta r \tan\tau \qquad (7.81)$$

Furthermore, taking the limits of Eqs. (7.80) and (7.81), respectively, it can get

$$\cot \sigma = \left[\frac{1}{r}\right] \frac{\partial r}{\partial \theta} \tag{7.82}$$

$$\cot \tau = \left[\frac{1}{r}\right] \frac{\partial r}{\partial \phi} \tag{7.83}$$

where $r$ can be determined by Eq. (7.72). Because $\varepsilon$ is a function of both $\phi$ and $\theta$, the Eq. (7.79) can be rewritten as

$$r = \frac{S \sin \theta}{\varepsilon(\phi, \theta)} \tag{7.84}$$

Find the partial derivatives with respect to $\phi$ and $\theta$, respectively; it gets

$$\frac{\partial r}{\partial \phi} = S \sin \theta \frac{-1}{\varepsilon^2} \frac{\partial \varepsilon}{\partial \phi} \tag{7.85}$$

$$\frac{\partial r}{\partial \theta} = S \left( \frac{\cos \theta}{\varepsilon} - \frac{\sin \theta}{\varepsilon^2} \frac{\partial \varepsilon}{\partial \theta} \right) \tag{7.86}$$

Note that the surface orientation determined by $\sigma$ and $\tau$ has nothing to do with the observer's movement speed $S$. Substituting Eq. (7.84) to Eq. (7.86) into Eq. (7.82) and Eq. (7.83), the equations for $\sigma$ and $\tau$ can be obtained:

$$\sigma = \text{arccot} \left[ \cot \theta - \frac{\partial(\ln \varepsilon)}{\partial \theta} \right] \tag{7.87}$$

$$\tau = \text{arccot} \left[ - \frac{\partial(\ln \varepsilon)}{\partial \phi} \right] \tag{7.88}$$

## 7.5   Key Points and References for Each Section

The following combines the main contents of each section to introduce some references that can be further consulted.

1. **Photometric Stereo**

    The use of photometric stereoscopic methods needs to control the lighting conditions; see also [1]. Using the symmetry of the bidirectional reflectance distribution function with respect to the incident and reflection directions, the 3-D scene can also be restored with the help of binocular Helmholtz stereo vision method, especially good for high-light scenes, as in [2].

2. **Shape from Illumination**

Restoring shape from light is a typical method of shape from $X$, which is introduced in many books about computer vision, such as [3].

3. **Optical Flow Equation**

The derivation of the optical flow equation can be seen in Sect. 5.3 and also in [4].

4. **Shape from Motion**

For the discussion of the boundary types and surface orientations of boundary points and surface points in the optical flow field, please refer to [5]. The discussion on obtaining structure from motion can also be found in [6].

## Self-Test Questions

The following questions include both single-choice questions and multiple-choice questions, so each option must be judged.

### 7.1 Photometric Stereo

7.1.1 Imaging involves light source, scenery, and lens, ($\cdot$).

   (a) The light emitted by the light source is measured by intensity, and the light received by the scenery is measured by illuminance.
   (b) The light emitted by the scenery is measured by intensity, and the light received by the lens is measured by illuminance.
   (c) The light from the light source incidents to the scenery at a certain angle.
   (d) The light from the scenery incidents to the lens at a certain angle.

[Hint] Refer to the flowchart from the light source through the scenery to the lens in Fig. 7.1.

7.1.2 The brightness of the image obtained after imaging a 3-D scenery is proportional to ($\cdot$).

   (a) The shape of the scenery itself and its posture in space
   (b) The intensity of light reflected when the surface of the scenery is illuminated by light
   (c) The light reflection coefficient of the surface of the scenery
   (d) The product of the light reflection coefficient on the surface of the scenery and the intensity of the light reflected on the surface of the scenery when illuminated by light

[Hint] The light reflection coefficient is related to the reflected light intensity.

7.1.3 For Lambertian surfaces, the incident and observation mode correspond to ($\cdot$).

(a) Fig. 7.6a
(b) Fig. 7.6b
(c) Fig. 7.6c
(d) Fig. 7.6d

[Hint] The Lambertian surface is also called the diffuse reflection surface.

7.1.4 For an ideal specular reflection surface, the incident and observation mode correspond to ($\cdot$).

(a) Fig. 7.6a
(b) Fig. 7.6b
(c) Fig. 7.6c
(d) Fig. 7.6d

[Hint] The ideal specular reflection surface can reflect all the incident light from the ($\theta_i$, $\phi_i$) direction to the ($\theta_e$, $\phi_e$) direction.

## 7.2 Shape from Illumination

7.2.1 To represent the orientation of each point on the surface of the scenery, ($\cdot$).

(a) One can use the orientation of the tangent surface corresponding to each point on the surface.
(b) One can use the normal vector of the tangent plane corresponding to each point on the surface.
(c) One can use two position variables corresponding to the intersection of the normal vector and the surface of the sphere.
(d) One can use the unit observation vector from the scenery to the lens.

[Hint] What is needed is to represent the characteristics of the scenery itself.

7.2.2 In the reflection image obtained by illuminating the Lambertian surface with a point light source, ($\cdot$).

(a) Each point corresponds to a specific surface orientation.
(b) Each circle corresponds to a specific surface orientation.
(c) It contains information on surface reflection characteristics and light source distribution.
(d) It contains the relationship between the brightness of the scenery and the surface orientation.

[Hint] The $R$ in the reflection image $R(p, q)$ corresponds to the surface brightness of the scenery, and ($p, q$) corresponds to the surface gradient of the scenery.

7.2.3 There is an ellipsoidal object $x^2/4 + y^2/4 + z^2/2 = 1$ with an ideal specular reflection surface. If the incident light intensity is 9 and the reflection coefficient is 0.5, the intensity of the reflected light observed at $(1, 1, 1)$ will be approximately $(\cdot)$.

    (a) 3.8
    (b) 4.0
    (c) 4.2
    (d) 4.4

[Hint] Calculate the intensity of reflected light specifically, and pay attention that the incident angle and the reflection angle of the specular reflection surface are equal.

## 7.3 Optical Flow Equation

7.3.1 The optical flow expresses the change of the image. The following cases where there is optical flow (optical flow is not 0) include $(\cdot)$.

    (a) The moving light source illuminates the object that is relatively stationary with the camera
    (b) The fixed light source illuminates the rotating object in front of the fixed camera
    (c) The fixed light source illuminates moving objects with different reflective surfaces
    (d) The moving light source illuminates a moving object with an invisible brightness pattern on the surface

[Hint] Consider the three key elements of optical flow.

7.3.2 Only one optical flow equation cannot uniquely determine the optical flow velocity in two directions, but $(\cdot)$.

    (a) If the object is regarded as a rigid body without deformation, then this condition can be used to help solve the optical flow equation.
    (b) If the ratio of the optical flow components in the two directions are known, the optical flow in the two directions can also be calculated.
    (c) If the acceleration of the object movement in the image is set to be very small, then this condition can be used to help solve the optical flow equation.
    (d) If the gray level changes uniformly but there are only a few sudden changes in the image, it can also be used to calculate the optical flow in two directions.

[Hint] The establishment of the optical flow equation does not mean that it is solvable.

7.3.3 In solving the optical flow equation, from the perspective of rigid body motion, the constraint that the spatial rate of change of the optical flow is zero is introduced; from the perspective of smooth motion, the constraint that the motion field changes slowly and steadily is introduced, (·).

(a) Compared with the two constraints, the former is weaker than the latter

(b) Compared with the two constraints, the former is as weak as the latter

(c) Compared with the two constraints, the former is stronger than the latter

(d) Compared with the two constraints, the former is as strong as the latter

[Hint] Compare the representations of two constraints.

## 7.4 Shape from Motion

7.4.1 If the longitude of a point in space is $30°$, the latitude is $120°$, and the distance from the origin is 2, then its Cartesian coordinates are: (·).

(a) $x = \sqrt{6}/2, y = \sqrt{3}, z = -1$

(b) $x = \sqrt{6}/2, y = \sqrt{3}/2, z = -1$

(c) $x = \sqrt{6}/2, y = \sqrt{3}/4, z = -2$

(d) $x = \sqrt{6}/2, y = \sqrt{3}, z = -2$

[Hint] Judge according to the coordinate conversion equation.

7.4.2 If the Cartesian coordinates of a point in space are $x = 6, y = 3, z = 2$, then its spherical coordinates are (·).

(a) $\phi = 30°, \theta = 67°, r = 10$

(b) $\phi = 40°, \theta = 73°, r = 9$

(c) $\phi = 50°, \theta = 67°, r = 8$

(d) $\phi = 60°, \theta = 73°, r = 7$

[Hint] Judge according to the coordinate conversion formula.

7.4.3 Consider Fig. 7.25, which is/are used to illustrate the finding of the surface direction? (·).

(a) In Fig. 7.25b, the ZOR plane coincides with the YZ plane.

(b) In Fig. 7.25b, the ZOR plane does not coincide with the YZ plane.

(c) In Fig. 7.25c, the ZOR' plane coincides with the XY plane.

(d) In Fig. 7.25c, the ZOR' plane does not coincide with the XY plane.

[Hint] Analyze according to Fig. 7.25a.

# References

1. Jähne B, Haußecker H, Geißler P. Handbook of Computer Vision and Applications: Volume 1: Sensors and Imaging. Academic Press. 1999.
2. Chen Z H, Zhang Y-J. A binocular Helmholtz stereo method for measuring objects with highlights. Journal of Image and Graphics, 2010, 15(3): 429-434.
3. Horn B K P. Robot Vision. MIT Press. 1986.
4. Zhang Y-J. Image Engineering, Vol.2: Image Analysis. De Gruyter, 2017.
5. Ballard D H, Brown C M. Computer Vision. Prentice-Hall. 1982.
6. Forsyth D, Ponce J. Computer Vision: A Modern Approach, 2nd Ed. Prentice Hall. 2012.

# Chapter 8
# Monocular Single Image Recovery

The scene restoration method introduced in Chap. 7 is based on redundant information in multiple monocular images. This chapter introduces the method based on monocular single image. In practice, when a 3-D scene is projected onto a 2-D image, the depth information in it will be lost. However, judging from the practice of the human visual system, especially the ability of spatial perception (see Appendix A), in many cases there are still many depth cues in the image, so under certain constraints or prior knowledge, it is still possible to recover the scene from it. In other words, in the process of acquiring 2-D images from 3-D scenes, some useful information is indeed lost due to projection, but some information with conversing forms is retained (or it can be said that the 3-D clues of scenes are still in 2-D images).

Many methods have been proposed for scene restoration from **monocular single image**. Some methods are more general (with certain generalization), and some methods need to meet specific conditions. For example, in the imaging process, some information about the shape of the original scenery will be converted into the brightness information corresponding to the shape of the original scenery in the image (or in the case of certain illumination, the brightness change in the image is related to the shape of the scenery), so the surface shape of the scenery can be restored according to the shading changes of the image, which is called shape restoration from shading (in short, shape from shading). For another example, under the condition of perspective projection, some information about the shape of the scenery will be retained in the change of the surface texture of the object (different orientation of the scenery surface will cause different surface texture changes), so the surface of the object can be determined by analyzing the texture change for different orientations and then trying to restore its surface shape; this is called shape restoration from texture (in short, shape from texture).

The sections of this chapter are arranged as follows:

Section 8.1 introduces the principle of shape restoration from shading, which uses the relationship between the tone on the image and the surface shape of the object in the scene to establish a brightness equation that links the gray scale of the pixel with the orientation. The gradient space method is specifically discussed, which can analyze and explain the structure formed by the intersection of planes.

Section 8.2 discusses the problem of solving the image brightness constraint equation and introduces the method and effect of the solution in the linear, rotationally symmetric, and general smooth constraint conditions.

Section 8.3 introduces the principle of shape restoration from texture. The essence is to infer the orientation of the surface according to the corresponding relationship between imaging and distortion, with the aid of prior knowledge of the surface texture of the object, and using the change after the texture change projection.

Section 8.4 further discusses how to calculate the vanishing point when the texture is composed of regular texture element grids, so as to restore the surface orientation information.

## 8.1  Shape from Shading

When objects in the scene are illuminated by light, various parts of the surface will appear to have different brightness due to their different orientations. This spatial change of brightness (shading change) after imaging appears as different tones on the image (also called different shadows). According to the distribution and changes of the tone, the shape information of the object can be obtained. This is called restoring the shape from the shading or **shape from shading**.

### 8.1.1  Shading and Orientation

First discuss the relationship between the shading on the image and the surface shape of the object in the scene, and then introduce how to represent the change of orientation.

**Shading** corresponds to different levels of brightness (represented by gray scale) formed by projecting a 3-D object onto a 2-D image plane. The change distribution of these levels depends on four factors:

1. The geometry of the visible (facing the observer) surface of the object (surface normal direction)
2. The incident intensity (energy) and direction of the light source
3. The position and distance of the observer (line of sight) relative to the object
4. The reflection characteristics of the surface of the object

The effect of these four factors can be introduced with the help of Fig. 8.1, where the object is represented by the surface element $S$; the normal direction of the surface element $N$ indicates the direction of the surface element, which is related to the local geometry of the object; the incident intensity and the direction of the light source are represented by the vector $I$; the position and distance of the observer relative to the

**Fig. 8.1** Four factors
affecting the change of
image gray scale

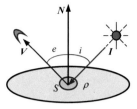

object are indicated by the line of sight vector $V$; the surface reflection characteristics
of the object $\rho$ depend on the material of the surface element, which is generally a
function of the spatial position of the element.

According to Fig. 8.1, if the incident light intensity on the 3-D object surface
element $S$ is $I$ and the reflection coefficient $\rho$ is a constant, then the reflection
intensity along $N$ is

$$E(x, y) = I(x, y)\rho \cos i \tag{8.1}$$

If the light source comes from behind the observer and is parallel light, then
$\cos i = \cos e$. Assuming that the line of sight intersects the imaged $XY$ plane
perpendicularly, and the object has a Lambertian scattering surface, that is, the
intensity of the surface reflection does not change due to changes in the observation
position, the observed light intensity can be written as

$$E(x, y) = I(x, y)\rho \cos e \tag{8.2}$$

To establish the relationship between the surface orientation and the image
brightness, the gradient coordinates $PQ$ are also arranged on the $XY$ plane; suppose
the normal is away from the observer along the observer's direction; according to
$N = [p \ q \ -1]^{\mathrm{T}}$ and $V = [0 \ 0 \ -1]^{\mathrm{T}}$, it can obtain

$$\cos e = \cos i = \frac{[p \ q \ -1]^{\mathrm{T}} \cdot [0 \ 0 \ -1]^{\mathrm{T}}}{|[p \ q \ -1]^{\mathrm{T}}| \cdot |[0 \ 0 \ -1]^{\mathrm{T}}|} = \frac{1}{\sqrt{p^2 + q^2 + 1}} \tag{8.3}$$

Substituting Eq. (8.3) into Eq. (8.1), the observed image gray scale is

$$E(x, y) = I(x, y)\rho \frac{1}{\sqrt{p^2 + q^2 + 1}} \tag{8.4}$$

Now consider the general case where the light is not incident at the angle $i = e$.
Let the incident light vector $I$ passing through the panel be $[p_i \ q_i \ -1]^{\mathrm{T}}$, because $\cos i$
is the cosine of the angle between $N$ and $I$, so it has

$$\cos i = \frac{[p \quad q \quad -1]^{\mathrm{T}} \bullet [0 \quad 0 \quad -1]^{\mathrm{T}}}{|[p \quad q \quad -1]^{\mathrm{T}}| \bullet |[0 \quad 0 \quad -1]^{\mathrm{T}}|} = \frac{pp_i + qq_i + 1}{\sqrt{p^2 + q^2 + 1}\sqrt{p_i^2 + q_i^2 + 1}} \tag{8.5}$$

Substituting Eq. (8.5) into Eq. (8.1), the gray level of the image observed when the light is incident at any angle is

$$E(x,\, y) = I(x,\, y)\rho = \frac{pp_i + qq_i + 1}{\sqrt{p^2 + q^2 + 1}\sqrt{p_i^2 + q_i^2 + 1}} \tag{8.6}$$

Equation (8.6) can also be written in a more abstract general form

$$E(x,\, y) = R(p,\, q) \tag{8.7}$$

This is the same **image brightness constraint equation** as Eq. (7.22).

### 8.1.2  Gradient Space Method

Now consider the change of the image gray level due to the change of surface element orientation. A 3-D surface can be expressed as $z = f(x,\, y)$, and the surface element normal on it can be represented as $\boldsymbol{N} = [p \; q \; -1]^{\mathrm{T}}$. It can be seen that the surface in 3-D space is just a point $G(p,\, q)$ in 2-D gradient space from its orientation, as shown in Fig. 8.2. In other words, only two variables are needed to represent the orientation of the 3-D surface. Using this **gradient space** method to study 3-D surfaces can play a role in dimensionality reduction (to 2-D), but the representation of gradient space does not determine the position of 3-D surfaces in 3-D coordinates. In other words, a point in the gradient space represents all surface elements with the same orientation, but the spatial positions of these surface elements can be different.

With the aid of gradient space method, the structure formed by the intersection of planes can be analyzed and explained.

**Example 8.1 Determine the Convex or Concave Structure Formed by the Intersection of Planes**
The intersection of multiple planes can form a convex structure or a concave structure. To determine whether it is a convex structure or a concave structure, the

**Fig. 8.2** The representation of 3-D surface in 2-D gradient space

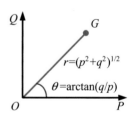

**Fig. 8.3** Example of the intersection of two spatial planes

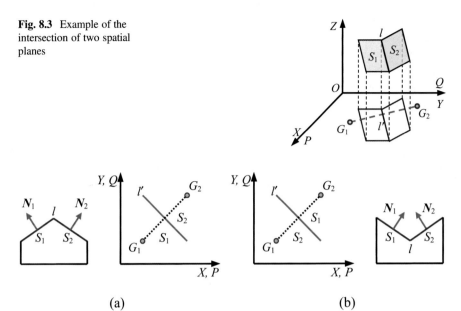

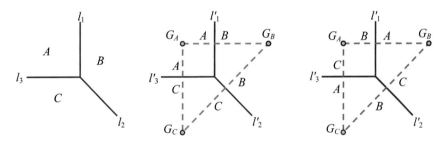

(a)          (b)

**Fig. 8.4** The convex structure (**a**) and concave structure (**b**) composed by two spatial planes

**Fig. 8.5** Two situations where three space planes intersect

gradient information can be used. First look at the situation where two planes $S_1$ and $S_2$ intersect to form a line of intersection $l$, as shown in Fig. 8.3 (where the gradient coordinate $PQ$ coincides with the spatial coordinate $XY$). Here $G_1$ and $G_2$, respectively, represent the gradient space points corresponding to the two normal lines of the two planes, and the line between them is perpendicular to the projection $l'$ of $l$.

If $S$ and $G$ of the same face have the same sign (on the same side of the projection $l'$ of $l$), it indicates that the two faces form a convex structure, as shown in Fig. 8.4a. If the $S$ and $G$ on the same face have different signs, it indicates that the two faces form a concave structure, as shown in Fig. 8.4b.

Further consider the case where three planes $A$, $B$, and $C$ intersect and their intersection lines are $l_1$, $l_2$, and $l_3$; see Fig. 8.5a. If the faces on both sides of each intersection line have the same sign as the corresponding gradient points (each face is arranged clockwise as AABBCC), it indicates that the three faces form a convex structure, as shown in Fig. 8.5b. If the faces on both sides of each intersection line have different signs with that of the corresponding gradient points (each face is arranged clockwise as CBACBA), it means that the three faces form a concave structure, as shown in Fig. 8.5c.

Now go back to Eq. (8.4) and rewrite it as

$$p^2 + q^2 = \left[\frac{I(x,\ y)\rho}{E(x,\ y)}\right]^2 - 1 = \frac{1}{K^2} - 1 \tag{8.8}$$

In Eq. (8.8), $K$ represents the relative reflection intensity observed by the observer. The map based on the contour line of the relative reflection intensity is called the **reflection map**. Equation (8.8) corresponds to the equations of a series of concentric circles on the $PQ$ plane, and each circle represents the observed orientation track of the same gray level panel. When $i = e$, the reflection image is composed of concentric circles. For the general case of $i \neq e$, the reflection map consists of a series of ellipses and hyperbolas.

### Example 8.2 Application Example of Reflection Map

Assuming that the observer can see three planes $A$, $B$, and $C$, they form the plane intersection as shown in Fig. 8.6a, but the actual degree of inclination is unknown. Using the reflection map, the angle between the three planes can be determined. Suppose $I$ and $V$ are in the same direction, it can get (the relative reflection intensity can be measured from the image) $K_A = 0.707$, $K_B = 0.807$, $K_C = 0.577$. According to the characteristic that the line between the $G(p, q)$ of the two faces is perpendicular to the intersection of the two faces, the triangle shown in Fig. 8.6b can be obtained (i.e., the conditions satisfied by the orientation of the three planes). Now find $G_A$, $G_B$, $G_C$ on the reflection map shown in Fig. 8.6c. Substituting each $K$ value into Eq. (8.8), the following two sets of solutions are obtained:

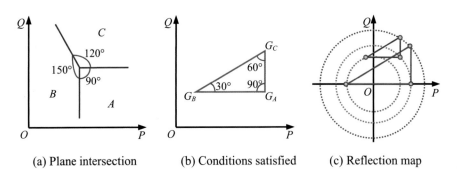

(a) Plane intersection          (b) Conditions satisfied          (c) Reflection map

**Fig. 8.6** (a–c) Application example of reflection map

$$(p_A, q_A) = (0.707, 0.707) \quad (p_B, q_B) = (-0.189, 0.707) \quad (p_C, q_C) = (0.707, 1.225)$$

$$(p'_A, q'_A) = (1, 0) \quad (p'_B, q'_B) = (-0.732, 0) \quad (p'_C, q'_C) = (1, 1)$$

The first set of solutions corresponds to the small triangles in Fig. 8.6c, and the second set of solutions corresponds to the big triangles in Fig. 8.6c. Both sets of solutions satisfy the condition of relative reflection intensity. In fact, there are two possible combinations for the orientation of the three planes, corresponding to the convex and concave structures of the three intersections.

## 8.2 Solving Brightness Equation

Since the image brightness constraint equation relates the gray level of the pixel to the orientation of the pixel, the gray level $I(x, y)$ of the pixel at $(x, y)$ in the image can be considered to find the orientation $(p, q)$ there. But there is a problem here, that is, the brightness measurement of a single point on the image can only provide one constraint, and the orientation of the surface has two degrees of freedom. In other words, suppose that the visible surface of the object in the image is composed of $N$ pixels, and each pixel has a gray value $I(x, y)$. The solution of Eq. (8.7) is the required value at the pixel position $(p, q)$. Because according to $N$ pixels, only $N$ equations can be formed from the image brightness equation, but there are $2N$ unknowns, that is, there are two gradient values for each gray value to be solved, this is an ill-conditioned problem, and no unique solution can be obtained. It is generally necessary to add additional conditions to establish additional equations to solve this ill-conditioned problem. In other words, if there is no additional information, although the image brightness equation establishes the relationship between the image brightness and the surface orientation, the surface orientation cannot be restored based on the image brightness equation alone.

A simple way to consider additional information is to use the constraints in the monocular image. The main considerations include uniqueness, continuity (surface, shape), compatibility (symmetry, epipolar line), etc. In practical applications, there are many factors that affect the brightness, so it is only possible to restore the shape of the object from the shading if the environment is highly controlled.

In practice, people can often estimate the shape of each part of the human face only by observing a plane picture. This shows that the picture contains enough information or people have implicitly introduced additional assumptions based on empirical knowledge when observing the picture. In fact, the surface of many real objects is smooth, or continuous in depth, and further partial differentials are also continuous. A more general situation is that the object has a continuous surface with slices and only the edges are not smooth. The above information provides a strong constraint. There is a certain connection between the orientation of two adjacent elements on the surface, and together they should give a continuous smooth surface. It can be seen that the macro-smooth constraint method can be used to provide additional information to help solve the **image brightness constraint equation**. The following three cases are introduced from simple to complex:

## 8.2.1   Linearity Case

First consider the special case of linear reflection; suppose

$$R(p, q) = f(ap + bq) \tag{8.9}$$

where $a$ and $b$ are constants. At this time, the reflection map is shown in Fig. 8.7, and the contour lines in the gradient space in the map are parallel lines.

The function $f$ in Eq. (8.9) is a strictly monotonic function (see Fig. 8.8). In addition, its inverse function $f^{-1}$ exists. Knowing from the image brightness equation

$$s = ap + bq = f^{-1}[E(x, \ y)] \tag{8.10}$$

Note that it is not possible to determine the gradient $(p, q)$ of a particular image point only by measuring the gray level of the image, but an equation that restricts the possible value of the gradient can be obtained. For a surface with an angle $\theta$ to the $X$ axis, its slope is

**Fig. 8.7** Reflection map of linear combination of gradient elements

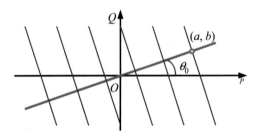

**Fig. 8.8** The $s = ap + bq$ can be restored from $E(x, y)$

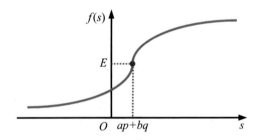

**Fig. 8.9** Restoring the surface according to the parallel surface profile lines

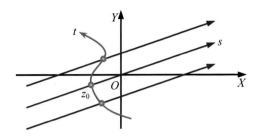

$$m(\theta) = p\cos\theta + q\sin\theta \tag{8.11}$$

Now choose a specific direction $\theta_0$ (see Fig. 8.7), $\tan\theta_0 = b/a$, that is

$$\cos\theta_0 = \frac{a}{\sqrt{a^2 + b^2}} \qquad \sin\theta_0 = \frac{b}{\sqrt{a^2 + b^2}} \tag{8.12}$$

The slope in this direction is

$$m(\theta_0) = \frac{ap + bq}{\sqrt{a^2 + b^2}} = \frac{1}{\sqrt{a^2 + b^2}} f^{-1}[E(x, \ y)] \tag{8.13}$$

Starting from a specific image point, if one takes a small step $\delta s$, then the change of $z$ at this time is $\delta z = m\delta s$, that is,

$$\frac{dz}{ds} = \frac{1}{\sqrt{a^2 + b^2}} f^{-1}[E(x, \ y)] \tag{8.14}$$

where $x$ and $y$ are linear functions of $s$:

$$x(s) = x_0 + s\cos\theta \qquad y(s) = y_0 + s\sin\theta \tag{8.15}$$

First find the solution at a point $(x_0, \ y_0, \ z_0)$ on the surface, and integrate the previous differential equation over $z$ to get

$$z(s) = z_0 + \frac{1}{\sqrt{a^2 + b^2}} \int_0^s f^{-1}[E(x, \ y)]\,ds \tag{8.16}$$

In this way, a surface profile line along the straight line given above (one of the parallel straight lines in Fig. 8.9) can be obtained. When the reflection map is a function of the linear combination of gradient elements, the surface profile lines are parallel straight lines. As long as the initial height $z_0(t)$ is given, the surface can be restored by integrating along these lines. Of course, in practice, the integral is calculated by a numerical algorithm.

Note that if one wants to know the absolute distance, one needs to know the $z_0$ value at a certain point, but one can restore the (surface) shape without this absolute distance. In addition, the absolute distance cannot be determined only by the integral constant $z_0$. This is because $z_0$ itself does not affect the shading, and only the changes in depth can affect the shading.

## 8.2.2  Rotational Symmetry Case

Now consider a more general situation. If the distribution of the light source has **rotational symmetry** with respect to the observer, then the reflection map is also rotationally symmetric. For example, when the observer views the hemispherical sky from bottom to top, the obtained reflection map is rotationally symmetric; and when the point light source and the observer are at the same position, the obtained reflection map is also rotationally symmetric. In these cases

$$R(p, q) = f\left(p^2 + q^2\right) \tag{8.17}$$

Now assuming that the function $f$ is strictly monotonic and derivable, and the inverse function is $f^{-1}$, then according to the image brightness equation, it has

$$p^2 + q^2 = f^{-1}[E(x, y)] \tag{8.18}$$

If the angle between the fastest rising direction of the surface and the $X$ axis is $\theta_s$, where $\tan\theta_s = p/q$, then

$$\cos\theta_s = \frac{p}{\sqrt{p^2 + q^2}} \qquad \sin\theta_s = \frac{q}{\sqrt{p^2 + q^2}} \tag{8.19}$$

According to Eq. (8.11), the slope in the direction of steepest ascent is

$$m(\theta_s) = \sqrt{p^2 + q^2} = \sqrt{f^{-1}[E(x, y)]} \tag{8.20}$$

In this case, if one knows the brightness of the surface, one can know its slope, but one doesn't know the direction of the fastest rising, that is, one doesn't know the respective values of $p$ and $q$. Now suppose that the direction of the steepest ascent is given by $(p, q)$. If a small step length of $\delta s$ is taken in the direction of the steepest ascent, the resulting change in $x$ and $y$ should be

$$\delta x = \frac{p}{\sqrt{p^2 + q^2}}\delta s \qquad \delta y = \frac{q}{\sqrt{p^2 + q^2}}\delta s \tag{8.21}$$

And the change of $z$ is

$$\delta z = m\delta s = \sqrt{p^2 + q^2}\delta s = \sqrt{f^{-1}[E(x,\ y)]}\delta s \tag{8.22}$$

To simplify these equations, the step size can be taken as $\sqrt{p^2 + q^2}\delta s$, so it has

$$\delta x = p\delta s \qquad \delta y = q\delta s \qquad \delta z = (p^2 + q^2)\delta s = \{f^{-1}[E(x,\ y)]\}\delta s \tag{8.23}$$

In addition, a horizontal surface is a region of uniform brightness on the image, so only the brightness gradient of the curved surface is not zero. To determine the brightness gradient, the image brightness equation can be derived with respect to $x$ and $y$. Let $u$, $v$, and $w$ be the second-order partial derivatives of $z$ with respect to $x$ and $y$ respectively, namely,

$$u = \frac{\partial^2 z}{\partial x^2} \qquad \frac{\partial^2 z}{\partial x \partial y} = v = \frac{\partial^2 z}{\partial y \partial x} \qquad w = \frac{\partial^2 z}{\partial y^2} \tag{8.24}$$

Then according to the chain rule of the derivative, one can get

$$E_x = 2(pu + qv)f' \qquad E_y = 2(pv + qw)f' \tag{8.25}$$

where $f'(r)$ is the derivative of $f(r)$ with respect to its unique variable $r$.

Now let's determine the changes in $\delta p$ and $\delta q$ due to the step size $(\delta x, \delta y)$ in the image plane. By differentiating $p$ and $q$, one can get

$$\delta p = u\delta x + v\delta y \qquad \delta q = v\delta x + w\delta y \tag{8.26}$$

According to Eq. (8.23), one can get

$$\delta p = (pu + qv)\delta s \qquad \delta q = (pv + qw)\delta s \tag{8.27}$$

Or further by Eq. (8.25), one can get

$$\delta p = \frac{E_x}{2f'}\delta s \qquad \delta q = \frac{E_y}{2f'}\delta s \tag{8.28}$$

In this way, in the limit case of $\delta s \to 0$, the following set of five differential equations can be obtained (differentiation is performed on $s$):

$$\dot{x} = p \qquad \dot{y} = q \qquad \dot{z} = p^2 + q^2 \qquad \dot{p} = \frac{E_x}{2f'} \qquad \dot{q} = \frac{E_y}{2f'} \tag{8.29}$$

If the initial value is given, the above five ordinary differential equations can be solved numerically to get a curve on the object surface. The curve obtained in this way is called the characteristic curve, and it happens to be the fastest rising curve here. This kind of curve is perpendicular to the contour lines point by point. Note that when $R(p, q)$ is a linear function of $p$ and $q$, the characteristic curve is parallel to the surface of the object.

In addition, if $\dot{x}=p$ and $\dot{y}=q$ in Eq. (8.29) are differentiated once again to $s$, another set of equations can be obtained:

$$\ddot{x}=\frac{E_x}{2f'} \qquad \ddot{y}=\frac{E_y}{2f'} \qquad z=f^{-1}[E(x, y)] \tag{8.30}$$

Since both $E_x$ and $E_y$ are measures of image brightness, the above equations need to be solved by numerical solutions.

### 8.2.3   The General Case of Smoothness Constraints

Under normal circumstances, the surface of the object is relatively smooth (although there are discontinuities between the objects); this **smoothness constraint** can be used as an additional constraint. If it is considered that the surface of the object (within the contour of the object) is smooth, the following two equations hold:

$$(\nabla p)^2 = \left(\frac{\partial p}{\partial x} + \frac{\partial p}{\partial y}\right)^2 = 0 \tag{8.31}$$

$$(\nabla q)^2 = \left(\frac{\partial q}{\partial x} + \frac{\partial q}{\partial y}\right)^2 = 0 \tag{8.32}$$

If they are combined with the brightness constraint equation, solving the surface orientation problem can be transformed into a problem that minimizes the following total error:

$$\varepsilon(x, y) = \sum_x \sum_y \left\{ [E(x, y) - R(p, q)]^2 + \lambda\left[(\nabla p)^2 + (\nabla q)^2\right] \right\} \tag{8.33}$$

Equation (8.33) can be regarded as follows: Find the orientation distribution of the surface elements of the object, so that the weighted sum of the overall grayscale error and the overall smoothness error is the smallest. Let $\bar{p}$ and $\bar{q}$ denote the mean values in the $p$ neighborhood and $q$ neighborhood, respectively, take the derivative of $\varepsilon$ with respect to $p$ and $q$, respectively, and take the derivative to zero, and then substitute $\nabla p = p - \bar{p}$ and $\nabla q = q - \bar{q}$ to obtain

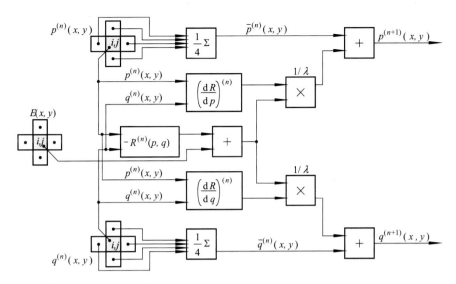

**Fig. 8.10** Flowchart for solving constraint equations

$$p(x, y) = \bar{p}(x, y) + \frac{1}{\lambda}[E(x, \ y) - R(p, q)]\frac{\partial R}{\partial p} \tag{8.34}$$

$$q(x, y) = \bar{q}(x, y) + \frac{1}{\lambda}[E(x, \ y) - R(p, q)]\frac{\partial R}{\partial q} \tag{8.35}$$

The equations for iteratively solving Eqs. (8.34) and (8.35) are as follows (the initial value of the iteration can be the boundary point value):

$$p^{(n+1)} = \bar{p}^{(n)} + \frac{1}{\lambda}\left[E(x, \ y) - R\left(p^{(n)}, q^{(n)}\right)\right]\frac{\partial R^{(n)}}{\partial p} \tag{8.36}$$

$$q^{(n+1)} = \bar{q}^{(n)} + \frac{1}{\lambda}\left[E(x, \ y) - R\left(p^{(n)}, q^{(n)}\right)\right]\frac{\partial R^{(n)}}{\partial q} \tag{8.37}$$

Here one should pay attention to the unevenness between the inside and outside of the contour of the object, and there are jumps.

**Example 8.3 Flowchart for Solving the Brightness Constraint Equation**
The flowchart for solving Eqs. (8.36) and (8.37) is shown in Fig. 8.10. Its basic framework can also be used to solve the relaxation iteration Eqs. (7.47) and (7.48) of the optical flow equation.

**Example 8.4 Example of Shape Restoration from Shading**
Figure 8.11 shows two examples of restoring shapes from shading. Figure 8.11a is an image of a sphere; Fig. 8.11b is the (needle) image of the surface orientation of the sphere obtained from Fig. 8.11a using shading information; Fig. 8.11c is another

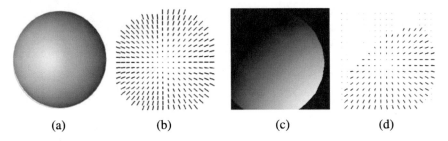

(a)                    (b)                    (c)                    (d)

**Fig. 8.11** (a–d) Example of shape restoration from shading (see text)

sphere image; Fig. 8.11d is the (needle) image of the surface orientation obtained from Fig. 8.11c using shading information. In the group of Fig. 8.11a, b, the direction of the light source is relatively close to the direction of the line of sight, so basically the direction of each point can be determined for the entire visible surface. Figure 8.11c, d has a relatively large angle between the direction of the light source and the direction of the line of sight, so the direction of the visible surface that cannot be illuminated by light cannot be determined (as shown in Fig. 8.11d, corresponding to the upper left parts of the image in Fig. 8.11c).

## 8.3  Shape from Texture

The representation, description, segmentation, and classification of textures in images have been introduced in Chap. 11 of *2D Computer Vision: Principles, Algorithms and Applications*. Here we discuss the problem of restoring **shape from texture**.

When people observe a textured surface, they can observe the degree of inclination of the surface with only one eye, because the texture of the surface will look distorted due to the inclination. The role of texture in restoring surface orientation has been discussed as early as 1950. The method of estimating the surface orientation based on the observed surface texture distortion will be described below.

### 8.3.1  Monocular Imaging and Distortion

In perspective projection imaging, the farther the scene is from the observation point or the collector, the smaller the image will be, and vice versa. This can be seen as a kind of dimensional **distortion** during imaging. This kind of imaging distortion actually contains the spatial and structural information of the 3-D scenery. It needs to be pointed out here that unless the X or Y of the scenery coordinates is known, the absolute distance between the collector and the scenery cannot be directly obtained from the 2-D image (only the relative distance information is obtained).

The geometric outline of an object can be regarded as composed of straight-line segments. Next, consider some distortions that occur when a straight line of 3-D space is perspectively projected onto a 2-D image plane. According to the camera model, the projection of a point is still a point. A straight line is composed of its end points and intermediate points, so the projection of a straight line can be determined based on the projections of these points. There are two points in space (points at both ends of the straight line) $W_1 = [X_1 \ Y_1 \ Z_1]^T$, $W_2 = [X_2 \ Y_2 \ Z_2]^T$; the points in between can be represented as $(0 < s < 1)$

$$sW_1 + (1-s)W_2 = s \begin{bmatrix} X_1 \\ Y_1 \\ Z_1 \end{bmatrix} + (1-s) \begin{bmatrix} X_2 \\ Y_2 \\ Z_2 \end{bmatrix} \tag{8.38}$$

The above two end points, after projection $P$, can be represented as $PW_1 = [kX_1 \ kY_1 \ kZ_1 \ q_1]^T$, $PW_2 = [kX_2 \ kY_2 \ kZ_2 \ q_2]^T$, where $q_1 = k(\lambda - Z_1)/\lambda$, $q_2 = k(\lambda - Z_2)/\lambda$. The point on the line between the original $W_1$ and $W_2$ can be represented as $(0 < s < 1)$ after being projected:

$$P[sW_1 + (1-s)W_2] = s \begin{bmatrix} kX_1 \\ kY_1 \\ kZ_1 \\ q_1 \end{bmatrix} + (1-s) \begin{bmatrix} kX_2 \\ kY_2 \\ kZ_2 \\ q_2 \end{bmatrix} \tag{8.39}$$

In other words, the image plane coordinates of all points on this space straight line can be obtained by dividing the first three terms by the fourth term of homogeneous coordinates, which can be represented as $(0 \le s \le 1)$

$$w = [x \ y]^T = \left[ \frac{s X_1 + (1-s)X_2}{s q_1 + (1-s)q_2} \quad \frac{s Y_1 + (1-s)Y_2}{s q_1 + (1-s)q_2} \right]^T \tag{8.40}$$

The above is the result of projection transformation using $s$ to represent the spatial point. On the other hand, on the image plane, $w_1 = [\lambda X_1/(\lambda - Z_1) \ \lambda Y_1/(\lambda - Z_1)]^T$, $w_2 = [\lambda X_2/(\lambda - Z_2) \ \lambda Y_2/(\lambda - Z_2)]^T$; the point on the line between them can be represented as $(0 < t < 1)$

$$tw_1 + (1-t)w_2 = t \begin{bmatrix} \dfrac{\lambda X_1}{\lambda - Z_1} \\ \dfrac{\lambda Y_1}{\lambda - Z_1} \end{bmatrix} + (1-t) \begin{bmatrix} \dfrac{\lambda X_2}{\lambda - Z_2} \\ \dfrac{\lambda Y_2}{\lambda - Z_2} \end{bmatrix} \tag{8.41}$$

Therefore, the coordinates (indicated by $t$) of the points on the image plane of $w_1$ and $w_2$ as well as the line between them are $(0 \le t \le 1)$

$$w = [x \quad y]^T = \left[ t\frac{\lambda X_1}{\lambda - Z_1} + (1-t)\frac{\lambda X_2}{\lambda - Z_2} \quad t\frac{\lambda Y_1}{\lambda - Z_1} + (1-t)\frac{\lambda Y_2}{\lambda - Z_2} \right]^T \quad (8.42)$$

If the projection result represented by $s$ is the image point coordinate represented by $t$, then Eqs. (8.40) and (8.42) should be equal, so that one can get

$$s = \frac{tq_2}{tq_2 + (1-t)q_1} \quad (8.43)$$

$$t = \frac{sq_1}{sq_1 + (1-s)q_2} \quad (8.44)$$

It can be seen from Eqs. (8.43) and (8.44) that $s$ and $t$ have single-valued relationships. In 3-D space, the point represented by $s$ corresponds to one and only one point represented by $t$ in the 2-D image plane. All the spatial points represented by $s$ are connected to form a straight line, and all the image points represented by $t$ are connected to form a straight line. It can be seen that after a straight line in the 3-D space is projected onto the 2-D image plane, as long as it is not a vertical projection, the result is still a straight line (but the length may vary). If it is a vertical projection, the projection result is just a point (this is a special case). The inverse proposition is also true, that is, a straight line on the 2-D image plane must be produced by a straight line projection in the 3-D space (in special cases it can also be produced by a plane projection).

Next, consider the distortion of parallel lines, because parallel is a very characteristic relationship between lines in a straight line system. In 3-D space, a point $(X, Y, Z)$ on a straight line can be represented as

$$\begin{bmatrix} X \\ Y \\ Z \end{bmatrix} = \begin{bmatrix} X_0 \\ Y_0 \\ Z_0 \end{bmatrix} + k\begin{bmatrix} a \\ b \\ c \end{bmatrix} \quad (8.45)$$

Among them, $(X_0, Y_0, Z_0)$ represents the starting point of the straight line; $(a, b, c)$ represents the direction cosines of the straight line; $k$ is any coefficient.

For a group of parallel lines, their $(a, b, c)$ are the same; only $(X_0, Y_0, Z_0)$ are different. The distance between the parallel lines is determined by the difference between different $(X_0, Y_0, Z_0)$. If the parallel line is extended to both ends infinitely, it can be seen that the projected trajectory of the parallel line is only related to $(a, b, c)$ and has nothing to do with $(X_0, Y_0, Z_0)$. In other words, parallel lines with the same $(a, b, c)$ will intersect at one point after extending infinitely. This point can be in the image plane or outside the image plane, so it is also called **vanishing point**. The calculation of the vanishing point will be introduced in Sect. 8.4.

## 8.3.2   Orientation Restoration from the Change of Texture

Using the texture on the surface of the object can help determine the orientation of the surface and further restore the shape of the surface. The description of texture here is mainly based on the idea of structural method: complex texture is composed of some simple texture primitives (**texture element**, or **texel**) repeatedly arranged and combined in a certain regular form. In other words, texture elements can be regarded as visual primitives with repeatability and invariance in a region. Here the repeatability refers to the repeated occurrence of these primitives in different positions and directions. Of course, this kind of repetition is possible only at a certain resolution (the number of texels in a given visual range). The invariance refers to the pixel composition of the same primitive having some basically similar characteristics. These characteristics may be only related to the gray scale or may depend also on the certain characteristics such as its shape.

### 8.3.2.1   Three Typical Methods

Using the texture of the surface of an object to determine its orientation should consider the influence of the imaging process, which is specifically related to the relationship between the texture of the scenery and the texture of the image. In the process of acquiring the image, the texture structure on the original scenery may change in the image (generating gradient changes in both size and direction). This change may be different depending on the orientation of the surface where the texture is located and have 3-D information about the orientation of the object's surface. Note that this is not to say that the surface texture itself carries 3-D information but that the changes produced by the texture during the imaging process carry 3-D information. The texture changes can be divided into three categories (here, assuming that the texture is limited to a flat surface), referring to the schematic diagram in Fig. 8.12. The commonly used methods for restoring orientation based on texture information can also be divided into the following three categories:

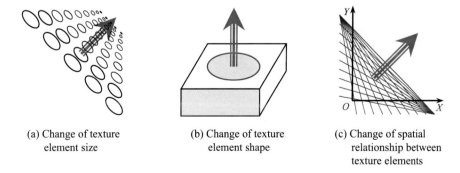

(a) Change of texture        (b) Change of texture        (c) Change of spatial
element size                 element shape                relationship between
                                                          texture elements

**Fig. 8.12**  (**a**–**c**) Texture change and surface orientation

1. Use the Change of Texture Element Size

In perspective projection, there is a law of near-large and far-small, so texture elements with different positions may have different sizes after projection. This is obvious when looking along the direction of the floor or floor tiles. According to the maximum value of the change rate of the projection size of the texture element, the orientation of the plane where the texture element is located can be determined. See Fig. 8.12a; the direction of this maximum value is the direction of the texture gradient. Assuming that the image plane coincides with the paper surface and the line of sight comes out of the paper, then the direction of the texture gradient depends on the rotation angle of the texture element around the **camera line of sight**, and the value of the texture gradient gives the degree of inclination of the texture element relative to the line of sight. Therefore, the orientation of the texture element and the plane of texture element can be determined with the aid of the geometric information of the camera placement.

It should be noted that the regular texture on the surface of the 3-D scene will produce a texture gradient in the 2-D image, but the texture gradient in the 2-D image does not necessarily come from the regular texture on the surface of the 3-D scene.

**Example 8.5 The Change of Texture Element Size Provides the Depth of the Scenery**

Figure 8.13 shows two pictures. The front part of Fig. 8.13a has many petals (they are equivalent to texels of similar size), and the petal size gradually decreases from front to back (from near to far). This change in the size of texture elements gives a sense of depth to the scene. The building in Fig. 8.13b has many columns and windows (they are equivalent to regular-shaped texture elements). The changes in their size also give people a sense of depth in the scene, and it is easy to help the observer to make the judgment that the farthest distance is from the corners.

(a)                                                                (b)

**Fig. 8.13** (**a, b**) The change of texture element size gives the depth of the scene

2. Use the Change of Texture Element Shape

The shape of the texel on the surface of the object may change after imaging with **perspective projection** and **orthogonal projection**. If the original shape of the texel is known, the direction of the surface can also be calculated from the result of the change of the texel shape. The orientation of the plane is determined by two angles (the angle of rotation relative to the camera axis (line of sight) and the angle of inclination relative to the camera axis). For the given original texture elements, these two angles can be determined according to the change results after imaging. For example, on a plane, the texture composed of circles will become ellipse on an inclined plane, as shown in Fig. 8.12b. At this time, the orientation of the main axis of the ellipse determines the angle of rotation relative to the camera axis, and the ratio of the lengths of the long and short axis reflects the angle of tilt relative to the camera axis. This ratio is also called the **aspect ratio**. The calculation process is described below. Suppose the equation of the plane where the circular texture primitives are located is

$$ax + by + cz + d = 0 \tag{8.46}$$

The circle that constitutes the texture can be regarded as the line of intersection between the plane and the sphere (the line of intersection between the plane and the sphere is always a circle, but when the line of sight is not perpendicular to the plane, the line of intersection seen by the deformation is always an ellipse). The spherical equation is

$$x^2 + y^2 + z^2 = r^2 \tag{8.47}$$

Solve the above two equations together (equivalent to projecting a sphere onto a plane)

$$\frac{a^2 + c^2}{c^2}x^2 + \frac{b^2 + c^2}{c^2}y^2 + \frac{2adx + 2bdy + 2abxy}{c^2} = r^2 - \frac{d^2}{c^2} \tag{8.48}$$

This is an elliptic equation, which can be further transformed into

$$\left[(a^2 + c^2)x + \frac{ad}{a^2 + c^2}\right]^2 + \left[(b^2 + c^2)y + \frac{bd}{b^2 + c^2}\right]^2 + 2abxy = c^2r^2$$
$$- \left[\frac{a^2d^2 + b^2d^2}{a^2 + c^2}\right]^2 \tag{8.49}$$

From the above equation, the coordinates of the center point of the ellipse can be obtained, and the semimajor axis and semiminor axis of the ellipse can be determined, so that the rotation angle and the tilt angle can be calculated.

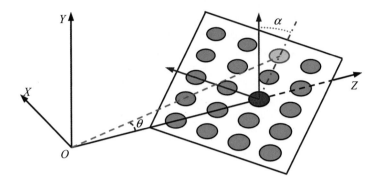

**Fig. 8.14** The position of the circular texture primitive plane in the coordinate system

Another way to judge the deformation of circular texture is to calculate the semimajor axis and semiminor axis of different ellipses. See Fig. 8.14 (where the world coordinates coincide with the camera coordinates), the angle between the plane where the circular texture primitives are located and the $Y$ axis is $\alpha$ (it is also the angle between the texture plane and the image plane). In the image obtained at this time, not only the circular texture primitive becomes an ellipse, but the density of the upper primitive is greater than that of the middle part, forming a density gradient. In addition, the aspect ratio of each ellipse, that is, the ratio of the length of the semiminor axis to the length of the semimajor axis, is not constant, forming a gradient of the aspect ratio. At this time, there are changes in both the size of the texel and the shape of the texel.

If the diameter of the original circle is $D$, for the circle at the center of the scenery, the long axis of the ellipse in the image can be obtained according to the perspective projection relationship as

$$D_{\text{major}}(0, \ 0) = \lambda \frac{D}{Z} \tag{8.50}$$

where $\lambda$ is the focal length of the camera and $Z$ is the object distance. The aspect ratio at this time is the cosine of the tilt angle, that is,

$$D_{\text{minor}}(0, 0) = \lambda \frac{D}{Z} \cos \alpha \tag{8.51}$$

Now consider the primitives on the scenery that are not on the optical axis of the camera (the light-colored ellipse in Fig. 8.14). If the $Y$ coordinate of the primitive is $y$ and the angle between the line to the origin and the $Z$ axis is $\theta$, then one can get

$$D_{\text{major}}(0, \ y) = \lambda \frac{D}{Z}(1 - \tan \theta \tan \alpha) \tag{8.52}$$

$$D_{\text{minor}}(0, y) = \lambda \frac{D}{Z} \cos \alpha (1 - \tan \theta \tan \alpha)^2 \qquad (8.53)$$

The aspect ratio at this time is $\cos\alpha(1 - \tan\theta \tan\alpha)$, which will decrease with the increase of $\theta$, forming a gradient of the aspect ratio.

3. Use the Change of Spatial Relationship Between Texture Elements

If the texture is composed of **regular grids of texels**, the surface orientation information can be recovered by calculating its **vanishing point** (see Sect. 8.4). The vanishing point is the common intersection point of each line segment in the set of intersecting line segments. For a perspective image, the vanishing point on the plane is formed by the projection of the texel at infinity to the image plane in a certain direction, or is the convergence point of parallel lines at infinity, which can be seen in Eq. (8.39).

**Example 8.6 Texture Element Grid and Vanishing Point**

Figure 8.15a shows a perspective view of a cuboid with parallel grid lines on each surface, and Fig. 8.15b is a schematic diagram of the vanishing point of each surface texture.

If one looks along the surface to its vanishing point, one can see the change in the spatial relationship between texture elements, that is, the increase in the distribution density of texture elements. Two vanishing points obtained from the same surface texture element grid can be used to determine the orientation of the surface. The line where these two points are located is also called **vanishing line**, which is composed of vanishing points of parallel lines in different directions on the same plane (e.g., the vanishing points of parallel lines in different directions on the ground constitute the horizon). The direction of the vanishing line indicates the rotation angle of the texture element relative to the camera axis, and the intersection of the vanishing line and $x = 0$ indicates the tilt angle of the texture element relative to the line of sight; see

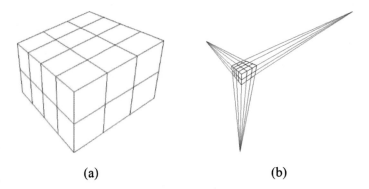

(a)  (b)

**Fig. 8.15** Texture element grid (**a**) and vanishing point (**b**)

**Table 8.1** Comparison of three methods for determining the surface orientation of objects using texel changes

| Method | Rotation angle of the texel relative to the camera axis | Tilt angle of the texel relative to the camera axis |
|---|---|---|
| Use the change of texel size | Texture gradient direction | Texture gradient value |
| Use the change of texel shape | Texel main axis direction | The ratio of the long axis and short axis of the texel |
| Use the change of spatial relationship between texels | The direction of the line between the two vanishing points | The intersection of the line between two vanishing points and $x = 0$ |

**Table 8.2** Overview of some methods to obtain shapes from textures

| Surface cue | Surface type | Original texture | Projection model | Analysis method | Analysis unit | Unit attribute |
|---|---|---|---|---|---|---|
| Texture gradient | Plane | Unknown | Perspective | Statistics | Wave | Wavelength |
| Texture gradient | Plane | Unknown | Perspective | Structure | Region | Area |
| Texture gradient | Plane | Uniform density | Perspective | Statistics/ structure | Edge/ region | Density |
| Convergence line | Plane | Parallel lines | Perspective | Statistics | Edge | Direction |
| Normalized texture feature map | Plane | Known | Orthogonal | Structure | Line | Length |
| Normalized texture feature map | Curved surface | Known | Spherical | Structure | Region | Axis |
| Shape distortion | Plane | Isotropic | Orthogonal | Statistics | Edge | Direction |
| Shape distortion | Plane | Unknown | Orthogonal | Structure | Region | Shape |

Fig. 8.12c. The above situation can be easily explained by the perspective projection model.

Finally, the above three methods of using the changes of texture element to determine the surface orientation of an object can be summarized in Table 8.1.

### 8.3.2.2  Shape from Texture

The specific effect of determining the surface orientation and restoring the surface shape by texture is related to the gradient of the surface itself, the distance between the observation point and the surface, and the angle between the line of sight and the image. Table 8.2 gives an overview of some typical methods, which also lists various terms for obtaining shapes from textures. The various methods that have been proposed to determine the surface by texture are mostly based on different combinations of them.

In Table 8.2, the difference between the different methods is mainly on the use of different surface orientation cues, namely, the texture gradient (referring to the maximum change rate and direction of the texture roughness on the surface), the convergence line (which can limit the flat surface in assuming that these lines are parallel in 3-D space and can determine the vanishing point of the image), the normalized texture characteristic map (the map is similar to the reflection map for the shape from shading), and the shape distortion (if knowing the original shape of a pattern on the surface, then the observable shape can be determined on the image for various orientations of the surface). The surface is flat in most cases, but it can also be curved; the analysis method can be either a structural method or a statistical method.

In Table 8.2, the projection type mostly uses **perspective projection**, but it can also be **orthogonal projection** or **spherical projection**. In spherical projection, the observer is at the center of the sphere, the image is formed on the sphere, and the line of sight is perpendicular to the sphere. When restoring the surface orientation from the texture, the 3-D volume should be reconstructed according to the distortion of the original texture element shape after projection. Shape distortion is mainly related to two factors: (1) the distance between the observer and the object, which affects the size of the texture element after distortion, and (2) the angle between the normal line of the object surface and the line of sight (camera axis, also called the surface inclination); it affects the deformed shape of the texture element. In orthogonal projection, the first factor does not work; only the second factor will work. In perspective projection, the first factor works, and the second factor only works when the surface of the object is curved (if the surface of the object is flat, it will not produce distortion that affects the shape). The projection form that can make the above two factors work together on the shape of the object is spherical perspective projection. At this time, the change of the distance between the observer and the object will cause the size of the texture element to change, and the change of the inclination of the object surface will cause the change of the object shape after projection.

In the process of restoring the surface orientation from the texture, it is often necessary to make certain assumptions about the texture pattern. Two typical assumptions are as follows:

Isotropic Assumption

The **isotropic assumption** holds that for an isotropic texture, the probability of finding a texture primitive on the texture plane has nothing to do with the orientation of the texture primitive. In other words, the probability model for isotropic texture does not need to consider the orientation of the coordinate system on the texture plane.

Homogeneity Assumption

The homogeneity of texture in an image means that no matter where the texture of a window is selected at any position in the image, it is consistent with the texture of the window selected at other positions. More strictly speaking, the probability distribution of a pixel value only depends on the nature of the pixel neighborhood and has nothing to do with the spatial coordinates of the pixel itself. According to the **homogeneity assumption**, if the texture of a window in the image is collected as a sample, the texture outside the window can be modeled according to the nature of the sample.

In an image obtained by orthogonal projection, even if the texture is assumed to be homogeneous, the orientation of the texture plane cannot be restored, because the homogeneous texture is still a homogeneous texture after viewing angle transformation. However, if the image obtained by perspective projection is considered, it is possible to restore the orientation of the texture plane.

This problem can be explained as follows: According to the assumption of homogeneity, and that the texture is composed of a uniform pattern of points, if the texture plane is sampled with equally spaced grids, then the number of texture points obtained by each grid should be the same or very close. However, if this texture plane covered with grids at equal intervals is perspectively projected, some grids will be mapped into larger quadrilaterals, while others will be mapped into smaller quadrilaterals. In other words, the texture on the image plane is no longer homogeneous. Since the grid is mapped to different sizes, the number of (originally homogeneous) texture patterns contained therein is no longer the same. According to this property, the relative orientation of the imaging plane and the texture plane can be determined by using the proportional relationship of the number of texture patterns contained in different windows.

### 8.3.2.3  Texture Stereo Technology

The combination of texture method and stereo vision method is called **texture stereo technique**. It estimates the direction of the surface of the scene by acquiring two images of the scene at the same time, avoiding the problem of complicated corresponding point matching. In this method, the two imaging systems used are connected by rotation transformation.

In Fig. 8.16, the straight line orthogonal to the texture gradient direction and parallel to the surface of the object is called the characteristic line, and there is no change in the texture structure on this line. The angle between the characteristic line and the $X$ axis is called the characteristic angle, which can be calculated by comparing the Fourier energy spectrum of the texture region.

According to the characteristic lines and characteristic angles obtained from the two images, the surface normal vector $N = [N_x\ N_y\ N_z]^{\mathrm{T}}$ can be determined:

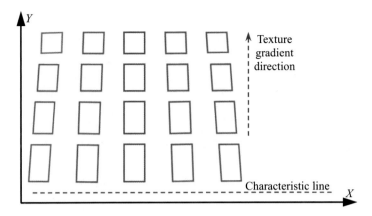

**Fig. 8.16** Characteristic lines of texture surface

$$N_x = \sin \theta_1 (a_{13} \cos \theta_2 + a_{23} \sin \theta_2) \tag{8.54}$$

$$N_y = - \cos \theta_1 (a_{13} \cos \theta_2 + a_{23} \sin \theta_2) \tag{8.55}$$

$$N_z = \cos \theta_1 (a_{21} \cos \theta_2 + a_{22} \sin \theta_2) - \sin \theta_1 (a_{11} \cos \theta_2 + a_{21} \sin \theta_2) \tag{8.56}$$

Among them, $\theta_1$ and $\theta_2$ are the angles formed by the characteristic line in the two images and the $X$ axis counterclockwise; the coefficient $a_{ij}$ is the directional cosine between the corresponding axes in the two imaging systems.

## 8.4 Detection of Texture Vanishing Points

When using changes in the spatial relationship between texture elements to estimate the surface orientation, it is necessary to detect/calculate the vanishing point.

### 8.4.1 Detecting the Vanishing Point of Line Segment Texture

If the texture pattern is composed of straight-line segments, the introduction for the method of detecting vanishing point can be conducted with the help of Fig. 8.17. Theoretically, this work can be carried out in two steps (each step requires one Hough transform):

1. Determine all the straight lines in the image (which can be done directly with the Hough transform).
2. Find those straight lines that pass through common points, and determine which points are the vanishing points (the peak accumulated in the parameter space indicating these points with the help of the Hough transform).

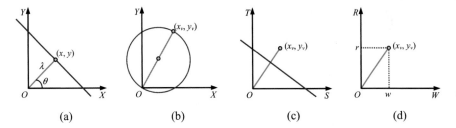

**Fig. 8.17** (a–d) Determine the vanishing point of line segment texture (see text)

According to the **Hough transform**, the straight line in the image space can be determined by detecting the parameters in the parameter space. As shown in Fig. 8.17a, in the polar coordinate system, a straight line can be represented as

$$\lambda = x \cos\theta + y \sin\theta \tag{8.57}$$

If the symbol "⇒" is used to represent the transformation from one set to another, the transformation $\{x, y\} \Rightarrow \{\lambda, \theta\}$ maps a straight line in the image space $XY$ to a point in the parameter space $\Lambda\Theta$, and the set of straight lines with the same vanishing point $(x_v, y_v)$ in the image space $XY$ is projected onto a circle in the parameter space $\Lambda\Theta$. To illustrate this point, $\lambda = \sqrt{x^2 + y^2}$ and $\theta = \arctan\{y/x\}$ can be substituted into the following equation:

$$\lambda = x_v \cos\theta + y_v \sin\theta \tag{8.58}$$

Transfer the result to the Cartesian coordinate system, and one can get

$$\left(x - \frac{x_v}{2}\right)^2 + \left(y - \frac{y_v}{2}\right)^2 = \left(\frac{x_v}{2}\right)^2 + \left(\frac{y_v}{2}\right)^2 \tag{8.59}$$

The above equation represents a circle with its center at $(x_v/2, y_v/2)$ and a radius of $\lambda = \sqrt{(x_v/2)^2 + (y_v/2)^2}$, as shown in Fig. 8.17b. This circle is the trajectory of all the line segments with $(x_v, y_v)$ as the vanishing point projected into the $\Lambda\Theta$ space. In other words, the transformation $\{x, y\} \Rightarrow \{\lambda, \theta\}$ can be used to map the set of line segments from $XY$ space to $\Lambda\Theta$ space to detect the vanishing point.

The above method of determining the vanishing point has two shortcomings: one is that the detection of a circle is more difficult than the detection of a straight line, and the amount of calculation is also large; the other is when $x_v \rightarrow \infty$ or $y_v \rightarrow \infty$, there are $\lambda \rightarrow \infty$ (here the symbol "→" indicates a trend). To overcome these shortcomings, the transformation $\{x, y\} \Rightarrow \{k/\lambda, \theta\}$ can be used instead, where $k$ is a constant ($k$ is related to the value range of the Hough transform space). At this time, Eq. (8.58) becomes

$$\frac{k}{\lambda} = x_v \cos \theta + y_v \sin \theta \tag{8.60}$$

Transfer Eq. (8.60) into the Cartesian coordinate system (let $s = \lambda \cos\theta$ and $t = \lambda \sin\theta$); then it gets

$$k = x_v s + y_v t \tag{8.61}$$

This is a line equation. In this way, the vanishing point at infinity can be projected to the origin, and the trajectory of the points corresponding to the line segments with the same vanishing point $(x_v, y_v)$ becomes a straight line in the $ST$ space, as shown in Fig. 8.17c. The slope of this line can be known from Eq. (8.61) as $-y_v/x_v$, so this line is orthogonal to the vector from the origin to the vanishing point $(x_v, y_v)$, and the distance from the origin is $k/\sqrt{x_v^2 + y_v^2}$. The Hough transform can be used another time to detect this line, that is, the space $ST$ where the line is located is regarded as the original space, and the detection is performed in the (new) Hough transform space $RW$. In this way, the straight line in the space $ST$ is a point in the space $RW$, as shown in Fig. 8.17d, and its position is

$$r = \frac{k}{\sqrt{x_v^2 + y_v^2}} \tag{8.62}$$

$$w = \arctan\left(\frac{y_v}{x_v}\right) \tag{8.63}$$

From Eqs. (8.62) and (8.63), the coordinates of the vanishing point can be solved as

$$x_v = \frac{k^2}{r^2\sqrt{1 + \tan^2 w}} \tag{8.64}$$

$$y_v = \frac{k^2 \tan w}{r^2\sqrt{1 + \tan^2 w}} \tag{8.65}$$

### 8.4.2   Determine the Vanishing Point Outside the Image

The above method has no problem when the vanishing point is in the range of the original image. But in practice, the vanishing point is often outside the image range (as shown in Fig. 8.18), or even at infinity. At this time, the normal image parameter space will encounter problems. For long-distance vanishing points, the peaks of the parameter space are distributed in a large distance range. As a result, the detection sensitivity will be poor, and the positioning accuracy will be low.

**Fig. 8.18** An example of
the vanishing point outside
the image

**Fig. 8.19** Use Gaussian
sphere to determine the
vanishing point

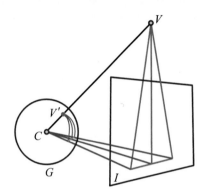

An improved method for this is to construct a **Gaussian sphere** $G$ around the
projection center of the camera, and use $G$ instead of the extended image plane as the
parameter space. As shown in Fig. 8.19, the vanishing point appears at a finite
distance (but it is also possible at infinity), and it has a one-to-one relationship ($V$ and
$V'$) with a point on the Gaussian sphere (the center is $C$). In reality, there will be
many unrelated points. To eliminate their influence, paired lines (lines in 3-D space
and lines projected onto the Gaussian sphere) need to be considered. If there are
$N$ lines in total, the total number of line pairs is $N(N - 1)/2$, that is, the magnitude is
$O(N^2)$.

Consider the situation where the ground is covered with floor tiles and the camera
is tilted to the ground and observed along the laying direction of the floor. At this
time, the configuration shown in Fig. 8.20 can be obtained (VL stands for vanishing
line), where $C$ is the center of the camera; $O$, $H_1$, and $H_2$ are on the ground; $O$, $V_1$, $V_2$,
and $V_3$ are on the imaging plane; and $a$ and $b$ (the length and width of the brick,
respectively) are known. The cross ratio obtained from points $O$, $V_1$, $V_2$, and $V_3$ is
equal to the cross ratio obtained from points $O$, $H_1$, and $H_2$ and the point at infinity
along the horizontal direction, so it gives

**Fig. 8.20** Determine the vanishing point by means of the cross ratio from the known intervals

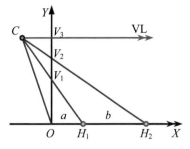

**Fig. 8.21** Calculate the offset of the circle center

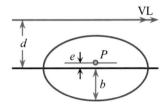

$$\frac{y_1(y_3 - y_2)}{y_2(y_3 - y_1)} = \frac{x_1}{x_2} = \frac{a}{a + b} \tag{8.66}$$

From Eq. (8.66), $y_3$ can be calculated:

$$y_3 = \frac{by_1 y_2}{ay_1 + by_1 - ay_2} \tag{8.67}$$

In practice, it should be possible to adjust the position and angle of the camera relative to the ground so that $a = b$; then one can get

$$y_3 = \frac{y_1 y_2}{2y_1 - y_2} \tag{8.68}$$

This simple equation shows that the absolute values of $a$ and $b$ are not important; as long as their ratio is known, it can be calculated. Furthermore, the above calculation does not assume that the points $V_1$, $V_2$, and $V_3$ are vertically above the point $O$, nor does it assume that the points $O$, $H_1$, and $H_2$ are on the horizontal line. It is only required that they are on two coplanar straight lines, and $C$ is also in this plane.

Under the condition of perspective projection, the ellipse is projected as an ellipse, but its center will be slightly offset. This is because the perspective projection does not maintain the length ratio (the midpoint is no longer the midpoint). Assuming that the position of the vanishing point of the plane can be determined from the image, the previous method can be used to easily calculate the center offset. First consider the special case of an ellipse, a circle, which is an ellipse after projection. Refer to Fig. 8.21; let $b$ be the short semiaxis of the ellipse after projection, $d$ be the

**Fig. 8.22** Calculate the offset of the center of the ellipse

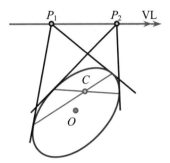

distance between the ellipse and the vanishing line after projection, $e$ be the offset of the center of the circle after projection, and point $P$ as the center of projection. Taking $b + e$ as $y_1$, $2b$ as $y_2$, and $b + d$ as $y_3$, then it can get from Eq. (8.68)

$$e = \frac{b^2}{d} \tag{8.69}$$

The difference from the previous method is that here $y_3$ is known and it is used to calculate $y_1$ and then to calculate $e$. If one doesn't know the vanishing line, but one knows the direction of the plane where the ellipse is located and the direction of the image plane, one can deduce the vanishing line and then makes the calculation as above.

If the original object is an ellipse, the problem is a little more complicated, because not only the longitudinal position of the center of the ellipse is not known, but also its horizontal position is also not known. At this time, two pairs of parallel tangents of the ellipse should be considered. After projection imaging, one pair intersects at $P_1$ and the other pair intersects at $P_2$. Both intersection points are on the vanishing line (VL), as shown in Fig. 8.22. Because for each pair of tangents, the chord connecting the tangent points passes through the center $O$ of the original ellipse (this characteristic does not change with the projection), the center of the projection should be on the chord. The intersection of the two chords corresponding to the two pairs of tangents is the projection center $C$.

## 8.5　Key Points and References for Each Section

The following combine the main contents of each section to introduce some references that can be further consulted:

1. **Shape from Shading**

      The principle and method of reconstructing the surface shape of the scene according to the image shading can also be found in many references, such as [1, 2].

2. **Solving Brightness Equation**

   The image brightness constraint equation establishes the relationship between the pixel brightness and the pixel gradient, but the gradient is 2-D and the brightness is 1-D, so an equation has two unknowns, and other constraints must be added to increase the number of equations to find the solutions. Refer to reference [2].

3. **Shape from Texture**

   For the content of the camera model and homogeneous coordinates, please refer to the document *2D Computer Vision: Principles, Algorithms and Applications*. Table 8.2 summarizes some typical methods of restoring shape from texture, which also lists various terms for obtaining shape from texture [3]. The idea of structural method is commonly used in texture analysis; please refer to the document *2D Computer Vision: Principles, Algorithms and Applications*. For the discussion of the assumption of texture patterns, please refer to reference [4].

4. **Detection of Texture Vanishing Points**

   An introduction to the Hough transform can be found in the document *2D Computer Vision: Principles, Algorithms and Applications*. For the discussion of cross ratio, please refer to reference [5].

# Self-Test Questions

The following questions include both single-choice questions and multiple-choice questions, so each option must be judged.

8.1. **Shape from Shading**

    8.1.1. 3-D objects are projected onto the 2-D image plane to form various brightness levels, and the distribution and changes of these levels depend on four factors. In Eq. (8.6), these four factors are, respectively, corresponding to (·).

        (a) $I(x, y)$, light source incident intensity and direction; $\rho(x, y)$, surface reflection characteristics; $(p, q)$, line of sight direction; $(p_i, q_i)$, surface normal direction.

        (b) $I(x, y)$, surface reflection characteristics; $\rho(x, y)$, light source incident intensity and direction; $(p, q)$, surface normal direction; $(p_i, q_i)$, line of sight direction.

        (c) $I(x, y)$, surface reflection characteristics; $\rho(x, y)$, light source incident intensity and direction; $(p, q)$, line of sight direction; $(p_i, q_i)$, surface normal direction.

        (d) $I(x, y)$, light source incident intensity and direction; $\rho(x, y)$, surface reflection characteristics; $(p, q)$, surface normal direction; $(p_i, q_i)$, line of sight direction.

        [Hint] Check these four factors in turn.

8.1.2. In gradient space method, (·).

(a) A point is used in the gradient space to represent a surface element.
(b) A point in the gradient space can only represent a surface element at one location.
(c) A point is used in the gradient space to represent all surface elements with the same orientation.
(d) A point in the gradient space may represent a surface element at different positions.

[Hint] Each point in the gradient space represents an orientation.

8.1.3. In the two sets of solutions of Example 8.2, (·).

(a) The first set of solutions corresponds to the convex structure of the converging point of three lines of intersection, and the second set of solutions corresponds to the concave structure of the converging point of three lines of intersection.
(b) The first set of solutions corresponds to the convex structure of the converging point of three lines of intersection, and the second set of solutions also corresponds to the convex structure of the converging point of three lines of intersection.
(c) The first set of solutions corresponds to the concave structure of the converging point of three lines of intersection, and the second set of solutions corresponds to the convex structure of the converging point of three lines of intersection.
(d) The first set of solutions corresponds to the concave structure of the converging point of three intersections, and the second set of solutions also corresponds to the convex structure of the converging point of three intersections.

[Hint] Refer to Fig. 8.5 for analysis.

## 8.2. Solving Brightness Equation

8.2.1. The image brightness constraint equation is compared with the optical flow constraint equation in Chap. 7; (·).

(a) The similarity is that there are both two unknown quantities.
(b) The difference is that the former only contains spatial information, while the latter also contains temporal information.
(c) The similarity is that both provide information to restore the 3-D scene from the 2-D image.
(d) The difference is that the former considers the brightness change rate, while the latter considers the speed of the imaging point.

[Hint] Analyze the meaning of each parameter in the two equations in detail.

8.2.2. Compare the optical flow constraint equation in Chap. 7 with the image brightness constraint equation here; (·).

(a) The similarity is that they both establish the relationship between the pixel characteristics in the image and the object characteristics in the scene.

(b) The difference is that the former is related to the movement speed of the imaging point, while the latter is related to the reflection characteristics of the imaging point.

(c) The similarity is that the grayscale gradient information at each pixel in the image is used.

(d) The difference is that the former considers the first-order time change rate of the pixel gray value, while the latter only considers the pixel gray value.

[Hint] Pay attention to distinguish between brightness gradient and orientation gradient.

8.2.3. Solving the image brightness constraint equation is to determine the orientation of the object surface according to the image grayscale information; (·).

(a) In the case of linear reflection, the grayscale function can be any monotonic function.

(b) In the case of linear reflection, the gradient of a particular image point can be determined by only measuring the gray level of the image.

(c) In the case of rotational symmetry, the grayscale reflection image obtained is also rotationally symmetric.

(d) In the case of rotational symmetry, the value of the object orientation gradient can be determined according only to the brightness of the object surface.

[Hint] Pay attention to the conditions for solving the image brightness constraint equation under specific circumstances.

## 8.3. Shape from Texture

8.3.1. Projecting the lines in the 3-D space by perspective projection onto the 2-D image plane will produce dimensional distortion; (·).

(a) The farther the line perpendicular to the line of sight is from the camera, the smaller the distortion.

(b) The distance from the straight line to the camera can be judged according to the magnitude of the distortion.

(c) If it is not a vertical projection, the projection result is still a straight line.

(d) If the projection result is not a straight line, it is not a vertical projection.

[Hint] Analyze how the line perspective projection produces distortion.

8.3.2. In the restoration of orientation from flat surface texture changes, (·).

(a) Suppose the surface texture itself has 3-D orientation information.
(b) Suppose the change of surface texture patterns carries 3-D orientation information.
(c) Assuming that the orientation change of the surface texture carries 3-D orientation information.
(d) Suppose that the size change of the surface texture carries 3-D orientation information.

[Hint] The surface texture and surface have the same orientation.

8.3.3. Among the three methods of using texture element changes to determine the surface orientation of an object, (·).

(a) The changes of the three texture elements are independent and will not occur in combination.
(b) If the direction of the texture gradient is determined, the change in the size of the texture element can be used to determine the orientation of the texture element.
(c) If the lengths of the long axis and short axis of the texture element are determined, the change in the shape of the texture element can be used to determine the orientation of the texture element.
(d) If the equation connecting the two vanishing points is determined, the change in the spatial relationship of the texels can be used to determine the orientation of the texels.

[Hint] To determine the orientation of the texture element, two angles need to be determined.

## 8.4. Detection of Texture Vanishing Points

8.4.1. Which of the following description(s) about vanishing points is/are incorrect? (·).

(a) The vanishing point is obtained by projecting the spatial point onto the image plane.
(b) The vanishing point is the intersection point of parallel lines with the same direction cosines after infinite extension.
(c) For any projection form, the vanishing point can be obtained by projecting the texture element at infinity to the image plane.
(d) As long as the surface is covered by texture, the surface orientation information can be restored by calculating the vanishing point.

[Hint] Analyze the principles and conditions of the vanishing point formation.

8.4.2. In determining the vanishing point of the line segment texture according to Fig. 8.17, (·).

(a) The reason that the detection of circles is more computationally expensive than the detection of straight lines is that the number of parameters of circles is more than those of straight lines.

(b) When $x_v \to \infty$ or $y_v \to \infty$, the circle becomes a straight line.

(c) The transformation $\{x, y\} \Rightarrow \{k/\lambda, \theta\}$ will transform the line segment to be detected back to the line segment in Fig. 8.17a.

(d) The transformation $\{x, y\} \Rightarrow \{k/\lambda, \theta\}$ will project the set of straight lines with the same vanishing point $(x_v, y_v)$ in the image space to a point in the parameter space.

[Hint] Analyze with reference to each space in Fig. 8.17.

8.4.3. Suppose that the texture is composed of regular texture element grids. The grid texture has a vanishing point in the perspective projection image. Suppose there are three known straight lines passing the vanishing point as $x = 0$, $y = 0$, and $y = 1 - x$; let $k = 1$; then the coordinates of the vanishing point are ($\cdot$).

(a) $x_v = \sqrt{2}$, $y_v = \sqrt{2}$.
(b) $x_v = \sqrt{2}/2$, $y_v = \sqrt{2}$.
(c) $x_v = \sqrt{2}$, $y_v = \sqrt{2}/2$.
(d) $x_v = \sqrt{2}/2$, $y_v = \sqrt{2}/2$.

[Hint] Calculate with the help of Hough transform.

# References

1. Jähne B, Haußecker H. Computer Vision and Applications: A Guide for Students and Practitioners. Academic Press. 2000.
2. Forsyth D, Ponce J. Computer Vision: A Modern Approach. Prentice Hall. 2003.
3. Tomita F, Tsuji S. Computer Analysis of Visual Textures. Kluwer Academic Publishers. 1990.
4. Forsyth D, Ponce J. Computer Vision: A Modern Approach, 2nd Ed. Prentice Hall. 2012.
5. Davies E R. Computer and Machine Vision: Theory, Algorithms, Practicalities, 4th Ed. Elsevier. 2012.

# Chapter 9
# Three-Dimensional Scenery Representation

After obtaining a 3-D image with various direct 3-D imaging methods or various scene restoration and reconstruction methods, it is necessary to represent the 3-D scenery in it.

Various representation methods for the 2-D regions segmented from the image have been introduced in *2D Computer Vision: Principles, Algorithms and Applications*. For the actual representation of 3-D sceneries, the 3-D representation method can be studied on this basis. It should be pointed out here that the changes brought by the development from the 2-D world to the 3-D world are not only quantitative but also a qualitative leap (e.g., in 2-D space, the region is enclosed by lines or curves; in 3-D space, only lines or curves cannot enclose the volume); it puts forward new requirements in theory and methods for the representation and processing of visual information.

There are multiple 3-D structures in the objective world, and they may correspond to different levels of abstraction. Different methods are often needed to represent various 3-D structures at different levels.

The sections of this chapter are arranged as follows:

Section 9.1 first introduces some concepts that represent and describe the local features of a surface, including surface normal section, surface principal normal curvature, average curvature, and Gaussian curvature.

Section 9.2 discusses how to represent a 3-D surface. On the one hand, one can use the parameter representation method of a curve or a curved surface. On the other hand, one can also represent the 3-D surface by representing the orientation of the surface.

Section 9.3 introduces two algorithms for constructing and representing iso-surfaces in 3-D space: the marching cube algorithm and the wrapper algorithm.

Section 9.4 discusses how to start from the parallel contour of the 3-D object, through interpolation, to represent the object surface with a set of mesh elements, and to realize the technology of surface titling.

Section 9.5 introduces several methods to directly represent 3-D entities (including surface and interior). In addition to some basic representation schemes, a generalized cylinder representation method is introduced in detail.

## 9.1  Local Features of the Surface

The surface of an object may be a flat surface or a curved surface, and a flat surface can be regarded as a special case of a curved surface. The curved surface is an important component that constitutes a 3-D (solid) **entity**, and it is also the first observed part when observing the entity. In order to represent and describe curved surfaces, it is necessary to study their local features. Differential geometry is an important tool for studying the local features of curved surfaces. In the following discussion, general curved surfaces are considered.

### 9.1.1  Surface Normal Section

In the following, the properties near a point $P$ on the surface $S$ are considered. It can be proved that for the curve $C$ passing through the point $P$ and on the surface $S$, all its tangent lines are on the same plane $U$, and the plane $U$ is the tangent plane passing through the point $P$ on the surface $S$. The straight line $N$ passing through the point $P$ and perpendicular to the surface $S$ is called the normal line of the surface $S$ at the point $P$, as shown in Fig. 9.1. The direction of the normal vector at the point $P$ can be

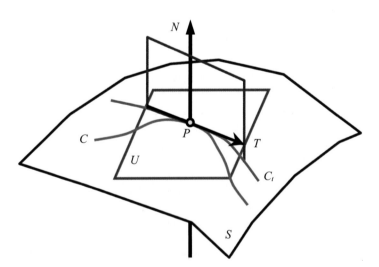

**Fig. 9.1**  The normal $N$, tangent $T$, tangent surface $U$, and normal section line $C_t$ of a point on the surface

taken as the local direction of the surface $S$ at the point $P$. It can be seen that at each point on the surface, there is only one normal, but there can be countless tangents.

Although there is only one normal at the point $P$ through the surface $S$, there can be an infinite number of planes containing the normal (and also a tangent); all these planes can be obtained by rotating any plane containing the normal around the normal. The intersection of these planes and the surface $S$ constitutes a single-parameter plane curve family, which can be called a **normal section** family. Figure 9.1 also shows a normal section $C_t$ (it is completely in surface $S$, but it can be different from curve $C$) corresponding to the tangent of curve $C$.

In general, the normal section of the surface $S$ is regular at the point $P$, and sometimes it is an inflection point. The curvature of the normal section at the point $P$ is called the normal curvature of the surface $S$ in the corresponding tangent direction at the point $P$. If the normal section line is on the same side of the tangent plane as the surface normal pointing to the inside, the normal curvature is said to be positive; if they are separately on both sides, the normal curvature is said to be negative. If the point $P$ is the inflection point of the corresponding normal section, then the normal curvature of the surface $S$ in the corresponding tangent direction at the point $P$ is zero.

## 9.1.2 Surface Principal Curvature

Since there may be an infinite number of curves passing through the same point on the surface, it is not possible to directly extend the curvature definition of the above plane curve to the surface. However, for each surface, at least one direction with the maximum curvature $K_1$ can be determined on it, and a direction with the minimum curvature $K_2$ can also be determined (for a relatively flat surface, there may be multiple directions of maximum curvature and minimum curvature, any of which could be selected at this time). In other words, the normal curvature of the normal section line at the point $P$ on the surface will have a maximum value $K_1$ in a certain direction around the normal line, and a minimum value $K_2$ in another certain direction. Generally speaking, these two directions are called the **principal directions** of the surface $S$ at the point $P$. It can be proved that they are orthogonal to each other (unless the normal curvature takes the same value in all directions, which corresponds to a plane). Figure 9.2 shows an example. $T_1$ and $T_2$ represent the two principal directions.

**Fig. 9.2** Principal curvature direction

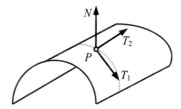

According to the similarities and differences of the two principal curvature signs in the neighborhood of the point $P$ on the surface $S$, three different shapes of the neighborhood can be judged. If the signs of the two principal curvatures are the same, the surface of the neighborhood at point $P$ is elliptical and does not cross the tangent plane. When the sign of curvature is positive, point $P$ is convex; when the sign of curvature is negative, point $P$ is concave. If the signs of the two principal normal curvatures are opposite, then the surface of the neighborhood at point $P$ is hyperbolic, and the surface $S$ is partially saddle-shaped and passes through the tangent plane along the two curves. The corresponding normal section line has an inflection point at point $P$. Their tangents are in the asymptotic direction of the surface $S$ at the point $P$, and these directions are separated by the principal direction. Elliptical points and hyperbolic points form blocky regions on the surface. These regions are generally separated by a curve composed of parabolic points. On these curves, one of the two principal curvatures is zero. The corresponding principal direction is also the asymptotic direction, and there is a sharp point along this direction at the intersection of the surface and its tangent plane.

### 9.1.3  Mean Curvature and Gaussian Curvature

Combining the principal curvatures $K_1$ and $K_2$ introduced above can form the **mean curvature** $H$ and **Gaussian curvature** $G$:

$$H = \frac{K_1 + K_2}{2} = \frac{\mathrm{Tr}(K)}{2} \tag{9.1}$$

$$G = K_1 K_2 = \det(K) \tag{9.2}$$

The mean curvature determines whether the surface is locally convex (mean curvature is negative) or concave (mean curvature is positive). If the surface is locally elliptical, the Gaussian curvature is positive; if the surface is locally hyperbolic, the Gaussian curvature is negative.

Combining the sign analysis of Gaussian curvature and mean curvature, a classification description of the surface can be obtained, which is often called a topographical description; see Table 9.1. (These descriptions can also be used to segment depth images, often called surface segmentation.)

In mathematical language, the gradient at the peak point is zero, and all secondary directional derivatives are negative. The gradient at the pit point is also zero, but all

**Table 9.1** Eight surface types determined by Gaussian curvature $G$ and mean curvature $H$

| Curvature | $H < 0$ | $H = 0$ | $H > 0$ |
| --- | --- | --- | --- |
| $G < 0$ | Saddle ridge | Minimal | Saddle valley |
| $G = 0$ | Ridge/ridge surface | Plane | Valley/valley surface |
| $G > 0$ | Peak | | Pit |

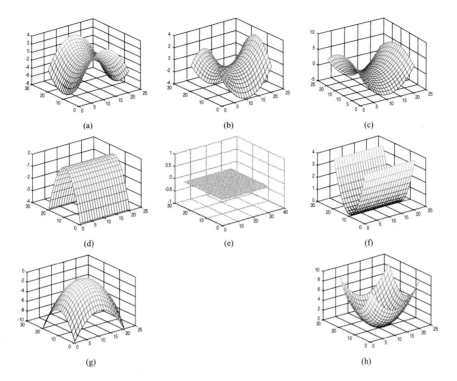

**Fig. 9.3** (a–h) Examples of eight surface types

the secondary directional derivatives are positive. Ridges can be divided into ridge points and ridge lines. A ridge point is also a kind of peak point, but unlike an isolated peak point, it only has a negative secondary directional derivative in a certain direction. Adjacent ridge points are connected to form a ridge line. The ridge line can be a flat straight line or a curved line (including non-flat straight lines). The gradient along the flat ridge line is zero, and the secondary directional derivative is also zero, while the secondary directional derivative in the direction intersecting the ridge line is negative. There must be a negative second derivative along the direction that intersects the curved ridge, and the first derivative in that direction must be zero. A valley is also called a ditch. It is different from an isolated pit. It only has a positive second derivative in certain directions (change the second derivative in the description of the ridge line from negative to positive to obtain the right description of valley line). The gradient at the saddle point is zero, and the extreme values of its two quadratic directional derivatives (there are a local maximum in one direction and a local minimum in the other direction perpendicular to it) must have different signs. Saddle ridge and saddle valley, respectively, correspond to the situations where the two extreme values take different signs.

**Example 9.1 Eight Kinds of Surface Types Examples**
From Table 9.1 it can be seen that there are eight different types of surfaces. Figure 9.3 shows an example of each of these eight surface types.

The relative arrangement positions of the example images in Fig. 9.3 are the same as those in Table 9.1, where Fig. 9.3a corresponds to the saddle ridge, Fig. 9.3b corresponds to the minimal direction, Fig. 9.3c corresponds to the saddle valley, Fig. 9.3d corresponds to the ridge/ridge surface, Fig. 9.3e corresponds to the plane, Fig. 9.3f corresponds to the valley/valley surface, Fig. 9.3g corresponds to the peak, and Fig. 9.3h corresponds to the pit.

## 9.2  Three-Dimensional Surface Representation

When people observe a 3-D scene, the first thing they see is the outer surface of the object. In general, the outer surface is composed of a set of curved surfaces. In order to represent the outer surface of 3-D objects and describe their shape, the outer contour line or outer contour surface of the object can be used. If the outer contour line is given, the outer contour surface can also be obtained by interpolation or "surface overlay" method. The **surface model** is mainly used here.

### 9.2.1  Parameter Representation

The parameter representation is a general analytical representation.

#### 9.2.1.1  The Parameter Representation of the Curve

The outline of an object is an important clue to express the shape of an object. For example, the commonly used **wireframe** representation method is an approximate method for representing 3-D objects with a set of outer contour lines. The outline of some objects can be obtained directly from the image. For example, when using the structured light method to collect depth images, the 3-D coordinates of the points where the light plane intersects the outer surface of the object can be obtained. If the points on the same plane are connected with smooth curves and the series of curves are displayed in sequence, the shape of the object surface can be represented. The outline of some objects needs to be calculated from the image. For example, in order to observe the inside of a biological specimen, the specimen is cut into a series of slices, and an image is collected for each slice. Through the segmentation of each image, the boundary of each specimen can be obtained, that is, the contour line of the cross-section of the organism. Here, if one wants to restore the 3-D shape of the original specimen, it is needed to align and combine these contour lines.

**Example 9.2 Wireframe Representation Example**
Figure 9.4 shows several examples of wireframe representations. This is the result of the biomedical cells sliced into thin slices, first acquiring a 2-D image for each slice,

**Fig. 9.4** Example of wireframe representation method

then detecting the cell profile, obtaining the contour of each cell, and then aligning and representing the result with a wireframe representation method. From these wireframe representations, information about the shape and structure of 3-D cells can be obtained.

The contour line of the object is generally a 3-D curve, which can often be represented by a parametric spline, written in the form of a matrix (using $t$ to indicate the normalized length from a certain point along the curve) as

$$P(t) = [x(t) \ \ y(t) \ \ z(t)]^{\mathrm{T}} \ \ 0 \le t \le 1 \tag{9.3}$$

Any point on the curve is described by a function of three parameters $t$. The curve starts at $t = 0$ and ends at $t = 1$. In order to represent a universal curve, make the first and second derivatives of the parametric spline continuous, and the order of $P(t)$ is at least 3. The cubic polynomial curve can be written as

$$P(t) = at^3 + bt^2 + ct + d \tag{9.4}$$

where

$$a = [a_x \ \ a_y \ \ a_z]^{\mathrm{T}} \tag{9.5}$$

$$b = [b_x \ \ b_y \ \ b_z]^{\mathrm{T}} \tag{9.6}$$

$$c = [c_x \ \ c_y \ \ c_z]^{\mathrm{T}} \tag{9.7}$$

$$d = [d_x \ \ d_y \ \ d_z]^{\mathrm{T}} \tag{9.8}$$

The cubic spline curve can be represented as

$$x(t) = a_x t^3 + b_x t^2 + c_x t + d_x \tag{9.9}$$

$$y(t) = a_y t^3 + b_y t^2 + c_y t + d_y \tag{9.10}$$

$$z(t) = a_z t^3 + b_z t^2 + c_z t + d_z \tag{9.11}$$

The cubic polynomial can represent the curve passing through a specific tangent point, and it is also the lowest-order polynomial that represents a nonplanar curve.

In addition, a 3-D curve can be implicitly represented as a set of points $(x, y, z)$ satisfying the following equation:

$$f(x, y, z) = 0 \tag{9.12}$$

### 9.2.1.2   Parameter Representation of Curved Surface

The outer surface of the object is also an important clue to represent the shape of the object. The outer surface of an object can be represented by a collection of patches, and each patch can be represented as

$$P(u, v) = [x(u, \ v) \ \ y(u, \ v) \ \ z(u, \ v)]^{\mathrm{T}} \quad 0 \le u, v \le 1 \tag{9.13}$$

If the first derivatives of $P(u, v)$ in two directions are calculated, then $P_u(u, v)$ and $P_v(u, v)$ can be obtained, both of which are on the tangent plane passing through the surface point $(x, y, z) = P(u, v)$; the normal vector $N$ at this point can be calculated by $P_u(u, v)$ and $P_v(u, v)$:

$$N(P) = \frac{P_u \times P_v}{\|P_u \times P_v\|} \tag{9.14}$$

A 3-D surface can also be implicitly represented as a set of points $(x, y, z)$ satisfying the following equation:

$$f(x, y, z) = 0 \tag{9.15}$$

For example, a sphere of radius $r$ with its center at $(x_0, y_0, z_0)$ can be represented as

$$f(x, y, z) = (x - x_0)^2 + (y - y_0)^2 + (z - z_0)^2 = 0 \tag{9.16}$$

The explicit representation of a 3-D surface is

$$z = f(x, y) \tag{9.17}$$

Surface elements can be represented by bivariate polynomials of different orders. The simplest **bilinear patch** (any section parallel to the coordinate axis is a straight line) can be represented as

$$z = a_0 + a_1 x + a_2 y \qquad (9.18)$$

The curved surface can be represented by high-order polynomials, for example, **biquadratic patch**

$$z = a_0 + a_1 x + a_2 y + a_3 xy + a_4 x^2 + a_5 y^2 \qquad (9.19)$$

and **bi-cubic patch**

$$z = a_0 + a_1 x + a_2 y + a_3 xy + a_4 x^2 + a_5 y^2 + a_6 x^3 + a_7 x^2 y + a_8 xy^2 + a_9 y^3 \quad (9.20)$$

In addition, the representation of the surface can also be converted into the representation of the curve with the help of the concept of surface element. If each surface element is surrounded and bounded by four curves, then the entire surface can be represented by determining the four curves of each surface element.

## 9.2.2 Surface Orientation Representation

The appearance and shape of the object can be outlined by representing the orientation of each surface of the 3-D object, and the surface normal can be used to represent the orientation of the surface.

### 9.2.2.1 Extended Gaussian Image

The **extended Gaussian image** is a model for representing 3-D objects. Its two characteristics are approximation and abstraction. The extended Gaussian image of an object gives the distribution of the normal of the object surface, and thus the direction of each point on the surface. If the object is a convex multi-cone, then the object and its extended Gaussian image have one-to-one correspondence, but one extended Gaussian image may correspond to an infinite number of concave objects.

In order to calculate the extended Gaussian image, the concept of **Gaussian sphere** can be used. The Gaussian sphere is a unit sphere. Given a point on the 3-D object surface as shown in Fig. 9.5a, the point corresponding to the point on the sphere with the same surface normal can be used to obtain the Gaussian sphere, as shown in Fig. 9.5b. In other words, put the end of the orientation vector of the object surface point at the center of the sphere, and the top of the vector intersects the sphere at a specific point. This intersection point can be used to mark the orientation of the original object surface point. The position of the intersection point on the sphere can be represented by two variables (with two degrees of freedom), such as polar angle and azimuth angle or longitude and latitude. If all points on the Gaussian sphere are

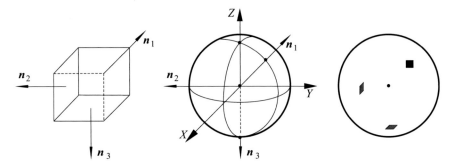

**Fig. 9.5** Gaussian sphere and extended Gaussian image

placed with a mass equal in value to the corresponding surface area, an extended Gaussian image can be obtained, as shown in Fig. 9.5c.

Consider the case where the object is a convex polyhedron and all its surfaces are flat. The convex polyhedron can be completely determined by the area and orientation of its various surfaces. The direction of each surface plane (the direction of the normal vector) can be used to obtain the Gaussian sphere of the convex polyhedron. Because points on different surfaces of the convex polyhedron will not have the same surface normal vector, each point on the Gaussian sphere corresponds to a specific surface orientation. The expanded Gaussian image obtained in this way has the following characteristics: the total mass on the expanded Gaussian image is numerically equal to the sum of the area of the polyhedron surface regions; if the polyhedron is closed, the same region can be projected from any opposite direction.

The above method can be extended to smooth curved surfaces. Define the limit of the ratio of the region $\delta S$ on the Gaussian sphere to the corresponding region $\delta O$ on the object when $\delta O$ tending to zero is the **Gaussian curvature** $G$, namely,

$$G = \lim_{\delta O \to 0} \frac{\delta S}{\delta O} = \frac{dS}{dO} \tag{9.21}$$

If the integration for a region $O$ on the object is made, it will get the **integral curvature**:

$$\iint_O G dO = \iint_S dS = S \tag{9.22}$$

where $S$ is the corresponding region on the Gaussian sphere. Equation (9.22) allows the treatment of surfaces with discontinuous normal lines.

If the integration for the above region $S$ on the Gaussian sphere is made, it gives

$$\iint_S \frac{1}{G}\,dS = \iint_O dO = O \tag{9.23}$$

where $O$ is the corresponding region on the object.

Equation (9.23) shows that the extended Gaussian image can be defined by the reciprocal of Gaussian curvature, specifically mapping the reciprocal of Gaussian curvature at a point on the object surface to the corresponding point on the unit ball. If $u$ and $v$ are used to denote the coefficients of the object surface points, and $p$ and $q$ are used to denote the coefficients of the points on the Gaussian sphere, the extended Gaussian image is defined as

$$G_e(p, q) = \frac{1}{G(u, v)} \tag{9.24}$$

The above mapping is unique for convex objects. If the object is not convex, the following three situations may occur:

1. The Gaussian curvature of some points will become negative.
2. Multiple points on the object will contribute to the same point on the ball.
3. Some parts of the object will be obscured by other parts.

**Example 9.3 Calculation Example of Extended Gaussian Image**
Given a sphere with a radius of $R$, its extended Gaussian image $G_e(p, q) = R^2$; if the region $\delta O$ is observed from the center of the sphere, then the observed **solid angle** is $w = \delta O/R^2$; and the area of the region on the Gaussian sphere is $\delta S = w$.

### 9.2.2.2 Spherical Projection and Stereographic Projection

The surface orientation of the object has two degrees of freedom. To specify the orientation of the surface element, either gradient or unit normal can be used, where the direction pointed by the surface normal can be represented by the above Gaussian sphere. The Gaussian sphere itself has a curved outer surface. Generally, it can be projected onto a plane to obtain a gradient space, as shown in Fig. 9.6a.

Consider an axis that passes through the sphere and is parallel to the $Z$ axis. The center of the sphere can be used as the center of projection to project a point on the Northern Hemisphere onto a plane tangent to the North Pole. This is called **spherical projection**. It can be proved that the position of the point with gradient $(p, q)$ on this plane is equal to $(-p, -q)$. One disadvantage of using this plane to define the gradient space is that in order to avoid confusion, only a hemisphere can be projected onto this plane.

In many cases, the only concern is the surface visible to the observer, which corresponds to a point on the Northern Hemisphere. But there are other situations.

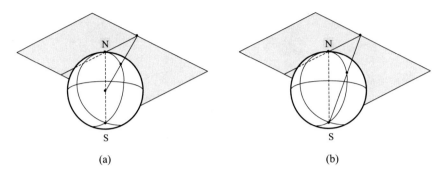

**Fig. 9.6**  Spherical projection (**a**) and stereographic projection (**b**)

For example, for a backlit scene, the direction to the light source needs to be represented by a point in the Southern Hemisphere. This encounters a difficulty in the gradient space, which is that the point on the equator corresponding to the surface of the Gaussian sphere will be projected to infinity in the gradient space.

One way to avoid such difficulties is to use **stereographic projection**. The destination of the projection here is still a plane tangent to the North Pole, but the center of the projection is the South Pole, as shown in Fig. 9.6b. In this way, except for the South Pole, all points on the sphere can be uniquely mapped to the plane. The projection of the equator will be a circle with a radius equal to the diameter of the sphere. If the coordinates in the stereographic projection are $s$ and $t$, it can be proved:

$$s = \frac{2p}{1 + \sqrt{1 + p^2 + q^2}} \qquad t = \frac{2q}{1 + \sqrt{1 + p^2 + q^2}} \qquad (9.25)$$

In turn:

$$p = \frac{4s}{4 - s^2 - t^2} \qquad q = \frac{4t}{4 - s^2 - t^2} \qquad (9.26)$$

Another advantage of the stereographic projection is that it is a conformal projection on the Gaussian sphere, that is, the angles on the spherical surface are the same angles after being projected to the plane. One disadvantage of stereographic projection is that some equations are more complicated than in spherical projection.

## 9.3   Construction and Representation of Iso-surfaces

The basic unit in a 3-D image is a **voxel**. If the contour voxels of a 3-D object all have a certain gray value, then these voxel points will form an equivalent surface (iso-surface), which is the interface of this object with other objects or background.

The following introduce two related algorithms for the construction and representation of equivalent surfaces:

### 9.3.1   Marching Cube Algorithm

Consider a cube with eight voxels forming vertices (see Fig. 9.7a) where black voxels represent the foreground and white voxels represent the background. The cube has six adjacent cubes (up, down, left, right, front, back). If all the eight voxels of the cube belong to the foreground or all belong to the background, then the cube is an internal cube. If some of the eight voxels of the cube belong to the foreground and some belong to the background, then the cube is a bounding cube. The equivalent surface should be in the bounding cube (passing through the bounding cube). For example, for the cube in Fig. 9.7a, the equivalent surface can be the shaded rectangle in Fig. 9.7b.

The **marching cube** (MC) algorithm is a basic method to determine the equivalent surface. The algorithm needs to check each cube in the image first and determine the bounding cube that intersects the object surface and at the same time determine their intersection. According to the intersection of the object surface and the cube, the part of the object surface inside the cube is generally a curved surface, but it can be approximated by a **patch**. Each such patch is easily decomposed into a series of triangles, and the triangles obtained in this way can easily further compose the triangular network of the object surface.

The algorithm checks each voxel one by one, traveling from one cube to another adjacent cube. In theory, each vertex voxel of the cube may be black voxel or white voxel, so for each cube, there may be $2^8 = 256$ different black and white voxel layouts/configurations. However, if considering the symmetry of the cube, there are only 22 different black and white voxel layouts. Among the 22 different layouts, 8 are the inversions of other layouts (black voxels are converted to white voxels or white voxels are converted to black voxels). In this way, only 14 different black and white voxel layouts are left, and there are only 14 different object surface patches, as shown in Fig. 9.8 (the first image represents the case where the object surface does not intersect the cube).

**Fig. 9.7**  A cube with eight voxels (**a**) forming vertices intersects with the object surface (**b**)

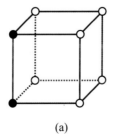
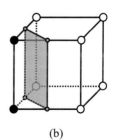

(a)                                    (b)

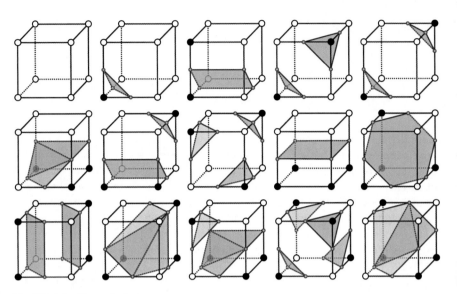

**Fig. 9.8** Marching cube layout

These conditions can be listed in a look-up table, and whenever a cube is checked, only the look-up table needs to be searched to determine the corresponding surface patch. The algorithm proceeds as follows: Starting from the upper left corner, scan the entire first layer of the 3-D image, and then start the entire scan from the upper left corner of the second layer after reaching the lower right corner, and proceed to the lower right corner of the last layer of image in turn. Every time a foreground voxel is scanned, check the cube of eight voxels that the voxel belongs to. As long as the object surface intersects the cube, it is one of the last 14 layout situations in Fig. 9.8. One can use the above look-up table to find each corresponding surface patch and further decompose it into a series of triangles. In practical applications, all 256 layout situations are often listed in the look-up table to avoid time-consuming verification of symmetry and reversibility.

Although the distributions of the above-mentioned various black and white voxels are different and easy to distinguish, in some cases, the part of the object surface intersecting the cube within the cube cannot be obtained from the distribution of black and white voxels only. In fact, among the last 14 layouts in Fig. 9.8, the six layouts of 3rd, 6th, 7th, 10th, 12th, and 13th (most of their diagonal vertices are voxels of the same color) correspond to more than one surface distribution; in other words, there is ambiguity to determine a certain plane. Figure 9.9 shows a pair of typical examples, they correspond to the same layout (the tenth layout), but there are two possible object surface distributions.

One way to solve the above-mentioned ambiguity problem is to expand the layouts by adding complementary layouts to those with ambiguity in the basic layouts. Figure 9.9a, b can be regarded as complementary layouts. The other five complementary layouts that extend the ambiguous layout can be seen in Fig. 9.10

**Fig. 9.9** (**a, b**) An example of an ambiguous marching cube layout

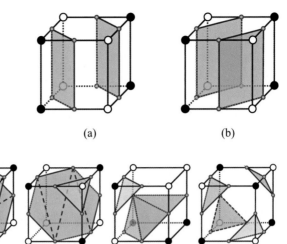

(a)                    (b)

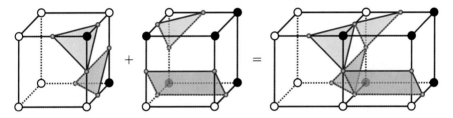

**Fig. 9.10** Five complementary layouts added to ambiguous layouts

**Fig. 9.11** The object surface is not closed from the marching cube

(the polygons in the first three figures have been triangulated). In practice, a sub-look-up table can be established for each of them. Each sub-look-up table contains two triangulation methods. In addition, a table must be stored to record the compatibility of these triangulation methods.

In addition, there are two other methods that correspond to the topology flow pattern. One is called the **surface average values**, which calculate the average value of four vertices on the ambiguity surface and compare the average value with a predetermined threshold, to select a possible topology flow pattern. The other is called the **gradient consistency heuristics**, which estimate the gradient of the center point of the ambiguity surface from the average of the gradients of the four corner points of the ambiguity surface and determine the topology flow pattern of ambiguity surface according to the direction of the gradient.

In addition to the above ambiguity problem, the marching cube algorithm only checks each cube separately and does not consider the topology of the overall object, so even if an ambiguous layout is not adopted, it cannot guarantee that a closed object surface will always be obtained. An example of using the marching cube method but not getting a closed object surface is shown in Fig. 9.11. The two initial

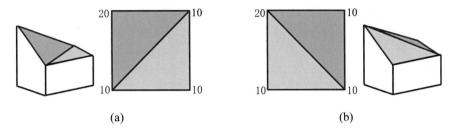

Fig. 9.12  (a, b) The combination of two kinds of triangular surface elements

layouts in the figure both get the correct decomposition without ambiguity, but combining them does not provide a closed object surface.

**Example 9.4 Different Combinations of Triangular Surface Elements**
There are two ways to use two triangles to connect the four vertices and form the surface part of the object. The resulting surface area and surface orientation are not the same. For example, in Fig. 9.12, for the same four vertices on a square (the number indicates the height of the point relative to the reference plane), Fig. 9.12a, b, respectively, gives two kinds of way. The surface area obtained according to Fig. 9.12a is 13.66, and the surface area obtained according to Fig. 9.12b is 14.14. There is a difference of about 3.5% between the two areas.

## 9.3.2  Wrapper Algorithm

The **wrapper algorithm** is also called the **marching tetrahedral** (MT) algorithm, which can solve the unclosed problem of the marching cube method described above, thereby ensuring a closed and complete triangular representation of the object surface. However, the disadvantage of this method is that it will normally generate up to three times the actual number of triangles required, so a post-processing step is required to simplify the polygon mesh, thereby reducing the number of triangles to an acceptable level.

In this algorithm, the cube with eight voxels (vertices) as shown in Fig. 9.7a is also considered each time. The first step of the algorithm is to decompose the voxel grid into a set of cubes. Each cube has six adjacent cubes (up, down, left, right, front, back). The second step of the algorithm decomposes each cube into five tetrahedrons, as shown in Fig. 9.13. The four tetrahedrons on the left have two sets of edges of the same length (three for each), and the fifth tetrahedron (the rightmost one in Fig. 9.13) has four faces of the same size. The voxels that belong to the tetrahedron can be regarded as inside the object, and the voxels that do not belong to the tetrahedron can be regarded as outside the object.

There are two solutions to the tetrahedron decomposition of the cube, as shown in Fig. 9.14. Among them, the two schemes shown in Fig. 9.14a, b can be called odd scheme and even scheme, respectively. The decomposition of the voxel grid is

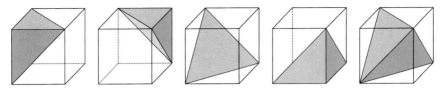

**Fig. 9.13** Each cube is decomposed into five tetrahedrons

**Fig. 9.14** (**a, b**) Two
solutions to decompose the
cube into tetrahedrons

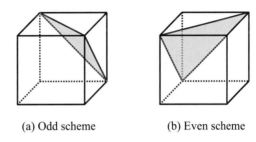

(a) Odd scheme  (b) Even scheme

carried out in odd phase and even phase, just like a chess board, alternating black and white. This ensures that the tetrahedrons in adjacent cubes can match each other, so as to finally get a consistent surface.

The third step of the algorithm is to determine whether the object surface intersects the tetrahedron. Note that each tetrahedron contains four voxels. If all four voxels of a tetrahedron are inside the object or none of the voxels are inside the object, then it can be said that the object surface does not intersect with the tetrahedron and can be ignored in subsequent processing.

The next step of the algorithm is to estimate the boundary between the object surface and each (polygon) face of the tetrahedron that intersects the object surface. The vertices at both ends of each pair of boundary lines can be linearly interpolated, and the intersection points on the edges connecting each pair of vertices can be obtained by approximation. If all four vertices are used for bilinear interpolation, it is possible to get better results. For six adjacent voxels, bilinear interpolation is equivalent to linear interpolation. For diagonal edges, set the gray values of the four vertices as $a$, $b$, $c$, and $d$; then the interpolation result is

$$I(u) = (a - b - c + d)u^2 + (-2a + b + c)u + a \qquad (9.27)$$

where the parameter $u$ changes from 0 to 1 along the diagonal. By calculating a $u_0$ value and making $I(u_0) = 0$, the intersection point can be calculated.

According to the intersection point, the vertices after surface titling (splicing) can be determined, as shown in Fig. 9.15. The orientation of the tiling surface is indicated by arrows. Orientation can help distinguish the inside and outside of each tiling surface. By convention, when viewed from the outside, the orientation is counterclockwise. In order to stabilize the topology of the object, the above conventions must be adopted in the entire surface mesh.

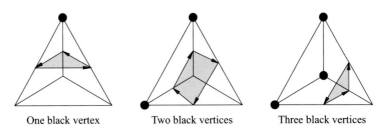

| One black vertex | Two black vertices | Three black vertices |

**Fig. 9.15** Three situations where the surface intersects

## 9.4 Interpolating Three-Dimensional Surfaces from Parallel Contours

For 3-D object surfaces, a common boundary representation method is to use polygon meshes. Here the polygon is composed of vertices, edges, and surfaces, and each mesh can be regarded as a surface element. Given a set of three-dimensional data, the process of obtaining the above-mentioned polygon mesh and representing the object surface with a set of surface elements is often called **surface tiling**. The two methods in the previous section are general methods for surface tiling of arbitrary 3-D grids. This section considers a special case.

### 9.4.1 Contour Interpolation and Tiling

In many 3-D imaging methods (such as CT, MRI, etc.), 2-D images are obtained layer by layer and then added together to obtain 3-D images. If the contour of the object is detected from each 2-D image, the 3-D object surface can be reconstructed based on the series of parallel contour lines. A common method here is to use (triangular) surface elements to interpolate between contours. In practice, contour lines are often given in the form of polygons to save the amount of representation data. The problem to be solved at this time can be described as using a series of triangular planes to form the surface between two adjacent polygons. If a triangle has a vertex on one polygon, the remaining two vertices must be on another polygon, and vice versa. There are two main steps here. The first step is how to determine an initial pair of vertices from two adjacent polygons, and the connection of these two vertices forms an edge of the triangle. The second step is how to select the next adjacent vertex based on a known vertex pair to form a complete triangle. By repeating the second step continuously, the work of constructing triangles can be continued to form a closed contour (often called a **wireframe**). This process can also be called **contour tiling**.

Look at the first step intuitively; the corresponding initial vertices on two adjacent polygons should have a certain similarity on their respective polygons, that is, they have similar features on their respective polygons. The features that can be

**Fig. 9.16** Selection from
the contour line to the vertex
in the contour surface

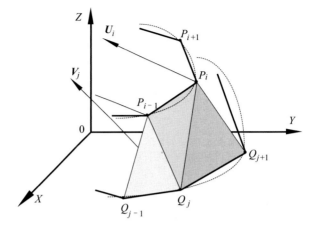

considered here include the geometric position of the vertices, the direction of the
edges connecting adjacent vertices, the angle between two adjacent edges, the
direction from the center of gravity to the edge point, etc. When the distance from
the center of gravity of the polygon to the edge point is relatively large, the direction
from the center of gravity to the edge point will be a relatively stable feature. As
shown in Fig. 9.16, if the vector from the edge point $P_i$ to the center of gravity of the
polygon in one polygon is $U_i$, and the vector from the edge point $Q_j$ to the center of
gravity of the polygon in another polygon is $V_j$, then the initial pair of vertices can be
determined according to the principle of maximizing the inner product of the vectors
$U_i$ and $V_j$. The maximum inner product here represents the situation where the two
vectors are as parallel as possible and the distance between the edge point and the
center of gravity is as large as possible. If the two polygons are similar, then select
the furthest vertex pair.

Look at the second step now. After selecting the first pair of vertices, it needs to
select another vertex to form the first triangle. There are many selection criteria, such
as the area of the triangle, the distance from the next pair of vertices, the orientation
of the line with the center of gravity, and so on. If it is based on the distance from the
next pair of vertices, the vertex pair with the shortest distance can be selected. But
sometimes just using this criterion is not enough, especially when the horizontal
positions of the vertices are different.

Figure 9.17 is used to introduce a vertex selection method used in the second step,
which is obtained by projecting the contour line of Fig. 9.16 to the $XY$ plane.
Suppose the current vertex pair is $P_i$ and $Q_j$. The $X$ axis coordinate of $P_i$ is smaller
than the $X$ axis coordinate of $Q_j$. In this case, $\overline{P_{i+1}Q_j}$ may be shorter than $\overline{P_iQ_{j+1}}$.
However, because the direction of $\overline{P_iP_{i+1}}$ is quite different from the direction of
$\overline{Q_{j-1}Q_j}$, from the perspective of surface continuity, people still tend to choose $Q_j + 1$
as the vertex of the next triangle. Specifically, in this case, the difference in direction
should also be taken into consideration. Suppose the direction difference between
$\overline{P_iP_{i+1}}$ and $\overline{Q_{j-1}Q_j}$ is $A_i$, and the direction difference between $\overline{P_{i-1}P_i}$ and $\overline{Q_jQ_{j+1}}$ is

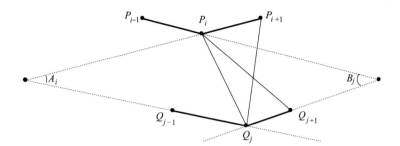

**Fig. 9.17** The result of projecting the contour line of Fig. 9.16 to the XY plane

**Fig. 9.18** Three problems
encountered when building
a 3-D surface from a plane
profile

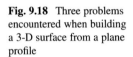

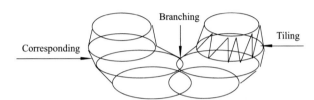

$B_j$, then the rule for selecting the next vertex when $\overline{P_{i+1}Q_j} < \overline{P_iQ_{j+1}}$ is as follows
($T$ represents a predetermined threshold):

1. If $\cos A_i > T$, it indicates that $A_i$ is smaller, $\overline{P_iP_{i+1}}$ and $\overline{Q_{j-1}Q_j}$ closer to parallel, so
   at this time the next vertex should be $P_{i+1}$.
2. If $\cos A_i \leq T$, and $\cos B_j > T$, it means that $B_j$ is smaller, $\overline{P_{i-1}P_i}$ and $\overline{Q_jQ_{j+1}}$ closer
   to parallel, so the next vertex should be $Q_{j+1}$ at this time.
3. If the above two conditions are not met, that is, $\cos A_i \leq T$ and $\cos B_j \leq T$, the
   distance factor is still considered, and $P_{i+1}$ is selected.

## 9.4.2   Problems That May Be Encountered

The above method of interpolating the contour to obtain the surface can be regarded
as extracting a grid of surface tiling from the plane contour represented by the vector.
This task is much more difficult than extracting a surface grid from a raster image
with a voxel data structure. There are several problems in creating a 3-D surface from
a plane profile, which can be explained with the help of Fig. 9.18.

### 9.4.2.1   Corresponding Problems

**Correspondence** includes two levels of problems. If there is only one contour in
each plane, then the corresponding problem only involves determining the relationship between the corresponding points in the contours of the adjacent planes. When

the distance between the planes is relatively small, the shape difference between the contours will be relatively small, and it is easier to find the match between the contour points. However, if the distance between the planes is relatively large and the contour shape is relatively complex, it is difficult to determine the correspondence. If there is more than one contour in the two adjacent planes, the problem will be more complicated. First, it is to determine the relationship of the corresponding contours in different planes. This not only needs to consider the local characteristics of the contour but also the global characteristics of the contour. Due to insufficient constraints, there is currently no very reliable fully automatic method to solve the corresponding problem, and manual intervention is still required in some situations.

### 9.4.2.2 Tiling Problem

**Tiling** is to use the triangular meshes to create a surface between two corresponding contours of adjacent planes. The basic idea is to generate a set of optimized triangular patches according to a certain criterion to approximate the object surface. The criteria here can vary according to different requirements, such as requiring the smallest surface area, the largest total volume, the shortest connection between contour points, and the most parallel connection between contour points and the center of gravity of the contour. Although there can be many criteria, the central problem is an optimization problem. In addition, in a general sense, tiling can also be used to fit the surface between the corresponding contours with curved surfaces (the above method of using triangular planes is a special case). At this time, the representation of parametric curved surfaces is often used to obtain higher-order continuity.

### 9.4.2.3 Branching Problem

The problem of **branching** (bifurcation) occurs when a contour is divided into two or more contours from one plane to an adjacent plane. In general, the contour corresponding relationship when the branching occurs cannot be determined only by the local information at the branching. It is often necessary to use the overall geometric information and topological relationship of the contour. A common way to solve this problem is to use the following Delaunay triangulation method to generate the triangle meshes from a given set of input vertices.

### 9.4.3 Delaunay Triangulation and Neighborhood Voronoï Diagram

In 1934, the Russian mathematician Delaunay pointed out: For a point set composed of $N$ points on a plane domain, there is one and only one type of triangulation, namely, **Delaunay triangulation**, so that the sum of smallest interior angles of all triangles is the largest. Delaunay triangulation can make each triangle obtained as close to an equilateral triangle as possible, but this definition is not complete.

According to the definition of Delaunay triangulation, it can be derived that Delaunay triangulation meets the following two criteria (they are the basis for constructing the triangulation algorithm):

1. **Common circle criterion**: That is, the circumcircle of any triangle will not contain any other data points. This criterion is often referred to as the property of an empty disc.
2. **Maximum and minimum angle criterion**: For a quadrilateral formed by any two adjacent triangles, Delaunay triangulation requires that all the minimum value of the six internal angles of the two triangles divided by a diagonal of the quadrilateral will be greater than the minimum value of all the six internal angles of the two triangles divided by the other diagonal of the quadrilateral. This criterion enables Delaunay triangulation to avoid producing narrow and ill-conditioned triangles with sharp internal angles as much as possible.

The Voronoï diagram and Delaunay's triangle are duals. The Voronoï neighborhood of a pixel provides an intuitive approximate definition of the pixel. The Voronoï neighborhood of a given pixel corresponds to the closest Euclidean plane region to the pixel, which is a set of finite independent points $P = \{p_1, p_2, \ldots, p_n\}$, where $n \geq 2$.

Let's first define the ordinary Voronoï diagram.

Utilize Euclidean distance:

$$d(p, q) = \sqrt{\left(p_x - q_x\right)^2 + \left(p_y - q_y\right)^2} \tag{9.28}$$

The Voronoï neighborhood of point $p_i$ can be defined as

$$V(p_i) = \left\{p \in \mathbb{R}^2 | \forall i \neq j : d(p, \ p_i) \leq d(p, p_j)\right\} \tag{9.29}$$

It contains the boundary $B_V(p_i)$ of the neighborhood, which contains equidistant points satisfying the following formula:

$$B_V(p_i) = \left\{p \in \mathbb{R}^2 | \exists i \neq j : d(p, \ p_i) = d(p, p_j)\right\} \tag{9.30}$$

The set of Voronoï neighborhoods for all points is

**Fig. 9.19** The vertical dichotomy method to construct the Voronoï diagram

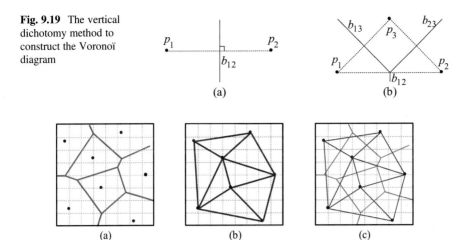

**Fig. 9.20** The duality (**c**) of the Voronoï diagram (**a**) and Delaunay triangle (**b**)

$$W(P) = \{V(p_1), \quad \cdots, \quad V(p_n)\} \tag{9.31}$$

This can be called the **ordinary Voronoï diagram** of the point set $P$, or Voronoï diagram for short. The edges in the Voronoï diagram represent the line segments of the boundary $B_V(p_i)$. The vertices in the Voronoï diagram are the points where the line segments intersect.

The vertices of the Delaunay diagram are all points in $P$. If and only if $V(p_i)$ and $V(p_j)$ are adjacent in the Voronoï diagram, the two points $p_i$ and $p_j$ form an edge in the Delaunay diagram.

When constructing the Voronoï diagram, it can start with the simplest case, that is, from only two different plane points $p_1$ and $p_2$, as shown in Fig. 9.19a. Equation (9.29) shows that the Voronoï neighborhood $V(p_1)$ of $p_1$ includes all points that are either closer to $p_1$ than $p_2$, or points that are equidistant from these two points. It can be seen from Fig. 9.19a that all the points equidistant from the two points $p_1$ and $p_2$ are exactly on the vertical dichotomy (bisecting) $b_{12}$ of the line segment from $p_1$ to $p_2$. According to Eq. (9.30) and the definition of the vertical dichotomy, the contour $B_V(p_1)$ of the Voronoï neighborhood of $p_1$ is $b_{12}$. All points on the half-plane containing $p_1$ defined by $b_{12}$ are closer to $p_1$ than $p_2$, and they will form the Voronoï neighborhood $V(p_1)$ of $p_1$.

If the third point $p_3$ is added to the construction of the Voronoï diagram, a triangle $\Delta_{123}$ can be constructed, as shown in Fig. 9.19b. Using the vertical dichotomy method for each side of the triangle again, a Voronoï diagram with $n = 3$ can be constructed.

Figure 9.20 gives an example of the **duality** of the Voronoï diagram and Delaunay triangle. Figure 9.20a is the Voronoï diagram of several plane points, Fig. 9.20b is its duality, namely, Delaunay triangle, and Fig. 9.20c shows the relationship between them.

According to Eqs. (9.28)–(9.31) used for the Voronoï diagram, it can be further extended to the **region Voronoï diagram**.

The region Voronoï diagram of an image unit $i_j$ is defined as

$$V_a(i_j) = \left\{ p \in \mathbb{R}^2 | \forall j \neq k : d_a(p, \ i_j) \leq d_a(p, \ i_k) \right\} \tag{9.32}$$

where the distance between image unit $i_j$ and point $p$ is

$$d_a(p, \ i_j) = \min_{q \in i_j} d(p, \ q) \tag{9.33}$$

The above equation gives the minimum Euclidean distance between the point $p$ and any point $q$ in the image unit $i_j$. The Voronoï neighborhood of an image unit is a point set, and the distance from this point set to $i_j$ is less than or equal to the distance from any other image unit to $i_j$. Similar to the Voronoï diagram, the boundary $B_{V_a}(i_j)$ of the region Voronoï diagram is given by

$$B_{V_a}(i_j) = \left\{ p \in \mathbb{R}^2 | \exists j \neq k : d_a(p, \ i_j) = d_a(p, \ i_k) \right\} \tag{9.34}$$

The boundary contains points that are equidistant from two or more image units (they are not closer to one of the image units). In the Voronoï diagram, the common boundary of two adjacent Voronoï neighborhoods is always a line or line segment, while in the region Voronoï diagram, the boundary is always a curve or curve segment.

The region Voronoï diagram $W_a$ of an image is the collection of the region Voronoï diagram of all image units, namely,

$$W_a(P) = \left\{ V_a(i_1), \ \cdots, \ V_a(i_n) \right\} \tag{9.35}$$

## 9.5   Three-Dimensional Entity Representation

For most objects in the real world, although they can only be seen on their surface, they are actually 3-D **entities**. These entities can be represented in a variety of ways according to specific applications. The **volumetric model** is mainly used here.

### 9.5.1   Basic Representation Scheme

There are many schemes for 3-D entity representation. The following is a brief introduction to the most basic and commonly used representation schemes.

### 9.5.1.1   Spatial Occupancy Array

Similar to the 2-D spatial occupancy array for the 2-D region, the 3-D **spatial occupancy array** can also be used to represent the 3-D object. Specifically, for any point $(x, y, z)$ in the image $f(x, y, z)$, if it is within a given entity, $f(x, y, z)$ is taken as 1; otherwise it is 0. In this way, the set of points where $f(x, y, z)$ is 1 represents the object to be represented. An example can be seen in Fig. 9.21, Fig. 9.21a is a schematic diagram of a 3-D stereoscopic region image, Fig. 9.21b is a schematic diagram of the corresponding 3-D spatial occupancy array, and the image voxel and the array element are one-to-one correspondence.

Because the size of the 3-D array here is the cube of the image resolution, the spatial occupancy array method is effective and practical only when the image resolution is low (and the shape of the object is irregular); otherwise the amount of data is too large. One of the advantages of representing objects with 3-D arrays is that it is easy to obtain various slices through the object, so as to display the information inside the object.

### 9.5.1.2   Cell Decomposition

**Cell decomposition** refers to a method of decomposing objects step by step until they are decomposed into cells that can be represented uniformly. The aforementioned spatial occupancy array representation can be regarded as a special case of unit decomposition, and the unit is a voxel. In general unit decomposition, the units can also have more complex shapes, but they still have the property of **quasi-disjoint**; in other words, different units do not share the volume. The only combination operation for the 3-D solid elements after decomposition is **glue**.

The **octree** method is a commonly used unit decomposition method, and its structure is shown in Fig. 9.22. The left side shows the octree decomposition diagram, and the right side shows the octree representation diagram.

The octree is a direct extension of the quadtree in 2-D images (see *2D Computer Vision: Principles, Algorithms and Applications*) in 3-D images, and it can be generated by recursive volume decomposition. The octree representation method converts the position of an object in a 3-D image into a position in a hierarchical structure tree. Similar to the analysis of the quadtree, it can be seen that for an octree

**Fig. 9.21  (a, b)**
Representing 3-D objects by
spatial occupancy array

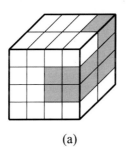 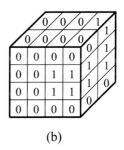

(a)                              (b)

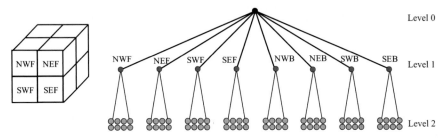

**Fig. 9.22** Octree structure

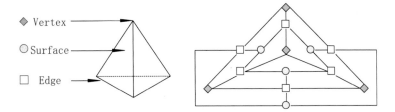

**Fig. 9.23** Surface decomposition example

with $n$ levels, the total number of nodes $N$ is at most (for practical applications, generally less than this number)

$$N = \sum_{k=0}^{n} 8^k = \frac{8^{n+1} - 1}{7} \approx \frac{8}{7} 8^n \tag{9.36}$$

The basic principle of unit decomposition is applicable to various forms of primitives. A typical example is surface decomposition, where the appearance of a 3-D structure is regarded as the combination of its various visible surfaces. Surface decomposition uses graphs to represent the surface of an object with nodes representing each surface, edges (intersections of surfaces) and vertices (intersections of edges), and a set of pointers that indicate the connection of these basic units. Figure 9.23 shows an example of the decomposition of a triangular pyramid. The three types of units are represented by three symbols (as shown on the left), and the pointers are represented by lines on the right.

The result of surface decomposition is the collection of all (basic) surfaces, and these surfaces can also be represented by a **region adjacency graph** (RAG). The region adjacency graph only considers the surface and its adjacency relationship (it implies the vertex and edge units), so it is simpler than the representation in Fig. 9.23.

### 9.5.1.3 Geometric Model Method

The **geometric model** method is often used in systems based on **computer-aided design** (CAD) models. It is also called the **rigid body model** method because it is used to represent rigid bodies (the representation of nonrigid bodies is still a challenging problem, and there is no unified method). The rigid body model system can be divided into two categories. In the boundary representation system, the rigid body is represented by the union of its various boundary surfaces. In the **constructive solid geometry** representation system, the rigid body is represented as a combination of other simple rigid bodies through a set of collective operations. The lowest level (simplest) is the primitive body, which can generally be represented by the analytical function $F(x, y, z)$, and is limited to the inside of the intersection of the closed half-space defined by $F(x, y, z) \geq 0$.

**Example 9.5 Example of Boundary Representation and Constructive Representation**
Figure 9.24a shows an object composed of two geometric bodies, Fig. 9.24b shows an example of the boundary representation of this object (ten boundary surfaces are used), and Fig. 9.24c gives an example of the constructive representation of this object (three simple rigid bodies are used).

## 9.5.2 Generalized Cylinder Representation

Many actual 3-D objects can be formed by moving a 2-D set along a 3-D curve (similar to build a series of flat plates). In a more general case, this set can also have parameter changes in motion. The rigid body representation method based on this mode is usually called the **generalized cylinder** method, and it is also called the generalized cone method. This is because the primitive body in this method is often a cylinder or cone of any size; of course, it can also be a cuboid or sphere of any size (a variation of a cylinder or a cone).

The generalized cylinder method usually uses a combination of a (generalized) cylinder with a certain axis (called **through-axis**) and a certain **cross-section** to

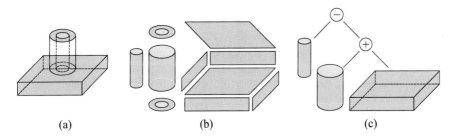

(a)　　　　　　　　　(b)　　　　　　　　　(c)

**Fig. 9.24** (**a–c**) Example of boundary representation and constructive representation

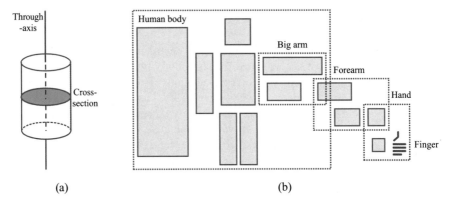

(a)                                               (b)

**Fig. 9.25**  (**a, b**) Example of the generalized cylinder method

represent a 3-D object. In other words, it has two basic units: a through-axis and a cross-section with a certain shape that moves along the through-axis; a schematic diagram is shown in Fig. 9.25a. Combining multiple such primitives can represent the different details of an object from high to low, level by level. Figure 9.25b gives an example of this representation (where each cylinder is represented by a rectangle in 2-D).

If the primitive is treated as a variable, that is, the through-axis and the moving cross-section are changed, a series of generalized cylinder variants can also be obtained. In fact, the through-axis can be divided into the following two categories:

1. The through-axis is a straight-line segment.
2. The through-axis is a curve (it can also be closed).

There are many types or forms of changes in the moving cross-section, mainly in the following three categories:

1. The boundary of the cross-section can be a straight line or a curve.
2. The cross-section can be rotationally and reflectively symmetrical or asymmetrical, or only rotationally or reflectively symmetrical.
3. The shape of the cross-section can be changed or unchanged when it moves. The size of the cross-section can also become larger, smaller, larger first and then smaller, smaller first and then larger, etc., when it moves.

Figure 9.26 shows some change cases. Combining these variants as **volumetric primitives** can represent even complex 3-D objects. Theoretically, there are infinitely many pairs of through-axes and cross-sections that can represent all kinds of 3-D object.

Projecting a basic 3-D generalized cylinder into a 2-D image will mainly produce two different results, namely, strips and ellipses. The strip is the result of projection along the length of the cylinder, and the ellipse is the result of the projection of the cross-section of the cylinder. If one considers various generalized cylinder variants, it is possible to produce any desired result.

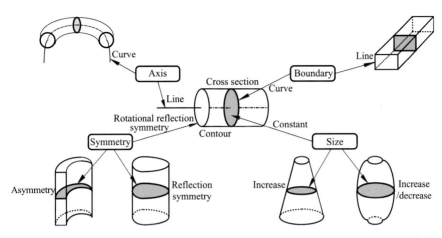

**Fig. 9.26** Variations of generalized cylinder

## 9.6 Key Points and References for Each Section

The following combine the main contents of each section to introduce some references that can be further consulted:

1. **Local Features of the Surface**

    The calculation and representation of local features of curved surfaces mainly involve differential geometry, as can be found in references [1, 2]. For the mean curvature and Gaussian curvature of the surface, please refer to reference [3].

2. **3-D Surface Representation**

    For the Gaussian map method of representing the surface orientation, please refer to reference [4]. More discussion on the Gaussian sphere can be found in reference [2]. The content of the 3-D edge representation model can also be found in the reference [5]. For the extended Gaussian image, several situations when the object is a non-convex body can be found in reference [6].

3. **Construction and Representation of Iso-surfaces**

    The marching cube algorithm can perform fast calculations with the help of a look-up table; the wrapping algorithm has a large amount of calculation, but it can overcome the ambiguity problem of the marching cube algorithm [3]. To solve the corresponding problems, tiling problems, and branching problems of these algorithms, please refer to reference [7].

4. **Interpolate 3-D Surfaces from Parallel Contours**

    The surface interpolation stitching of two adjacent parallel contours needs to solve the corresponding problem between contours. This is a problem of image registration in a more general sense. See the discussion in Sect. 10.1. For the content of using contours to represent 3-D shapes, please refer to references [8, 9]. The definition of the Voronoï region and the ordinary Voronoï diagram can be found in reference [10].

5. **3-D Entity Representation**

   The method of directly representing 3-D entities including surface and interior can be found in references [11, 12]. In addition, one can also refer to the literature of computer graphics, such as reference [13], which also provides many related C language programs.

# Self-Test Questions

The following questions include both single-choice questions and multiple-choice questions, so each option must be judged.

9.1. **Local Features of the Surface**

   9.1.1. Consider a point $P$ on the surface $S$; (·).

   (a) The tangent plane passing through this point contains all the tangent lines of the curve $C$ passing through the point $P$ and on the surface $S$.
   (b) The straight-line $N$ passing through this point and perpendicular to the surface $S$ is called the normal line of the surface $S$ at the point $P$.
   (c) The number of tangents passing through the point is equal to the number of normal lines.
   (d) Among the tangent lines passing through this point, at least one of the tangent lines is in the same plane as the normal line.

   [Hint] The tangent line and the normal line are perpendicular to each other.

   9.1.2. For each point on a surface, (·).

   (a) There is only one direction of maximum curvature.
   (b) There is only one direction of minimum curvature.
   (c) The maximum curvature will always be obtained in a certain direction.
   (d) The minimum curvature will always be obtained in a certain direction.

   [Hint] The curvature may be the same in different directions.

   9.1.3. Only considering the signs of mean curvature and Gaussian curvature can make the following judgments on the surface: (·).

   (a) As long as the mean curvature is positive, there is a local minimum point on the surface.
   (b) As long as the mean curvature is negative, there is a local maximum point on the surface.
   (c) As long as the Gaussian curvature is positive, there is a local minimum point on the surface.
   (d) As long as the Gaussian curvature is negative, there is a local maximum point on the surface.

   [Hint] Refer to the example in Fig. 9.3.

## 9.2. 3-D Surface Representation

9.2.1. To represent the outer surface of 3-D objects and describe their shape, (·).

(a) The outer contour line or outer contour surface of the object can be used.
(b) The outline of the object is obtained during image acquisition.
(c) The outer contour surface of the object can be decomposed into a collection of various surface elements.
(d) The representation of the outer contour surface of the object can be converted into the representation of the outer contour line of the object.

[Hint] Analyze the relationship between body, surface, and line.

9.2.2. Extended Gaussian image (·).

(a) Can represent the distribution of the normals of the 3-D object surface.
(b) Can accurately represent the orientation of each point on the surface.
(c) Has a one-to-one correspondence with the represented object.
(d) Can be used to restore the surface of the 3-D object.

[Hint] Refer to the description of the extended Gaussian image.

9.2.3. When projecting the Gaussian sphere onto a plane to obtain the gradient space, (·).

(a) The spherical projection projects the point with the gradient $(p, q)$ onto the position $(p, q)$ on the plane.
(b) The spherical projection uses the center of the Gaussian sphere as the center of projection to project all points on the spherical surface onto the plane.
(c) Stereographic projection uses the South Pole of the Gaussian sphere as the center of projection to project all points on the spherical surface onto the plane.
(d) Stereographic projection will project the point on the equator of the corresponding Gaussian sphere to the edge of the plane.

[Hint] Analyze according to the center position of the two projections.

## 9.3. Construction and Representation of Iso-surfaces

9.3.1. Equivalent surface (iso-surface) (·).

(a) Only exists at the junction of one object and other objects or backgrounds.
(b) Is always a 3-D curved surface in a 3-D image.
(c) Is composed of 3-D voxel points with a certain gray value.
(d) Constructs a closed and complete object surface.

[Hint] Pay attention to the definition of iso-surface.

9.3.2. In the marching cube algorithm, (·).

(a) The bounding cube is defined as the cube contained in the object.
(b) Determine the iso-surface according to the different situations where the object surface intersects the cube.
(c) Determine the boundary cube with voxel as the basic unit.
(d) The 14 different black and white voxel layouts shown in Fig. 9.7 contain all possible layouts of the cube.

[Hint] Distinguish between voxel and cube, cube and boundary cube.

9.3.3. Which of the following statement(s) is/are correct? (·).

(a) The object surface that is not closed by the marching cube algorithm is due to the ambiguity problem.
(b) The wrapper algorithm can always produce a closed object surface.
(c) The marching cube algorithm and the wrapper algorithm use cubes of different sizes.
(d) In the wrapper algorithm, all cube decomposition methods are the same.

[Hint] Compare the characteristics of the marching cube algorithm and the wrapper algorithm.

9.4. **Interpolate 3-D Surfaces from Parallel Contours**

9.4.1. Which of the following description(s) about tiling is/are correct? (·).

(a) Surface tiling is a method of representing the surface of 3-D object by using a set of surface elements.
(b) Each mesh in the polygon mesh is a three-dimensional structure composed of vertices, edges, and surfaces.
(c) The effect of surface tiling is consistent with the effect of contour tiling.
(d) The basic unit represented by the wireframe is the mesh in the polygonal mesh.

[Hint] Pay attention to the difference between line representation and surface representation.

9.4.2. Among the problems that may be encountered in the method of interpolating the contour to obtain the surface, (·).

(a) The corresponding problem only needs to consider determining the corresponding points in the corresponding contours.
(b) To solve the tiling problem, the corresponding problem needs to be solved first.
(c) The branching problem often needs to use the geometric information and topological relationship of the contour as a whole.
(d) To solve these problems, it is needed to use the global features of the contour.

[Hint] Analyze the characteristics of these problems separately.

9.4.3. Voronoï diagram and Delaunay triangle are related to each other and have their own characteristics: (·).

    (a) Given some plane points, Delaunay triangle takes these points as vertices.

    (b) Given a plane point, the Voronoï neighborhood corresponds to the Euclidean plane region closest to the point.

    (c) Given some plane points, the Voronoï diagram is the set of Voronoï neighborhoods of these points.

    (d) The Voronoï diagram and Delaunay triangle are duals, so their lines of intersection are perpendicular to each other.

    [Hint] Refer to Fig. 9.19.

## 9.5. **3-D Entity Representation**

9.5.1. Among the most basic and commonly used representation schemes, (·).

    (a) The amount of data required for the spatial occupancy array is more than that of the octree, but the representation accuracy is higher than that of the octree.

    (b) The amount of data required for the spatial occupancy array is more than that of the surface decomposition, but the representation accuracy is higher than that of the surface decomposition.

    (c) The boundary representation system of the rigid body model uses the boundary surface as the primitive, so the representation of the object is consistent with the surface decomposition method.

    (d) The simple rigid body is used as the primitive in the constructive solid geometry representation system, so the representation result of the object is consistent with the representation result of the spatial occupancy array.

    [Hint] Analyze the characteristics of each representation method.

9.5.2. The generalized cylinder method uses a through-axis and a cross-section as variables to represent 3-D objects; (·).

    (a) The through-axis can be a straight line segment or a curved segment of any shape.

    (b) The cross-section can be a plane of any shape and move along the through-axis.

    (c) Various combinations of through-axis and cross-section can form various basic three-dimensional primitives.

    (d) There is a special pair of through-axis and cross-section representations for each given 3-D object.

    [Hint] The generalized cylinder method has no restrictions on the through-axis and the cross-section.

9.5.3.  When using a generalized cylinder to represent a bicycle, (·).

(a)  The bell cover needs to use a circular threading axis and a circular cross-section.

(b)  The handlebar needs to use a curved through-axis and a circular cross-section.

(c)  The wheel needs to use a circular through-axis and asymmetrical cross-section.

(d)  The spokes need to use a straight through-axis and a rotationally symmetrical cross-section.

[Hint] The cross-section moves along the through-axis.

# References

1. Ma L. Concise differential geometry. Tsinghua University Press, 2004.
2. Forsyth D, Ponce J. Computer Vision: A Modern Approach. Prentice Hall. 2003.
3. Lohmann G. Volumetric Image Analysis. John Wiley & Sons and Teubner Publishers. 1998.
4. Shirai Y. Three-Dimensional Computer Vision. Springer-Verlag. 1987.
5. Zhang Y J. Quantitative study of 3-D gradient operators. IVC, 1993, 11: 611-622.
6. Horn B K P. Robot Vision. MIT Press. 1986.
7. Guan W G. Stereoscopic technology and its application. Publishing House of Industry Press, 1998.
8. Weiss I. 3D shape representation by contours. CVGIP, 1988, 41(1): 80-100.
9. Zhang Y J. 3-D image analysis system and megakaryocyte quantitation. Cytometry, 1991, 12: 308-315.
10. Kropatsch W G, Bischof H (eds.). Digital Image Analysis — Selected Techniques and Applications. Springer. 2001.
11. Haralick R M, Shapiro L G. Computer and Robot Vision, Vol. 2. Addison-Wesley. 1993.
12. Sonka M, Hlavac V, Boyle R. Image Processing, Analysis, and Machine Vision. 3rd Ed. Thomson. 2008.
13. Foley J D, Van Dam A, Feiner S K, et al. Computer Graphics: Principles and Practice in C, 2nd Ed. Addison-Wesley. 1996.

# Chapter 10
# Generalized Matching

The functions and goals to be achieved by computer vision are complex, including processes such as perception/observation, scene restoration, matching cognition, scene interpretation, etc. Among them, matching cognition tries to connect the unknown with the known through matching and then uses the known to explain the unknown. For example, the scene matching technology is a technology that uses the data of the scene reference map for autonomous navigation and positioning. It uses the image sensor mounted on the aircraft to collect the real-time scene during the flight and compare it with the pre-prepared reference scene. The real-time matching will obtain accurate navigation and positioning information.

For a complex computer vision system, there are often multiple image inputs and other forms of representation coexisting within it. **Matching** uses the existing representations and models stored in the system to perceive the information in the image input and finally establish the correspondence with the outside world, to realize the interpretation of the scene. The interpretation of the scene is a process of continuous cognition, so it is necessary to match the information obtained from the image with the existing model for explaining the scene. It can also be said that perception is the process of combining visual input with previous representations, and cognition also needs to establish or discover connections between various internal representations. For this reason, matching can be understood as a technique or process that combines various representations and knowledge to explain the scene.

Commonly used image-related matching methods and techniques can be classified into two categories: one is more specific and corresponds to the lower-level pixels or sets of pixels, which can be collectively referred to as image matching; the other is more abstract, mainly related to image objects or the nature and connection of objects, or even related to the description and interpretation of the scene, which can be collectively referred to as generalized matching. For example, the region-based stereo matching and feature-based stereo matching introduced in Chap. 6 belong to the former category. This chapter focuses on introducing some matching methods and techniques related to the latter type of scenery.

Y.-J. Zhang, *3-D Computer Vision*, https://doi.org/10.1007/978-981-19-7580-6_10

The sections of this chapter are arranged as follows:

Section 10.1 summarizes the basic concepts of various matching, compares and discusses matching and registration, and analyzes several commonly used image matching evaluation criteria.

Section 10.2 first discusses the measurement of matching and then introduces some typical object matching methods, including matching with landmarks or feature points on the object, matching the contours of the two object regions with the help of string representations, and matching by using the inertia equivalent ellipse and matching two object regions with the help of the shape matrix representation.

Section 10.3 introduces a method of dynamically establishing the pattern for object representation during the matching process and then matching these patterns. This dynamic idea/thinking can be extended to various occasions.

Section 10.4 uses the principle of graph theory and the properties of graphs to establish the correspondence between objects and uses graph isomorphism to match scenes at different levels.

Section 10.5 introduces the matching method that first constructs the line drawing of the object by projecting the (visible) surface observed on the 3-D scene onto the contour of the region formed by the 2-D image, and then marking the line drawing, and finally using this mark to match the 3-D scene with the corresponding model.

## 10.1   Matching Overview

In the understanding of images, matching technology plays an important role. From a visual point of view, vision includes sight and sense. The "sight" should be a purposeful "sight," that is, according to a certain knowledge (including the description of the object and the explanation of the scene), the image should be used to find the scenery that meets the requirements in the scene; the "sense" should be the "sense" with cognition, that is, the characteristics of the scenery should be extracted from the input image, and then matched with the existing scenery model, so as to achieve the purpose of understanding the meaning of the scene. Matching and knowledge are inherently related, and matching and interpretation are also inseparable.

### 10.1.1   Matching Strategies and Categories

In a broad sense, matching can be carried out at different (abstract) levels, because knowledge has different levels and can also be used at different levels. For each specific match, it can be seen as finding the correspondence between two representations. If the types of two representations are comparable, matching can be done in a similar sense. For example, when the two representations are both in image form, it

**Fig. 10.1** Matching and mapping

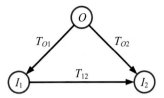

is called **image matching**; if the two representations represent the object in the image, it is called **object matching**; if the two representations represent the description of the scene, it is called **scene matching**; if both representations are relational structures, it is called **relational matching**; the latter three are **generalized matching**. If the two representation types are different (e.g., one is an image structure and the other is a relational structure), then it can also be matched in an extended sense, or it is called **fitting**.

To establish a connection between the two representation types, matching needs to be carried out through mapping. When reconstructing the scene, the image matching strategy can be divided into two situations according to the different mapping functions used; see Fig. 10.1.

### 10.1.1.1 Matching in Image Space

The image space matching directly connects the images $I_1$ and $I_2$ with the mapping function $T_{12}$. In this case, the object model is implicitly included in the establishment of $T_{12}$. The process is generally quite complicated, but if the object surface is relatively smooth, an affine transformation can be used to locally approximate it. At this time, the computational complexity can be reduced to a level comparable to that of the object space. In the case of occlusion, the smooth hypothesis will be affected and the image matching algorithm will encounter difficulties.

### 10.1.1.2 Matching in Object Space

In this case, the object $O$ is directly reconstructed by the inversion of the perspective transformations $T_{O1}$ and $T_{O2}$. An explicit representation model for object $O$ is needed here, and the problem is solved by establishing a correspondence between image features and object model features. The advantage of object space matching technology is that they are more consistent with the physical world, so if a more complex model is used, it can even deal with occlusion. If the object space is regarded as the transformation of the image space or the mapping space, the matching of the object space can also be extended to the generalized matching of more general and abstract level spaces.

Image matching algorithms can be further classified and hierarchized according to the image representation model they use.

### 10.1.1.3   Matching Based on Raster

Raster-based matching uses the raster representation of the image, that is, it tries to find the mapping function between image regions by directly comparing gray scale or grayscale functions. This type of method can be very accurate, but it is very sensitive to occlusion.

### 10.1.1.4   Feature-Based Matching

In feature-based matching, the symbolic description of the image is first decomposed by using the salient features extracted from the image with the feature extraction operator, and then the corresponding features of different images are searched for, according to the assumption of the local geometric properties of the object to be described. The further step is to perform geometric mapping. Compared with the methods based on raster matching, these methods are more suitable for situations with surface discontinuities and data approximation.

### 10.1.1.5   Matching Based on Relationship

Relation matching is also called structural matching. Its technology is based on the similarity of topological relationships between features (topological properties do not change under perspective transformation). These similarities exist in the **feature adjacency graph** rather than the similarity of grayscale or point distribution. The matching of the relationship description can be applied in many situations, but it may generate a very complicated search tree, so its computational complexity may be very large.

The (broad) **template matching** theory believes that in order to recognize the content of a certain image, there must be a "memory trace" or basic model in the past experience. This model is also called a "template." If the current stimulus matches the template in the brain, people can tell what the stimulus is. For example, the "template matching" introduced in Sect. 6.2 is actually a special case of using this theory, and it can also be called narrow template matching. In narrow template matching, the designed template comes from the past experience in the brain, and the large image to be matched corresponds to the current stimulus. However, the template matching theory says that the external stimulus must be in full compliance with the template. In reality, people can not only recognize images that are consistent with the basic model in real life but also can recognize images that are not completely consistent with the basic model.

Gestalt psychologists proposed the **prototype matching** theory. This theory believes that the currently observed image of a letter "A," no matter what shape it is or where it is placed, is similar to the "A" known in the past. Humans do not store countless templates of different shapes in long-term memory, but use the similarities abstracted from various images as prototypes to test the images they want for cognition. If one can find a prototype similar to the image one wants for cognition, then one can realize the cognition of this image. This kind of image cognition model is more suitable than template matching from the perspective of neurology and memory search process, and it can also explain the cognition process of some irregular images that are similar to the prototype in some aspects. According to this model, an idealized prototype of the letter "A" can be formed, which summarizes the common characteristics of various images similar to this prototype. On this basis, the matching cognition for all other "A"s becomes possible even though they are inconsistent with the prototype and only similar.

Although the prototype matching theory can explain some phenomena in image cognition more reasonably, it does not explain how humans can distinguish and process similar stimuli. Prototype matching theory does not give a clear model or mechanism of image cognition, and it is difficult to realize this theory in computer programs.

## 10.1.2  Matching and Registration

Matching and registration are two closely related concepts, and there are many similarities in technology. However, careful analysis shows that there are still certain differences between the two. The meaning of **registration** is generally narrow. It mainly refers to the establishment of the correspondence between images obtained in different time or space, especially the geometric correspondence (geometric correction). The final effect is often reflected in the pixel level. Matching can consider not only the geometric properties of the image but also the grayscale properties of the image, and even other abstract properties and attributes of the image. From this point of view, registration can be regarded as a matching of lower-level representations, and the generalized matching can include registration. The main difference between image registration and stereo matching is that the former requires not only the establishment of the relationship between the point pairs but also the calculation of the global coordinate transformation parameters between the two images from the corresponding relationship and the latter only requires the establishment of the corresponding relationship between the point pairs and then simply needs to calculate the parallax for each pair of points.

In terms of specific implementation technology, registration can often be achieved with the help of coordinate transformation and affine transformation. Most registration algorithms include three steps: (1) feature selection; (2) feature matching; and (3) calculation of the transformation function. The performance of registration technology is often determined by the following four factors:

1. The feature space of the features used for registration
2. A search space that makes the search process possible
3. Search strategy for scanning the search space

4. A similarity measure used to determine whether the registration correspondence is valid

The registration technology in the image space (such as stereo vision matching) can be divided into two categories similar to the matching technology (such as Sects. 6.2 and 6.3). The registration technology in the frequency domain is mainly carried out through related calculations in the frequency domain. Here, the image needs to be converted/transformed to the frequency domain through Fourier transform, and then the phase information or amplitude information of the spectrum is used to build the corresponding relationship between images in the frequency domain to achieve registration; they can be called phase correlation method and amplitude correlation method, respectively.

The following only takes the registration when there is a translation between the images as an example to introduce the calculation of the **phase correlation method** (PCM; for the calculation of rotation and scale changes, please refer to the ideas in Sect. 4.3). The phase correlation calculation between the two images can be carried out by means of the phase estimation of the cross power spectrum. Suppose two images $f_1(x, y)$ and $f_2(x, y)$ have the following simple translation relationship in the space domain:

$$f_1(x, y) = f_2(x - x_0, y - y_0)  \tag{10.1}$$

According to the translation theorem of the Fourier transform, it has

$$F_1(u, v) = F_2(x, y) \exp\left[-j2\pi(ux_0 + vy_0)\right]  \tag{10.2}$$

If the normalized cross power spectrum of the Fourier transform $F_1(u, v)$ and $F_2(u, v)$ of two images $f_1(x, y)$ and $f_2(x, y)$ is used for representation, the phase correlation between them can be calculated as follows:

$$\exp\left[-j2\pi(ux_0 + vy_0)\right] = \frac{F_1(x, y)F_2^*(x, y)}{|F_1(x, y)F_2^*(x, y)|}  \tag{10.3}$$

where the inverse Fourier transform of $\exp[-j2\pi(ux_0 + vy_0)]$ is $\delta(x - x_0, y - y_0)$. It can be seen that the relative translation of the two images $f_1(x, y)$ and $f_2(x, y)$ in space is $(x_0, y_0)$. The amount of translation can be determined by searching the position of the maximum value (caused by the pulse) in the image.

The following summarize the steps of the phase correlation algorithm based on the Fourier transform:

1. Calculate the Fourier transform $F_1(u, v)$ and $F_2(u, v)$ of the two images $f_1(x, y)$ and $f_2(x, y)$ to be registered.
2. Filter out the DC component and high-frequency noise in the spectrum, and calculate the product of the spectrum components.
3. Use Eq. (10.3) to calculate the normalized cross power spectrum.

4. Perform inverse Fourier transform on the normalized cross power spectrum.
5. Search the coordinates of the peak point in the image of inverse Fourier transform, which gives the relative translation amount.

The calculation amount of the above registration method is only related to the size of the image and has nothing to do with the relative position between the images or whether they overlap. This method only uses the phase information in the cross power spectrum, is easy to calculate, is insensitive to the brightness changes between images, and can effectively overcome the influences of illumination changes. Since the obtained correlation peaks are sharper and more prominent, higher registration accuracy can be obtained.

### *10.1.3 Matching Evaluation*

Commonly used image matching evaluation criteria include accuracy, reliability, robustness, and computational complexity.

**Accuracy** refers to the difference between the true value and the estimated value. The smaller the difference, the more accurate the estimation. In image registration, accuracy refers to the mean, median, maximum, or root mean square value of the distance between the reference image point and the registered image point (after resampling to the reference image space). When the correspondence has been determined, the accuracy can be measured from the synthesized image or the simulated image; another method is to place the fiducial mark in the scene and use the position of the fiducial mark to evaluate the accuracy of the registration. The unit of accuracy can be pixels or voxels.

**Reliability** refers to how many times the algorithm has achieved satisfactory results in the total tests performed. If $N$ pairs of images are tested and $M$ tests give satisfactory results, when $N$ is large enough and $N$ is representative of the image, then $M/N$ represents reliability. The closer the $M/N$ is to 1, the more reliable it is. The reliability of the algorithm is predictable.

**Robustness** refers to the degree of stability of accuracy or the reliability of an algorithm under different changing conditions of its parameters. Robustness can be measured in terms of noise, density, geometric differences, or the percentage of dissimilar regions between images. The robustness of an algorithm can be obtained by determining the stability of the accuracy of the algorithm or the reliability when the input parameters change (such as using their variance, the smaller the variance, the more robust the algorithm). If there are many input parameters, each of which affects the accuracy or reliability of the algorithm, then the robustness of the algorithm can be defined relative to each parameter. For example, an algorithm may be robust to noise, but not robust to geometric distortion. To say that an algorithm is robust generally means that the performance of the algorithm will not change significantly with the changes in the parameters involved.

**Computational complexity** determines the speed of the algorithm and indicates its practicality in specific applications. For example, in image-guided neurosurgery, it is necessary to register the image used to plan the operation with the image reflecting the operation condition at a specific time within a few seconds. However, matching aerial images acquired by aircraft often needs to be completed in the order of milliseconds. The computational complexity can be expressed as a function of the image size (considering the number of additions or multiplications required for each unit); it is generally hoped that the computational complexity of a good matching algorithm is a linear function of the image size.

## 10.2  Object Matching

Image matching uses pixels as a unit, the amount of calculation is generally large, and the matching efficiency is low. In practice, the object of interest is often detected and extracted first, and then the object is matched. If a concise object representation is used, the matching workload can be greatly reduced. Since the object can be represented in different ways, a variety of methods can also be used to match the object.

### 10.2.1  Measure of Matching

The effect of object matching should be judged by a certain measure, the core of which is mainly the degree of object similarity.

#### 10.2.1.1  Hausdorff Distance

In the image, the object is composed of points (pixels), and the matching of two objects is a match between two point sets in a certain sense. The method of using **Hausdorff distance** (HD) to describe the similarity between point sets and matching through feature point sets is widely used. Given two finite point sets $A = \{a_1, a_2, \ldots, a_m\}$ and $B = \{b_1, b_2, \ldots, b_n\}$, the Hausdorff distance between them is defined as follows:

$$H(A, B) = \max [h(A, B), h(B, A)] \tag{10.4}$$

where

**Fig. 10.2** Schematic diagram of Hausdorff distance

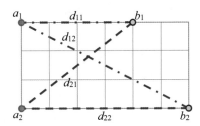

$$h(A, B) = \max_{a \in A} \min_{b \in B} \|a - b\| \qquad (10.5)$$

$$h(B, A) = \max_{b \in B} \min_{a \in A} \|b - a\| \qquad (10.6)$$

The norm $\|\cdot\|$ in Eqs. (10.5) and (10.6) can take different forms. The function $h(A, B)$ is called the directed Hausdorff distance from the set $A$ to set $B$, which describes the longest distance from point $a \in A$ to any point in the point set $B$; similarly, the function $h(B, A)$ is called the directed Hausdorff distance from set $B$ to set $A$, which describes the longest distance from point $b \in B$ to any point in point set $A$. Since $h(A, B)$ and $h(B, A)$ are asymmetric, the maximum value between them is generally taken as the Hausdorff distance between the two point sets.

The geometric meaning of the Hausdorff distance can be explained as follows: If the Hausdorff distance between two point sets $A$ and $B$ is $d$, then for any point in each point set, at least one point in another point set can be found in a circle centered on that point and with a radius of $d$. If the Hausdorff distance between two point sets is 0, it means that the two point sets are coincident. In the schematic diagram in Fig. 10.2, $h(A, B) = d_{21}$, $h(B, A) = d_{22} = H(A, B)$.

The Hausdorff distance defined above is very sensitive to noise points or the outline of a point set. A commonly used improvement method uses the concept of statistical average, replacing the maximum with the mean value, which is called the **modified Hausdorff distance** (MHD), that is, Eqs. (10.5) and (10.6) are, respectively, changed to

$$h_{\text{MHD}}(A, B) = \frac{1}{N_A} \sum_{a \in A} \min_{b \in B} \|a - b\| \qquad (10.7)$$

$$h_{\text{MHD}}(B, A) = \frac{1}{N_B} \sum_{b \in B} \min_{a \in A} \|b - a\| \qquad (10.8)$$

where $N_A$ represents the number of points in point set $A$ and $N_B$ represents the number of points in point set $B$. Substituting them into Eq. (10.4), it gives

$$H_{\text{MHD}}(A, B) = \max \left[ h_{\text{MHD}}(A, B), \; h_{\text{MHD}}(B, A) \right] \qquad (10.9)$$

When the Hausdorff distance is used to calculate the correlation matching between the template and the image, it does not require a clear point relationship between the template and the image. In other words, it does not need to establish a one-to-one relationship of point correspondence between the two point sets, which is an important advantage.

### 10.2.1.2   Structural Matching Measure

Objects can often be decomposed, that is, into their individual components. Different objects can have the same components but different structures. For **structural matching**, most of the matching measures can be explained by the so-called "template and spring" physical analogy model. Considering that the structure matching is the matching between the reference structure and the structure to be matched, if the reference structure is regarded as a structure depicted on the transparent film, the matching can be regarded as moving the transparent film on the structure to be matched and deforming it to get the fit of the two structures.

Matching often involves similarities that can be quantitatively described. A match is not a simple correspondence, but a correspondence quantitatively described according to a certain goodness index, and this goodness corresponds to a match measure. For example, the goodness of the fit of two structures depends on the degree of matching between the components of the two structures one by one, as well as the amount of work required to deform the transparencies.

In practice, to achieve deformation, the model is considered as a set of rigid templates connected by springs. For example, a face template and spring model can be seen in Fig. 10.3. Here the templates are connected by springs, and the spring function describes the relationship between the templates. The relationship between templates generally has certain constraints. For example, on a face image, the two eyes are generally on the same horizontal line, and the distance is always within a certain range. The quality of the matching is a function of the goodness of the local

**Fig. 10.3** The template and spring model of the human face

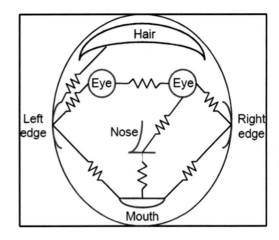

fitting of the template and the energy required to make the structure to be matched in fitting the reference structure by elongating the spring.

The matching measurement of template and spring can be represented in general form as follows:

$$C = \sum_{d \in Y} C_T[d, F(d)] + \sum_{(d,\ e) \in (Y \times E)} C_S[F(d), F(e)] + \sum_{c \in (N \cup M)} C_M(c) \qquad (10.10)$$

where $C_T$ represents the dissimilarity between the template $d$ and the structure to be matched, $C_S$ represents the dissimilarity between the structure to be matched and the object component $e$, $C_M$ represents the penalty for missing components, and $F(\bullet)$ is a mapping that transforms the reference structure template into a structural component to be matched. $F$ divides reference structures into two categories: structures that can be found in the structure to be matched (belonging to set $Y$) and structures that cannot be found in the structure to be matched (belonging to set $N$). Similarly, components can also be divided into two types: components that exist in the structure to be matched (belonging to set $E$) and components that do not exist in the structure to be matched (belonging to set $M$).

The normalization problem needs to be considered in the structural matching measurement, because the number of matched components may affect the value of the final matching metric. For example, if the "spring" always has a finite cost, so that the more elements that are matched, the greater the total energy, this does not mean that the more number of matched parts is worse than the less number of matched parts. Conversely, the delicate matching of a part of the structure to be matched with a specific reference object often makes the remaining part unmatched. At this time, this kind of "sub-matching" is not as good as the effect of making most of the parts to be matched close to matching. In Eq. (10.10), this situation is avoided by penalizing missing parts.

## 10.2.2   Corresponding Point Matching

When the matching between two objects (or a model and an object) has specific **landmark points** or characteristic points on the object (see Sect. 6.3), it can be carried out by means of the **correspondence** between them. If these landmark points or feature points are different from each other (with different attributes), there are two pairs of points that can be matched. If these landmark points or feature points are the same as each other (have the same attributes), at least three non-collinear corresponding points must be determined on the two objects (the three points must be coplanar).

In 3-D space, if perspective projection is used, since any set of three points can be matched with any other set of three points, the correspondence between the two sets

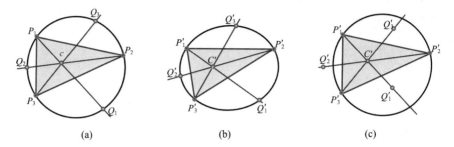

**Fig. 10.4** (a–c) Three-point matching under weak perspective projection (see text)

**Table 10.1** Ambiguity when using corresponding point matching

| Distribution of points | Coplanar | | | | | Non-coplanar | | | | |
|---|---|---|---|---|---|---|---|---|---|---|
| Number of corresponding point pairs | ≤2 | 3 | 4 | 5 | ≥6 | ≤2 | 3 | 4 | 5 | ≥6 |
| Perspective projection | ∞ | 4 | 1 | 1 | 1 | ∞ | 4 | 2 | 1 | 1 |
| Weak perspective projection | ∞ | 2 | 2 | 2 | 2 | ∞ | 2 | 1 | 1 | 1 |

of points cannot be determined at this time. If the weak perspective projection is used, the ambiguity of matching is much smaller.

Consider a simple situation below. Suppose a group of three points $P_1$, $P_2$, and $P_3$ on the object are on the same circle, as shown in Fig. 10.4a. Suppose the center of gravity of the triangle is $C$ and the straight line connecting $C$ and $P_1$, $P_2$, and $P_3$ intersects the circle at points $Q_1$, $Q_2$, and $Q_3$, respectively. Under weak perspective projection conditions, the distance ratio $P_iC:CQ_i$ remains unchanged after projection. In this way, the circle will become an ellipse after projection (but a straight line will still be a straight line after projection, and the distance ratio will not change), as shown in Fig. 10.4b. When $P'_1$, $P'_2$, and $P'_3$ are observed in the image, $C'$ can be calculated, and then the positions of points $Q'_1$, $Q'_2$, and $Q'_3$ can be determined. So there are six points to determine the position and parameters of the ellipse (actually at least five points are needed). Once the ellipse is known, the match becomes an ellipse match.

If the distance ratio is calculated incorrectly, $Q_i$ will not fall on the circle, as shown in Fig. 10.4c. In this way, the ellipses passing through $P'_1$, $P'_2$, and $P'_3$ as well as $Q'_1$, $Q'_2$, and $Q'_3$ cannot be obtained after projection, so the above calculation is impossible.

More general ambiguity can be found in Table 10.1, where the number of solutions obtained when matching the object with corresponding points in the image is given in various situations. The bold **1** means there is only one solution and no ambiguity. When the number of solutions ≥2, it shows that there is ambiguity. All 2s happen when they are coplanar, corresponding to perspective inversion. Any non-coplanar point (more than three points in the corresponding plane) provides enough information to eliminate ambiguity. Table 10.1 considers the two cases of coplanar points and non-coplanar points, respectively, and also compares perspective projection and weak perspective projection.

### 10.2.3   String Matching

**String matching** can be used to match the contours of two object regions. Suppose that two region contours $A$ and $B$ have been coded into character strings $a_1 a_2 \ldots a_n$ and $b_1 b_2 \ldots b_m$ (see the various contour representation methods in Chap. 9 of *2D Computer Vision: Principles, Algorithms and Applications* and the discussion about character string description in Chap. 10 of the book). Starting from $a_1$ and $b_1$, if there is $a_k = b_k$ at the $k$th position, it is said that the two contours have a match. If $M$ is used to represent the total number of matches between two strings, the number of unmatched symbols is

$$Q = \max \left( \left\| A \right\|, \ \left\| B \right\| \right) - M \tag{10.11}$$

where ‖arg‖ represents the length (number of symbols) of the string representation of arg. It can be proved that $Q = 0$ if and only if $A$ and $B$ are congruent.

   A simple similarity measure between $A$ and $B$ is

$$R = \frac{M}{Q} = \frac{M}{\max \left( \left\| A \right\|, \ \left\| B \right\| \right) - M} \tag{10.12}$$

   It can be seen from Eq. (10.12) that a larger value of $R$ indicates a better match. When $A$ and $B$ match exactly, the value of $R$ is infinite; and when there is no symbol match between $A$ and $B$ ($M = 0$), the value of $R$ is zero.

   Because string matching is performed symbol by symbol, the determination of the starting point is very important to reduce the amount of calculation. If the calculation is started from any point, and each time the calculation is made again after moving the position of one symbol; according to Eq. (10.12), the entire calculation will be very time-consuming (proportional to ‖A‖ × ‖B‖), so in practice, it is often necessary to normalize the string representation first.

   The similarity between two strings can also be described by Levenshtein distance (**edit distance**). The distance is defined as the (minimum) number of operations required to convert one string to another. The operations here mainly include editing operations on the string, such as deleting, inserting, and replacing. For these operations, one can also define weights, so that the similarity between two strings can be measured more finely.

### 10.2.4   Matching of Inertia Equivalent Ellipses

The matching between objects can also be carried out by means of their **inertia equivalent ellipse**, which has been used in the registration work of 3-D object reconstruction of sequence images. Different from the matching based on the object

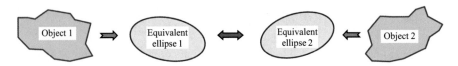

**Fig. 10.5** Matching with equivalent ellipse

contour, the matching based on the inertia equivalent ellipse is based on the entire object region. With the help of the inertia ellipse corresponding to the object, an equivalent ellipse can be further calculated for each object. From the perspective of object matching, since each object in the image pair to be matched can be represented by its equivalent ellipse, the problem of object matching can be transformed into the matching of its equivalent ellipse. A schematic diagram for this match is shown in Fig. 10.5.

In general object matching, the main considerations are the deviations caused by translation, rotation, and scale transformation. The goal is to obtain the corresponding geometric parameters needed. To this end, the parameters required for translation, rotation, and scale transformation can be calculated with the help of the center coordinates of the equivalent ellipse, the orientation angle (defined as the angle between the major principal axis of the ellipse and the positive $X$ axis), and the length of the major principal axis.

Firstly consider the center coordinates $(x_c, y_c)$ of the equivalent ellipse, that is, the center of gravity coordinates of the object. Assuming that the object region contains a total of $N$ pixels, then

$$x_c = \frac{1}{N} \sum_{i=1}^{N} x_i \tag{10.13}$$

$$y_c = \frac{1}{N} \sum_{i=1}^{N} y_i \tag{10.14}$$

The translation parameter can be calculated based on the difference between the center coordinates of the two equivalent ellipses. Secondly, the direction angle $\theta$ of the equivalent ellipse can be obtained by means of the slopes $k$ and $l$ of the two principal axes of the corresponding inertia ellipse (set $A$ is the moment of inertia when the object rotates around the $X$ axis, and $B$ is the moment of inertia when the object rotates around the $Y$ axis)

$$\theta = \begin{cases} \arctan(k) & A < B \\ \arctan(l) & A > B \end{cases} \tag{10.15}$$

The rotation parameter can be calculated based on the angle difference of the two ellipses. Finally, the two semimajor axis lengths ($p$ and $q$) of the equivalent ellipse reflect the information of the object size. If the object itself is an ellipse, it is exactly

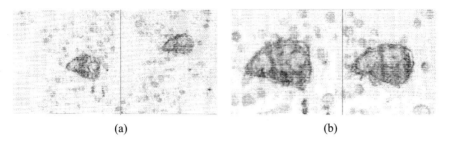

**Fig. 10.6**  Example of equivalent ellipse matching: before (**a**) and after (**b**)

the same in shape as its equivalent ellipse. In general, the equivalent ellipse of the object is the approximation of the object in terms of moment of inertia and area (but not at the same time). Here, the object area $M$ is needed to normalize the axis length. After normalization, when $A < B$, the length $p$ of the semimajor axis of the equivalent ellipse can be calculated by the following equation (suppose $H$ is the product of inertia):

$$p = \sqrt{\frac{2\left[(A + B) - \sqrt{(A - B)^2 + 4H^2}\right]}{M}} \qquad (10.16)$$

The scale transformation parameter can be calculated according to the length ratio of the major axes of the two ellipses. As the three transformation parameters of geometric correction required for the above two object matching can be calculated independently, so each transformation in the equivalent ellipse matching can be performed separately in order.

**Example 10.1 Equivalent Ellipse Matching Effect Example**
Using the inertia equivalent ellipse for matching is more suitable for irregular objects. Figure 10.6 shows a set of examples of matching cell images. Figure 10.6a shows two adjacent cell slice images. The cross-sectional size and shape of the two cells in the figure and the position and orientation of the two cells in the image are all different. Figure 10.6b shows the matching result after calculating the equivalent ellipse for the cell profile. It can be seen that the two cell profiles are well aligned, which also lays a solid foundation for the subsequent 3-D reconstruction.

## *10.2.5   Shape Matrix Matching*

The object regions that need to be matched in two images often have differences in translation, rotation, and scale. Taking into account the local characteristics of the

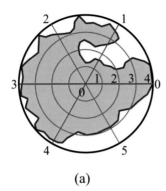

|   | 0 | 1 | 2 | 3 | 4 |
|---|---|---|---|---|---|
| 0 | 1 | 1 | 1 | 1 | 1 |
| 1 | 1 | 1 | 0 | 1 | 0 |
| 2 | 1 | 1 | 1 | 1 | 0 |
| 3 | 1 | 1 | 1 | 1 | 0 |
| 4 | 1 | 1 | 1 | 1 | 0 |
| 5 | 1 | 1 | 1 | 0 | 0 |

(a)                                        (b)

**Fig. 10.7**  An object (**a**) and its shape matrix (**b**)

image, if the image does not represent a deformed scene, the local non-linear geometric differences between the images can be ignored. In order to determine the correspondence between the objects that need to be matched in two images, it is necessary to seek the similarity between the objects that does not depend on translation, rotation, and scale differences. The **shape matrix** is a representation of the quantization of the object shape with polar coordinates. As shown in Fig. 10.7a, place the origin of the coordinates at the center of gravity of the object, and resample the object along the radial and circumferential directions. These sampled data are independent of the object's position and orientation. Let the radial increment be a function of the maximum radius, that is, always quantize the maximum radius into the same number of intervals, and the representation obtained in this way is called the shape matrix, as shown in Fig. 10.7b. The shape matrix is independent of scale.

The shape matrix contains both the boundary and internal information of the object, so it can also represent the object with holes (not just the outer contour). The shape matrix can represent all the projection, orientation, and scale of the object in a standardized way. Given two shape matrices $M_1$ and $M_2$ of size $m \times n$, the similarity between them is (note that the matrix is a binary matrix)

$$S = \sum_{i=0}^{m-1} \sum_{j=0}^{n-1} \frac{1}{mn} \left\{ [M_1(i, j) \wedge M_2(i, j)] \vee [\overline{M}_1(i, j) \wedge \overline{M}_2(i, j)] \right\} \quad (10.17)$$

where the upper horizontal line represents the logical NOT operation. When $S = 1$, it means that the two objects are exactly the same. As $S$ gradually decreases and tends to 0, the two objects become increasingly dissimilar. If the sampling is dense enough when constructing the shape matrix, the original object region can be reconstructed from the shape matrix.

If the shape matrix is sampled on a logarithmic scale along the radial direction when constructing the shape matrix, the scale difference between the two objects will be transformed into a positional difference along the horizontal axis in the logarithmic coordinate system. If one starts from any point in the object region (rather than from the maximum radius) when quantifying the region circumference, it will get the value along the vertical axis in the logarithmic coordinate system. Log polar coordinate mapping can convert the rotation difference and scale difference between two regions into translation difference, thus simplifying the work of object matching.

## 10.3   Dynamic Pattern Matching

In the previous discussion of various matches, the representations that need to be matched have been established in advance. In fact, sometimes the representation that needs to be matched is dynamically established during the matching process, or different representations for matching need to be established according to the data to be matched in the matching process. The following describes a method combined with a practical application, called **dynamic pattern matching**.

### *10.3.1   Matching Process*

In the process of reconstructing 3-D cells from serial medical slice images, judging the correspondence of each profile of the same cell in adjacent slices is a key step (this is the basis for contour interpolation in Sect. 9.4). Due to the complicated slicing process, thin slices, deformation, and other reasons, the number of cell profiles on adjacent slices may be different, and their distribution arrangements may also be different. To reconstruct the 3-D cells, it is necessary to determine the corresponding relationship between the various profiles of each cell, that is, to find the corresponding profiles of the same cell on each slice. The overall flowchart for completing this work can be seen in Fig. 10.8. Here, the two slices to be matched are called matched slice and matching slice, respectively. The matched slice is a

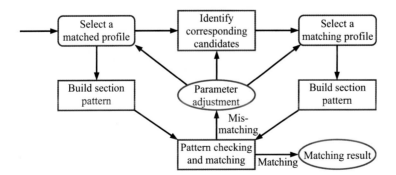

**Fig. 10.8** Flowchart of dynamic pattern matching process

reference slice. When each profile on the matching slice to be matched is registered with the corresponding matched profile on the matched slice, the matching slice becomes a matched slice and can be used as a reference slice for the next matching slice. By continuing to match in this way, all profiles on a sequence slice can be registered (Fig. 10.8 only takes one profile as an example). This sequence strategy can also be used for other matching tasks.

Refer to the flowchart in Fig. 10.8; it can be seen that there are six main steps in dynamic pattern matching:

1. Select a matched profile from the matched slice.
2. Construct the pattern representation of the selected matched profile.
3. Determine the candidate region on the matching slice (the prior knowledge can be used to reduce the amount of calculation and ambiguity).
4. Select the matching profile in the candidate region.
5. Construct the pattern representation of each selected matching profile.
6. Use the similarity between the profile patterns to test for determining the correspondence between the profiles.

## 10.3.2 Absolute Pattern and Relative Pattern

Since the distribution of cell profiles on the slices is not uniform, in order to complete the above matching steps, it is necessary to dynamically establish a pattern representation for each profile that can be used for matching. Here, the relative positional relationship between each profile and its several adjacent profiles can be used to construct the unique pattern of the profile. The pattern constructed in this way can be represented by a pattern vector. Assuming that the relationship used is the length and direction of the line between each profile and its adjacent profile (or the angle between the lines), then the two profile patterns (both are represented by vectors) $P_l$ and $P_r$ on two adjacent slices can be written as

$$P_l = [x_{l0}, y_{l0}, d_{l1}, \theta_{l1}, \cdots, d_{lm}, \theta_{lm}]^T \qquad (10.18)$$

$$P_r = [x_{r0}, y_{r0}, d_{r1}, \theta_{r1}, \cdots, d_{rn}, \theta_{rn}]^T \qquad (10.19)$$

In the formula, $x_{l0}$, $y_{l0}$, and $x_{r0}$, $y_{r0}$ are the center coordinates of the two slices, respectively; each $d$ represents the length of the connection line between other profiles on the same slice and the matching profile; each $\theta$ represents the angle between the lines from the matching profile to the surrounding two adjacent profiles in the same slice. Note that $m$ and $n$ can be different here. When $m$ and $n$ are different, it can also select parts of the points to construct the pattern for matching. In addition, the choice of $m$ and $n$ should be the result of the balance between the amount of calculation and the uniqueness of the pattern. The specific value can be adjusted by determining the pattern radius (i.e., the largest $d$, as shown in $d_2$ in

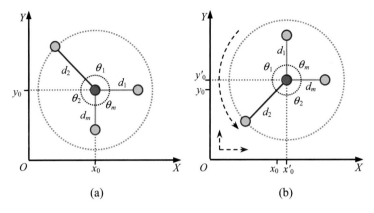

**Fig. 10.9** Absolute pattern: (**a**) original, (**b**) after rotation and translation

Fig. 10.9a). The entire pattern can be seen as contained in a circle with a definite radius of action.

In order to match between the profiles, the corresponding pattern needs to be translated and rotated. The pattern constructed above can be called an **absolute pattern** because it contains the absolute coordinates of the center profile. Figure 10.9a shows an example of $P_l$. Absolute pattern has rotation invariance to the origin (central profile), that is, after the entire mode is rotated, each $d$ and $\theta$ is unchanged; but from Fig. 10.9b, it can be seen that it does not have translation invariance, because after the entire pattern is translated, both $x_0$ and $y_0$ have changed.

In order to obtain translation invariance, the center point coordinates in the absolute pattern can be removed, and the **relative pattern** is constructed as follows:

$$Q_1 = [d_{11}, \theta_{11}, \cdots, d_{1m}, \theta_{1m}]^T \tag{10.20}$$

$$Q_r = [d_{r1}, \theta_{r1}, \cdots, d_{rn}, \theta_{rn}]^T \tag{10.21}$$

The relative pattern corresponding to the absolute pattern in Fig. 10.9a is shown in Fig. 10.10a.

It can be seen from Fig. 10.10b that the relative pattern has not only rotation invariance but also translation invariance. In this way, the two relative pattern representations can be matched by rotation and translation, and the similarity can be calculated, so as to obtain the goal of matching profile.

It can be seen from the analysis of dynamic pattern matching that its main characteristics are as follows: the pattern is dynamically established, and the matching is completely automatic. This method is more versatile and flexible, and its basic idea can be applied to a variety of applications.

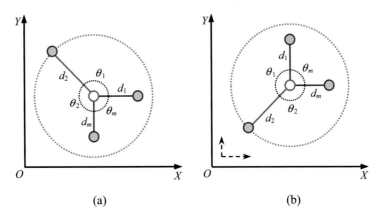

(a)                                                      (b)

**Fig. 10.10**  Relative pattern: (**a**) original, (**b**) after translation

## 10.4   Graph Theory and Graph Matching

Seeking correspondence is a key in relation matching. Because the corresponding relationship can have many different combinations, if the search method is not appropriate, the workload will be too large to be carried out. Graph isomorphism is a way to solve this problem.

### 10.4.1   Introduction to Graph Theory

Let's first introduce some basic definitions and concepts of graph theory.

#### 10.4.1.1   Basic Definition

In graph theory, a **graph** $G$ is defined as a finite non-empty **vertex set** $V(G)$ and a finite **edge set** $E(G)$, denoted as

$$G = [V(G), E(G)] = [V, E]  \tag{10.22}$$

Among them, each element of $E(G)$ corresponds to the unordered pair of vertices in $V(G)$, which is called the edge of $G$. Graph is also a relational data structure.

In the following, the elements in the set $V$ are represented by uppercase letters, and the elements in the set $E$ are represented by lowercase letters. Generally, the edge $e$ formed by the unordered pair of vertices $A$ and $B$ is denoted as $e \leftrightarrow AB$ or $e \leftrightarrow BA$, and $A$ and $B$ are called the end points of $e$; the edge $e$ is called **join** $A$ and $B$. In this case, vertices $A$ and $B$ are **incident** with edge $e$, and edge $e$ is incident with vertices $A$ and $B$. Two vertices incident with the same edge are **adjacent**, and similarly, two edges with a common vertex are also adjacent. If two edges have the same two end points, they are called **multiple edges** or **parallel edges**. If the two end points of an edge are the same, it is called a **loop**; otherwise it is called a **link**.

### 10.4.1.2 The Geometric Representation of the Graph

The vertices of the graph are represented by dots, and the edges are represented by straight lines or curves connecting the vertices, and the **geometric representation** or **geometric realization** of the graph can be obtained. A graph with edges greater than or equal to 1 can have an infinite number of geometric representations.

**Example 10.2 The Geometric Representation of a Graph**
Set $V(G) = \{A, B, C\}$, $E(G) = \{a, b, c, d\}$, where $a \leftrightarrow AB$, $b \leftrightarrow AB$, $c \leftrightarrow BC$, $d \leftrightarrow CC$. In this way, the graph $G$ can be represented by the graph given in Fig. 10.11.

In Fig. 10.11, the edges $a$, $b$, and $c$ are adjacent to each other, and the edges $c$ and $d$ are adjacent to each other, but the edges $a$ and $b$ are not adjacent to the edge $d$. Similarly, vertices $A$ and $B$ are adjacent, vertices $B$ and $C$ are adjacent, but vertices $A$ and $C$ are not adjacent. In terms of edge types, edges $a$ and $b$ are parallel edges, edge $d$ is a loop, and edges $a$, $b$, and $c$ are both links.

### 10.4.1.3 Colored Graph

In the definition of a graph, the two elements of each unordered pair (i.e., two vertices) can be the same or different, and any two unordered pairs (i.e., two edges) can be the same or different. Different elements can be represented by vertices of different colors, which are called the chromaticity of the vertices (referring to vertices marked with different colors). The different relationships between elements can be represented by edges of different colors, which are called the chromaticity of edges (referring to edges marked with different colors). So a generalized colored graph $G$ can be represented as

$$G = [(V,\ C), (E,\ S)] \tag{10.23}$$

where $V$ is the vertex set, $C$ is the vertex chromaticity set, $E$ is the edge set, and $S$ is the edge chromaticity set. They are

**Fig. 10.11** Geometric representation of a graph

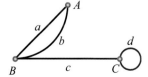

**Fig. 10.12** (**a. b**) Two objects to be represented by colored graphs

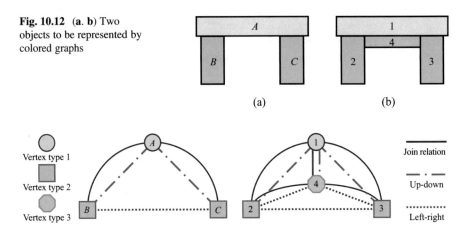

(a)                                                          (b)

**Fig. 10.13** The object representation with colored graph

$$V = \{V_1, \ V_2, \ \cdots, \ V_N\} \tag{10.24}$$

$$C = \{C_{V_1}, \ C_{V_2}, \ \cdots, \ C_{V_N}\} \tag{10.25}$$

$$E = \{e_{V_i V_j} | V_i, \ V_j \in \ V\} \tag{10.26}$$

$$S = \{s_{V_i V_j} | V_i, \ V_j \in \ V\} \tag{10.27}$$

Among them, each vertex can have a color, and each edge can also have a color.

**Example 10.3 Examples of Colored Graph Representation**
Consider the two objects in the image as shown in Fig. 10.12. The object on the left contains three elements, which can be represented as $Q_1 = \{A, B, C\}$; the object on the right contains four elements, which can be represented as $Q_r = \{1, 2, 3, 4\}$.

The two objects in Fig. 10.12 can be represented by two colored graphs as shown in Fig. 10.13, in which the vertex color is distinguished by the shape of the vertex and the edge color is distinguished by the line type. The information reflected by colored graphs is more comprehensive and intuitive.

#### 10.4.1.4   Sub-Graph

For two graphs $G$ and $H$, if $V(H) \subseteq V(G)$, $E(H) \subseteq E(G)$, then the graph $H$ is called a **sub-graph** of graph $G$, denoted as $H \subseteq G$. In turn, call graph $G$ the **mother graph** of graph $H$. If the graph $H$ is a sub-graph of the graph $G$, but $H \neq G$, then the graph $H$ is called the **proper sub-graph** of the graph $G$, and the graph $G$ is called the **proper mother graph** of the graph $H$.

If $H \subseteq G$ and $V(H) = V(G)$, call graph $H$ the **spanning sub-graph** of graph $G$, and call graph $G$ the **spanning mother graph** of graph $H$. For example, in Fig. 10.14, Fig. 10.14a shows graph $G$, while Fig. 10.14b–d, respectively, shows

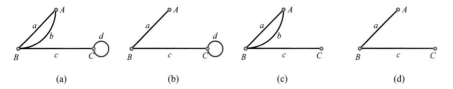

**Fig. 10.14** Examples of graph (**a**) and spanning sub-graphs (**b–d**)

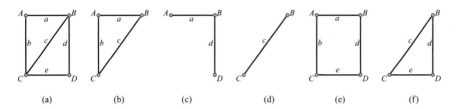

**Fig. 10.15** (**a–f**) Several operations to obtain sub-graphs (see text)

the various spanning sub-graphs of graph $G$ (they are all spanning sub-graphs of graph $G$ but are different from each other).

If all the multiple edges and loops are removed from a graph $G$, the resulting simple spanning sub-graph is called the **underlying simple graph** of the graph $G$. The three spanning sub-graphs shown in Fig. 10.14b–d have only one underlying simple graph, that is, Fig. 10.14d. The following four operations to obtain an underlying simple graph will be introduced with the help of graph $G$ given in Fig. 10.15a.

1. For the non-empty vertex subset $V'(G) \subseteq V(G)$ of graph $G$, if there is a sub-graph of graph $G$ with $V'(G)$ as the vertex set, and all edges with the two end points in graph $G$ as the edge set, then this sub-graph is called the **induced sub-graph** of graph $G$, denoted as $G[V'(G)]$ or $G[V']$. Figure 10.15b shows the graph of $G[A, B, C] = G[a, b, c]$.

2. Similarly, for the non-empty edge subset $E'(G) \subseteq E(G)$ of graph $G$, if there is a sub-graph of graph $G$ with $E'(G)$ as the edge set, and the end points of all the edges in this set as vertex set, then this sub-graph is called the **edge-induced sub-graph** of graph $G$, denoted as $G[E'(G)]$ or $G[E']$. Figure 10.15c shows the graph of $G[a, d] = G[A, B, D]$.

3. For the proper subset of non-empty vertices $G[a, d] = G[A, B, D]$ of graph $G$, if there is a sub-graph of graph $G$ that takes the vertex set after removing $V'(G) \subset V(G)$ as the vertex set, and takes the edge set after removing all the edges incident with $V'(G)$ in the graph $G$ as the edge set, then this sub-graph is the remaining sub-graph of the graph $G$, denoted as $G - V'$. Here $G - V' = G[V \setminus W']$ holds. Figure 10.15d shows the graph of $G - \{A, D\} = G[B, C] = G[\{A, B, C, D\} - \{A, D\}]$.

4. For the proper subset of non-empty edges $E'(G) \subseteq E(G)$ of graph $G$, if there is a sub-graph of graph $G$ that takes the edge set after removing $E'(G) \subset E(G)$ as the

edge set, then this sub-graph is a spanning sub-graph of graph $G$, denoted as $G -$ $E'$. Note that here $G - E'$ and $G[E\backslash E']$ have the same edge set, but the two are not necessarily identical. Among them, the former is always a spanning sub-graph, while the latter is not necessarily a spanning sub-graph. Figure 10.15e gives an example of the former, $G - \{c\} = G[a, b, d, e]$. Figure 10.15f gives an example of the latter, $G[\{a, b, c, d, e\} - \{a, b\}] = G - A \neq G - [\{a, b\}]$.

## 10.4.2  Graph Isomorphism and Matching

The matching of graphs is achieved with the help of graph isomorphism.

### 10.4.2.1  The Identity and Isomorphism of Graph

According to the definition of graphs, for two graphs $G$ and $H$, if and only if $V(G) = V(H)$ and $E(G) = E(H)$, the graphs $G$ and $H$ are called **identical**, and the two graphs can be represented by the same geometric representation. For example, the graphs $G$ and $H$ in Fig. 10.16 are identical. However, if two graphs can be represented by the same geometric representation, they are not necessarily identical. For example, the graphs $G$ and $I$ in Fig. 10.16 are not identical (the vertices and edges have different labels), although they can be represented by two geometric representations with the same shape.

For two graphs that have the same geometric representation but are not identical, as long as the labels of the vertices and edges of one of the graphs are appropriately renamed, a graph identical to the other graph can be obtained. These two graphs can be called isomorphic, or they are isomorphism. In other words, the isomorphism of two graphs means that there is a one-to-one correspondence between the vertices and edges of the two graphs. The isomorphism of two graphs $G$ and $H$ can be denoted as $G \cong H$. The necessary and sufficient condition is that the following mapping exists between $V(G)$ and $V(H)$ as well as $E(G)$ and $E(H)$:

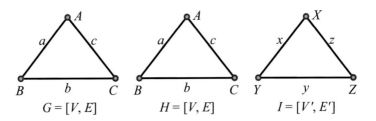

Fig. 10.16  The identity of the graphs

**Fig. 10.17** Graph
isomorphism

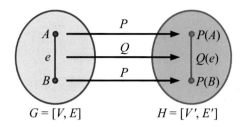

$$G = [V, E] \qquad\qquad H = [V', E']$$

$$P : \quad V(G) \rightarrow V(H) \qquad\qquad (10.28)$$

$$Q : \quad E(G) \rightarrow E(H) \qquad\qquad (10.29)$$

In addition, the mapping $P$ and $Q$ maintain an induced relationship, that is, $Q(e) = P(A)P(B)$, $\forall e \leftrightarrow AB \in E(G)$, as shown in Fig. 10.17.

### 10.4.2.2 Determination of Isomorphism

It can be seen from the previous definition that isomorphic graphs have the same structure and the only difference is that the labels of the vertices or edges are not exactly the same. The comparison of graph isomorphism focuses on describing mutual relationships, so graph isomorphism can have no geometric requirements, that is, more abstract (of course, there can also be geometric requirements, that is, more specific). Graph isomorphism matching is essentially a tree search problem, in which different branches represent trials of different combinations of corresponding relationships.

Now consider the situation of isomorphism between several graphs. For the sake of simplicity, all vertices and edges of the graphs are not labeled here, that is, all vertices are considered to have the same color, and all edges also have the same color. For clarity, it takes a single-color line diagram (a special case of $G$)

$$B = [(V), (E)] = [V, E] \qquad\qquad (10.30)$$

to illustrate. $V$ and $E$ in Eq. (10.30) are still given by Eqs. (10.24) and (10.26), respectively, but all elements in each set are the same here. In other words, there are only one type of vertex and one type of edge. Refer to Fig. 10.18; given two graphs $B_1 = [V_1, E_1]$ and $B_2 = [V_2, E_2]$, the isomorphism between them can be divided into the following types:

1. Graph Isomorphism

    The **graph isomorphism** refers to one-to-one mapping between $B_1$ and $B_2$. For example, Fig. 10.18a, b shows cases of graph isomorphism. Generally speaking, if the mapping is represented by $f$, then for $e_1 \in E_1$ and $e_2 \in E_2$,

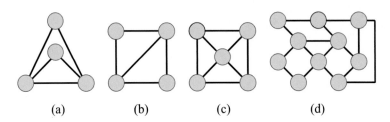

**Fig. 10.18** (**a–d**) Several cases of graph isomorphism

$f(e_1) = e_2$ must exist, and for each join line in $E_1$ connecting any pair of vertices $e_1$ and $e_1'$ ($e_1$, $e_1' \in E_1$), there must be a join line connecting $f(e_1)$ and $f(e_1')$ in $E_2$. When recognizing the object, it is necessary to establish a full-graph isomorphism relationship between the graph representing the object and the graph of the object model.

2. Sub-Graph Isomorphism

   **Sub-graph isomorphism** refers to the isomorphism between a part of graph $B_1$ (sub-graph) and the whole graph of $B_2$. For example, the multiple sub-graphs in Fig. 10.18c are isomorphic with Fig. 10.18a. When detecting objects in the scene, the object model needs to be used to search for isomorphic sub-graphs in the scene graph.

3. Double-Sub-Graph Isomorphism

   **Double-sub-graph isomorphism** refers to all isomorphism between each sub-graph of $B_1$ and each sub-graph of $B_2$. For example, in Fig. 10.18a, d, there are several double-sub-graphs that are isomorphic. Generally, when a common object needs to be found in two scenarios, the task can be transformed into a problem of isomorphism of double-sub-graphs.

   There are many algorithms for finding isomorphism of graphs. For example, each graph to be determined can be converted into a certain type of standard form, so that the isomorphism can be determined more conveniently. In addition, it is also possible to perform an exhaustive search on the trees that may match between the corresponding vertices in the line graph, but this method requires a lot of calculation when the number of vertices in the line graph is large.

   A method with fewer restrictions and faster convergence than the isomorphic method is **association graph matching**. In association graph matching, the graph is defined as $G = [V, P, R]$, where $V$ represents a set of nodes, $P$ represents a set of unit predicates for nodes, and $R$ represents a set of binary relations between nodes. Here the predicate represents a sentence that only takes one of the two values TRUE or FALSE, and the binary relationship describes the attributes of a pair of nodes. Given two graphs, an association graph can be constructed. Association graph matching is the matching between the nodes and nodes as well as two-value relationship and two-value relationship in the two graphs.

## 10.5 Line Drawing Signature and Matching

When observing a 3-D scene, what one sees is its (visible) surface. When a 3-D scene is projected onto a 2-D image, each surface will form a region. The boundaries of each surface will be displayed as contours in the 2-D image, and the line drawing of the object is formed by using these contours to represent the object. For relatively simple scenes, line drawings can be marked, that is, 2-D images with outline markings can be used to represent the relationship between the surfaces of the 3-D scenes. With the help of this mark, the 3-D scene can also be matched with the corresponding model to further explain the scene.

### *10.5.1 Contour Marking*

First give some definitions of the nouns/concepts in the contour marking.

#### 10.5.1.1 Blade

If a continuous surface (called the occluding surface) in the 3-D scene occludes a part of another surface (called the occluded surface), the change in the direction of the normal of the surface is smooth and continuous when advancing along the contour of the former surface. At this time, the contour line is called the blade (the blade of the 2-D image is a smooth curve). To indicate the blade, an arrow "←" or "→" can be added to the contour line. Generally, it is agreed that the direction of the arrow indicates that when advancing in the direction of the arrow, the occluding surface is on the right side of the blade. On both sides of the blade, the direction of the occluding surface and the direction of the occluded surface can be independent.

#### 10.5.1.2 Limb

If a continuous surface in a 3-D scene not only occludes a part of another surface but also occludes other parts of itself, that is, **self-occlusion**, the change of the normal direction of the surface is smooth and continuous and perpendicular to the line of sight; the contour line at the time is called the limb (usually formed when a smooth 3-D surface is viewed from the side). To indicate the limb, double arrows "↔" can be added to the contour line. When traveling along the limb, the direction of the 3-D surface does not change; while traveling in a direction that is not parallel to the limb, the direction of the 3-D surface changes continuously.

The blade is the true (physical) edge of the 3-D scene, while the limb is only the (apparent) edge. When the blade or limb crosses the boundary or contour between the occluding object surface and the occluded background surface, a **jump edge** with discontinuous depth will be produced.

### 10.5.1.3   Crease

If the orientation of the 3-D visible surface changes suddenly or if two 3-D surfaces meet at an angle, a crease is formed. On both sides of the crease, the points on the surface are continuous, but the direction of the surface normal is not continuous. If the surface of the crease is convex, it is generally indicated by "+"; if the surface of the crease is concave, it is generally indicated by "−."

### 10.5.1.4   Mark

If the parts of the 3-D surface have different reflectivity, marks will be formed. The marks are not caused by the shape of the 3-D surface. It can use "$M$" to indicate marks.

### 10.5.1.5   Shade/Shadow

If a continuous surface in a 3-D scene does not occlude a part of the other surface from the viewpoint, but blocks the light from the light source to this part, it will cause shadows on this part of the second surface. The shadow on the surface is not caused by the shape of the surface itself, but is the result of the influence of other parts on the light. The shadow can be marked with "$S$." The sudden change of light at the shadow boundary is called the light boundary.

**Example 10.4 Contour Marking Example**
Figure 10.19 shows some examples of above contour markings. In the picture, a hollow cylinder is placed on a platform. There is a mark $M$ on the cylinder, and the cylinder creates a shadow $S$ on the platform. There are two limbs on the side of the cylinder. The upper contour is divided into two parts by the two limbs. The upper contour side occludes the background (platform), and the lower contour side occludes the inside of the cylinder. The creases of the platform are convex, and the creases between the platform and the cylinder are concave.

## 10.5.2   Structural Reasoning

In the following, consider using the contour structure in the 2-D image to reason about the structure of the 3-D object. It is assumed that the surface of the object is a flat surface and all the corner points after the intersection are formed by the

**Fig. 10.19** Example of
contour marking

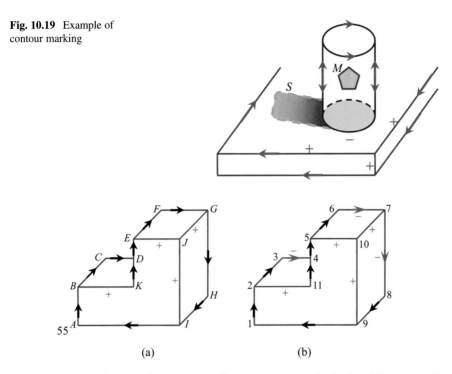

(a)                                        (b)

**Fig. 10.20**   Different interpretations of the same line drawing: (**a**) Floating in air, (**b**) Pasted on wall

intersection of three surfaces. Such a 3-D object can be called a **trihedral corner**
object, as shown by the two line drawings in Fig. 10.20. At this time, a small change
in the viewpoint will not cause a change in the topological structure of the line
drawing, that is, it will not cause the disappearance of surfaces, edges, or joins. In
this case, the object is said to be **in general position**.

The two line drawings in Fig. 10.20 are geometrically the same, but there are two
different 3-D interpretations for them. The difference is that Fig. 10.20b marks three
more concave creases than Fig. 10.20a, so that the object in Fig. 10.20a appears to be
floating in the air, while the object in Fig. 10.20b appears to be pasted on the
back wall.

In the graph marked with only $\{+, -, \rightarrow\}$, "+" represents an unclosed convex
line, "−" represents an unclosed concave line, and "→" represents a closed line/
curve. At this time, there are four types of (topological) combination of line joins: six
types of L joins, four types of T joins, three types of arrow joins, and three types of
fork joins (Y joins), as shown in Fig. 10.21.

If one considers the vertices formed by the intersection of all three faces, there
should be a total of 64 marking methods, but only the above 16 join methods are
reasonable. In other words, only the line drawings that can be marked with the
16 join types shown in Fig. 10.21 can physically exist. When a line drawing can be
marked, its marking can provide a qualitative interpretation of the drawing.

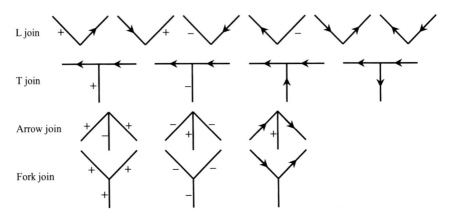

**Fig. 10.21** Sixteen join types of trihedral corner object

### 10.5.3  Labeling via Backtracking

To automatically mark the line drawing, different algorithms can be used. The following describes a method of **labeling via backtracking**. Formulate the problem to be solved as follows: Given a set of edges in a 2-D line drawing, a mark should be assigned to each edge (the type of join used must satisfy Fig. 10.21) to explain the 3-D situation. The method of labeling via backtracking arranges the edges in a sequence (as far as possible, put the edges with the most constraints on the mark in front), it generates a path in a depth-first manner, mark each edge in turn with all possible labels, and check the new label with other edge labels for consistency. If the join created with the new label is inconsistent or does not conform to the situation in Fig. 10.21, then fall back to consider another path; otherwise continue to consider the next edge. If the labels assigned to all edges in this way satisfy the consistency, then a labeling result is obtained (a complete path to the leaf is obtained). Generally, more than one marking result can be obtained for the same line drawing. At this time, it is necessary to use some additional information or prior knowledge to obtain the final unique judgment result.

**Example 10.5 Marking Example with Labeling via Backtracking**
Consider the pyramid shown in Fig. 10.22, and the interpretation tree (including the steps and final results) obtained by using the method of labeling via backtracking for labeling is shown in Table 10.2.

As can be seen from the interpretation tree, there are three complete pathways (marked up to the leaves), which give three different interpretations of the same line drawing. The search space of the entire interpretation tree is quite small, which indicates that the trihedral corner object has a fairly strong constraint mechanism.

**Fig. 10.22** Pyramid

**Table 10.2** Interpretation tree for pyramid line drawing

| | A | B | C | D | Result and interpretation |
|---|---|---|---|---|---|
| Interpretation tree | *(diagram: + ∧ +)* | *(diagram: + − +)* | *(diagram: + )* | − | C is not a reasonable L join |
| | | *(diagram: − +)* | − | − | The interpretation of edge AB is contradictory |
| | | *(diagram: +)* | − | − | |
| | *(diagram: − + )* | *(diagram: + +)* | − | − | The interpretation of edge AB is contradictory |
| | | *(diagram: − + −)* | *(diagram)* | − | C is not a reasonable L join |
| | | *(diagram: +)* | *(diagram: < >)* | *(pyramid diagram)* | Pasted on wall |
| | *(diagram: +)* | *(diagram: + +)* | − | − | The interpretation of edge AB is contradictory |
| | | *(diagram: − +)* | *(diagram: < >)* | *(pyramid diagram)* | Put on table |
| | | *(diagram: +)* | *(diagram: < >)* | *(pyramid diagram)* | Floating in air |

## 10.6  Key Points and References for Each Section

The following combine the main contents of each section to introduce some references that can be further consulted:

1. **Matching Overview**

The discussion of matching and mapping can also be found in reference [1]. The four factors describing the performance of registration technology can be found in reference [2]. The discussion on the evaluation criteria of image matching can also be found in reference [3].

2. **Object Matching**

For further analysis of the modified Hausdorff distance, please refer to reference [4]. A detailed explanation of the physical analogy model of "template and spring" can be found in reference [5]. An introduction to landmarks can be found in the document *2D Computer Vision: Principles, Algorithms and Applications.* The discussion about weak perspective projection can also be found in reference [6]. The matching and application of inertia equivalent ellipse can be found in reference [7]. For the specific calculation of the inertia ellipse, please refer to the document *2D Computer Vision: Principles, Algorithms and Applications.* For further analysis of the shape matrix, please refer to reference [3].

3. **Dynamic Pattern Matching**

A detailed introduction to dynamic pattern matching can be found in reference [8]. For the discussion and application of the generality of dynamic pattern matching, please refer to reference [7].

4. **Graph Theory and Graph Matching**

The detailed introduction of graph theory can be found in reference [9]. An introduction to several types of isomorphism can be found in reference [5]. For more description of association graph matching, please refer to reference [10].

5. **Line Drawing Signature and Matching**

For the introduction of the principle of line drawing marking and the specific method of labeling via backtracking, please refer to reference [11].

## Self-Test Questions

The following questions include both single-choice questions and multiple-choice questions, so each option must be judged.

10.1. **Matching Overview**

10.1.1. Matching is to find the correspondence between two representations; (·).

(a) Image matching is to find the correspondence between two image representations, such as the left and right image functions in binocular stereo vision.

(b) Object matching is to find the correspondence between two object representations, such as two persons in the two consecutive video frames.

(c) The scene matching is looking for the correspondence between two scene descriptions, such as the scenery on both sides of a highway.

(d) Relationship matching is to find the correspondence between two relationship descriptions, such as the mutual positions of two persons at different moments.

[Hint] The object hierarchy of different matches is different.

10.1.2. Matching and registration are two closely related concepts; (·).

(a) The concept of matching is larger than the concept of registration.
(b) The registration considers more image properties than matching.
(c) Image registration and stereo matching both need to establish the correspondence between point pairs.
(d) The goal of matching and registration is to establish content correlation between two images.

[Hint] Registration mainly considers low-level representation, while matching covers more levels.

10.1.3. Various evaluation criteria for image matching are both related and different; (·).

(a) For a matching algorithm, the higher the accuracy, the higher the reliability.
(b) For a matching algorithm, the higher the reliability, the higher the robustness.
(c) For a matching algorithm, the robustness can be judged with the help of accuracy.
(d) For a matching algorithm, the reliability can be judged with the help of robustness.

[Hint] Analyze according to the self-definition of the criteria.

## 10.2. Object Matching

10.2.1. Hausdorff distance (·).

(a) Can only describe the similarity between two pixel sets.
(b) Is the distance between the closest two points in the two point sets.
(c) Is the distance between the two points that are the furthest apart in the two point sets.
(d) Being 0 indicates that the two point sets do not overlap.

[Hint] Judge according to the definition of Hausdorff distance.

10.2.2. Suppose that the contours $A$ and $B$ encoded as character strings are matched. It is known that $\|A\| = 10$, $\|B\| = 15$, and (·).

(a) If $M = 5$ is known, then $R = 1/2$.
(b) If $M = 5$ is known, then $R = 1/4$.
(c) If $M = 10$ is known, then $R = 2$.
(d) If $M = 10$ is known, then $R = 1$.

[Hint] Calculate directly according to Eq. (10.12).

10.2.3. Inertia equivalent ellipse matching method can be applied to object matching; (·).

   (a) Each inertia equivalent ellipse corresponds to a specific object.

   (b) Representing the object with its inertia equivalent ellipse can reduce the complexity of representing the object.

   (c) When the object is not an ellipse, the inertia equivalent ellipse of the object is only equal to the area of the object.

   (d) For this, four parameters of the ellipse are calculated, which shows that an ellipse can be completely determined by four parameters.

[Hint] See the calculation of inertia and equivalent ellipse (Chap. 12 of *2D Computer Vision: Principles, Algorithms and Applications*).

## 10.3. Dynamic Pattern Matching

10.3.1. In the dynamic pattern matching method, (·).

   (a) The grayscale information of the pixels to be matched has been used.

   (b) The position information of the pixel to be matched has been used.

   (c) Two point sets can be matched.

   (d) The Hausdorff distance can be used to measure the effect of matching.

[Hint] Analyze according to the construction method of dynamic pattern.

10.3.2. In the dynamic pattern matching method, the absolute pattern refers to the pattern (·).

   (a) Whose number of units used is determined.

   (b) That can be realized with a fixed size template.

   (c) That is determined in space.

   (d) That is constant throughout the matching process.

[Hint] See the pattern example in Fig. 10.9.

10.3.3. Comparing absolute pattern and relative pattern, (·).

   (a) The representation of absolute pattern is simpler than that of relative pattern.

   (b) The absolute pattern has more units than the relative pattern has.

   (c) The absolute pattern and the relative pattern have the same properties.

   (d) The absolute pattern and relative pattern can have different pattern radii.

[Hint] Analyze the difference between absolute pattern and relative pattern.

## 10.4. Graph Theory and Graph Matching

10.4.1. In the geometric representation of the graph, (·).

(a) A graph with number of edges one can have an infinite number of geometric representations.

(b) The graph with the number of vertices one can have an infinite number of geometric representations.

(c) If edges $a$ and $b$ are adjacent, it indicates that edges $a$ and $b$ are incident with vertex $A$.

(d) If vertices $A$ and $B$ are adjacent, it indicates that the edge $e$ is incident with the vertices $A$ and $B$.

[Hint] Adjacent only involves any two edges or two vertices, and the incident also considers a specific vertex or a specific edge.

10.4.2. Which of the following statement(s) about colored graphs is/are wrong? (·).

(a) A graph is composed of two sets, and a colored graph is composed of two sets.

(b) A graph is composed of two sets, and a colored graph is composed of four sets.

(c) The number of edges in the colored graph is the same as the chromaticity number of the edges.

(d) The number of vertices in the colored graph is the same as the chromaticity number of the vertices.

[Hint] Different vertices can have the same color, and different edges can also have the same color.

10.4.3. Which of the following statement(s) about the identity and isomorphism of graphs is/are correct? (·).

(a) The two graphs of identity have the same geometric representation.

(b) The two graphs of isomorphism have the same geometric representation.

(c) Two graphs with the same geometric representation are identical.

(d) Two graphs with the same geometric representation are isomorphic.

[Hint] Analyze the difference between identities and isomorphism and their relationship with geometric representations.

10.4.4. Which of the following statement(s) about graph isomorphism is/are correct? (·).

(a) The graph isomorphism of two graphs indicates that the two graphs have the same geometric representation.

(b) The sub-graph isomorphism of two graphs indicates that the two graphs have the same geometric expression.

**Fig. 10.23** A line drawing
of a square

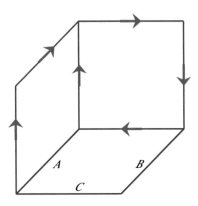

   (c) The sub-graph isomorphism of two graphs indicates that the two
       graphs are isomorphic.
   (d) The double-sub-graph isomorphism of the two sub-graphs indi-
       cates that the two sub-graphs are isomorphic.

     [Hint] Distinguish between isomorphism and geometric represen-
tation, and distinguish between graphs and sub-graphs.

## 10.5. **Line Drawing Signature and Matching**

10.5.1. Some of the blades of the square in Fig. 10.23 have marks, and the
       remaining marks are as follows: (·).

     (a) $A$ is $\nearrow$, $B$ is $\swarrow$, and $C$ is $\rightarrow$.
     (b) $A$ is $\nearrow$, $B$ is $\nearrow$, and $C$ is $\leftarrow$.
     (c) $A$ is $\swarrow$, $B$ is $\swarrow$, and $C$ is $\leftarrow$.
     (d) $A$ is $\nearrow$, $B$ is $\swarrow$, and $C$ is $\leftarrow$.

     [Hint] Pay attention to the agreement on the direction of the arrow.
10.5.2. For the object in Fig. 10.19a, if it is to be pasted on the left wall, it
       should be as follows: (·).

     (a) Figure 10.24a.
     (b) Figure 10.24b.
     (c) Figure 10.24c.
     (d) Figure 10.24d.

     [Hint] The concave creases should be on the same vertical plane.
10.5.3. When performing structural reasoning and labeling via backtracking,
       the issues to be noted include: (·).

     (a) Only one mark can be assigned to each edge of the line graph.
     (b) Do not use the join types not shown in Fig. 10.21.

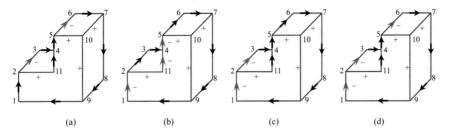

**Fig. 10.24** (**a–d**) Various line drawing objects

    (c) Two graphs with the same geometric structure may have different interpretations.

    (d) Sort the vertices first, list all possible constraints for each vertex in turn, and verify them one by one.

    [Hint] Refer to the example in Table 10.2 for analysis.

# References

1. Kropatsch W G, Bischof H (eds.). Digital Image Analysis – Selected Techniques and Applications. Springer. 2001.
2. Lohmann G. Volumetric Image Analysis. John Wiley & Sons and Teubner Publishers. 1998.
3. Goshtasby A A. 2-D and 3-D Image Registration – for Medical, Remote Sensing, and Industrial Applications. Wiley-Interscience. 2005.
4. Dubuisson M, Jain A K. A modified Hausdorff distance for object matching. Proc. 12ICPR, 1994, 566-568.
5. Ballard D H, Brown C M. Computer Vision. Prentice-Hall. 1982.
6. Zhang Y-J. Image Engineering, Vol. 3: Image Understanding. De Gruyter, 2017.
7. Zhang Y J. 3-D image analysis system and megakaryocyte quantitation. Cytometry, 1991, 12: 308-315.
8. Zhang Y J. Automatic correspondence finding in deformed serial sections. Scientific Computing and Automation (Europe) 1990, Chapter 5 (39-54).
9. Sun H Q. Graph Theory and Applications. Science Press, 2004.
10. Snyder W E, Qi H. Machine Vision. Cambridge University Press. 2004.
11. Shapiro L, Stockman G. Computer Vision. Prentice Hall. 2001.

# Chapter 11
# Knowledge and Scene Interpretation

The high-level goal of computer vision is to achieve an understanding of the scene. The understanding of visual scenes can be expressed as based on the visual perception of scene environment data, combined with various image technologies, mining features, and patterns in visual data from different perspectives such as computational statistics, behavioral cognition, and semantics, so as to realize the effective scene analysis and understanding. From a certain point of view, scene understanding is based on the analysis of the scene to achieve the purpose of explaining the semantic of the scene.

**Scene interpretation** needs to be based on existing knowledge and with the help of reasoning. **Knowledge** is the result of previous human understanding of the objective world and a summary of experience, which can guide the current knowing and understanding of new changes in the objective world. The analysis of the scene should be combined with high-level semantics, and the marking and classification of scenes are both semantic interpretation-oriented scene analysis methods. In addition, to explain the semantics of the scene, it is necessary to further reason/infer based on the analysis results of the image data. **Reasoning** is the process of collecting information, learning, and making decisions based on logic.

The high-level explanation of the scene is based on the analysis and semantic description of the scene. This includes methods for fuzzy reasoning using fuzzy sets and fuzzy operation concepts, methods for classifying scenes based on bag-of-words models/feature package models, and probabilistic hidden semantic analysis models.

The sections of this chapter are arranged as follows:

Section 11.1 introduces the representation methods for scene knowledge and models and discusses some problems in knowledge modeling.

Section 11.2 introduces the predicate logic and system, which is a well-organized type of knowledge that is widely used in proposition representation and knowledge inference. It specifically analyzes the predicate calculus rules and the basic method of using theorem proof to reason.

Section 11.3 introduces the fuzzy logic principles and fuzzy operation rules required
for fuzzy inference. It also discusses the basic model of fuzzy inference, as well as
combination rules and de-fuzzification methods to help make decisions.

Section 11.4 discusses two widely used models in scene classification: bag-of-words
model/bag-of-feature model and probabilistic latent semantic analysis model.

## 11.1   Scene Knowledge

The knowledge of the scene mainly includes the factual characteristics of the scenery
in the objective world. This kind of knowledge is generally limited to certain
determined scenes, and it can also be called a priori knowledge of the scene.
Common knowledge refers to this kind of knowledge.

### *11.1.1   Model*

**Scene knowledge** is closely related to the model. On the one hand, knowledge is
often represented by models, so it is often referred to directly as models. On the other
hand, in practical applications, knowledge is often used to build models to help
restoring scenes and realizing the purpose of image understanding. For example, a
scene model can be built to describe the 3-D world with the help of objects and their
surfaces; a lighting model can be built to describe the intensity, color, position, and
range of the light source; a sensor model can be built to describe the optics of the
imaging device and geometric properties.

The word **model** reflects the fact that any natural phenomenon can only be
described to a certain degree (precision or accuracy). In the research of natural
sciences in seeking the simplest and most versatile description that can minimize
the deviation of observation facts, the use of models is a basic and effective principle.
However, one must be very careful when using the model, and even when the data
seems to be very consistent with the model assumptions, as there is no guarantee that
the model assumptions will always be correct. This is because it is possible to obtain
the same data based on different model assumptions.

Generally speaking, there are two issues to pay attention to when building a
model. An issue is called an **overdetermined inverse problem**, when a model is
described by only a few parameters but there are a lot of data to verify it. A common
example is fitting a straight line through a large number of data points. In this case, it
may not be possible to determine the exact solution of the straight line through all the
data points, but it is possible to determine the straight line that minimizes the total
distance from all the data points. In many cases, the reverse situation is encountered,
that is, too little data can be obtained. A typical example is to calculate the dense
motion vector of an image sequence, and another example is to calculate a depth map

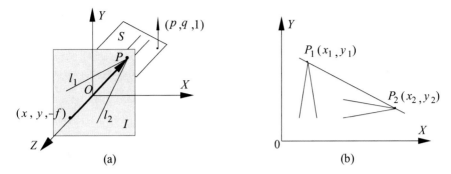

**Fig. 11.1** (**a, b**) Get the surface orientation of the object with the help of geometric constraints (see text)

from a pair of stereo images. Mathematically speaking, this is an **under-determined problem**, and it is necessary to increase the limited conditions to solve the problem.

In image understanding, models can be divided into 2-D model and 3-D model. The 2-D model represents the characteristics of the image. The advantage is that it can be directly used for the matching of images or image features. The disadvantage is that it is not easy to fully represent the geometric characteristics of objects in 3-D space and the connections between objects. They are generally only used when the line of sight or object orientation is given. The 3-D model contains the characteristics of the position and shape of the 3-D object in the scene and the relationship between them, so it can be used in many different occasions. The problem with this flexibility and versatility is that it is difficult to establish a matching connection between the model and the scene description. In addition, the amount of calculation required to build these models is often very large.

Commonly used 2-D models can be divided into two types: image models and object models. The image model matches the description of the entire image with the model of the scene. This is generally suitable for relatively simple scenes or images. When there are multiple objects with uncertain interrelationships in the image, this model is not suitable. This is because the 2-D model is the result of projection and does not completely represent the geometric relationship of the actual 3-D space. The object model only matches the description of the partial image with the model, that is, a model must be prepared for each object and matched with the description of the partial image to identify the object.

Scene knowledge is very important for image understanding. Scene knowledge can help to give the only explanation of the scene in many cases, because the conditions of the problem and the types of changes can often be determined according to the model.

### Example 11.1 Get the Orientation of the Object with the Help of Geometric Constraints

As shown in Fig. 11.1a, two parallel lines on the 3-D space plane $S$ are given. Projecting them onto the image $I$ by perspective projection, the result is still two parallel lines, denoted as $l_1$ and $l_2$, respectively, and they have the same vanishing point $P$ (see Sect. 8.4). Because each vanishing point corresponds to a point at infinity on the plane $S$, all lines of sight passing through this point are parallel to $S$. If the focal length of the camera is $\lambda$, the direction of the line of sight can be represented by $(x, y, -\lambda)$. Let the normal direction of the plane $S$ be $(p, q, 1)$, while $p$ and $q$ correspond to the gradient map of $S$. Because the sight direction vector and the normal direction vector of $S$ are orthogonal, their inner product is zero, that is, $xp + yq = \lambda$, which can also be regarded as the linear equation of $p$ and $q$.

Now consider Fig. 11.1b; suppose that a vanishing point $P_1$ is determined by two parallel lines. If it is known that there are two parallel lines on $S$, another vanishing point $P_2$ can be obtained. By solving the two linear equations together, $p$ and $q$ can be determined, so as to finally determine the direction of the normal line.

It can be further proved that for any parallel line on $S$, their $p$ and $q$ are the same, so their vanishing points are on the line connecting the above two points. Here, because it is known that the two lines on the image are derived from parallel lines in the scene (scene knowledge), the orientation of the object surface can be constrained. Scene knowledge has the effect of limiting the types of changes.

## 11.1.2   Attribute Hypergraph

In order to understand the image, it is necessary to link the input image with the scene knowledge. The representation of scene knowledge is closely related to the representation of 3-D objects. The **attribute hypergraph** is a way to represent the attributes of 3-D objects. In this representation, objects are represented in the form of attribute pairs. An attribute pair is an ordered pair, which can be recorded as $(A_i, a_i)$, where $A_i$ is the attribute name and $a_i$ is the attribute value. An attribute set can be represented as $\{(A_1, a_1), (A_2, a_2), \ldots, (A_n, a_n)\}$. The entire attribute graph is represented as $G = [V, A]$, where $V$ is a set of hyper nodes and $A$ is a set of hyper arcs. Each hyper node or hyper arc has an attribute set associated with it.

**Example 11.2 Attribute Hypergraph Example**
Figure 11.2 shows a tetrahedron and its attribute hypergraph. In Fig. 11.2a, the five visible edge lines are represented by numbers 1–5, and the two visible surfaces $S_1$

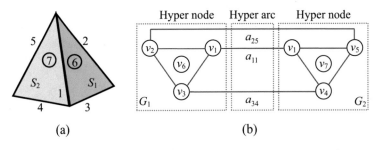

(a)                                                                (b)

**Fig. 11.2**   (**a**) Tetrahedron, (**b**) Attribute hypergraph

and $S_2$ are represented by circled numbers 6 and 7, respectively (they also represent the orientation of the surface). In the attribute hypergraph in Fig. 11.2b, the nodes correspond to the edges and surfaces, the arcs correspond to the connections between them, and the subscripts of the symbols correspond to the numbers of the edges and surfaces.

The surface $S_1$ can be represented by an attribute graph as

$$G_1 = [V_1, A_1]$$

$v_1 = \{(\text{type, line}), (\text{length, } 10)\}$
$v_2 = \{(\text{type, line}), (\text{length, } 10)\}$
$v_3 = \{(\text{type, line}), (\text{length, } 9)\}$
$v_6 = \{(\text{type, circle}), (\text{radius, } 1)\}$
$a_{12} = \{(\text{type, connection}), (\text{line1, } v_1), (\text{line2, } v_2), (\text{angle, } 54°)\}$
$a_{13} = \{(\text{type, connection}), (\text{line1, } v_1), (\text{line2, } v_3), (\text{angle, } 63°)\}$
$a_{23} = \{(\text{type, connection}), (\text{line1, } v_2), (\text{line2, } v_3), (\text{angle, } 63°)\}$

The surface $S_2$ can be represented by an attribute graph as

$$G_2 = [V_2, A_2]$$

$v_1 = \{(\text{type, line}), (\text{length, } 10)\}$
$v_4 = \{(\text{type, line}), (\text{length, } 8)\}$
$v_5 = \{(\text{type, line}), (\text{length, } 12)\}$
$v_7 = \{(\text{type, circle}), (\text{radius, } 1)\}$
$a_{14} = \{(\text{type, connection}), (\text{line1, } v_1), (\text{line2, } v_4), (\text{angle, } 41°)\}$
$a_{15} = \{(\text{type, connection}), (\text{line1, } v_1), (\text{line2, } v_5), (\text{angle, } 82°)\}$
$a_{45} = \{(\text{type, connection}), (\text{line1, } v_4), (\text{line2, } v_5), (\text{angle, } 57°)\}$

The attribute graphs $G_1$ and $G_2$ are both basic attribute graphs, which describe the surfaces $S_1$ and $S_2$, respectively. In order to combine them to form a complete description of the object, an attribute hypergraph can be used. In the attribute hypergraph, each hyper node corresponds to a basic attribute graph, and each hyper arc connects two basic attribute graphs corresponding to two hyper nodes. The hyper arcs of the above attribute graphs $G_1$ and $G_2$ are

$a_{11} = \{(\text{type, connection}), (\text{line1, } v_1)\}$
$a_{25} = \{(\text{type, connection}), (\text{line1, } v_2), (\text{line2, } v_5), (\text{angle, } 85°)\}$
$a_{34} = \{(\text{type, connection}), (\text{line1, } v_3), (\text{line2, } v_4), (\text{angle, } 56°)\}$

The attribute hypergraph obtained is shown in Fig. 11.2b, where the hyper node set $V = \{G_1, G_2\}$ and the hyper arc set $A = \{a_{11}, a_{25}, a_{34}\}$.

For a scene with multiple objects, an attribute graph can be constructed for each object first, and then they can be used as the hyper nodes of a higher layer of the hypergraph to further construct the attribute hypergraph. By iterating in this way, an attribute hypergraph of a complex scene can be constructed.

The matching of attribute hypergraphs can be carried out with the help of graph isomorphism (see Sect. 10.4).

### *11.1.3  Knowledge-Based Modeling*

Starting from the existing knowledge of the 3-D world, the models of 3-D scenes and objects can be built and stored in the computer as high-level knowledge. By comparing and matching these models with the descriptions of 3-D scenes and objects obtained through low-level image processing and analysis, the recognition of 3-D objects and even the understanding of 3-D scenes can be realized.

In addition, the establishment of the model can also be gradually established based on the image data obtained from the object. Such a modeling process is essentially a learning process, and this process is more consistent with the human cognitive process, because after seeing an object many times, people will abstract the various features of the object. Thus, the description of the object is obtained and stored in the brain for future use. It is worth pointing out here that **learning** means thinking and purpose, and learning without purpose can only be counted as training. In learning, the purpose is the learner's purpose, and in training, the purpose is the teacher's purpose.

In some specific applications, especially in some object recognition applications, it is not necessary to build a complete 3-D model; only the model can describe the salient features of the object to be recognized and help identify the object is required. But in the case of general scene interpretation, modeling is a complicated problem, and there are two main difficulties:

1. The model should contain all the information of the scene. However, it is difficult to obtain complete information. For example, it is difficult to obtain all the information of a complex scene, especially when a part of the scene is occluded; the information of occluded part needs often to be obtained from other sources. In addition, people often use multi-level methods with different levels of abstraction to describe and represent scenes based on specific situations. How to establish these levels and obtain corresponding information often requires special methods.
2. The complexity of the model is also difficult to determine, and it is often necessary to build a complex model for complex scenes. But if the model is too complex, the model may not be practical even if enough information can be obtained.

In modeling, the use of model knowledge or scene knowledge related to the application domain is very important. In many practical applications, making full use of prior knowledge is an important guarantee for solving the problem of image understanding. For example, in many industrial designs, the object model is established during the design process, and this structured knowledge can help greatly simplify the processing of information. In recent years, systems based on

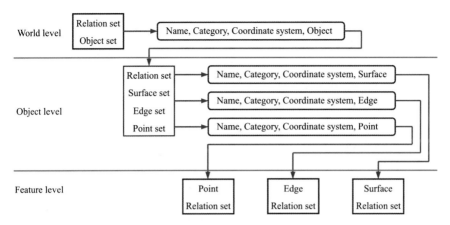

**Fig. 11.3** Example of a multi-level model

**computer-aided design** (CAD) models have been greatly developed, among which the **geometric model** method is mainly used; see Sect. 9.5.

When establishing a scene model based on the geometric model method, the following issues should be considered:

1. The objective world is composed of objects, and each object can be decomposed into geometric elements at different levels, such as curved surfaces and lines of intersection (using a boundary representation system) or basic unit (using a constructive solid geometry representation system). The data structure of the model should reflect these levels.
2. The representation of any geometric element must use a certain coordinate system. For the convenience of representation, the coordinate system of each level can be different. In this way, there should be information required for coordinate conversion between every level of the model.
3. It is best to use the same data structure at the same level.
4. The representation of features by the model can be divided into two types: explicit and implicit. For example, the explicit representation of the surface directly gives the conditional equations that each point on the surface should satisfy. Since the intersection of each surface can be calculated according to the equation of each surface, it can be considered that the explicit representation of the surface is also the implicit representation of the intersection of the surface. However, in practice, in order to reduce online calculations, implicit features are often calculated and stored in the model during modeling.

### Example 11.3 Multi-Level Model Example
Figure 11.3 shows an example of a multi-level model, which is basically divided into three levels:

1. The world level is the highest level, corresponding to the 3-D environment or scene.
2. The object level is the middle level, corresponding to each independent object that composes the 3-D environment or scene.
3. The feature level is the lowest level, corresponding to the various basic elements that make up the object. From a geometric point of view, the basic elements can be divided into surfaces, edges, and points. The surface can be a plane or a curved surface; an edge can be a curve or a straight line; a point can be a vertex or an inflection point; etc. For various basic elements, sometimes they can be further decomposed as needed to establish more basic and lower levels.

Each of the above levels can adopt its own data structure to indicate the corresponding name, category, characteristics, coordinate system, etc.

## 11.2  Logic System

**Predicate logic**, also called first-order logic, has a history of hundreds of years. It is a well-organized and widely used knowledge type. This type of knowledge is very useful in representing propositions and introducing new facts with the help of fact knowledge bases. One of the most powerful elements is predicate calculus. In most cases, logic systems are based on first-order predicate calculus, which can represent almost anything. First-order predicate calculus is a symbolic formal language (symbol logic), which can be used to represent a wide range of numerical formulas or statements in various natural languages and can also represent statements from simple facts to complex representations. With the help of it, logical reasoning in mathematics can be symbolized, knowledge can be represented by logical rules, and these rules can be used to prove whether logical representations are valid or not. This is a natural way of representing knowledge in the form of a formula. Its characteristic is that it can represent knowledge accurately and flexibly (meaning that the method of knowledge representation can be independent of the method of reasoning).

### 11.2.1  Predicate Calculation Rules

There are four basic elements of **predicate calculus**:

1. Predicate symbols: Generally represented by uppercase strings (including letters and digits).
2. Function symbols: Generally, lowercase strings were used to represent functions (symbols).
3. Variable symbols: Generally, lowercase characters were used to represent variables (symbols).

**Table 11.1** Example of predicate

| Statement | Predicate |
|-----------|-----------|
| Image $I$ is a digital image | DIGITAL($I$) |
| Image $J$ is a scan image | SCAN($J$) |
| Combine digital image $I$ and scan image $J$ | COMBINE[DIGITAL($I$), SCAN($J$)] |
| There is a pixel $p$ in image $I$ | INSIDE($p$, $I$) |
| Object $x$ is behind object $y$ | BEHIND($x$, $y$) |

**Table 11.2** Examples of clauses

| Statement | Predicate |
|-----------|-----------|
| Image $I$ is a digital image and a scan image | DIGITAL($I$) $\wedge$ SCAN($I$) |
| Image $I$ is a digital image or an analogue image | DIGITAL($I$) $\vee$ ANALOGUE($I$) |
| Image $I$ is not a digital image | ~DIGITAL($I$) |
| If image $I$ is a scan image; then image $I$ is a digital image | SCAN($I$) $\Rightarrow$ DIGITAL($I$) |
| An image is either a digital image or an analogue image | $(\forall x)$DIGITAL($x$) $\vee$ ANALOGUE($x$) |
| There is an object inside image | $(\exists x)$INSIDE($x$, $I$) |

4. Constant symbol: Also known as constant symbol, generally represented by uppercase character string.

A predicate symbol indicates a relationship in the domain in question. For example, the proposition "1 is less than 2" can be represented as LESSHAN(1, 2), where LESSHAN is a predicate symbol and 1 and 2 are both constant symbols.

**Example 11.4 Example of Basic Elements of Predicate Calculus**
Table 11.1 gives some examples of the basic elements of predicate calculus. In these examples, the predicate includes the predicate symbol and one or more of its variables. These variables can be constants or functions of other variables.

Predicates are also called atoms, and the atoms are combined with logical conjunctions to get clauses. Commonly used logical conjunctions are "$\wedge$" (AND), "$\vee$" (OR), "~" (NOT), and "$\Rightarrow$" (IMPLIES). In addition, there are two quantifiers that indicate quantity: "$\forall$" is called **universal quantifier**, $\forall x$ represents all $x$, "$\exists$" is called **existential quantifier**, and $\exists x$ represents the existence of an $x$. For logical representations, the representations obtained by connecting other representations with $\wedge$ or $\vee$ are called **conjunctive** representations or **disjunctive** representations, respectively. Legal predicate calculus representations are called **well-formed formulas** (WFFs).

**Example 11.5 Use Logical Conjunctions to Combine Atoms to Get Clauses**
Table 11.2 gives examples of using logical conjunctions to combine atoms to obtain clauses. The first four examples are related to constant symbols, and the last two examples also include variable symbols.

Logical representations can be divided into two categories. If a logical representation is in the form of $(\forall x_1 x_2 \ldots x_k)[A_1 \wedge A_2 \wedge \ldots \wedge A_n \Rightarrow B_1 \vee B_2 \vee \ldots \vee B_m]$,

**Table 11.3** The truth table of logical connector

| A | B | ~A | A ∧ B | A ∨ B | A ⇒ B |
|---|---|----|-------|-------|-------|
| T | T | F  | T     | T     | T     |
| T | F | F  | F     | T     | F     |
| F | T | T  | F     | T     | T     |
| F | F | T  | F     | F     | T     |

where $A$ and $B$ are atoms, then it is said to follow the **clausal form syntax**. The left and right parts of a clause are, respectively, called the condition and conclusion of the clause. If a logical representation includes atoms, logical conjunctions, existential quantifiers, and universal quantifiers, then it is said that the representation follows the **non-clausal form syntax**.

Now consider the proposition: For each $x$, if $x$ represents an image and a digit, then $x$ is either black and white or colored. In clause syntax, this proposition can be written as the following representation:

$$(\forall x)[\text{IMAGE}(x) \land \text{DIGITAL}(x) \Rightarrow \text{GRAY}(x) \lor \text{COLOR}(x)] \qquad (11.1)$$

In non-clause syntax, this proposition can be written as the following representation:

$$(\forall x)[\text{IMAGE}(x) \land \text{DIGITAL}(x) \lor \text{GRAY}(x) \lor \text{COLOR}(x)] \qquad (11.2)$$

It is easy to verify that the above two representations are equivalent or that the above two representations have the same representative ability (it can use the truth table of the logical connector in Table 11.3 to prove). In fact, it is always possible to switch from clause form to non-clause form, or vice versa.

Table 11.3 shows the relationship between the aforementioned logical connectors. The first five columns are the basic logic operations, and the sixth column is the implicit operation. For an implicit operation, the left part is called the **antecedent**, and the right part is called the **consequent**. If the antecedent is empty, the representation "⇒$P$" can be regarded as representing $P$; conversely, if the consequent is empty, the representation "$P$⇒" represents the negation of $P$, that is, "~$P$." Table 11.3 indicates that if the consequent is $T$ (regardless of the antecedent at this time) or the antecedent is $F$ (regardless of the consequent at this time), then the implicit value is $T$; otherwise, the implicit value is $F$. In the above definition, for an implicit operation, as long as the antecedent is $F$, the implicit value is $T$. This definition often creates confusion and leads to strange propositions. For example, consider a meaningless statement: "If the image is round, then all objects are green." Because the antecedent is $F$, the representation result of the predicate calculus of the statement will be $T$, but it is obviously not true here. However, in practice, considering that logically implicit operations in natural languages do not always make sense, the above problems do not always arise.

**Table 11.4** Some important equivalent relations

| Relation | Definition | | |
|---|---|---|---|
| Basic logic | $\sim(\sim A)$ | $\Leftrightarrow$ | $A$ |
| | $A \vee B$ | $\Leftrightarrow$ | $\sim A \Rightarrow B$ |
| | $A \Rightarrow B$ | $\Leftrightarrow$ | $\sim B \Rightarrow \sim A$ |
| De Morgan's law | $\sim(A \wedge B)$ | $\Leftrightarrow$ | $\sim A \vee \sim B$ |
| | $\sim(A \vee B)$ | $\Leftrightarrow$ | $\sim A \wedge \sim B$ |
| Distribution law | $A \wedge (B \vee C)$ | $\Leftrightarrow$ | $(A \wedge B) \vee (A \wedge C)$ |
| | $A \vee (B \wedge C)$ | $\Leftrightarrow$ | $(A \vee B) \wedge (A \vee C)$ |
| Commutative law | $A \wedge B$ | $\Leftrightarrow$ | $B \wedge A$ |
| | $A \vee B$ | $\Leftrightarrow$ | $B \vee A$ |
| Associative law | $(A \wedge B) \wedge C$ | $\Leftrightarrow$ | $A \wedge (B \wedge C)$ |
| | $(A \vee B) \vee C$ | $\Leftrightarrow$ | $A \vee (B \vee C)$ |
| Others | $\sim(\forall x)P(x)$ | $\Leftrightarrow$ | $(\exists x)[\sim P(x)]$ |
| | $\sim(\exists x)P(x)$ | $\Leftrightarrow$ | $(\forall x)[\sim P(x)]$ |

## Example 11.6 Logical Representation Example

The following examples of logical representations can help explain the concepts discussed earlier.

1. If the image is digital, then it has discrete pixels:

$$\text{DIGITAL}(\text{image}) \Rightarrow \text{DISCRETE}(x)$$

2. All digital images have discrete pixels:

$$(\forall x)\{[\text{IMAGE}(x)\text{DIGITAL}(x)] \Rightarrow (\exists y)[\text{PIXEL\_IN}(y,\ x) \wedge \text{DISCRETE}(y)]\}$$

The representation reads: For all $x$, $x$ is an image and digital, then there is always $y$, $y$ is the pixel in $x$, and it is discrete.

3. Not all images are digital:

$$(\forall x)[\text{IMAGE}(x)] \Rightarrow (\exists y)[\text{IMAGE}(y) \wedge \sim \text{DIGITAL}(y)]$$

The representation reads: For all $x$, if $x$ is an image, then there is $y$, and $y$ is an image, but not a digital.

4. Color digital images carry more information than monochrome digital images:

$$(\forall x)(\forall y)\{[\text{IMAGE}(x) \wedge \text{DIGITAL}(x) \wedge \text{COLOR}(x)]$$

$$\wedge[\text{IMAGE}(y) \wedge \text{DIGITAL}(y) \wedge \text{MONOCHROME}(y)] \Rightarrow \text{MOREINFO}(x, y)\}$$

The representation reads: For all $x$ and all $y$, if $x$ is a color digital image and $y$ is a monochrome digital image, then $x$ carries more information than $y$.

Table 11.4 gives some important equivalent relations (here $\Leftrightarrow$ stands for equivalence), which can help realize the conversion between clause form and non-clause form. The rationality of these equivalent relations can be verified with the help of the truth table of logical connectors in Table 11.3.

## 11.2.2  Inference by Theorem Proving

In predicate logic, the rules of **inference** can be applied to certain WFFs and sets of WFFs to generate new WFFs. Table 11.5 gives some examples of inference rules (*W* stands for WFFs). In the table, *c* is a constant symbol. The general statement "infer *G* from *F*" indicates $F \Rightarrow G$ is always true, so *G* can replace *F* in logical representations.

Inference rules can generate "derived WFFs" from given WFFs. In predicate calculus, "derived WFFs are called theorems," and in the derivation, the sequential application of inference rules constitutes the proof of the theorem. Many work of image understanding can be represented in the form of theorem proving through predicate calculus. In this way, a set of known facts and some rules of inference can be used to obtain new facts or prove the rationality (correctness) of the hypothesis.

In predicate calculus, two basic methods can be used to prove the correctness of logical representations: the first is to use a process similar to proving mathematical representations to directly operate on non-clause forms, and the second is to match item in the form of a clause in a representation.

**Example 11.7 Prove the Correctness of Logical Representations**
Suppose the following facts are known: (1) There is a pixel *p* in the image *I*; (2) the image *I* is a digital image. Also suppose the following "physics" law holds: (3) If the image is digital, then its pixels are discrete. Both aforementioned facts (1) and (2) vary with the application problem, but condition (3) is knowledge that has nothing to do with the application.

The above two facts can be written as INSIDE(*p*, *I*) and DIGITAL(*I*). According to the description of the problem, the above two facts are connected by the logical conjunction $\wedge$, namely, INSIDE(*p*, *I*) $\wedge$ DIGITAL(*I*). The law of "physics" represented in clauses (i.e., condition (3)) is $(\forall x, y)$[INSIDE(*x*, *y*) $\wedge$ DIGITAL $(y) \Rightarrow$ DISCRETE(*x*)].

Now use clause representation to prove that the pixel *p* is indeed discrete. The idea of proof is to first prove that the nonconformity of the clause is inconsistent with the fact, so that it can show that the clause to be proved is valid. According to the

**Table 11.5** Example of inference rules

| Inference rule | Definition | | |
|---|---|---|---|
| Modus ponens | From $W_1 \wedge (W_1 \Rightarrow W_2)$ | deduce | $W_2$ |
| Modus tollens | From $\sim W_2 \wedge (\sim W_1 \Rightarrow W_2)$ | deduce | $W_1$ |
| Projection | From $W_1 \wedge W_2$ | deduce | $W_1$ |
| Universal specialization | From $(\forall x)W(x)$ | deduce | $W(c)$ |

previous definition, the knowledge about this problem can be represented in the form of the following clauses:

1. $\Rightarrow$INSIDE($p$, $I$)
2. $\Rightarrow$DIGITAL($I$)
3. ($\forall x$, $y$)[DIGITAL($y$) $\Rightarrow$ DISCRETE($x$)]
4. DISCRETE($p$)$\Rightarrow$

Note that the negation of the predicate DISCRETE($p$) can be represented as DISCRETE($p$)$\Rightarrow$.

After representing the basic elements of the problem in clause form, the empty clause can be achieved by matching the left and right sides of each implicit representation, thereby using the contradiction that arises to obtain proof. The matching process relies on variable substitution to make the atoms equal. After matching, one can get a clause called **resolvent**, which contains the left and right sides that do not match. If one replaces $y$ with $I$ and replaces $x$ with $p$, the left side of (3) matches the right side of (2), so the resolvent is

5. $\Rightarrow$DISCRETE($p$)

However, because the left side of (4) and the right side of (5) are congruent, the solution of (4) and (5) is an empty clause. This result is contradictory. It shows that DISCRETE($p$)$\Rightarrow$ cannot be established, which proves the correctness of DIS-CRETE($p$).

Now use non-clause representation to prove that the pixel $p$ is indeed discrete. First, according to the relationship introduced in Table 11.4, $\sim A \Rightarrow B \Leftrightarrow A \vee B$, condition (3) is converted into a non-clause form, namely, ($\forall x$, $y$)[$\sim$INSIDE ($x$, $y$) $\wedge$ $\sim$DIGITAL($y$) $\vee$ DISCRETE($x$)].

The following use a modus ponens form to represent the knowledge about this problem:

1. ($\forall x$, $y$)[INSIDE($x$, $y$) $\wedge$ DIGITAL($y$)] $\wedge$ [$\sim$INSIDE($x$, $y$) $\wedge$ $\sim$DIGITAL($y$) $\vee$ DIS-CRETE($x$)]

    Replace $y$ with $I$ and $x$ with $p$ to get

2. [INSIDE($p$, $I$) $\wedge$ DIGITAL($I$)] $\wedge$ [$\sim$INSIDE($p$, $I$) $\wedge$ $\sim$DIGITAL($I$) $\vee$ DIS-CRETE($p$)]

    Using projection rules, it can deduce

3. INSIDE($p$, $I$) $\wedge$ [$\sim$INSIDE($p$, $I$) $\vee$ DISCRETE($p$)]

    Then, use the distribution law to get $A \wedge (\sim A \vee B) = (A \wedge B)$. This gives a simplified representation:

4. INSIDE($p$, $I$) $\wedge$ DISCRETE($p$)

    Using the projection rule again, it gets

5. DISCRETE($p$).

This proves that the original representation in (1) is completely equivalent to the representation in (5). In other words, in this way, the conclusion that the pixel $p$ is discrete is inferred or deduced based on the given information.

A basic conclusion of predicate calculus is that all theorems can be proved in a finite time. People have already proposed an inference rule called **resolution** to prove this conclusion. The basic step of this analysis rule is to first represent the basic elements of the problem in the form of clauses, and then seek the antecedent and consequent of the implicit representation that can be matched, and then match by substituting variables to make the atoms equal. The clause (called the **resolvent**) obtained after matching includes the left and right sides that do not match. The proof of the theorem is now transformed into a clause to be solved to produce an empty clause, and the empty clause gives contradictory results. From the point of view that all correct theorems can be proved, this resolution rule is complete; from the point of view that all wrong theorems are impossible to prove, this resolution rule is correct.

**Example 11.8 Interpret the Image Based on the Knowledge Base Solution**
Suppose that the knowledge base in an aerial image interpretation system has the following information: (1) There are runways in all commercial airport images. (2) There are planes in all commercial airport images. (3) There are buildings in all commercial airport images. (4) In a commercial airport, at least one of the buildings is the terminal building. (5) The building surrounded by and pointed by the airplanes is the terminal building. This information can be put into a "model" of a commercial airport in the form of clauses:

$$(\forall x)[\text{CONTAINS}(x, \text{runways}) \land \text{CONTAINS}(x, \text{airplanes})$$
$$\land \text{CONTAINS}(x, \text{buildings}) \land \text{POINT}-\text{TO}(\text{airplanes, buildings})]$$
$$\Rightarrow \text{COM} - \text{AIRPORT}(x)$$

Note that the information in (4) is not directly used in the model, but its meaning is implicit in the two conditions that the building and the airplanes point to the building in the model; condition (5) clearly indicates what kind of building is the terminal building.

Suppose there is an aerial image and a recognition engine can distinguish different objects in the aerial image. From the perspective of image interpretation, two types of questions can be asked:

1. What kind of image is this?
2. Is this an image of a commercial airport?

Under normal circumstances, the first question cannot be answered with current technology. The second question is generally more difficult to answer, but it will become easier if the scope of the discussion is narrowed. Specifically, the model-driven approach shown above has obvious advantages, and it can be used to guide the work of the recognition engine. In this example, the recognition engine should be able to recognize three types of objects, namely, runways, airplanes, and buildings. If, as is common, the height of the acquired image is known, the task of finding the object can be further simplified, because the relative scale of the object can be used to guide the recognition process.

The recognizer that works according to the above model will have the following output: CONTAINS(image, runway), CONTAINS(image, airplanes), CONTAINS (image, buildings). On the basis of object recognition, the authenticity of the clause POINT-TO(airplanes, buildings) can be further judged. If the clause is false, the process stops; if the clause is true, the process will continue to determine whether the given image is an image of a commercial airport by judging the correctness of the clause COM-AIRPORT(image).

If one wants to use the method of analyzing and proving theorem to solve the above problem, one can start to work according to the following four pieces of information obtained from the image: (1) ⇒CONTAINS(image, runway); (2) ⇒CONTAINS(image, airplanes); (3) ⇒CONTAINS(image, buildings); and (4) ⇒POINT-TO(airplanes, buildings). The negation of the clause to be proved here is (5) COM-AIRPORT(image)⇒. First notice that if the $x$ is replaced with image, one of the clauses on the left side of the model will match the right side of (1). The resolvent is

$$[\text{CONTAINS(image, airplanes)} \land \text{CONTAINS(image, buildings)} \land \text{POINT}$$
$$- \text{TO(airplanes, buildings)}]$$
$$\Rightarrow \text{COM} - \text{AIRPORT(image)}$$

Similarly, one of the clauses on the left side of the above resolvent will match the right side of (2), and the new resolvent is

$$[\text{CONTAINS(image, buildings)} \land \text{POINT-TO(airplanes, buildings)}]$$
$$\Rightarrow \text{COM-AIRPORT(image)}$$

Next, the resolvent obtained by using (3) and (4) is ⇒COM-AIRPORT(image).

Finally, the resolvent of this result and (5) give an empty clause (the right side of the resolvent is the same as the left side of (5)), which creates a contradiction. This proves the correctness of COM-AIRPORT(image), which means that the given image is indeed an image of a commercial airport (it matches the model of the commercial airport).

## 11.3 Fuzzy Reasoning

**Fuzzy** is a concept often opposed to clarity or crisp. In daily life, many vague things are often encountered, without clear quantitative or quantitative boundaries, which need to use some vague words and sentences to describe. Using fuzzy concepts can represent a variety of loose, uncertain, and imprecise knowledge and information (e.g., fuzzy mathematics uses uncertain things as its research objects) and can even represent knowledge that is obtained from conflicting sources. Determinants or modifiers similar to those in human language can be used here, such as high gray scale, medium gray scale, low gray scale, etc., to form a fuzzy set to represent and describe related image knowledge. Based on the representation of knowledge, further reasoning can be carried out. Fuzzy reasoning needs to be carried out with the help of fuzzy logic and fuzzy operations.

### 11.3.1  Fuzzy Sets and Fuzzy Operations

A **fuzzy set** $S$ in fuzzy space $X$ is a set of ordered pairs:

$$S = \{[x, M_S(x)] | x \in X\} \tag{11.3}$$

where the **membership function** $M_S(x)$ represents the membership degree of $x$ in $S$.

The value of the membership function is always a nonnegative real number, usually limited to [0, 1]. Fuzzy sets can often be uniquely described by their membership functions. Figure 11.4 shows several examples of using exact set and fuzzy set to represent the gray level as "dark," where the horizontal axis corresponds to the image gray level $x$, for the fuzzy set is the definition domain of its membership function $M_S(x)$. Figure 11.4a is described by the exact set, and the result given is binary (less than 127 is completely "dark," and greater than 127 is not "dark" at all). Figure 11.4b is a typical fuzzy set membership function, from 0 to 255 along the horizontal axis, its membership degree along the vertical axis from 1 (corresponding to a gray level of 0, completely belonging to the "dark" fuzzy set) to 0 (corresponding to a gray scale of 255, which is not part of the "dark" fuzzy set at all). The gradual transition in the middle shows that the $x$ between them is partly "dark" and partly not "dark." Figure 11.4c gives an example of a non-linear membership function, which is somewhat like the combination of Fig. 11.4a, b, but still represents a fuzzy set.

The operation on fuzzy sets can be carried out with the help of fuzzy logic operations. **Fuzzy logic** is a science based on multivalued logic that uses fuzzy sets to study fuzzy thinking, language forms, and their laws. Fuzzy logic operations have names similar to general logic operations but define different operations. Let $M_A(x)$ and $M_B(y)$ denote the membership functions corresponding to fuzzy sets $A$ and $B$, and their domains are $X$ and $Y$, respectively. The fuzzy intersection

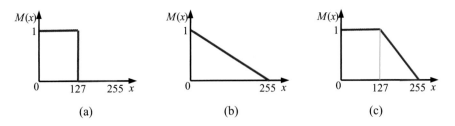

**Fig. 11.4**  Schematic representation of exact set (**a**) and fuzzy set (**b, c**)

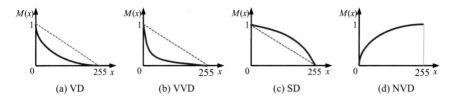

Fig. 11.5 (a–d) Some calculation results of the original fuzzy set D in Fig. 11.4b

operation, fuzzy union operation, and fuzzy complement operation can be defined point by point as follows:

$$\text{Intersection } A \cap B: \quad M_{A \cap B}(x, y) = \min\left[M_A(x), M_B(y)\right]$$
$$\text{Union } A \cup B: \quad M_{A \cup B}(x, y) = \max\left[M_A(x), M_B(y)\right] \tag{11.4}$$
$$\text{Complement } A^c: \quad M_{A^c}(x) = 1 - M_A(x)$$

The operation on the fuzzy set can also be carried out by changing the shape of the fuzzy membership function point by point with the help of general algebraic operations. Assuming that the membership function in Fig. 11.4b represents a fuzzy set D (dark), then the membership function of the enhanced fuzzy set VD (very dark) is shown in Fig. 11.5a.

$$M_{VD}(x) = M_D(x) \bullet M_D(x) = M_D^2(x) \tag{11.5}$$

This type of operation can be repeated. For example, the membership function of the fuzzy set VVD (very very dark) is shown in Fig. 11.5b.

$$M_{VVD}(x) = M_D^2(x) \bullet M_D^2(x) = M_D^4(x) \tag{11.6}$$

On the other hand, it can also define a weakened fuzzy set SD (somewhat dark), and its membership function is shown in Fig. 11.5c.

$$M_{SD}(x) = \sqrt{M_D(x)} \tag{11.7}$$

Logic operations and algebraic operations can also be combined. For example, the complement of the enhanced fuzzy set VD, that is, the membership function of the fuzzy set NVD (not very dark), is shown in Fig. 11.5d.

$$M_{NVD}(x) = 1 - M_D^2(x) \tag{11.8}$$

Here NVD can be regarded as N[V(D)], that is, $M_D(x)$ corresponds to D, $M_D{}^2(x)$ corresponds to V(D), and $1 - M_D{}^2(x)$ corresponds to N[V(D)].

## *11.3.2   Fuzzy Reasoning Method*

In fuzzy reasoning, the information in each fuzzy set must be combined with certain rules to make a decision.

### 11.3.2.1   Basic Model

The basic model and main steps of fuzzy reasoning are shown in Fig. 11.6. Starting from the **fuzzy rules**, determining the basic relationship of membership in the related membership function is called combination, and the result of using **fuzzy composition** is a **fuzzy solution space**. In order to make a decision based on the solution space, there must be a process of **de-fuzzification**.

Fuzzy rules refer to a series of unconditional and conditional propositions. The form of the unconditional fuzzy rule is

$$x \text{ is } A \tag{11.9}$$

The form of conditional fuzzy rule is

$$\text{if } x \text{ is } A \quad \text{then } y \text{ is } B \tag{11.10}$$

where $A$ and $B$ are fuzzy sets, while $x$ and $y$ represent scalars in their corresponding domains.

The degree of membership corresponding to the unconditional fuzzy rule is $M_A(x)$. Unconditional fuzzy rules are used to limit the solution space or define a default solution space. Since these rules are unconditional, they can directly act on the solution space with the help of the operation of fuzzy sets.

Now consider conditional fuzzy rules. Among the various existing methods for realizing decision-making, the simplest is **monotonic fuzzy reasoning**, which can directly obtain the solution without using the fuzzy combination and de-fuzzification described below. For example, let $x$ represent the illuminance value of the outside world and $y$ represent the gray value of the image; then the fuzzy rule representing the high-low degree of the image grayscale is as follows: if $x$ is DARK, then $y$ is LOW.

Figure 11.7 shows the principle of monotonic fuzzy reasoning. Assume that according to the determined external illuminance value (where $x = 0.3$), the membership value $M_D(0.3) = 0.4$ can be obtained. If one uses this value to represent the

**Fig. 11.6**  Model and steps for fuzzy reasoning

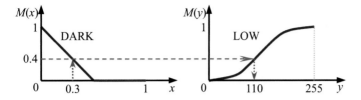

**Fig. 11.7** Monotonic fuzzy reasoning based on a single fuzzy rule

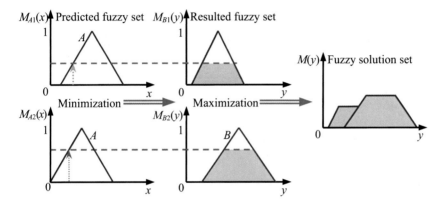

**Fig. 11.8** Fuzzy min-max combination using minimum correlation

membership value $M_L(y) = M_D(x)$, one can get the expected gray level of the image to be $y = 110$ (range 0–255), which is at lower range.

### 11.3.2.2 Fuzzy Combination

Knowledge related to the decision-making process is often contained in more than one fuzzy rule. But not every fuzzy rule has the same contribution to decision-making. There are different combining mechanisms that can be used to combine rules; the most commonly used is the **min-max rule**.

In the min-max combination, a series of minimization and maximization processes are used. Refer to Fig. 11.8; first use the minimum value of the predicted true value, also called the **correlation minimum** $M_A(x)$, to define the membership function $M_B(y)$ of the fuzzy result. Then, update the membership function of the fuzzy result point by point to get the fuzzy membership function

$$M(y) = \min \{M_A(x), \ M_B(y)\} \tag{11.11}$$

If there are $N$ rules, do this for each rule (two rules are taken as an example in the figure). Finally, the fuzzy membership function of the solution is obtained by maximizing the minimized fuzzy set point by point:

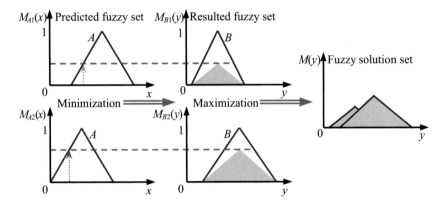

**Fig. 11.9** Fuzzy min-max combination using correlation products

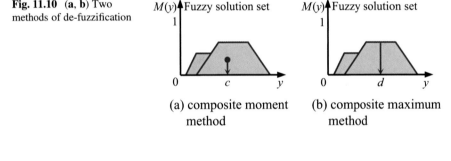

**Fig. 11.10 (a, b)** Two methods of de-fuzzification

(a) composite moment method

(b) composite maximum method

$$M_S(y) = \max_n \{M_n(y)\} \tag{11.12}$$

Another method is called **correlation product**, which scales the original result fuzzy membership function instead of truncating it. The minimum correlation calculation is simple, and the de-fuzzification is simple, while the correlation product can maintain the shape of the original fuzzy set (see Fig. 11.9).

### 11.3.2.3 De-fuzzification

Fuzzy combination gives a fuzzy membership function of a single solution for each solution variable. In order to determine the exact solution for decision-making, it is necessary to determine a vector containing multiple scalars (each scalar corresponds to a solution variable) that can best represent the information in the fuzzy solution set. This process is performed independently for each solution variable and is called **de-fuzzification**. Two commonly used de-fuzzification methods are **composite moment** method and **composite maximum** method.

The composite moment method first determines the center of gravity $c$ of the membership function of the fuzzy solution and transforms the fuzzy solution into a clear solution $c$, as shown in Fig. 11.10a. The composite maximum method determines the domain point with the maximum membership value in the membership function of the fuzzy solution. If the maximum value is on a platform, the center of the platform gives a clear solution $d$, as shown in Fig. 11.10b. The result of the composite moment method is sensitive to all rules (take a weighted average), while the result of the composite maximum method depends on the single rule with the highest predicted true value. The composite moment method is often used in control applications, and the composite maximum method is often used in identification applications.

## 11.4 Scene Classification

**Scene classification** is to determine various specific regions (including position, relationship, attribute/property, etc.) in the image based on the principle of visual perception organization and give the semantic and conceptual explanation of the scene. Its specific means and goal are to automatically classify and label images according to a given set of semantic categories and provide effective contextual information for object recognition and interpretation of the scene content.

Scene classification is related to but different from object recognition. On the one hand, there are often many types of objects in a scene. To achieve scene classification, it is often necessary to recognize some of these objects (but generally it is not necessary to recognize all objects). On the other hand, in many cases, only a certain understanding of the object is needed for classification (e.g., in some cases, only the underlying information, such as color, texture, etc., can meet the classification requirements). With reference to the human visual cognition process, the preliminary object recognition can often meet the specific classification requirements of the scene. At this time, the connection between the low-level features and the high-level cognition must be established to determine and explain the semantic category of the scene.

The classified scene has a certain guiding effect on object recognition. In the nature world, most objects only appear in specific scenes. The correct judgment of the global scene can provide a reasonable context constraint mechanism for the local analysis of the image (including object recognition).

### 11.4.1 Bag-of-Words/Feature Model

The **bag-of-words model** or **bag-of-features model** is derived from the processing of natural language, and it is often called the bag-of-features model after it is introduced into the image domain. The bag-of-features model is named after the category features belong to the same object group to form a bag. The model usually adopts a directed graph structure (the relationship between the undirected graph nodes is a probability constraint relationship, while the relationship between the directed graph nodes is a causal relationship; and an undirected graph can be regarded as a special kind of directed graph, symmetric directed graph). The conditional independence between the image and the visual vocabulary in the bag-of-features model is the theoretical basis of the model, but there is no strict geometric information about the object component in the model.

The original bag-of-words model only considers the symbiotic relationship and the **topic** logical relationship between the features corresponding to the words and ignores the spatial relationship between the features. In the image field, not only the image features themselves but also the spatial distributions of image features are also very important. In recent years, many local feature descriptors (such as SIFT; see Sect. 6.3) have relatively high dimensionality, which can more comprehensively and explicitly represent the special properties of key points in the image and the small region around it (different from the corner points representing only position information while keeping the nature of itself implicitly represented), and are obviously different from other key points and the small regions around them. Moreover, these feature descriptors can overlap and cover each other in the image space, so that the nature of the relationship can be better preserved. The use of these feature descriptors improves the ability to describe the spatial distribution of image features.

Representing and describing the scene with the bag-of-features model requires extracting local region description features from the scene, which can be called **visual vocabulary**. The scene has some basic components, so the scene can be decomposed. Applying the concept of a document, a book is composed of many words. Returning to the image domain, it can be considered that the image of the scene is composed of many visual words. From a cognitive perspective, each visual word corresponds to a feature (more precisely, a feature that describes the local characteristics of a scene) in the image, which is a basic unit that reflects the content of the image or the meaning of the scene. Constructing a collection of visual words (visual vocabulary) to represent and describe the scene can include the following aspects: (1) extracting features; (2) learning visual vocabulary; (3) obtaining quantified features of visual vocabulary; and (4) using the frequency of visual vocabulary to represent images.

A specific example is shown in Fig. 11.11. First, perform region (the neighborhood of key points) detection on the image, and divide and extract regions of different categories (see Fig. 11.11a, where the regions take small squares for ease of use); then calculate the feature vector for each region to represent the region, as shown in Fig. 11.11b; next quantize the feature vector to obtain visual words and build a codebook, as shown in Fig. 11.11c; and finally count the occurrence frequency of specific words in each region image. Here several examples of using histograms are shown in Fig. 11.11d–f. Combining them together can give the representation of the whole image.

After the image is divided into multiple subregions, each subregion can be given a semantic concept, that is, each subregion is used as a visual unit to make it have a unique semantic meaning. Since similar scenes should have similar concept collections and distributions, scenes can be divided into specific semantic categories based on the regional distribution of semantic concepts. If semantic concepts can be

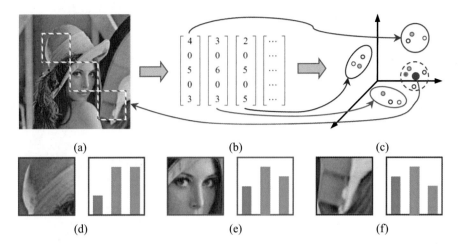

(a)                                    (b)                                    (c)

(d)                                    (e)                                    (f)

**Fig. 11.11** (**a–f**) The process of obtaining the description features of the local region in the image (see text)

connected with visual vocabulary, then the classification of scenes can be carried out with the help of vocabulary representation and description models.

Visual vocabulary can directly represent the object or only represent the middle-level concepts in the neighborhood of key points. The former needs to detect or segment the object in the scene and further classify the scene by classifying the object. For example, if the sky is detected, the image should be outdoor. The latter does not need to segment the object directly, but uses the local descriptor obtained by training to determine the label of the scene. There are generally three steps:

1. Feature point detection: Commonly used methods include image grid method and Gaussian difference method. The former divides the image according to the grid and takes the center of the grid to determine the feature points. The latter uses the **difference of Gaussian** (DoG) operator (see Sect. 6.3) to detect local features of interest, such as corner points.
2. Feature representation and description: Use the nature of the feature point itself and the nature of the neighborhood to carry out. In recent years, the **Scale Invariant Feature Transformation** (SIFT) operator (see Sect. 6.3) is often used, which actually combines feature point detection and feature representation and description.
3. Generate dictionary: Cluster local description results (such as using $K$-means clustering method), and take cluster centers to form a dictionary.

**Example 11.9 Visual Vocabulary**
In practice, the selection of the local region can be done with the help of the SIFT local descriptor. The selected local region is a circular region with key points as the center and has some invariant characteristics, as shown in Fig. 11.12a. The constructed visual vocabulary is shown in Fig. 11.12b, where each sub-image

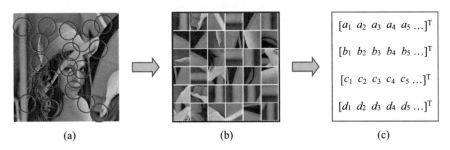

$$[a_1 \ a_2 \ a_3 \ a_4 \ a_5 \ ...]^\mathrm{T}$$

$$[b_1 \ b_2 \ b_3 \ b_4 \ b_5 \ ...]^\mathrm{T}$$

$$[c_1 \ c_2 \ c_3 \ c_4 \ c_5 \ ...]^\mathrm{T}$$

$$[d_1 \ d_2 \ d_3 \ d_4 \ d_5 \ ...]^\mathrm{T}$$

(a)                              (b)                              (c)

**Fig. 11.12** (**a–c**) Obtaining visual vocabulary with the help of SIFT local descriptors (see text)

represents a basic visual word (a key point feature cluster), and can be represented by a vector, as shown in Fig. 11.12c. The visual word dictionary can be used to represent the original image with a combination of visual words, and the frequency of use of various visual words reflects the characteristics of the image.

In the actual application process, firstly represent the image with visual vocabulary through feature detection operators and feature descriptors, form the parameter estimation and probabilistic reasoning of the visual vocabulary model, obtain parameter iteration formulas and probabilistic analysis results, and finally carry out the analysis and explanation of the trained model.

Bayesian correlation models are most commonly used in modeling; typical models include **probabilistic latent semantic analysis** (pLSA) model and **latent Dirichlet allocation** (LDA) model. According to the framework of the bag-of-features model, the image is regarded as text, and the topics found in the image are regarded as object classes (such as classrooms, sports fields); then a scene containing multiple objects is regarded as a composition of probabilistic models constructed by mixing a set of topics, which can be divided into semantic categories by analyzing the distribution of scene topics.

### 11.4.2  pLSA Model

The probabilistic latent semantic analysis (pLSA) model is derived from the **Probabilistic Latent Semantic Index** (pLSI), which is a graph model established to solve the classification of objects and scenes. This model was originally used for learning natural language and text. Its original noun definitions all used concepts in the text, but it is also easy to generalize to the image field (especially with the help of the framework of the bag-of-features model).

### 11.4.2.1 Model Description

Suppose there is an image set $T = \{t_i\}$; $i = 1, \ldots, N$, $N$ is the total number of images; the visual words contained in $T$ come from the word set, i.e., dictionary (visual vocabulary) $S = \{s_j\}$; $j = 1, \ldots, M$, $M$ is the total number of words; a statistical co-occurrence matrix $P$ of size $N \times M$ can be used to describe the properties of the image set; each element $p_{ij} = p(t_i, s_j)$ in the matrix indicates that the frequency of word $s_j$ appears in the image $t_i$. The matrix is actually a sparse matrix.

The pLSA model uses a latent variable model to describe the data in the co-occurrence matrix. It associates each observation (the word $s_j$ appears in the image $t_i$) with a latent variable (called a topic variable) $z \in Z = \{z_k\}$, $k = 1, \ldots, K$. Use $p(t_i)$ to represent the probability of the word appearing in the image $t_i$, $p(z_k|t_i)$ to represent the probability that the topic $z_k$ appears in the image $t_i$ (i.e., the probability distribution of the image in the topic space) and $p(s_j|z_k)$ to represent the probability that the word $s_j$ appears under a specific topic $z_k$ (i.e., the topic probability distribution in the dictionary); then by selecting an image $t_i$ with a probability of $p(t_i)$ and a topic with a probability of $p(z_k|t_i)$, one can generate the word $s_j$ with a probability of $p(s_j|z_k)$. In this way, the conditional probability model based on the topic and word co-occurrence matrix can be defined as

$$p(s_j|t_i) = \sum_{k=1}^{K} p(s_j|z_k)p(z_k|t_i) \qquad (11.13)$$

That is, the words in each image can be mixed by $K$ latent topic variables $p(s_j|z_k)$ according to the coefficient $p(z_k|t_i)$. In this way, the elements of the co-occurrence matrix $P$ are

$$p(t_i, s_j) = p(t_i)p(s_j|t_i) \qquad (11.14)$$

The **graph** representation of the pLSA model is shown in Fig. 11.13, where the boxes represent collections (large boxes represent image collections, and small boxes represent repeated selection of topics and words in images); arrows represent the dependencies between nodes; and nodes are a random variable—the left observation node $t$ (shaded) corresponds to the image, the right observation node

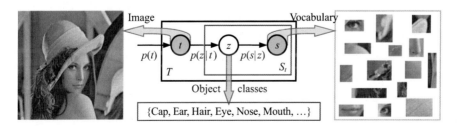

**Fig. 11.13** Schematic diagram of pLSA model

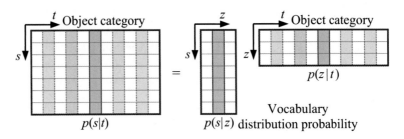

**Fig. 11.14** Decomposition of the co-occurrence matrix

$s$ (shaded) corresponds to the visual vocabulary described by the descriptor, and the middle node $z$ is the (unobserved) latent node that indicates the object category corresponding to the image pixel, that is, the topic. The model is to establish the probability mapping relationship between the topic $z$ and the image $t$ and the visual vocabulary $s$ through training and to select the category corresponding to the maximum posterior probability as the final classification decision result.

The goal of the pLSA model is to search for the vocabulary distribution probability $p(s_j|z_k)$ under a specific topic $z_k$ and the corresponding mixing ratio $p(z_k|t_i)$ in the specific image, so as to obtain the vocabulary distribution $p(s_j|t_i)$ in the specific image. Equation (11.13) represents each image as a convex combination of $K$ topic vectors, which can be illustrated by matrix operations, as shown in Fig. 11.14. Among them, each column in the left matrix represents a visual vocabulary in a given image, each column in the middle matrix represents a visual vocabulary in a given topic, and each column in the right matrix represents a topic (object category) in a given image.

### 11.4.2.2 Model Calculation

Here it is necessary to determine the topic vector common to all images and the special mixing ratio coefficient for each image. The purpose is to determine the model with high probability for the words appearing in the image, so that the category corresponding to the maximum posterior probability can be selected as the final object category. This can be achieved by optimizing the following objective function to obtain the maximum likelihood estimation of the parameters:

$$L = \prod_{j=1}^{M} \prod_{i=1}^{N} p\left(s_j|t_i\right)^{p\left(s_j,\, t_i\right)} \tag{11.15}$$

The maximum likelihood estimation of the latent variable model can be calculated using the **maximum expectation** or **expectation maximization** (EM) algorithm. The EM algorithm is an algorithm for finding the maximum likelihood estimation or maximum a posteriori estimation of parameters in a probability model (depending on unobservable latent variables) in statistical calculations. It is an iterative technique that estimates unknown variables when a part of the relevant variables is known. The algorithm has two alternate iterative calculation steps:

1. Calculate expectation (E step), that is, use the existing estimated value of the latent variable to calculate its maximum likelihood estimation.
2. Maximize (M step), that is, to estimate the value of the required parameter on the basis of the obtained maximum likelihood value in E step, and the obtained parameter estimation value is used in the next E step.

Here, the E step is to calculate the posterior probability of the latent variable on the basis of the known parameter estimation, which can be represented as (by Bayesian formula)

$$p(z_k|t_i, s_j) = \frac{p(s_j|z_k)p(z_k|t_i)}{\sum_{l=1}^{K} p(s_j|z_l)p(z_l|t_i)} \qquad (11.16)$$

The M step is to maximize the likelihood of the completely expected data in the posterior probability obtained from the E step, and its iterative formula is

$$p(s_j|z_k) = \frac{\sum_{i=1}^{N} p(s_j|z_k)p(z_k|t_i)}{\sum_{l=1}^{K} p(s_j|z_l)p(z_l|t_i)} \qquad (11.17)$$

The formulas of the E step and the M step are operated alternately until the termination condition is met. The final decision on the category can be made with the help of the following formula:

$$z^* = \arg \max_{z} \{p(z|t)\} \qquad (11.18)$$

### 11.4.2.3  Model Application Example

Consider an image classification problem based on emotional semantics. The image contains not only the intuitive scene information but also various emotional semantic information. In addition to representing the scenery, state, and environment of the objective world, it can also bring strong emotional reactions to people. Different emotion categories can generally be represented by adjectives. There is an emotion classification framework that divides all emotions into ten categories, including five positive (joy, satisfaction, excitement, awe, and unbiased positive) and five negative (anger, sadness, disgust, panic, and unbiased negative). An **International Affective Picture System** (IAPS) database has been established internationally. There are a total of 1182 color pictures with a wide range of object categories. Some pictures belonging to the above ten emotional categories are shown in Fig. 11.15.

(a) Joy

(f) Anger

(b) Satisfaction

(g) Sadness

(c) Excitement

(h) Disgust

(d) Awe

(i) Panic

(e) Unbiased positive

(j) Unbiased negative

**Fig. 11.15** (**a–j**) Examples of ten emotion category pictures in the International Affective Picture System database

Figure 11.15a–e corresponds to five positive emotions and Fig. 11.15f–j corresponds to five negative emotions.

In image classification based on emotional semantics, the image is the picture in the library, the words are selected from emotional category vocabulary, and the topic is the **latent emotional semantic factor** (representing an intermediate semantic layer concept between the underlying image features and the high-level emotional category). First, the $K$-means algorithm is used to cluster the underlying image features obtained by the SIFT operator into an emotional dictionary. Then, the pLSA model is used to learn the latent emotional semantic factors, so as to obtain the probability distribution $p(s_j|z_k)$ of each latent emotional semantic factor on the emotional word and the probability distribution of each picture on the latent emotional semantic factor $p(z_k|t_i)$. Finally, the **support vector machine** (SVM) method is used to train the emotional image classifier and used to classify different emotion categories.

**Example 11.10 Classification Test Results**
Some experimental results of classification using the above method are shown in Table 11.6, in which 70% of the pictures of each emotion category are used as the

**Table 11.6**  Example of classification

|         | $s = 200$ | $s = 300$ | $s = 400$ | $s = 500$ | $s = 600$ | $s = 700$ | $s = 800$ |
|---------|-----------|-----------|-----------|-----------|-----------|-----------|-----------|
| $z = 10$ | 24.3 | 29.0 | 33.3 | 41.7 | 35.4 | 36.1 | 25.5 |
| $z = 20$ | 38.9 | 45.0 | 52.1 | 69.5 | 62.4 | 58.4 | 45.8 |
| $z = 30$ | 34.0 | 36.8 | 43.8 | 58.4 | 55.4 | 49.1 | 35.7 |
| $z = 40$ | 28.4 | 30.7 | 37.5 | 48.7 | 41.3 | 40.9 | 29.8 |
| $z = 50$ | 26.5 | 30.8 | 40.7 | 48.9 | 39.5 | 37.1 | 30.8 |
| $z = 60$ | 23.5 | 27.2 | 31.5 | 42.0 | 37.7 | 38.3 | 26.7 |
| $z = 70$ | 20.9 | 22.6 | 29.8 | 35.8 | 32.1 | 23.1 | 21.9 |

The shaded rows and columns show the best effect obtained at the cross of $s = 500$ and $z = 20$

training set and the remaining 30% of the pictures are used as the test set. The training and testing process is repeated ten times. The table shows the average correct classification rate (%) of the ten categories. The value of the emotional word $s$ is between 200 and 800 (interval 100), and the value of the latent emotional semantic factor $z$ is between 10 and 70 (interval 10).

From Table 11.6, it can be seen the influence of different numbers of latent emotional semantic factors and emotional vocabulary on the image classification effect. When the value of the latent emotional semantic factor is fixed, as the number of emotional words increases, the classification performance gradually increases and then gradually decreases, and the value of $s$ is best when the value of $s$ is 500. Similarly, when the number of emotional words is fixed, as the latent emotional semantic factor increases, the classification performance gradually improves and then gradually decreases, and the value of $z$ is best when the value of $z$ is 20. Therefore, when $s = 500$ and $z = 20$, the best classification effect that can be achieved by the above method can be obtained.

## 11.5  Key Points and References for Each Section

The following combine the main contents of each section to introduce some references that can be further consulted:

1. **Scene Knowledge**

    For more discussion on the concept of the model, see reference [1]. More discussion on learning and training purposes can be found in reference [2].

2. **Logic System**

    The details of the description of predicate calculus and the use of theorem proof for inference can be found in references [3, 4].

3. **Fuzzy Reasoning**

The discussion of various rules of fuzzy reasoning can be found in reference [5].

4. **Scene Classification**

Scene classification is a step further than object recognition. To give the semantic and conceptual explanation of the scene, various models are often used. The bag-of-words model is often referred to as the bag-of-features model in the image field, which can be found in reference [6]. Probabilistic latent semantic analysis is a graph model established to solve the classification of objects and scenes, which can be found in reference [7]. For more information about the International affective picture system (IAPS) database, please refer to reference [8], and the use of this database for image classification problems based on emotional semantics can be found in reference [9].

## Self-Test Questions

The following questions include both single-choice questions and multiple-choice questions, so each option must be judged.

11.1. **Scene Knowledge**

11.1.1. Analyze the following statements; which one(s) is/are wrong? ($\cdot$).

(a) It is possible to obtain the same data according to different model assumptions.
(b) The same data may meet different model assumptions.
(c) One way to solve the under-determined problem is to increase the limiting conditions.
(d) One way to solve the overdetermined inverse problem is to reduce the limiting conditions.

[Hint] Consider the relationship between the model and the data.

11.1.2. For the tetrahedron given in Fig. 11.2a, if the invisible surface and ridge line are also considered, the attribute hypergraph will have ($\cdot$).

(a) Four super nodes, six super arcs.
(b) Four super nodes, 12 super arcs.
(c) Four super nodes, 18 super arcs.
(d) Four super nodes, 24 super arcs.

[Hint] Each super node corresponds to an attribute graph, and super arc connections are required between each other.

11.1.3. The following statements correspond in pairs, of which the incorrect one/ones is/are ($\cdot$).

(a) The learner's purpose in learning is his own purpose.
(b) The purpose of the learner in training is the purpose of others.

(c) The complete 3-D model should contain all the information of the scene.

(d) A model that does not contain all the information of the scene cannot solve the 3-D problem.

[Hint] Model building and problem-solving are not equivalent.

## 11.2. Logic System

11.2.1. Point out the following incorrect description: (·).

(a) The four basic elements of predicate calculus can be divided into two groups.

(b) The four basic elements of predicate calculus are all used in representing a statement.

(c) Conjunctive representations and disjunctive representations are both well-formed formulas.

(d) Both conjunctive representations and disjunctive representations can represent the same statement.

[Hint] Pay attention to the difference between general conditions and special cases.

11.2.2. Compare clause form syntax and non-clause form syntax: (·).

(a) Representations in clause form can be converted to representations in non-clause form.

(b) Representations in clause form and representations in non-clause form can represent the same proposition.

(c) Representations obtained by following the clause form syntax include atoms, logical conjunctions, existential quantifiers, and universal quantifiers.

(d) Representations that follow the non-clause form syntax include atoms, logical conjunctions, existential quantifiers, and universal quantifiers.

[Hint] The existential quantifiers are not considered in the clause form syntax.

11.2.3. In predicate calculus, to prove the correctness of logical representations, (·).

(a) One can directly operate on non-clause forms.

(b) The logical representation to be proved is obtained by reasoning on the non-clause form.

(c) One can match items in the clause form of the representation.

(d) The logical representation to be proved is obtained by matching the clause form.

[Hint] The ideas of the two proofs are different.

**Fig. 11.16** The
membership functions of
three fuzzy sets

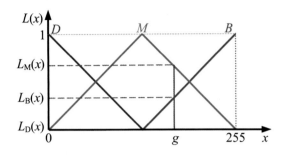

## 11.3. Fuzzy Reasoning

11.3.1. Fuzzy is the opposite of exact. Which of the following statement
(s) about fuzziness is/are correct? (·).

(a) The fuzzy set contains the exact set.
(b) There is a one-to-one correspondence between fuzzy sets and their
membership functions.
(c) The membership function of fuzzy sets is derivable point by point.
(d) Because fuzzy concepts represent loose, uncertain, and imprecise
knowledge and information, fuzzy reasoning is approximate.

[Hint] Fuzzy is related to exact.

11.3.2. Consider the operation on fuzzy sets; (·).

(a) This can be done with the help of fuzzy logic operations.
(b) This can be done with the help of fuzzy algebraic operations.
(c) Fuzzy logic operations and fuzzy algebra operations can be
combined.
(d) Fuzzy logic operations and fuzzy algebra operations can be
repeated.

[Hint] Fuzzy logic operations and fuzzy algebra operations have
their own characteristics.

11.3.3. Figure 11.16 gives the membership functions of dark gray fuzzy set D,
bright gray fuzzy set B, and medium gray fuzzy set M; if $L_M(x) = 2/3$,
$L_B(x) = 1/3$, then what is the grayscale $g$? (·).

(a) 43.
(b) 85.
(c) 170.
(d) 213.

[Hint] Judge according to Fig. 11.16.

### 11.4. **Scene Classification**

11.4.1.  Scene classification is related to but different from object recognition; (·).

   (a) The recognition of the object is often the basis of the scene classification.
   (b) The classification result of the scene can help identify the object.
   (c) The scene can be classified before the object is recognized.
   (d) The object recognition can be performed before the scene is classified.

   [Hint] The scene classification is generally at a higher level than the object recognition.

11.4.2.  The bag-of-features model is a bag-of-words model in the image field; (·).

   (a) Itself considers the spatial relationship between the features.
   (b) Itself considers the symbiotic relationship between the characteristics.
   (c) The features in the bag-of-features model are all local features.
   (d) Each local feature is a visual vocabulary.

   [Hint] Consider the composition of the bag-of-features.

11.4.3.  Consider the solid circles and ellipses in Fig. 11.11c; (·).

   (a) Each of them corresponds to a square region in Fig. 11.11a.
   (b) Each of them is related to each square region in Fig. 11.11a.
   (c) Each of them corresponds to a feature vector in Fig. 11.11b.
   (d) Each of them is related to a bin in Fig. 11.11d.

   [Hint] Each square region corresponds to a histogram.

# References

1. Jähne B. Digital Image Processing – Concepts, Algorithms and Scientific Applications. Springer. 1997.
2. Witten I H, Frank E. Data Mining: Practical Machine Learning Tools and Techniques. 2nd Ed. Elsevier Inc. 2005.
3. Robison J A. A machine-oriented logic based on the resolution principle. J. ACM, 1965, 12(1): 23-41.
4. Gonzalez R C, Woods R E. Digital Image Processing. 3rd Ed. Addison-Wesley. 1992.
5. Sonka M, Hlavac V, Boyle R. Image Processing, Analysis, and Machine Vision. 3rd Ed. Thomson. 2008.
6. Sivic J, Zisserman A. Video Google: A text retrieval approach to object matching in videos. Proc. ICCV, 2003, II: 1470-1477.
7. Sivic J, Russell B C, Efros A A, et al. Discovering objects and their location in images. Proc. ICCV, 2005, 370-377.
8. Lang, P J, Bradley, M M, Cuthbert, B N. International affective picture system (IAPS): Technical manual and affective ratings, NIMH Center for the Study of Emotion and Attention. 1997.
9. Li S, Zhang Y J, Tan H C. Discovering latent semantic factors for emotional picture categorization. Proc. 17th ICIP, 2010, 1065-1068.

# Chapter 12
# Spatial-Temporal Behavior Understanding

An important task of image understanding is to interpret the scene and guide actions by processing the images obtained from the scene. To this end, it is necessary to determine which sceneries are in the scene and how they change their position, posture, speed, relationship, etc., in space over time. In short, it is necessary to grasp the movement of the scenery in time and space, determine the purpose of the movement, and then understand the semantic information they convey.

Automatic object behavior understanding based on image/video is a very challenging research problem. It includes obtaining objective information (collecting image sequences), processing related visual information, analyzing (representation and description) to extract information content, and interpreting image/video information on this basis to achieve learning and recognition behavior.

The above-mentioned work spans a wide range, among which motion detection and recognition have recently received a lot of attention and research, and significant progress has also been made. Relatively speaking, research on high-level abstract behavior recognition and description (related to semantics and intelligence) is still underway, the definition of many concepts is not very clear, and many technologies are still being developed.

The sections of this chapter are arranged as follows:

Section 12.1 defines spatial-temporal technology and spatial-temporal behavior understanding and introduces their development and hierarchical research state.
Section 12.2 discusses how to detect the key points (spatial-temporal interest points) that reflect the concentration and change of spatial-temporal motion information.
Section 12.3, from point to line, further introduces the learning and analysis of dynamic trajectories and activity paths formed by connecting points of interest.
Section 12.4 introduces the technology of modeling and recognizing actions and activities that are still under constant research and development.

Y.-J. Zhang, *3-D Computer Vision*, https://doi.org/10.1007/978-981-19-7580-6_12

## 12.1   Spatial-Temporal Technology

Spatial-temporal technique is the technology oriented to the understanding of spatial-temporal behavior, and it is a relatively new research field. **Spatial-temporal behavior understanding** is based on spatial-temporal technology for image understanding. Current work is being carried out at different levels. Here are some general situations.

### 12.1.1   New Research Field

The image engineering review series mentioned in Chap. 1 has been conducted for 27 years since the 1995 literature statistics. When the image engineering review series entered its second decade (starting with the 2005 literature statistics), with the emergence of new hotspots in image engineering research and application, a new subcategory was added to the image understanding category—C5: space-time technology (3-D motion analysis, posture detection, object tracking, behavior judgment and understanding). The emphasis here is to comprehensively use all kinds of information in the image/video to make corresponding judgments and explanations on the scene and the dynamics of the target in it.

In the past 17 years, the number of literatures collected for subcategory C5 in the review series is 279, and their distribution in each year is shown by the histogram bins in Fig. 12.1. In the first 8 years, there were about 11 articles per year on average, and about 21 articles per year in the last 9 years. The figure also shows the change trend obtained by fitting the number of documents in each year with a fourth-order polynomial curve. Generally speaking, this is still a relatively new research field, and the research results are not too many, and the development trend has also fluctuated. In recent years, however, the number of publications of related literature has been relatively stable, and a rapid growth momentum has appeared.

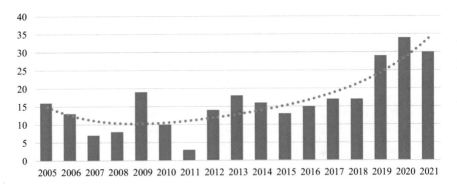

**Fig. 12.1**  The literature number and change of spatial-temporal technology in each year

### 12.1.2 Multiple Levels

At present, the main objects of research on spatial-temporal technology are moving people or objects and the changes in the scenery (especially people) in the scene. According to the level of abstraction of its representation and description, it can be divided into multiple levels from bottom to top:

1. **Action primitive**: Refers to the atomic unit used to construct the action, generally corresponding to the brief and specific movement information in the scene.
2. **Action**: A meaningful aggregate (ordered combination) composed of a series of action primitives of the subject/initiator. In general, actions represent simple exercise patterns that are often performed by one person and generally only last on the order of seconds. The result of human movement often leads to changes in human posture.
3. **Activity**: A combination of a series of actions performed by the subject/initiator in order to complete a certain task or achieve a certain goal (mainly emphasizing logical combination). Activities are relatively large-scale movements that generally depend on the environment and interacting people. Activities often represent complex sequences of (possibly interactive) actions performed by multiple people and often last for a long period of time.
4. **Events**: It refers to certain activities occurred at special circumstance (particular position, time, environment, etc.). Usually, the activity is performed by multiple subjects/initiators (group activity) and/or having the interaction with external world. Detection of specific events is often associated with abnormal activity.
5. **Behavior**: It emphasizes the subject/initiator (mainly human being), dominated by ideological movements, to change action, perform sustained activity, describe events, etc., in a specific environment/context.

In the following, the sport of table tennis is taken as an example to give some typical pictures at all the above levels, as shown in Fig. 12.2. Player's venue, swing, etc. can be seen as typical action primitives, as shown in Fig. 12.2a. Players serve a ball (including drop, windup, jitter wrist, hitting, *etc.*) and return a ball (including the venue, outriggers, palming, pumping balls, *etc.*) are typical actions, as shown in Fig. 12.2b. However, the whole process of a player running to the fence and picking up the ball is usually regarded as an activity. The two players hitting the ball back and forth in order to win points is a typical scene of activity, as shown in Fig. 12.2c.

(a) Action primitive    (b) Action    (c) Activity    (d) Event    (e) Behavior

**Fig. 12.2** (a–e) Several screens in the table tennis match

The competition between two or several sport teams is generally seen as an event, and awarding the players after the game is also a typical event, as shown in Fig. 12.2d, which leads to the ceremony. After winning, though the player making a fist and self-motivation gesture can be regarded as an action, this more often is seen as a behavior of the players. In addition, when players perform good exchange, the audience applauded, shouted, and cheered, which are also attributed to the behavior of the audience, as shown in Fig. 12.2e.

It should be noted that the concepts of last three layers are often not strictly distinguished and are used in many studies without distinction. For example, the activity may be called event, when it refers to some unusual activities (such as the disputes between two persons, the elder person falling during walk, etc.); the activity may be called behavior, when the emphasis is mainly on the meaning of activity (behavior), or the nature of the activity (such as shoplifting actions or activities over the wall burglary called theft). In the following discussion, unless special emphasis is being made, the (generalized) activities will be used unevenly to represent the last three layers.

## 12.2   Spatial-Temporal Interest Point Detection

The change of scenery usually comes from the motion (especially accelerated motion) of objects. Accelerated motion of local structure in video images corresponds to the objects with accelerated motion in scenes; they are at the locations with unconventional moving values in the image. It is expected, at these positions (image points), there are information of object movement in physical world and of force for changing object structure in scene, so they are helpful in understanding the scene.

In spatial-temporal scene, the detection of the **point of interest** (POI) has a tendency of expansion from space to space-time.

### 12.2.1   Detection of Points of Interest in Space

In the image space, the image modeling can be performed by using the **linear scale-space representation**, namely, $L^{SP}: R^2 \times R_+ \rightarrow R$, with $f^{SP}: R^2 \rightarrow R$.

$$L^{SP}\left(x, y; \sigma_z^2\right) = g^{SP}\left(x, y; \sigma_z^2\right) \otimes f^{SP}(x, y) \tag{12.1}$$

that is, making convolution of $f^{SP}$ by using a Gaussian kernel with a variance of $\sigma_z^2$:

$$g^{\text{SP}}\left(x, y; \sigma_z^2\right) = \frac{1}{2\pi\sigma_z^2} \exp\left[-\left(x^2 + y^2\right)/2\sigma_z^2\right] \tag{12.2}$$

Next, use **Harris interest point detector** to detect interest points. The idea of detection is to determine the spatial position of $f^{\text{SP}}$ with obvious changes in both horizontal and vertical directions. For a given observation scale $\sigma_z^2$, these points can be calculated with the help of a matrix of second moments obtained by summing in a Gaussian window with variance $\sigma_z^2$:

$$
\begin{aligned}
\mu^{\text{SP}}\left(\bullet; \sigma_z^2, \sigma_i^2\right) &= g^{\text{SP}}\left(\bullet; \sigma_i^2\right) \otimes \left\{\left[\nabla L\left(\bullet; \sigma_z^2\right)\right]\left[\nabla L\left(\bullet; \sigma_z^2\right)\right]^{\text{T}}\right\} \\
&= g^{\text{SP}}\left(\bullet; \sigma_i^2\right) \otimes \begin{bmatrix} \left(L_x^{\text{SP}}\right)^2 & L_x^{\text{SP}} L_y^{\text{SP}} \\ L_x^{\text{SP}} L_y^{\text{SP}} & \left(L_y^{\text{SP}}\right)^2 \end{bmatrix}
\end{aligned}
\tag{12.3}
$$

Among them, $L_x^{\text{SP}}$ and $L_y^{\text{SP}}$ are the Gaussian differential calculated at the local scale $\sigma_z^2$ according to $L_x^{\text{SP}} = \partial_x[g^{\text{SP}}(\bullet; \sigma_z^2) \otimes f^{\text{SP}}(\bullet)]$ and $L_y^{\text{SP}} = \partial_y[g^{\text{SP}}(\bullet; \sigma_z^2) \otimes f^{\text{SP}}(\bullet)]$.

The second-order moment descriptor in Eq. (12.3) can be regarded as the orientation distribution covariance matrix of a 2-D image in the local neighborhood of a point. Therefore, the eigenvalues of $\mu^{\text{SP}}$, $\lambda_1$, and $\lambda_2$ ($\lambda_1 \leq \lambda_2$) constitute a descriptor of $f^{\text{SP}}$, which changes along the two image directions. If the values of $\lambda_1$ and $\lambda_2$ are both large, it indicates that there is a point of interest. In order to detect such a point, the positive value of the corner point function can be detected:

$$H^{\text{SP}} = \det(\mu^{\text{SP}}) - k \bullet \text{trace}^2(\mu^{\text{SP}}) = \lambda_1\lambda_2 - k(\lambda_1 + \lambda_2)^2 \tag{12.4}$$

At the point of interest, the ratio of eigenvalues $a = \lambda_2/\lambda_1$ should be large. According to Eq. (12.4), for the positive local extremum of $H^{\text{SP}}$, $a$ should satisfy $k \leq a/(1 + a)^2$. Therefore, if $k = 0.25$, the positive maximum value of $H$ will correspond to an ideal isotropic interest point (at this time $a = 1$, that is, $\lambda_1 = \lambda_2$). A smaller value of $k$ is more suitable for the detection of sharper interest points (corresponding to a larger value of $a$). The commonly used value of $k$ in the literature is $k = 0.04$, which corresponds to detecting interest points with $a < 23$.

## 12.2.2   Detection of Points of Interest in Space and Time

The detection of point of interest in space is extended to space and time, that is, it is considered to detect the position in the local space-time volume that has significant changes in image value both in space and time. A point with this property will correspond to a point of interest in space with a specific position in time, which is in a temporal and spatial neighborhood with nonconstant motion value. Detecting spatial-temporal interest points is a method of extracting underlying motion features,

**Fig. 12.3** Example of
points of interest in time and
space

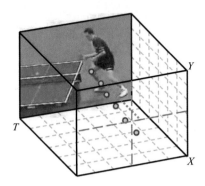

and does not require background modeling. Here, a given video can be convolved
with a 3-D Gaussian kernel at different spatial-temporal scales. Then the spatial-
temporal gradients are calculated in each layer of the scale-space representation, and
they are combined in the neighborhood of each point to obtain the stability estimation of the spatial-temporal second-order moment matrix. Local features can be
extracted from the matrix.

### Example 12.1 Examples of Points of Interest in Time and Space

Figure 12.3 shows a segment of a player swinging and hitting the ball in a table
tennis match. Several points of interest in time and space are detected from this
picture. The density of spatial-temporal interest points along the time axis is related
to the frequency of the action, while the position of the spatial-temporal interest
points in space corresponds to the motion trajectory and amplitude of the beat.

To model the spatial-temporal image sequence, one can use the function $f$:
$R^2 \times R \to R$ and construct its linear scale-space representation, by convolving
$f$ with the isotropic Gaussian kernel (uncorrelated spatial variance $\sigma_z^2$ and time
variance $\tau_z^2$), $L: R^2 \times R \times R_+^2 \to R$:

$$L\left(\bullet; \sigma_z^2, \tau_z^2\right) = g\left(\bullet; \sigma_z^2, \tau_z^2\right) \otimes f(\bullet) \qquad (12.5)$$

Among them, the space-time separated Gaussian kernel is

$$g\left(x, y, t; \sigma_z^2, \tau_z^2\right) = \frac{1}{\sqrt{(2\pi)^3 \sigma_z^4 \tau_z^2}} \exp\left[-\frac{x^2 + y^2}{2\sigma_z^2} - \frac{t^2}{2\tau_z^2}\right] \qquad (12.6)$$

The use of a separate scale parameter for the time domain is very critical, because
events in the time and space domains are generally independent. In addition, the
event detected by the interest point operator depends simultaneously on the observation scale of space and time domains, so the scale parameters $\sigma_z^2$ and $\tau_z^2$ need to be
treated separately.

Similar to the space domain, consider a matrix of second-order moments in the
time-space domain. It is a $3 \times 3$ matrix, including the first-order space and the

first-order time differentiation convolution with the Gaussian weight function $g(\bullet; \sigma_i^2, \tau_i^2)$:

$$\mu = g\left(\bullet; \sigma_i^2, \tau_i^2\right) \otimes \begin{bmatrix} L_x^2 & L_x L_y & L_x L_t \\ L_x L_y & L_y^2 & L_y L_t \\ L_x L_t & L_y L_t & L_t^2 \end{bmatrix} \tag{12.7}$$

Among them, the integration scales $\sigma_i^2$ and $\tau_i^2$ are connected with the local scales $\sigma_z^2$ and $\tau_z^2$ according to $\sigma_i^2 = s\sigma_z^2$ and $\tau_i^2 = s\tau_z^2$. The first-order differentiation is defined as

$$\begin{aligned} L_x\left(\bullet; \sigma_z^2, \tau_z^2\right) &= \partial_x(g \otimes f) \\ L_y\left(\bullet; \sigma_z^2, \tau_z^2\right) &= \partial_y(g \otimes f) \\ L_t\left(\bullet; \sigma_z^2, \tau_z^2\right) &= \partial_t(g \otimes f) \end{aligned} \tag{12.8}$$

In order to detect points of interest, search for regions with significant eigenvalues $\lambda_1$, $\lambda_2$, and $\lambda_3$ of $\mu$ in $f$. This can be achieved by extending the Harris corner detection function defined in space, that is, Eq. (12.4), to the spatial-temporal domain by combining the determinant and rank of $\mu$:

$$H = \det(\mu) - k \bullet \mathrm{trace}^3(\mu) = \lambda_1 \lambda_2 \lambda_3 - k(\lambda_1 + \lambda_2 + \lambda_3)^3 \tag{12.9}$$

To prove that the positive local extremum of $H$ corresponds to points with large values of $\lambda_1$, $\lambda_2$, and $\lambda_3$ ($\lambda_1 \leq \lambda_2 \leq \lambda_3$), it can define the ratio $a = \lambda_2/\lambda_1$ and $b = \lambda_3/\lambda_1$, and rewrite $H$ as

$$H = \lambda_1^3 \left[ ab - k(1 + a + b)^3 \right] \tag{12.10}$$

Because $H \geq 0$, there is $k \leq ab/(1 + a + b)^3$, and $k$ will get its maximum possible value $k = 1/27$ when $a = b = 1$. For a significantly large value of $k$, the positive local extremum of $H$ corresponds to a point where the image value changes significantly along both time and space axes. Especially, if the maximum value of $a$ and $b$ is 23 as in space domain, the value of $k$ used in Eq. (12.9) will be $k \approx 0.005$. Therefore, the spatial-temporal interest points in $f$ can be obtained by detecting the positive local spatial-temporal maxima in $H$.

## 12.3   Spatial-Temporal Dynamic Trajectory Learning and Analysis

Dynamic trajectory learning and analysis in time and space attempts to provide a grasp of the state of the monitoring scene through the understanding and characterization of the behavior of each moving object in the scene. Figure 12.4 shows the flowchart of the dynamic trajectory learning and analysis of the video. Firstly, the object is detected (such as pedestrian detection from the car) and tracked, then the obtained trajectory is used to automatically construct the scene model, and finally the model is used to describe the monitoring status and provide annotations to activities.

In scene modeling, first define the image region where the activity/event occurs as the **point of interest** (POI), and then define the **activity path** (AP) in the next learning step, which describes how the object moves/travels between the points of interest. The model built in this way can be called a POI/AP model.

The main work in POI/AP learning includes:

1. **Activity learning**: Activity learning can be carried out by comparing **trajectories**; although the length of the trajectories may be different, the key is to maintain an intuitive understanding of similarity.
2. **Adaptation**: Study on the technology of managing the POI/AP model. These technologies need to be able to adapt online how to add new activities, remove activities that are no longer continuing, and validate the model.
3. **Feature selection**: Determine the correct dynamic representation level for a specific task. For example, only spatial information can be used to determine the route that a car travels, but speed information is often needed to detect accidents.

### 12.3.1   Automatic Scene Modeling

The automatic modeling of the scene with the help of dynamic trajectory includes the following three points:

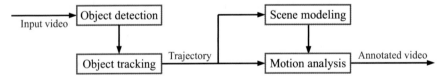

**Fig. 12.4** Flowchart of dynamic trajectory learning and analysis

### 12.3.1.1   Object Tracking

Object **tracking** (see Chap. 5) requires the identity maintenance of each observable object in each frame. For example, an object tracked in a $T$-frame video will generate a series of inferred tracking states:

$$S_T = \{s_1, \quad s_2, \quad \cdots, \quad s_T\} \qquad (12.11)$$

Among them, each $s_t$ can describe object characteristics such as position, speed, appearance, and shape. This trajectory information forms the cornerstone of further analysis. Through careful analysis of this information, activities can be identified and understood.

### 12.3.1.2   Point of Interest Detection

The first task of scene modeling is to find the region of interest in the image. In the topographic map indicating the tracking object, these regions correspond to the nodes in the map. Two types of nodes that are often considered include the entry/exit region and the stop region. Take a teacher to give a lecture in the classroom as an example. The former corresponds to the classroom door and the latter corresponds to the podium.

The entry/exit region is the location where the object enters or leaves the **field of view** (FOV) or the tracked object appears or disappears. These regions can often be modeled with the help of a 2-D **Gaussian mixture model** (GMM), $Z \sim \sum_{i=1}^{W} w_i N(\mu_i, \sigma_i)$, in which there are $W$ components. This can be solved by the EM algorithm (see Sect. 11.4). The entry point data is included in the position determined by the first tracking state, and the exit point data is included in the position determined by the last tracking state. They can be distinguished by a density criterion, and the mixing density in state $i$ is defined as

$$d_i = \frac{w_i}{\pi \sqrt{|\sigma_i|}} > T_d \qquad (12.12)$$

It measures the compactness of the Gaussian mixture. Among them, the threshold

$$T_d = \frac{w}{\pi \sqrt{|C|}} \qquad (12.13)$$

indicates the average density of signal clusters. Here, $0 < w < 1$ is the user-defined weight, and $C$ is the covariance matrix of all points in the region data set. Tight mixing indicates the correct region and loose mixing indicates tracking noise due to tracking interruption.

The stop region is derived from the scene landmark point, that is, the object tends to be a fixed position for a period of time. These stopping regions can be determined by two different methods, namely, (1) the speed of the tracked point in the region is lower than a certain low threshold determined in advance, and (2) all tracked points remain at one limited distance in the ring at least for a certain period of time. By defining a radius and a time constant, the second method can ensure that the object is indeed kept in a specific range, while the first method may still include slow-moving objects. For activity analysis, in addition to determining the location, it is also necessary to grasp the time spent in each stop region.

### 12.3.1.3　Activity Path Learning

To understand behavior, it is needed to determine the **activity path**. The POI can be used to filter out false alarms or track interrupted noise from the training set and only retain the trajectories that start after entering the active region and end before leaving out the active region. The tracking trajectory through the active region is divided into two segments corresponding to entering the active region and leaving the active region. An activity should be defined between the two points of interest at the start and end of the object.

In order to distinguish action objects that change over time (such as pedestrians walking or running along the sidewalk), time dynamic information needs to be added to the path learning. Figure 12.5 shows the three basic structures of the path learning algorithm. Their main differences include the type of input, motion vector, trajectory (or video clip), and the way of motion abstraction. In Fig. 12.5a, the input is a single trajectory at time $t$, and the points in the path are implicitly ordered in time. In Fig. 12.5b, a complete trajectory is used as the input of the learning algorithm to directly establish the output path. In Fig. 12.5c, what is drawn is the decomposition of the path according to the video sequence. The video clip (VC) is broken down into a set of action words to describe the activity, or the video clip is assigned a certain activity label according to the appearance of the action word.

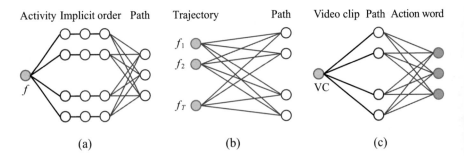

**Fig. 12.5**　(**a–c**) Trajectory and path learning plan (see text)

## 12.3.2 *Path Learning*

Since the path describes the movement of the object, an original trajectory can be represented as a sequence of dynamic measurements. For example, a commonly used trajectory representation is a motion sequence

$$G_T = \{g_1, g_2, \ldots, g_T\} \qquad (12.14)$$

where the motion vector

$$g_t = \left[ x^t, y^t, v_x^t, v_y^t, a_x^t, a_y^t \right]^T \qquad (12.15)$$

represents the dynamic parameters of the object obtained from tracking at time $t$, including position $[x, y]^T$, velocity $[v_x, v_y]^T$, and acceleration $[a_x, a_y]^T$.

It is possible to learn AP in an unsupervised way just by using the trajectory. The basic flow is shown in Fig. 12.6. The preprocessing step is to establish the trajectory for clustering, and the clustering step can provide a global and compact path model representation. Although there are three separate sequential steps in the figure, they are often combined together.

Here are some detailed explanations for each of the three steps.

### 12.3.2.1 Trajectory Preprocessing

Most of the work in path learning research is to obtain trajectories suitable for clustering. The main difficulty when tracking is due to the time-varying characteristics, which leads to inconsistent trajectory lengths. At this point, steps need to be taken to ensure that meaningful comparisons can be made between inputs of different sizes. In addition, the trajectory representation should intuitively maintain the similarity of the original trajectory in the clustering.

The **trajectory preprocessing** mainly includes two contents:

1. Normalization: The purpose of normalization is to ensure that all trajectories have the same length $L_t$. Two simple techniques are zero-filling and expansion. Zero-filling is to add some items equal to zero at the rear of the shorter trajectory. Expansion is to extend the part at the last moment of the original trajectory to the

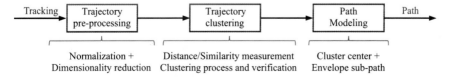

**Fig. 12.6** Trajectory learning steps

required length. They are all likely to expand the trajectory space very large. In addition to checking the training set to determine the length of the trajectory, $L_t$, prior knowledge can also be used for resampling and smoothing. Resampling combined with interpolation can ensure that all trajectories have the same length $L_t$. Smoothing can be used to eliminate noise, and the smoothed trajectory can also be interpolated and sampled to a fixed length.

2. Dimensionality reduction: Dimensionality reduction maps the trajectory to a new low-dimensional space, so that a more robust clustering method can be used. This can be achieved by assuming a trajectory model and determining the parameters that best describe the model. Commonly used techniques include vector quantization, polynomial fitting, multi-resolution decomposition, hidden Markov model, subspace method, spectrum method, and kernel method.

Vector quantization can be achieved by limiting the number of unique trajectories. If the trajectory dynamics are ignored and only based on spatial coordinates, the trajectory can be regarded as a simple 2-D curve and can be approximated by a least mean square polynomial of order $m$ (each $w$ is a weight coefficient):

$$x(t) = \sum_{k=0}^{m} w_k t^k \tag{12.16}$$

In the spectrum method, a similarity matrix $S$ can be constructed for the training set, where each element $s_{ij}$ represents the similarity between trajectory $i$ and trajectory $j$. It is also possible to construct a Laplacian matrix $L$:

$$L = D^{-1/2} S D^{-1/2} \tag{12.17}$$

where $D$ is a diagonal matrix and the $i$th diagonal element is the sum of the $i$th row elements in $S$.

The largest $K$ eigenvalues can be determined by decomposing $L$. Put the corresponding eigenvectors into a new matrix, the rows of which correspond to the trajectories after spectral space transformation, and the spectral trajectories can be obtained by $K$-means method.

Most researchers combine trajectory normalization and dimensionality reduction to treat the original trajectory to ensure that standard clustering techniques can be used.

### 12.3.2.2   Trajectory Clustering

Clustering is a common machine learning technique for determining structure in unlabeled data. When observing the scene, the motion trajectories are collected and combined into similar categories. In order to generate meaningful clusters, the process of **trajectory clustering** must consider three issues: (1) Define a distance (corresponding similarity) measure; (2) cluster update strategy; and (3) cluster verification.

1. Distance/Similarity Measurement

The clustering technique relies on the definition of distance (similarity) measurement. As mentioned earlier, one of the main problems of trajectory clustering is that the trajectories generated by the same activity may have different lengths. To solve this problem, either a preprocessing method can be used, or a distance measure independent of the size can be defined (if the two trajectories $G_i$ and $G_j$ have the same length):

$$d_E(G_i, G_j) = \sqrt{(G_i - G_j)^T (G_i - G_j)} \qquad (12.18)$$

If the two trajectories $G_i$ and $G_j$ have different lengths, the improvement to the Euclidean distance that does not change with size is to compare two trajectory vectors of length $m$ and $n$ ($m > n$), and use the last point $g_{j,n}$ to cumulate distortion:

$$d_{ij}^{(c)} = \frac{1}{m} \left\{ \sum_{k=1}^{n} d_E(g_{i,k}, g_{j,k}) + \sum_{k=1}^{m-n} d_E(g_{i,n+k}, g_{j,n}) \right\} \qquad (12.19)$$

The Euclidean distance is relatively simple, but it is not effective when there is a time offset, because only the aligned sequence can be matched. Here one can consider using the Hausdorff distance (see Sect. 10.2). In addition, there is a distance metric that does not depend on the complete trajectory (outliers are not considered). Assuming that the lengths of trajectories $G_i = \{g_{i,k}\}$ and $G_j = \{g_{j,l}\}$ are $T_i$ and $T_j$, respectively, then

$$D_o(G_i, G_j) = \frac{1}{T_i} \sum_{k=1}^{T_i} d_o(g_{i,k}, G_j) \qquad (12.20)$$

where

$$d_o(g_{i,k}, G_j) = \min_l \left[ \frac{d_E(g_{i,k}, g_{j,l})}{Z_l} \right] \quad l \in \{\lfloor (1-\delta)k \rfloor \cdots \lceil 1+\delta \rceil k\} \qquad (12.21)$$

where $Z_l$ is the normalization constant, which is the variance at point $l$.

$D_o(G_i, G_j)$ is used to compare trajectories with existing clusters. If two trajectories are compared, $Z_l = 1$ can be used. The distance metric defined in this way is the average normalized distance from any point to the best match with it. At this time, the best match is in a sliding time window centered at point $l$ with a width of $2\delta$.

2. Clustering Process and Verification

The preprocessed trajectories can be combined with unsupervised learning techniques. This will decompose the trajectory space into perceptually similar clusters (such as roads). There are many methods for clustering learning: (1) iterative optimization; (2) online adaptation; (3) hierarchical method; (4) neural network; and (5) symbiotic decomposition.

The path learned with the aid of the clustering algorithm needs further verification, because the actual number of categories is not known. Most clustering algorithms require an initial choice of the desired number of categories $K$, but this is often incorrect. For this reason, the clustering process can be performed on different $K$ separately, and the $K$ corresponding to the best result is taken as the true number of clusters. The judgment criterion here can use the **Tightness and Separation Criterion** (TSC), which compares the distance between trajectories in a cluster with the distance between trajectories in different clusters. Given the training set $D_T = \{G_1, \ldots, G_M\}$, there are

$$\text{TSC}(K) = \frac{1}{M} \frac{\sum_{j=1}^{K} \sum_{i=1}^{M} f_{ij}^2 d_E^2 (G_i, c_j)}{\min_{ij} d_E^2 (c_i, c_j)} \tag{12.22}$$

where $f_{ij}$ is the fuzzy membership degree of the trajectory $G_i$ to the cluster $C_j$ (the samples are denoted by $c_j$).

### 12.3.2.3  Path Modeling

After trajectory clustering, a graph model can be established according to the obtained path for effective reasoning. The path model is a compact representation of clustering. There are two ways to achieve **path modeling**. The first method considers the complete path, in which the path from the end to the end not only has an average centerline but also has an envelope indicating the path range on both sides. There may be some intermediate states along the path that give the measurement sequence, as shown in Fig. 12.7a; the second method decomposes the path into some sub-paths, or represents the path as a tree containing sub-paths, and predicts the probability of the path from the current node to the leaf node, as shown in Fig. 12.7b.

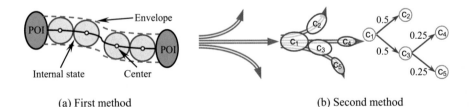

(a) First method                                             (b) Second method

**Fig. 12.7**  (**a, b**) Two ways to model the path

### *12.3.3  Automatic Activity Analysis*

Once the scene model is established, the behavior and activities of the object can be analyzed. A basic function of surveillance video is to verify events of interest. Generally speaking, it is only possible to define interest in certain circumstances. For example, the parking management system pays attention to whether there are vacant spaces for parking, while in the intelligent conference room system, it is concerned with the communication between personnel. In addition to only identifying specific behaviors, all atypical events also need to be checked. Through long-term observation of a scene, the system can perform a series of activity analysis, thereby learning which events are of interest.

Some typical activities are analyzed as follows:

1. **Virtual fence**: Any surveillance/monitoring system has a surveillance/monitoring range, and a sentry can be set up on the boundary of the range to give early warning of events within the range. This is equivalent to establishing a virtual fence at the boundary of the surveillance region and triggering analysis once there is an intrusion, such as controlling a high-resolution **pan-tilt-zoom** (PTZ) **camera** to obtain the details of the intrusion, starting to count the number of intrusions, etc.

2. **Speed analysis**: The virtual fence only uses position information. With the help of tracking technology, dynamic information can also be obtained to realize speed-based early warning, such as vehicle speeding or road blockage.

3. **Path classification**: The speed analysis only uses the current tracked data. In practice, the active path (AP) obtained from the historical movement pattern can also be used. The behavior of newly emerging objects can be described with the help of the maximum a posteriori (MAP) path:

$$L^* = \arg \max_k p(l_k|G) = \arg \max_k p(G, l_k)p(l_k) \tag{12.23}$$

   This can help determine which activity path best interprets the new data. Because the prior path distribution $p(l_k)$ can be estimated with the training set, the problem is simplified to use HMM for maximum likelihood estimation.

4. **Anomaly detection**: The detection of abnormal events is often an important task of the monitoring system. Because the activity path can indicate a typical activity, an abnormality can be found if a new trajectory does not match the existing one. Abnormal patterns can be detected with the help of intelligent thresholding:

$$p(l^*|G) < L_l \tag{12.24}$$

   where the value of the active path $l^*$ most similar to the new trajectory $G$ is still less than the threshold $L_l$.

5. **Online activity analysis**: Being able to analyze, identify, and evaluate activities online is more important than using the entire trajectory to describe the

**Fig. 12.8** Using path for collision assessment

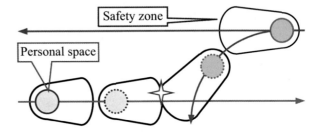

movement. A real-time system must be able to quickly reason about what is happening based on incomplete data (usually based on graph models). Two situations are considered here—(1) Path prediction: One can use the tracking data so far to predict future behavior and refine the prediction when more data is collected. The use of incomplete trajectories to predict activities can be represented as

$$\widehat{L} = \arg\max_j p\left(l_j | W_t G_{t+k}\right) \tag{12.25}$$

where $W_t$ represents the window function and $G_{t+k}$ is the trajectory up to the current time $t$ and $k$ predicted future tracking states. (2) Tracking anomalies: In addition to classifying the entire trajectory as anomalies, it is also necessary to detect abnormal events as soon as they occur. This can be achieved by replacing $G$ in Eq. (12.24) with $W_t G_{t+k}$. The window function $W_t$ does not have to be the same as in the prediction, and the threshold may need to be adjusted according to the amount of data.

6. **Object interaction characterization**: Higher-level analysis is expected to further describe the interaction between objects. Similar to abnormal events, it is difficult to strictly define object interactions. In different environments, there are different types of interactions between different objects. Take a car collision as an example. Each car has its own space size, which can be regarded as its personal space. When a car is driving, its personal space must increase a minimum safety distance (minimum safety zone) around the car, so the space-time personal space will change with movement; the faster the speed, the more the minimum safety distance increases (especially in the direction of travel). A schematic diagram is shown in Fig. 12.8, where the personal space is represented by a circle and the safe region changes as the speed (including size and direction) changes. If the two vehicles meet in a safe region, there is a possibility of a collision, which can help plan driving routes.

Finally, it needs to be pointed out that for simple activities, the analysis can be performed only based on the object position and speed, but for more complex activities, more measurements may be required, such as adding the curvature of the section to identify odd motion trajectories. To provide more comprehensive coverage of activities and behaviors, it is often necessary to use a multi-camera network. The activity trajectory can also be derived from an object composed of interconnected components (such as a human body), where the activity needs to be defined relative to a set of trajectories.

## 12.4 Spatial-Temporal Action Classification and Recognition

Vision-based human action recognition is a process of marking image sequences (videos) with action (class) labels. Based on the representation of the observed image or video, human action recognition can be turned into a classification problem.

### 12.4.1 Motion Classification

Various techniques can be used to classify spatial-temporal actions.

#### 12.4.1.1 Direct Classification

In the direct classification method, no special attention is paid to the time domain. These methods add the information of all frames in the observation sequence to a single representation or recognition and classify actions on each frame.

In many cases, the representation of images is high-dimensional. This leads to a very large amount of matching calculations. In addition, the representation may also include features such as noise. Therefore, it is necessary to obtain compact and robust feature representation in low-dimensional space for classification. The dimensionality reduction technology can use either a linear method or a non-linear method. For example, **principal component analysis** (PCA) is a typical linear method, and **local linear embedding** (LLE) is a typical non-linear method.

The classifier used for direct classification can also be different. Discriminative classifiers focus on how to distinguish different categories, rather than model each category; SVM is such a typical classifier. Under the bootstrap framework, a series of weak classifiers (each one often only represented in 1-D) are used to construct a strong classifier. **Adaptive booting** (AdaBoost; see Section 13.2 of *2D Computer Vision: Principles, Algorithms and Applications*) is a typical method.

#### 12.4.1.2 Time State Model

The **generative model** learns the joint distribution between observations and actions, modeling each action class (taking into account all changes). **Discriminant**

**models** learn the probability of action categories under observation conditions. They do not model categories but focus on the differences between different categories.

The most typical generative model is the **hidden Markov model** (HMM), where the hidden state corresponds to each step of the action. The hidden state models the state transition probability and the observation probability. There are two independent assumptions here. One is that the state transition only depends on the previous state, and the other is that the observation depends only on the current state. The variants of HMM include **maximum entropy Markov model** (MEMM), **factored-state hierarchical hidden Markov model** (FS-HHMM), and **hierarchical variable transition hidden Markov model** (HVT-HMM).

On the other hand, the discriminative model models the conditional distribution after a given observation, combining multiple observations to distinguish different action categories. This model is more useful for distinguishing related actions. **Conditional random field** (CRF) is a typical discriminative model, and its improvements include **factorial conditional random field** (FCRF), **generalization of conditional random field**, and so on.

### 12.4.1.3  Motion Detection

The method based on action detection does not explicitly model the representation of the object in the image, nor does it model the action. It links the observation sequence to the numbered video sequence to directly detect (already defined) actions. For example, a video segment can be described as a bag of words encoded on different timescales, and each word corresponds to the gradient orientation of a partial patch. Partial patches with slow time changes can be ignored, so that the representation will mainly focus on the moving region.

When the movement is periodic (such as walking or running), the movement is cyclic, that is, **cyclic action**. At this time, time domain segmentation can be performed by analyzing the self-similarity matrix. Further, a marker can be added to the athlete, and a self-similarity matrix can be constructed by tracking the marker and using an affine distance function. Perform frequency transformation on the self-similarity matrix, and the peaks in the frequency spectrum correspond to the frequency of the movement (if one wants to distinguish between a walking person or a running person, one can calculate the gait period). Analysis of the matrix structure can determine the type of action.

The main methods of representing and describing human actions can be divided into two categories—(1) Appearance-based methods: It directly uses the description of the image's foreground, background, contour, optical flow and changes, and so on. (2) Human model-based methods: It uses the human body model to represent the structural characteristics of the actor, such as describing the action with a sequence of human joint points. No matter what kind of method is adopted, it will play an important role to realize the detection of the human body and the detection and tracking of important parts of the human body (such as the head, hands, feet, etc.).

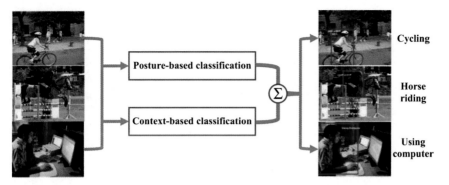

**Fig. 12.9** Action classification and recognition combining posture and context information

**Example 12.2 Action Classification Example**
The classification of actions should consider not only the posture of the actor but also the environment (context) of the action. The process of combining the two to classify images and some effects are shown in Fig. 12.9.

## 12.4.2  Action Recognition

The representation and recognition of actions and activities are a relatively new but not yet mature field. Most of the methods used depend on the researcher's purpose. In scene interpretation, the representation can be independent of the object that produces the activity (such as a person or car); while in monitoring applications, the most concerned are person's activities and interactions between persons. In the holistic approach, the global information is better than component information, for example, when the gender of a person needs to be determined. For simple actions such as walking or running, one may also consider using local/partial methods, where more attention is paid to detailed actions or action primitives.

### 12.4.2.1  Holistic Recognition

The **holistic recognition** emphasizes the recognition of the entire human body or various parts of a single human body. For example, a person's walking, walking gait, etc. can be recognized based on the structure of the entire body and the dynamic information of the entire body. Most of the methods here are based on the silhouette or contour of the human body and do not distinguish various parts of the body. For example, there is a human body-based identification technology that uses a silhouette of a person and uniformly samples the silhouette and then processes the decomposed silhouette with PCA. To calculate the time-space correlation, the trajectories can be compared in the eigen-space. On the other hand, the use of

**Fig. 12.10** Sample pictures of actions in the Weizmann action recognition database

dynamic information can not only identify the identity but also determine what the person is doing. Body part-based recognition uses the position and dynamic information of body parts to recognize actions.

**Example 12.3 Example of Action Recognition Database**
Figure 12.10 shows sample pictures of some actions in the Weizmann action recognition database. These pictures are divided into ten categories. In Fig. 12.10, from top to bottom, the left column shows head clap (jack), lateral movement (side), bend, walk, and run, and the right column shows slaps, play with one hand (wave1), waving both hands (wave2), one forward hop (skip), both feet jump (jump), and two feet jump in place (p-jump).

### 12.4.2.2  Posture Modeling

The recognition of human actions is closely related to the estimation of human posture. Human body posture can be divided into action posture and postural posture. The former corresponds to a person's action behavior at a certain moment, and the latter corresponds to the direction of the human body in 3-D space.

The representation and calculation methods of human body posture can be divided into three types:

1. Appearance-based method: Instead of directly modeling the physical structure of a person, it uses color, texture, contour, and other information to analyze the posture of the human body. Since only the apparent information in the 2-D image is used, it is difficult to estimate the postural posture of the human body.
2. Human body model-based method: First use the line drawing model (see Sect. 10.5), 2-D model, or 3-D model to model the human body, and then estimate the

human body posture by analyzing these parameterized human body models. Such methods usually require high image resolution and accuracy of object detection.
3. 3-D reconstruction-based method: Firstly, the 2-D moving object obtained by multiple cameras at different positions is reconstructed into a 3-D moving object through corresponding point matching, and then the human posture in 3-D space is estimated using camera parameters and imaging formulas.

The posture can be modeled based on points of interest in time and space (see Sect. 12.2). If only the spatial-temporal Harris interest point detector is used, most of the spatial-temporal interest points obtained are in the region of sudden motion. The number of such points is small and belongs to the sparse type, and it is easy to lose important motion information in the video, resulting in detection failure. In order to overcome this problem, some dense spatial-temporal interest points can also be extracted with the help of motion intensity to fully capture the changes caused by movement. Here, the image can be convolved with the spatial Gaussian filter and the temporal Gabor filter to calculate the motion intensity. After extracting the spatial-temporal interest points, a descriptor is established for each point, and then each posture is modeled. A specific method is to first extract the spatial-temporal feature points of the postures in the training sample library as the underlying features, and let one posture correspond to a set of spatial-temporal feature points. Then an unsupervised classification method is used to classify the posture samples to obtain clustering results of typical postures. Finally, the Gaussian mixture model based on EM is used to achieve modeling for each typical posture category.

A recent trend in posture estimation in natural scenes is to overcome the problem of tracking with a single view in unstructured scenes, and more use of single-frame images for posture detection. For example, based on robust component detection and probabilistic combination of components, a better estimate of 2-D posture can be obtained in complex movies.

### 12.4.2.3 Activity Reconstruction

Action leads to a change in posture. If each static posture of the human body is defined as a state, then with the help of state space method (also known as probabilistic network method), the state is transferred by transition probability; then the construction of an activity sequence can be obtained by traversing between the states of the corresponding posture.

Based on the estimation of posture, significant progress has also been made in automatically reconstructing human activities from video. The original model-based analysis-synthesis scheme uses multi-view video capture to effectively search the posture space. Many current methods pay more attention to obtaining the overall body movement rather than the precise construction of details.

Single-view human activity reconstruction has also made a lot of progress with the help of **statistical sampling techniques**. At present, more attentions are paid to the use of learned models to constrain activity-based reconstruction. Research has shown that using a strong prior model is helpful for tracking specific activities in a single-view image.

### 12.4.2.4  Interactive Activities

Interactive activities are more complex activities. It can be divided into two categories: (1) the interaction between people and the environment, such as when people drive a car or take a book, and (2) interpersonal interaction, which often refers to the communication activities or contact behaviors of two persons (or multiple persons). It is obtained by combining the (atomic) activities of a single person. Single-person activities can be described with the help of a probability graph model. Probabilistic graph model is a powerful tool for modeling continuous dynamic feature sequences and has a relatively mature theoretical basis. Its disadvantage is that the topological structure of its model depends on the structural information of the activity itself, so a large amount of training data is required to learn the topological structure of the graph model for complex interactive activities. In order to combine single-player activities, **statistical relational learning** (SRL) methods can be used. SRL is a machine learning method that integrates relational/logical representation, probabilistic reasoning, machine learning, and data mining to obtain a likelihood model of relational data.

### 12.4.2.5  Group Activities

Quantitative changes cause qualitative changes. A substantial increase in the number of participating activities will bring new problems and new research. For example, the analysis of group object movement mainly takes people flow, traffic flow, and dense biological groups in nature as objects, studies the representation and description methods of group object movement, and analyzes the influence of group object movement characteristics and boundary constraints on group object movement. At this time, the grasp of the unique behavior of special individuals is weakened, and more attentions are paid to the abstraction of individuals and the description of the entire collective activity. For example, some research draws on the theory of macro-kinematics, explores the motion law of particle flow, and establishes the motion theory of particle flow. On this basis, a semantic analysis of the dynamic evolution phenomena of aggregation, dissipation, differentiation, and merging in group object activities is carried out in order to explain the trend and situation of the entire scene.

Figure 12.11 shows a screen for counting the number of people in a monitoring scene.

In the analysis of group activities, the statistics of the number of individuals participating in the activity is a basic data. For example, in many public places, such as squares, stadium entrances, etc., it is necessary to have certain statistics on the number of people in the flow. Although there are many people in the scene and their

**Fig. 12.11** Statistics of the number of people in crowd monitoring

**Fig. 12.12** The monitoring geometry when the optical axis of the camera is horizontal

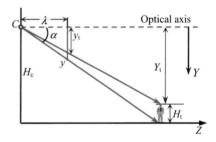

actions are different, the concern here is the number of people in a certain range (in the region enclosed by a frame).

## Example 12.4 Placement of Cameras in Surveillance

Consider the basic geometry for counting the number of people in monitoring. Place the camera (height is $H_c$) diagonally above the pedestrian, as shown in Fig. 12.12, and it can see the position of the pedestrian's feet on the ground. Suppose the optical axis of the camera is along the horizontal direction, the focal length is $\lambda$, and the angle of observing human feet is $\alpha$. Suppose the vertical downward direction of the coordinate system is the $Y$ axis, and the $X$ axis comes out of the paper.

In Fig. 12.12, the horizontal depth $Z$ is

$$Z = \lambda H_c / y \tag{12.26}$$

The height of the upper part of the pedestrian in image is

$$y_t = \lambda Y_t / Z = y Y_t / H_c \tag{12.27}$$

The height of the pedestrian itself can be estimated as follows:

**Fig. 12.13** The monitoring
geometry when the optical
axis of the camera is tilted
downward

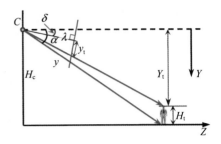

$$H_t = H_c - Y_t = H_c(1 - y_t/y) \tag{12.28}$$

In practice, the optical axis of the camera generally tilts downward slightly to increase the observation range (especially for observing objects close and below the camera), as shown in Fig. 12.13.

The calculation formula here is more complicated. First of all, it can be seen from Fig. 12.13:

$$\tan \alpha = H_c/Z \tag{12.29}$$

$$\tan (\alpha - \delta) = y/\lambda \tag{12.30}$$

where $\delta$ is the downward tilt angle of the camera. Eliminate $\alpha$ from the above two equations to get $Z$ as a function of $y$:

$$Z = H_c \frac{(\lambda - y \tan \delta)}{(y + f \tan \delta)} \tag{12.31}$$

In order to estimate the height of pedestrians, replace $H_c$ and $y$ in the above equation with $Y_t$ and $y_t$, respectively; then it gives

$$Z = Y_t \frac{(\lambda - y_t \tan \delta)}{(y_t + \lambda \tan \delta)} \tag{12.32}$$

Combine both Eqs. (12.31) and (12.32), and eliminate $Z$ to get

$$Y_t = H_c \frac{(\lambda - y \tan \delta)(y_t + \lambda \tan \delta)}{(y + \lambda \tan \delta)(\lambda - y_t \tan \delta)} \tag{12.33}$$

Next, consider the optimal downward tilt angle $\delta$. Refer to Fig. 12.14; the angle of view of the camera is $2\gamma$. It is required to include the closest point $Z_n$ and the farthest point $Z_f$, which correspond to $\alpha_n$ and $\alpha_f$, respectively.

Write for the closest point and the farthest point:

**Fig. 12.14** Calculate the monitoring geometry of the optimal tilt angle when the camera's optical axis is tilted downward

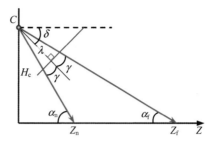

$$H_c/Z_n = \tan \alpha_n = \tan (\delta + \gamma) \tag{12.34}$$

$$H_c/Z_f = \tan \alpha_f = \tan (\delta - \gamma) \tag{12.35}$$

Take the ratio of the two equations to get

$$\eta = \frac{Z_n}{Z_f} = \frac{\tan (\delta - \gamma)}{\tan (\delta + \gamma)} \tag{12.36}$$

If taking $Z_f = \infty$, then $\delta = \gamma$, $Z_n = H_c \cot^2 \gamma$. The limit case is $Z_f = \infty$, $Z_n = 0$, that is, $\delta = \gamma = 45°$, which covers all points on the ground. In practice, $\gamma$ should be small, and $Z_n$ and $Z_f$ are determined by $\delta$. For example, when $\gamma = 30°$, the optimal $\eta$ is zero; at this time $\delta = 30°$ or $\delta = 60°$; the worst $\eta$ is 0.072; at this time $\delta = 45°$.

Finally, consider the nearest pedestrian distance $Z_s$ so that pedestrians do not block each other. According to Eq. (12.29), let $\tan \alpha = H_t/Z_s$ and $\tan \alpha = H_c/Z$, respectively; one can solve

$$Z_s = H_t Z/H_c \tag{12.37}$$

It can be seen that the distance is proportional to the height of pedestrians.

### 12.4.2.6 Scene Interpretation

Different from the recognition of the object in the scene, the **scene interpretation** mainly considers the whole image without verifying the specific object or person. Many methods actually used only consider the results captured by the camera and learn and recognize activities by observing the movement of the object without necessarily determining the identity of the object. This strategy is more effective when the object is small enough to be represented as a point in the 2-D space.

For example, a system for detecting abnormal conditions includes the following modules. The first is to extract the 2-D position and velocity and size and binary silhouette of object and use vector quantization to generate a sample codebook. In order to consider the temporal relationship between each other, the statistics of symbiosis can be used. By iteratively defining the probability function between the examples in the two codebooks and determining a binary tree structure, the leaf nodes correspond to the probability distribution in the co-occurrence statistical matrix. The higher-level nodes correspond to simple scene activities (such as the movement of car or pedestrian). They can be further combined to give an explanation of the scene.

## 12.5  Key Points and References for Each Section

The following combine the main contents of each section to introduce some references that can be further consulted:

1. **Spatial-Temporal Technology**

   A review series of image engineering for more than quarter century can be found in reference [1]. For a discussion on adding the subcategory of space-time technology to this series, please refer to reference [2]. More on the understanding of spatial-temporal behavior can be found in reference [3].

2. **Spatial-Temporal Interest Point Detection**

   In spatial-temporal scenes, the discussion of the trend of the detection of interest points from space to space-time can be found in reference [3]. The representation of linear scale space can be found in reference [4]. For an introduction to the Harris interest point detector, please refer to the document *2D Computer Vision: Principles, Algorithms and Applications*.

3. **Spatial-Temporal Dynamic Trajectory Learning and Analysis**

   More information about the learning and analysis of spatial-temporal dynamic trajectory can be found in reference [5]. An example of using a vehicle-mounted camera to detect pedestrians on the road can be found in reference [6]. The automatic modeling of the scene with the help of dynamic trajectory can be found in reference [7].

4. **Spatial-Temporal Action Classification and Recognition**

   More techniques and discussions on the classification of spatial-temporal actions can be found in reference [8]. For more information on the Weizmann action recognition database, please refer to [9]. The representation and recognition of actions and activities can also be found in reference [10]. An introduction to the Gabor filter can be found in reference [11]. An example of counting people in monitoring scenarios can be found in reference [12].

## Self-Test Questions

The following questions include both single-choice questions and multiple-choice questions, so each option must be judged.

## 12.1. Spatial-Temporal Technology

12.1.1. Spatial-temporal behavior understanding technology involves multiple levels: (·).

(a) The action primitive emphasizes the momentary movement information.
(b) The action primitives will not be the same in the actions of multiple people.
(c) The action is composed of a series of orderly action primitives.
(d) Different actions do not have the same action primitive.

[Hint] The action level is higher than the action primitive level.

12.1.2. Some people refer to the bag-of-words model to describe the relationship between action primitives and actions. At this time, the action primitives can be regarded as a word, and the action can be regarded as a bag of words: (·).

(a) A set of given action primitives corresponds to only one action.
(b) An action always corresponds to a given set of action primitives.
(c) The action primitives have a symbiotic relationship, so multiple action primitives can only constitute one action.
(d) Action primitives have a symbiotic relationship, so one action can contain multiple action primitives.

[Hint] Analyze according to the definition of bag-of-words model.

12.1.3. There are many cross-connections in the last three levels of spatial-temporal behavior understanding; (·).

(a) The behavior is the result of action.
(b) An event is a combination of a series of actions.
(c) The action is initiated by one person, and the activity is initiated by multiple persons.
(d) The relationship between two tuples (action primitives, action) and (action, activity) is the same.

[Hint] Grasp the basic meaning of each concept.

## 12.2. Spatial-Temporal Interest Point Detection

12.2.1. $L^{SP}$: $R^2 \times R_+ \to R$ and $f^{SP}$: $R^2 \to R$; then according to Eq. (12.1), (·).

(a) $g^{SP}(x, y; \sigma_z^2)$: $R_+ \to R$.
(b) $g^{SP}(x, y; \sigma_z^2)$: $R^2_+ \to R$.
(c) $g^{SP}(x, y; \sigma_z^2)$: $R^2 \times R_+ \to R$.
(d) $g^{SP}(x, y; \sigma_z^2)$: $R^2 \times R_+ \to R^2$.

[Hint] $g^{SP}(x, y; \sigma_z^2)$ is a Gaussian kernel with variance $\sigma_z^2$.

12.2.2. When detecting the large positive value of the corner point function, a larger value of $a$ is suitable for the detection of sharper points of interest. If $k = 0.16$, then (·).

(a) $a = 2$.
(b) $a = 4$.
(c) $a = 6$.
(d) $a = 8$.

[Hint] Calculate according to the relationship between $a$ and $k$.

12.2.3. When the method of detecting interest points in 2-D space is extended to space-time for 3-D interest point detection, it will encounter the problem of anisotropy (different resolution in the three directions). To solve this problem, one can (·).

(a) First, perform interest point detection in 2-D space at each moment, and then perform interest point detection in 1-D time.
(b) Adjust the ratio of space variance and time variance according to the anisotropy.
(c) Calculate the eigenvalues of the three directions according to the anisotropy.
(d) Resample (or interpolate) the original data to convert anisotropic data into isotropic data.

[Hint] Anisotropy is a problem caused by different resolutions.

## 12.3. Spatial-Temporal Dynamic Trajectory Learning and Analysis

12.3.1. Consider the three basic structures of the path learning algorithm given in Fig. 12.5; (·).

(a) In Fig. 12.5a, the time dynamic information is added in the sorting of the trajectory at each time.
(b) In Fig. 12.5b, the time dynamic information is added when constructing the path.
(c) In Fig. 12.5c, the time dynamic information is added in the process of decomposing the video segment.
(d) In the three basic structures, all of them have added time dynamic information.

[Hint] Analyze the location where the time dynamic information is added.

12.3.2. Consider the trajectory learning steps given in Fig. 12.6; (·).

(a) In the normalization method of trajectory preprocessing, zero-filling is a special case of extension.
(b) Zero-filling will make the length of all trajectories the same as the length of the original longest trajectory.

      (c) Resampling combined with interpolation can also make all trajectories have the same length, which is also the length of the original longest trajectory.

      (d) Resampling combined with interpolation can also solve the problem that the trajectories generated by the same activity in trajectory clustering have different lengths.

      [Hint] Compare the different characteristics of zero-filling and resampling in adjusting trajectory length.

12.3.3. In automatic activity analysis, (·).

      (a) The virtual fence directly considers the location information of the boundary of the monitoring range.

      (b) The speed analysis directly uses the position change information of the object movement.

      (c) The path classification directly considers the location information of the object in space.

      (d) The path classification directly uses the speed information of the object movement.

      [Hint] The path itself is defined by the spatial location.

## 12.4. Spatial-Temporal Action Classification and Recognition

12.4.1. In the time state model for action classification, (·).

      (a) The hidden Markov model models the state transition probability and observation probability of each action.

      (b) The hidden Markov model assumes that both the state transition probability and the observation probability only depend on the previous state.

      (c) The conditional random field model learns the joint distribution between observations and actions.

      (d) The conditional random field model learning models the conditional distribution after a given observation.

      [Hint] Contrast the generative model and the discriminant model.

12.4.2. In the working method of motion recognition, (·).

      (a) The human body posture estimation method based on appearance usually has higher requirements for image resolution.

      (b) The holistic recognition based on dynamic information is closer to the posture modeling of the action posture.

      (c) The method of posture modeling based on time and space interest points belongs to the method based on human body model.

      (d) The method based on 3-D reconstruction needs to reconstruct 3-D moving objects, so it focuses more on the modeling of postural posture.

[Hint] Analyze the main characteristics of various action recognition methods, respectively.

12.4.3. Suppose a camera with a focal length of 0.05 m is placed (height is 4 m) diagonally above the pedestrian as shown in Fig. 12.11, and a pedestrian's foot is observed with 45°. If the pedestrian's imaging height is 0.02 m, then the height of the pedestrian is ($\cdot$).

(a) 1.8 m.
(b) 1.7 m.
(c) 1.6 m.
(d) 1.5 m.

[Hint] It can be calculated according to the imaging model.

# References

1. Zhang Y-J. Image Engineering in China: 2021. Journal of Image and Graphics, 2022, 27(4): 1009-1022.
2. Zhang Y-J. Image Engineering in China: 2005. Journal of Image and Graphics, 2006, 11(5): 601-623.
3. Zhang Y-J. The Understanding of Spatial-Temporal Behaviors. Encyclopedia of Information Science and Technology, 4th Edition, Chapter 115 (1344-1354), 2018.
4. Laptev I. On space-time interest points. International Journal of Computer Vision, 2005, 64(2/3): 107-123.
5. Morris B T, Trivedi M M. A survey of vision-based trajectory learning and analysis for surveillance. IEEE-CSVT, 2008, 18(8): 1114-1127.
6. Jia H X. Zhang Y-J. A Survey of Computer Vision Based Pedestrian Detection for Driver Assistance Systems. ACTA AUTOMATICA SINICA, 2007, 33(1): 84-90.
7. Makris D, Ellis T. Learning semantic scene models from observing activity in visual surveillance, IEEE-SMC-B, 2005, 35(3): 397-408.
8. Poppe R. A survey on vision-based human action recognition. Image and Vision Computing, 2010, 28: 976-990.
9. Blank B, Gorelick L, Shechtman E, et al. Actions as space-time shapes. ICCV, 2005, 2: 1395-1402.
10. Moeslund T B, Hilton A, Krüger V. A survey of advances in vision-based human motion capture and analysis. Computer Vision and Image Understanding, 2006, 104: 90-126.
11. Zhang Y-J. Image Engineering: Processing, Analysis, and Understanding. Cengage Learning, 2009..
12. Jia H X. Zhang Y-J. Automatic People Counting Based on Machine Learning in Intelligent Video Surveillance. Video Engineering, 2009, (4): 78-81.

# Appendix A: Visual Perception

The high level of vision is visual perception. Typical visual perception mainly includes shape perception, space perception, and motion perception.

## A.1 Shape Perception

**Shape perception** mainly discusses the perception of the shape of the object one wants to observe or pay attention to. When people observe a scene, they often call the objects they want to observe or pay attention to as figure (foreground, object), and classify other parts into the background. Distinguishing between figure and background is the basis for understanding shape perception, and the first step in shape perception is to separate and extract objects from the background.

The structure of the object shape has certain rules. **Gestalt theory** in psychology believes that the perception of stimuli has a tendency of self-organizing, and the shape will follow a certain law when organizing basic visual units (such as points and lines) into meaningful blocks (connected components) or regions. Commonly used laws include the following:

1. Proximity: Elements that are close in space are more likely to be perceived as belonging to a common shape than elements that are separated.
2. Similarity: Elements with similar shapes or sizes are more likely to be perceived as belonging to similar collective shapes.
3. Continuation: If a shape is incomplete, there is a natural tendency to regard (connect) it as complete.
4. Closure: When a shape is moved, the elements that move at the same time are regarded as belonging to the same shape.

The most basic concept in shape perception is the **contour** (outline, the closed boundary of the object). People always see the outline before perceiving the shape. In fact, people see the shape of an object because they first see the contour that

Y.-J. Zhang, *3-D Computer Vision*, https://doi.org/10.1007/978-981-19-7580-6

distinguishes the object from other background parts in the field of vision. Intuitively speaking, the perception of shape generally requires a clear contour between visible regions of different brightness.

In mathematical language, the composition of the contour is the second derivative of the corresponding brightness of the contour. In other words, only a (linear) change in brightness does not produce a contour, and only an accelerated change in brightness can produce a contour. In addition, when the acceleration of the brightness change is lower than the threshold of the perceptual contour, although the eyes are looking at the object, its shape cannot be seen.

The contour is closely related to the shape, but the contour is not equal to the shape. When the two parts of the field of view are separated by contours, even though they have the same contour lines, they can be seen as having different shapes. The difference between contour and shape can also be explained in this way: When people pay attention to the shape of an object, they tend to look at certain regions (usually key parts derived from experience); when people pay attention to the contour, the contour is seen as a route to be traced, there is a process of "shape formation" from the contour to the perception of shape. It can be said that the contour is only the boundary, a partial concept, while the shape is the whole, which is a global concept.

Contours have "directivity" in helping to form shapes. Contours usually tend to affect the space it encloses, that is, contours generally play a role in forming shapes inward rather than outward. When the field of view is divided into an object and a background by a contour, the contour usually only helps the object to form a shape, and the background does not seem to have a shape. For example, if one digs out a small piece from a big picture, these two have the same contour, but few people can see that they form the same shape. This can explain that in jigsaw **puzzles**, the parts with specific patterns are better for splicing than those with large blue sky or sea water. This is because in the former case, it can rely on the understanding of the picture, while in the latter case, only the contour of the drawing board plays a role.

In shape perception, the perception of contours is often different from the actual situation due to psychological factors. In addition to the previous **Mach band effect** (see Sect. 1.2), there is an interesting phenomenon called subjective contour. People can see a certain contour or shape for some reason without a difference in brightness. This kind of contour perception produced without direct stimulation is called **subjective contour** or illusion contour.

### Example A.1 Subjective Contour Example

One can see a weak subjective contour (there is no closed boundary in practice) between the three fan-shaped discs in Fig. A.1a. The equilateral triangle surrounded by this subjective contour looks brighter than the actual background with equal brightness. It feels like a white triangle plane is located between the obscured triangle composed of the other three corners and the observer. Figure A.1b, c give two other examples, where Fig. A.1b is not as vivid as Fig. A.1c. The subjective

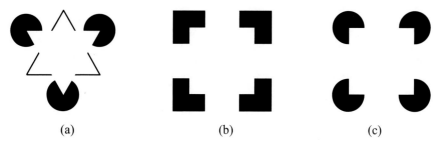

**Fig. A.1** (**a–c**) Example of subjective contour (see text)

contour indicates that the perception of shape depends on the extraction of edges. In Fig. A.1, although there are only discontinuous edges and lines, people can still see objects with shapes.

## A.2  Spatial Perception

The human eye retina is a curved surface. From the imaging point of view, it is equivalent to a plane with only height and width in the 2-D space. However, people can perceive a 3-D space from the visual image formed on it, that is, the depth and distance information might be obtained. This ability is the so-called **spatial perception**. Spatial perception is essentially a matter of depth perception, because the observation of the other two dimensions is often more direct and certain (less ambiguity).

There are many clues in the 2-D retinal image that can help people perceive and interpret the 3-D scene. Human beings do not have an organ directly or exclusively used to perceive distance, and the perception of space often does not rely solely on vision. In spatial vision, people use some external objective conditions called **indices of depth** and internal conditions of their own bodies to help judge the spatial position of objects. These conditions include nonvisual indices of depth, binocular indices of depth, and monocular indices of depth.

### A.2.1  Nonvisual Indices of Depth

**Nonvisual indices of depth** have their physiological basis (their principles have also been used in robot vision in recent years), and there are two common ones:

1. **Eye Focus Adjustment**

   When viewing objects at different distances, the eye adjusts its lens (equivalent to a lens in a camera) through the eye muscles to obtain a clear image on the retina. The signal transmitted to the brain by this regulatory activity provides information about the distance of the object, and the brain can give an estimate of the distance of the object based on this.

2. **Convergence of the Visual Axes of Two Eyes**

   When viewing objects at different distances, the two eyes will adjust themselves to align their respective **fovea** to the object, so that the object is mapped to the most receptive zone of the retina. In order to align the two eyes with the object, the visual axes of the two eyes must complete a certain convergent motion, which tends to be concentrated when looking near and scattered when looking far away. The eye muscle movement that controls the convergence of the visual axis can also provide the brain with information about the distance of the object.

**Example A.2 Binocular Convergence of Visual Axes and Object Distance**

Refer to Fig. A.2, set the object at point $P$, the points $L$ and $R$ represent the positions of the left and right eyes, and $d$ is the distance between $L$ and $R$, that is, the eye distance (usually 65 mm). When the original parallel viewing axes (as shown by the dashed arrow) converge to point $P$, the left eye's inward rotation angle is $\theta_L$, and the right eye's inward rotation angle is $\theta_R$, and it has $\theta = \theta_L + \theta_R$. It can be seen that if the angle of rotation $\theta$ is known, the object distance $D$ can be calculated. In addition, if the object distance $D$ is known, the angle $\theta$ can also be calculated.

### A.2.2 Binocular Indices of Depth

People's perception of the depth of a space scene mainly relies on **binocular vision**. In binocular vision, each eye observes from a different angle, forming a different and independent vision on its respective retina. Specifically, the left eye sees more points

**Fig. A.2** Schematic diagram of the visual axes of both eyes

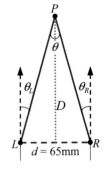

on the left side of the object, and the right eye sees more points on the right side of the object. In other words, the image of the center of attention on the object will fall on the corresponding points of the retina of the two eyes, while other points fall on the noncorresponding parts. This is binocular disparity (parallax), which provides main **binocular indices of depth**.

Binocular disparity is an important cause of stereo perception or depth perception. With the help of binocular disparity, the relative distance can be perceived more accurately than with the help of physiological conditions such as adjustment of eyes and convergence of visual axes. However, it should be noted that when two objects are located at different distances, these distances must exceed a certain limit before the observer can distinguish the difference in distance between the two. This discrimination ability is called **deep acuity**. To determine the depth acuity is to determine the minimum discrimination threshold of binocular disparity. Depth acuity can also be measured by aberration angle. The minimum limit of binocular depth acuity of a normal person is 0.0014–0.0028 rad.

When a person is in a normal body posture, the parallax between the eyes is along the horizontal direction, which is called **lateral aberration**. Human depth perception is mainly produced by lateral aberrations. The parallax along the up and down direction of the retina is called longitudinal aberration, it rarely appears in life, and people are not sensitive to it.

Da Vinci has long discovered the basic problem in binocular vision: the two retinal images obtained by observing the same object at a fixed focal length are different, so how do people perceive that they are the same object? Here it needs to use the concept of **corresponding points** (see Chap. 6 for more content). It can be geometrically proved that there are many points in the binocular field of view that can be perceived as one point. The geometric trajectory of these points is called **binocular single vision (horopter)**, and the left and right retinal images of these points form corresponding point pairs. The above-mentioned perception process is carried out in the cerebral cortex, and the two retinal images are combined after being transmitted to the cerebral cortex to produce a single image with a sense of depth.

In practice, when the observer focuses the vision of both eyes on a closer object, there is a certain angle between the visual axes of the two eyes, and neither of them is straightforward. However, when looking at the object, the eyes face a common visual direction through the combination of the frame, and the image obtained is single, as if it is seen by one eye. From the perspective of subjective perception, two eyes can be regarded as a single organ. A theoretically imaginary single eye in the middle of the two eyes can be used to represent this organ, called the **cyclopean eye**.

### Example A.3 Cyclopean Eye

Each pair of corresponding points on the retina of both eyes has a common visual direction. As shown in Fig. A.3, when the object is directly in front at $C$, it acts on the fovea $C_L$ and fovea $C_R$ of the left and right eyes, respectively. When $C_L$ and $C_R$ are hypothetically overlapped, the location of the object at point $C$ is on the fovea $F_C$ of the cyclopean eye, and its direction is in the center of the cyclopean eye, that is, the subjective visual direction is straightforward. When the object is at $S$, it acts on the $S_L$

**Fig. A.3** Schematic
diagram of the
cyclopean eye

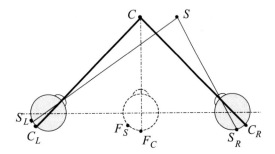

and $S_R$ of the left and right eyes, respectively. For the cyclopean eye, the object is positioned at the $F_S$.

The cyclopean eye is a very useful concept when people deal with spatial perception. When people are spatially orienting objects, they regard themselves as the center of the visual space, and the direction from the fovea toward the front of the cyclopean eye is regarded as the forward direction of vision to determine the orientation of the object. Since the object is viewed in a single direction subjectively, this direction is called the subjective direction, which connects the object with the cyclopean eye in the middle of the two eyes in the above imagination. All objects falling in two visual directions (corresponding to two optical axes) are perceived as being in the same subjective direction. It looks like two points corresponding to two retinas have the same direction value.

The subjective visual direction may be inconsistent with the actual position of the stimulus acting on any pair of corresponding points on the retina. In other words, there will be a difference between the objective visual space and the subjective visual space. Here the corresponding points on the retina refer to those units that produce the same visual direction when the stimulus is felt on the two retinas, that is to say, the retinal units on the two retinas that have the same visual direction are called the corresponding retina points. In fact, the foveae of the two eyes are the corresponding points on the retina of the two eyes. The visual direction of the fovea is the main visual direction. People rely on the main visual direction of the cyclopean eye to determine the position of an object in space.

### A.2.3  Monocular Indices of Depth

People's perception of the depth of a space scene can sometimes be achieved by **monocular vision** (only one eye is needed). In monocular vision, some physical conditions of the stimulus itself, through the experience and learning of the observer, can also become the indices of depth and distance of perception under certain conditions (see Chap. 8). The main **monocular indices of depth** include the following:

### 1. Size and Distance

According to the principle of viewing angle measurement, if the visual image size on the retina is maintained, the ratio of the object size to the object distance does not change. This is called Euclidean's law and is represented by equation as

$$s = \frac{S}{D} \tag{A.1}$$

Among them, $S$ is the size of the object; $D$ is the object distance; $s$ is the size of the visual image on the retina (the eyeball size is a constant, here is taken as 1).

This phenomenon in which the size of an object on the retina is inversely proportional to the distance of the object is called **perspective scaling**. Based on this, when the actual size of the object is known, the object distance can be calculated by visual observation. When observing two objects of similar size, which one produces a larger image on the retina, which one appears closer together. Observing the same object at an acute angle to the axis of the object has a smaller visual image on the retina than observing it at a right angle. This is also called **foreshortening**.

### 2. Lighting Changes

Illumination changes include: (1) The distribution of light and shadow: generally bright objects appear close, and dark or shadowed objects appear far away; (2) Color distribution: in people's experience, distant objects are generally blue, and close objects appear to be yellow or red. Based on this, people often think that yellow or red objects are closer, and blue objects are far away; (3) Atmospheric perspective: Because there are many related atmospheric factors (such as fog, etc.) between the observer and the object, people observe that the contours of distant objects are relatively not as clear as the contours of closer objects. These lighting variation factors provide important indices of depth.

### 3. Linear Perspective

According to the laws of geometric optics, rays passing through the center of the pupil generally give a true image projected by the center. Roughly speaking, this projection transformation can be described as a projection from a point to a plane, called **linear perspective**. Due to the existence of linear perspective, closer objects occupy a larger viewing angle and appear to be larger in size; distant objects occupy a smaller viewing angle and appear to be smaller in size.

### 4. Texture Gradient

The surface of the object in the scene is always textured. For example, a brick wall has a double texture, the pattern between the bricks contains a **macro texture**, and the surface of each brick has a **micro texture**. When a person observes a surface that contains a certain texture and that is not perpendicular to the line of sight, the texture is projected to the retina and gives a gradual change in the corresponding **texture gradient** in the visual image. This sparse near and dense far away structure density difference gives some clues to the distance (see Sect. 8.3).

5. **Object Occlusion**

The mutual occlusion between objects is an important condition for judging the relationship between objects. Using it to judge the context of objects depends entirely on physical factors. When the observer or the observed object is in motion, the change of occlusion makes it easier for people to judge the front and back relationship of the object. When an object occludes another object, the **inter-position** phenomenon occurs. At this time, it can be known that the distance between the occluding object and the observer is shorter than the distance between the occluded object and the observer. However, it is more difficult to judge the absolute distance between objects by occlusion.

6. **Motion Parallax**

When the observer moves in a fixed environment, the angle of view changes quickly due to the different distances of objects (the angle of view of closer objects changes quickly, and the angle of view of farther objects changes slowly), which causes the perception of relative motion. As shown in Fig. A.4, when the observer moves from left to right at speed $v$ and observes objects $A$ and $B$, the images obtained at $f_1$ are $A_1$ and $B_1$, respectively; and the images obtained at $f_2$ are $A_2$ and $B_2$, respectively. The observer perceives that the visual size of object $A$ changes faster than the visual size of object $B$, and the (stationary) objects $A$ and $B$ appear to be gradually moving away from each other (as if they are moving).

The above motion situation is related to the observer's gaze point, and the motion felt in reality is a rotation around the gaze point. As shown in Fig. A.5, when the observer moves from top to bottom at the speed $v$, if the gaze point is $P$, then the closer point $A$ can be observed to move in the opposite direction to the observer, and the far point $B$ moves in the same direction as the observer. It should be said that these are the indices of depth caused by the perception of the cerebral cortex.

It should be pointed out that although the motion parallax is caused by the movement of the observer, if the observer is stationary and the object or environment moves, a similar effect will be obtained. In addition, since the principle of perspective projection is the same, motion parallax is related to perspective scaling and perspective shortening.

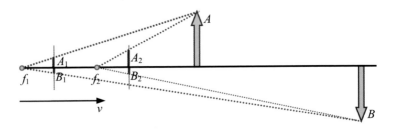

**Fig. A.4** Geometric interpretation of the distance motion parallax

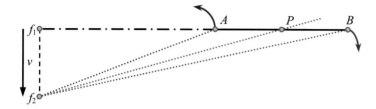

**Fig. A.5** The geometric explanation of the directional motion parallax

## A.3 Motion Perception

The perception of motion is also one of the important functions of the visual system. If vision is the general term for sensory **modalities** caused by light passing through the visual organs, then detecting the movement of objects in the visual field is one of the submodalities. The following gives some representations about the relationship between motion and motion vision and discusses some characteristics of motion perception.

### A.3.1 The Condition of Motion Perception

At present, the most widely accepted theory of visual motion perception has two keys:

1. There is a motion detection unit in the vision system, which includes two detection channels. One is a static channel, which detects spatial frequency information and has low-pass filtering characteristics in temporal frequency; the other is a dynamic channel, which has band-pass characteristics in time and frequency. If and only if the two channels have a response at the same time, the human eye can perceive the motion and detect the speed of the motion, as shown in Fig. A.6.

   This motion detector model correctly explains the visual choice of time frequency and motion speed. Obviously, the condition for obtaining good motion vision is that the speed of motion can be sensed if and only when both channels have a response. Such a zone can only be the overlapping part of the two response curves, that is, the shadow zone in Fig. A.6, and can be called the motion vision zone.

   When the time frequency of the object change is lower than the $T_{db}$ point, it can only cause a static channel response, while the dynamic channel response is zero. The result is that the output of the motion detector is zero, that is, the vision cannot perceive the change of the object. Reflected in the speed, the object will be perceived as static, such as the movement of the hour hand, the movements of the

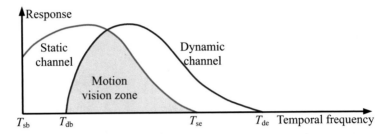

**Fig. A.6** Static and dynamic channels jointly determine motion vision

sun and the moon, etc. If the time frequency of the movement change is higher than $T_{se}$ and lower than $T_{de}$, it can only cause the response of the dynamic channel, while the response of the static channel is zero. At this time, although the vision can perceive the movement of the object, it cannot calculate its speed, nor can it distinguish the structural details of the object, such as the trees passing by at a high speed outside the window of a quickly run train, and the high-speed rotating fan blades. Motion with higher speed, that is, when the time frequency is higher than $T_{de}$, neither the dynamic channel nor the static channel responds, indicating that vision can neither calculate the speed nor perceive the movement of the object, or even the existence of the object, such as the movement of a bullet out of the chamber of gun. Therefore, only when the time frequency is in the motion vision zone between $T_{db}$ and $T_{se}$ can the dynamic channel and the static channel have a good response at the same time, and the vision can effectively perceive the movement of the object and calculate the speed of its movement. Therefore, the selectivity of the human eye to the speed of motion depends on the response of the motion detector inside the visual system to the time frequency.

It can be seen from the above that motion perception is closely related to motion speed. The upper and lower limits of the motion speed are affected by many factors, including: the size of the object, a large-sized object needs more movement to be considered as a movement; brightness and contrast, the greater the brightness and contrast, the more obvious the movement is perceived; the environment, there is a certain degree of relativity in the motion perception, if there is a fixed reference point, the movement is easy to be perceived.

2. The knowledge of human's own motion, which avoids attributing the motion of the human body or eyes to the motion of the scene. There are many kinds of human eye movements, including rapid movement, tracking movement, compensation movement, and drifting movement. These movements will make the retina perceive the motion relative to the environment, which is equivalent to the noise source of visual observation and needs to be eliminated.

## A.3.2 Detection of Moving Objects

When a person observes a moving object, the eyeball will automatically follow its movement. This phenomenon is called **eye pursuit movement**. At this time, the relative speed of the eyeball and the object will be reduced, so that people can recognize the object more clearly. For example, when watching some ball games (such as table tennis), although the movement speed of table tennis is very fast, people can still see the approximate trajectory of the ball due to eye pursuit movement. For another example, if one turns his/her eyes to follow the direction of rotation of the fan, one will find that the details of the fan can be seen more clearly. The maximum speed that the eyeball can follow is 4–5°/s, so it is impossible to see the flight of a bullet clearly.

## A.3.3 Depth Motion Detection

Humans can not only obtain depth distance information from the equivalent of 2-D retina, but also depth motion information. This shows that there is a mechanism for monocular depth motion detection, which can be explained with the help of Fig. A.7. First generate a rectangular pattern on the computer screen, and make its sides move in the 2-D plane along the direction of the arrow in Fig. A.7a. Observers looking at Fig. A.7a, b will feel that the rectangle is stretched in the horizontal and vertical directions, respectively, but there is no depth motion in both cases. But if the two are combined, that is, when the left and right sides of the rectangle and the top and bottom sides of the rectangle are moved in the horizontal and vertical directions at the same time as shown in Fig. A.7c, the observer can perceive the obvious depth motion even if he/she observes with a single eye: The rectangle moves from far to near to the front of the screen.

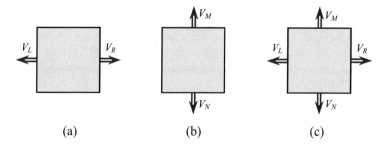

$$(a) \qquad (b) \qquad (c)$$

**Fig. A.7** (**a–c**) Monocular depth motion detection (see text)

## *A.3.4   Real Motion and Apparent Motion*

Under certain conditions, motion may be sensed when there is no scenery motion in the scene, which is called **apparent motion**. For example, the observer watches two relatively close points in space, and lights them with two flashes at different times. If the time difference between two flashes is small, they will be sensed at the same time. If the time difference between two flashes is large, they will be perceived one after the other. Only when the time difference between the two flashes is between 30 and 200 μs will the apparent motion be perceived (that is, feeling the motion of a light spot to another position). Apparent motion can be divided into several categories and marked with Greek letters. For example, α motion refers to the action of expansion or contraction (two flash points are different in size); β motion refers to the motion from one point to another. If some phenomena are very different but related, it is called the φ **effect**.

## *A.3.5   Correspondence Matching of Apparent Motion*

Which parts of the two successively presented patterns can be correspondingly matched will affect the effect of apparent motion. Since visual stimulation involves many factors, there are many types of **correspondence matching**. Experiments on the correspondence matching of apparent motion show that some common factors can be ranked as follows: (1) the proximity of the spatial position; (2) the similarity of the shape and structure; (3) the priority of the 2-D plane relative to the 3-D volume.

First consider the proximity of the spatial location. Suppose that the line segment *L* in Fig. A.8a is initially generated by a computer, displayed for 100 ms and then erased, and then line segments *M* and *N* are sequentially generated, and displayed for 100 ms and then erased. In this cycle, one can notice the line segments moving back and forth on the screen. So is the direction of movement perceived by the human eye from $L \rightarrow M$ or $L \rightarrow N$? Experiments show that this kind of motion matching mainly depends on the distance between the subsequent line segments *M* and *N* and the starting line segment *L*. Based on this, there is the corresponding matching rule 1: in the two successively presented patterns, the closest spatial position of the pixel corresponds to the matching (as shown in the figure by the double-headed arrow in the middle).

Figure A.8b shortens the line segment *N*. At this time, the sensed motion always goes back and forth between *L* and *M*. Based on this, there is the corresponding matching rule 2: the pixels with the most similar shape and structure in the two successively presented patterns are matched correspondingly.

Figure A.8c does not shorten the line segment *N*, but introduces a cube structure so that *L* and *M* appear to be on the same plane, while *N* is on another plane. At this time, it is noticed that the line segment *N* was flashing in the original place, while the

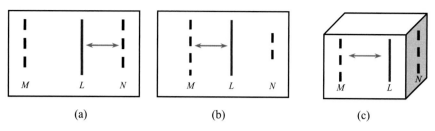

Fig. A.8 (a–c) Spatial location proximity and shape similarity (see text)

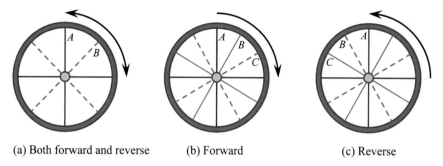

(a) Both forward and reverse          (b) Forward                    (c) Reverse

Fig. A.9 (a–c) Different presentation orders cause the motion perception of spoke rotation

other line segment was moving back and forth between $L$ and $M$. Based on this, there is the corresponding matching rule 3: In the presence of 3-D structure and motion cues, pixels in plane motion are matched first.

The above discussions are the most basic corresponding matching rules. Violating any of them will lead to the illusion motion. Using the rules of corresponding matching can easily explain the wheel reversal phenomenon in the movie. In Fig. A.9, the two cross-shaped spokes that appear one after another are represented by solid and dashed lines, respectively. When two adjacent spokes form an angle of 45° as shown in Fig. A.9a, the motion of the spokes will turn forward for a while and reverse for a while. This phenomenon can be easily explained by the first corresponding matching rule mentioned above. At this time, the spokes represented by the dashed lines can be formed by rotating the spokes represented by solid lines through 45° clockwise or 45° counterclockwise. Since the shapes of the two spokes are exactly the same, both forward and reverse rotation are possible.

Now use the computer to change the space interval displayed by the spokes, and use different display order to present three kinds of cross-shaped spokes $A$ (represented by thick lines), $B$ (represented by thin lines), and $C$ (represented by dashed lines). The motion direction of spokes is fixed. If the presentation order is $A \rightarrow B \rightarrow C$, then the spokes are perceived to rotate clockwise, and the direction of rotation is unique, as shown in Fig. A.9b. Because according to the corresponding matching rule 1, the order of $A \rightarrow B \rightarrow C$ is the closest in space. In the same way, the direction of rotation of the spokes as seen in Fig. A.9c is counterclockwise. In some movies, the spokes turned upside down because the shooting frame rate was not synchronized with the wheel speed. As a result, the fast-rotating wheel was shot into the display sequence of Fig. A.9c. According to the above-mentioned corresponding matching rule, the illusion of turning the wheel is caused.

### A.3.6  Aperture Problem

The aperture problem is an important issue to be considered in motion detection. The **aperture problem** can be represented as: when observing the motion of a certain object (such as a line segment group) through a circular small hole, the direction of motion perceived by the human eye is perpendicular to the line segment. The reason here is that the local motion of the line segment in the small hole is regarded as the overall motion. Take Fig. A.10a as an example. Regardless of whether the line segment moves to the left or upwards, it can only see the line segment moving in the direction pointed by the arrow (toward the upper left direction) through the small hole. This is a subjective apparent motion.

The above phenomenon can also be explained based on the corresponding matching rules of apparent motion. It can be seen from the figure that each line segment has two intersections with the small hole. According to the matching rule, the two intersections of the current line segment will match the two intersections of the nearest line segment at the next moment. Although the motion directions of these intersections are all along the circle, the visual system always tends to regard each line segment as a whole, so the perceived motion direction of the line segment will be the composite direction of the two intersections, that is, perpendicular to the direction of motion of the two intersections. Therefore, the strict representation of the aperture problem should be that the perceived motion direction of the line segment is the composite direction of the motion direction of its two intersection points.

It is deduced from this example that when the shape of the small hole changes, the apparent motion direction of the line segment will change to the left, as shown in

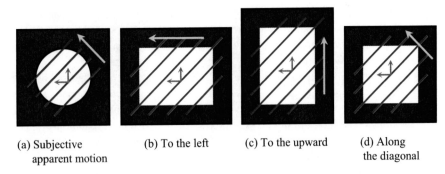

(a) Subjective          (b) To the left          (c) To the upward          (d) Along
    apparent motion                                                         the diagonal

**Fig. A.10** (a–d) The apparent motion direction under different small holes

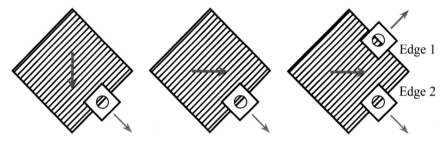

**Fig. A.11** A way to solve the aperture problem

Fig. A.10b; upward, as shown in Fig. A.10c; and along the diagonal direction, as shown in Fig. A.10d. Figure A.10c can well explain the illusion motion of the barber shop sign. From the perspective of the observer's retinal projection image, the cylindrical frame of the barber shop sign is equivalent to a rectangular hole. When the cylinder rotates, the motion direction of the color bar is determined by the two intersection points. According to the corresponding matching rule, the motion direction of the intersection of the left and right rows of the color bar is upwards, so the composite direction is also upwards (downward if reversed).

On the other hand, the "aperture problem" can also be used to illustrate how the human brain detects motion. As shown in Fig. A.11a, b, when the observer watches the motion of a larger diagonal grating pattern through a small circular hole, no matter if the pattern moves downward, toward right, or to the lower right, the observed motion direction seems to be the same, that is, the pattern moves to the lower right. This phenomenon shows a basic uncertainty in motion detection. One way to solve this problem is to watch through two small circular holes at the same time, as shown in Fig. A.11c, so that the motion of the two edges of the pattern can be detected separately, and two motion components can be obtained, so as to make correct judgments on the direction of motion.

It is seen from this method that the detection of motion information can be divided into two levels. The first level detects motion components, and the second level integrates motion components to detect more complex motions.

## A.3.7 Dynamic Indices of Depth

The indices of depth listed in Sect. A.2 can also provide depth information when the retina is moving, which is called **dynamic indices of depth**. For example, linear perspective often appears in the form of dynamic perspective in perception: when a person in the car moves with the car, the continuous change of the field of view produces a flow (flux, a continuous gradient change) on the retina. The speed of the flow is inversely proportional to the distance, so distance information is provided.

There is some other information related to motion, such as **motion parallax**, which is the information generated by the relative movement of the image and the retina when a person moves to both sides (lateral movement). Rotation and radial motion (when the object moves toward or away from the eye) can also provide information about space and the objects in it. There are two things to note:

1. These cues are both geometrical and dynamic. They are mainly perceived in the cerebral cortex rather than in the retina.
2. These clues are completely absent in the flat image. When a person moves in front of the portrait in the museum, the person neither perceives the parallax movement nor the dynamic perspective in the image. The image is treated as a single object and moves like a rigid body.

This is also the case for motion images. It is necessary to distinguish between the representation of dynamic cues (for example, a picture taken by a moving camera) and the dynamic cues caused by the observer's own motion. If the observer moves in front of the camera, then there is no dynamic perspective or parallax caused by its own movement. If an object is obscured by another object in the captured image, only the observer who relies on the movement of the camera can see the object, and it is useless for the observer to work hard.

## A.4   Key Points and References for Each Section

The following combines the main contents of each section to introduce some references that can be further consulted.

1. **Shape Perception**
   The vividness of subjective contours to shape perception can also be found in reference [1]. Discussing shape vision often involves many phenomena and problems of optical illusion, which can be found in reference [2].
2. **Spatial Perception**
   More discussion about lighting changes in monocular indices of depth can be found in reference [3].
3. **Motion Perception**
   More discussion on apparent motion can be found in reference [3].

## References

1. Finkel L H, Sajda P. Constructing visual perception. American Scientist, 1994, 82(3): 224-237.
2. Zakia R D. Perception and Imaging. Focal Press. 1997.
3. Aumont J. The Image. Translation: Pajackowska C. British Film Institute. 1994,

# Answers to Self-Test Questions

Some answers have explanations.

## Chapter 1 Computer Vision Overview

### 1.1. Human Vision and Characteristics

1.1.1. (C).
1.1.2. (B).
1.1.3. (C).

### 1.2. Computer Vision Theory and Model

1.2.1. (B); (C); (D).
1.2.2. (A); (B).
1.2.3. (B).

### 1.3. Three-Dimensional Vision System and Image Technology

1.3.1. (C).
1.3.2. (C).
1.3.3. (B); (C).

### 1.4. Overview of the Structure and Content of This Book

1.4.1. (A); (C).
1.4.2. (B).
1.4.3. (A); (C).

# Chapter 2 Camera Calibration

## 2.1. Linear Camera Model

2.1.1. (A), Two equations can be obtained from one space point.
2.1.2. (B); (C).
2.1.3. (D).

## 2.2. Nonlinear Camera Model

2.2.1. (A); (C).
2.2.2. (A); (D).
2.2.3. (B); (D).
2.2.4. (C).

## 2.3. Traditional Calibration Methods

2.3.1. (A); (B).
2.3.2. (C).
2.3.3. (A); (D).

## 2.4. Self-Calibration Methods

2.4.1. (A); (B); (C).
2.4.2. (C).
2.4.3. (D).

# Chapter 3 Three-Dimensional Image Acquisition

## 3.1. High-Dimensional Image

3.1.1. (A); (B); (C); (D).
3.1.2. (C); (D).
3.1.3. (A); (C); (D).

## 3.2. Depth Image

3.2.1. (A); (D).
3.2.2. (C); (D).
3.2.3. (B); (C); (D).
3.2.4. (C).

### 3.3. **Direct Depth Imaging**

3.3.1. (C).

3.3.2. (D), The depth is inversely proportional to the modulation frequency, and proportional to the speed of light and the phase difference; in addition, the phase difference has a period of $2\pi$.

3.3.3. (A).

### 3.4. **Stereo Vision Imaging**

3.4.1. (B).

3.4.2. (A); (D).

3.4.3. (B); (D).

# Chapter 4 Video Image and Motion Information

### 4.1. **Video Basic**

4.1.1. (D).

4.1.2. (C).

4.1.3. (B).

### 4.2. **Motion Classification and Representation**

4.2.1. (A); (D).

4.2.2. (B); (C).

4.2.3. (D).

### 4.3. **Motion Information Detection**

4.3.1. (D).

4.3.2. (A).

4.3.3. (B).

### 4.4. **Motion-Based Filtering**

4.4.1. (A); (C).

4.4.2. (B).

4.4.3. (D).

# Chapter 5 Moving Object Detection and Tracking

### 5.1. **Differential Image**

5.1.1. (A); (C).

5.1.2. (C); (D).

5.1.3. (A); (D).
5.1.4. (B); (C); (D).

## 5.2. Background Modeling

5.2.1. (A); (B); (C); (D).
5.2.2. (D).
5.2.3. (B); (C), This is not always true, because not every moving object will pass every pixel.

## 5.3. Optical Flow Field and Motion

5.3.1. (C); (D).
5.3.2. (C).
5.3.3. (B).

## 5.4. Moving Object Tracking

5.4.1. (A); (D).
5.4.2. (A); (C).
5.4.3. (B).

# Chapter 6 Binocular Stereo Vision

## 6.1. Stereo Vision Process and Modules

6.1.1. (A); (D).
6.1.2. (B); (C).
6.1.3. (B); (C).

## 6.2. Region-Based Stereo Matching

6.2.1. (C); (D).
6.2.2. (A); (D).
6.2.3. (B); (C); (D).
6.2.4. (B); (D).

## 6.3. Feature-Based Stereo Matching

6.3.1. (B); (D).
6.3.2. (A); (B).
6.3.3. (B); (C).

## 6.4. Error Detection and Correction of Parallax Map

6.4.1. (A); (C).
6.4.2. (B); (D).
6.4.3. (B).
6.4.4. (D).

# Chapter 7 Monocular Multiple Image Recovery

## 7.1. Photometric Stereo

7.1.1. (A); (C).
7.1.2. (B); (C).
7.1.3. (A).
7.1.4. (D).

## 7.2. Shape from Illumination

7.2.1. (A); (B); (C).
7.2.2. (A); (C); (D).
7.2.3. (C).

## 7.3. Optical Flow Equation

7.3.1. (A); (C).
7.3.2. (A); (B); (C).
7.3.3. (C).

## 7.4. Shape from Motion

7.4.1. (B).
7.4.2. (D).
7.4.3. (B); (C).

# Chapter 8 Monocular Single Image Recovery

## 8.1. Shape from Shading

8.1.1. (D).
8.1.2. (C); (D).
8.1.3. (B).

## 8.2. Solving Brightness Equation

8.2.1. (A); (B); (C).
8.2.2. (A); (B); (D).
8.2.3. (C).

## 8.3. Shape from Texture

8.3.1. (A); (C).
8.3.2. (B); (C); (D).
8.3.3. (D).

### 8.4. Detection of Texture Vanishing Points

8.4.1. (B).

8.4.2. (A), The parameter space of a circle is 3-D, while the parameter space of a straight line is 2-D.

8.4.3. (D).

# Chapter 9 Three-Dimensional Scene Representation

### 9.1. Local Features of the Surface

9.1.1. (A); (B); (D).

9.1.2. (C); (D).

9.1.3. (A); (B).

### 9.2. 3-D Surface Representation

9.2.1. (A); (C); (D).

9.2.2. (A).

9.2.3. (C).

### 9.3. Construction and Representation of Iso-Surfaces

9.3.1. (B); (C); (D).

9.3.2. (B).

9.3.3. (B).

### 9.4. Interpolate 3-D Surfaces from Parallel Contours

9.4.1. (B).

9.4.2. (C).

9.4.3. (A); (B); (C).

### 9.5. 3-D Entity Representation

9.5.1. (B); (D).

9.5.2. (A); (B); (C).

9.5.3. (B); (D).

# Chapter 10 Scene Matching

### 10.1. Matching Overview

10.1.1. (A); (B); (C); (D).

10.1.2. (A); (C).

10.1.3. (C).

## 10.2. **Object Matching**

10.2.1. (D).
10.2.2. (A); (C).
10.2.3. (B).

## 10.3. **Dynamic Pattern Matching**

10.3.1. (B); (C).
10.3.2. (C).
10.3.3. (B); (D).

## 10.4. **Graph Theory and Graph Matching**

10.4.1. (A).
10.4.2. (A); (C); (D).
10.4.3. (A); (B); (D).
10.4.4. (D).

## 10.5. **Line Drawing Signature and Matching**

10.5.1. (D).
10.5.2. (C).
10.5.3. (D).

# Chapter 11 Knowledge and Scene Interpretation

## 11.1. **Scene Knowledge**

11.1.1. (D).
11.1.2. (C).
11.1.3. (A); (B); (C).

## 11.2. **Logic System**

11.2.1. (B); (C).
11.2.2. (C).
11.2.3. (D).

## 11.3. **Fuzzy Reasoning**

11.3.1. (A); (B).
11.3.2. (D).
11.3.3. (C).

## 11.4. **Scene Classification**

11.4.1. (A); (B); (D).
11.4.2. (B); (C).
11.4.3. (A); (C).

# Chapter 12 Spatial-Temporal Behavior Understanding

## 12.1. Spatial-Temporal Technology

12.1.1. (A); (C).
12.1.2. (B); (D).
12.1.3. (B).

## 12.2. Spatial-Temporal Interest Point Detection

12.2.1. (C).
12.2.2. (B).
12.2.3. (B); (D).

## 12.3. Spatial-Temporal Dynamic Trajectory Learning and Analysis

12.3.1. (A); (C); (D).
12.3.2. (A); (B); (D).
12.3.3. (A); (B); (C).

## 12.4. Spatial-Temporal Action Classification and Recognition

12.4.1. (A); (D).
12.4.2. (B).
12.4.3. (C).

# Index

Printed in the United States
by Baker & Taylor Publisher Services